MTM
'Quality Television'

MTM
'Quality Television'

edited by
Jane Feuer, Paul Kerr and Tise Vahimagi

BFI Publishing

First published in 1984 by the British Film Institute
127 Charing Cross Road
London WC2H OEA

This is an unofficial history of MTM compiled from public sources. The principals and employees of MTM have not participated in its preparation.

British Library Cataloguing in Publication Data

MTM: quality television
1. Television broadcasting – United States
I. Feuer, Jane II. Kerr, Paul III. Vahimagi, Tise
IV. British Film Institute
384.55'4'0973 HE8700.8

ISBN 0 85170 162 0
ISBN 0 85170 163 9 Pbk

Cover design by John Gibbs

Printed in Great Britain by W. S. Cowell Ltd, London and Ipswich

Contents

Acknowledgments

We would like to thank a number of people who directly or indirectly contributed to the making of this book. First of all we would like to express our gratitude to Jay Sandrich, Mark Tinker, Michael Kozoll and Jerry McNeely, who were generous with their answers to our questions. We are also grateful to Joe Spano, whom Paul Kerr interviewed in London, to Michele Gallery and Robert Butler, both of whom were interviewed by Stephen Dark in Los Angeles, and to James L. Brooks, whom Sheila Johnstone talked with in London.

We would also like to thank Ruth Baumgarten, Marcie Bloom, Jeremy Boulton (Granada Television), William Boddy, Gretchen Bonsall (Gilson International), Ed Buscombe, Olive Campbell, Margaret Catchick (Viacom International), Stephen Dark, Lucy Douch, Maxine Fleckner (Wisconsin Center for Film and Theater Research), Roma Gibson, Ross Howard, Sue Huxley, Ruth Jacobs, Sheila Johnstone, Barbara Klinger, Jerry Leichter (TV Index Inc.), Tony Mechele, Ian Macdonald, Richard Paterson, Lionel Perry, Jayne Pilling, *Primetime* magazine, David Rodowick, Markku Salmi, Ron Simon (Museum of Broadcasting), Michelle Snapes, John Stewart, *Stills* magazine, Peter Tasker, Paul Taylor, Robert Thompson, Michael Tracey, Christopher Wicking, Stephen Woolley, John Wyver.

Introduction

MTM Enterprises Inc. is an independent production company set up in 1970 to produce television programmes, on a commission basis, for the American network TV system. For the most part, the television system in the United States is markedly different from that in Britain: the American networks produce comparatively little of their own programming, while in Britain both the ITV companies and the BBC have historically combined the dual functions of production and network transmission. Indeed, until the advent of Channel Four almost the only exceptions to the exercise of this oligopoly have been bought-in programmes. Under a strict quota system, such imports are not permitted to exceed about 15% of the total output. Not surprisingly the main supplier of such imports has been the United States.

American programmes began to appear on British screens in the mid- to late-fifties when the newly-founded ITV network discovered that imported US series were not only an inexpensive way of filling out schedules but also popular. But it was not until the late 1960s that American television programming could be said to occupy a permanent place in British schedules and ratings. Among the 'classic' US series screened in Britain during that decade was CBS' *The Dick Van Dyke Show*, a long-running, popular situation comedy featuring Van Dyke and Mary Tyler Moore. In 1970 CBS offered Ms Moore her own comedy series, and on the strength of that offer MTM Enterprises (bearing her initials) was formed to produce the show. The resulting series, *The Mary Tyler Moore Show*, alongside such successors – and successes – as *Lou Grant* and *Hill Street Blues*, gradually established MTM's reputation as *the* 'quality' company in the American television industry. The screening of those same series in Britain, notwithstanding their suffering from indifferent schedulers and reviewers (the invariable fate of American programmes on British television), has finally begun to build a similar status for MTM in the UK.

This book has, primarily, two ambitions. The first – and the initial impetus for the project – is the desire to chronicle and in some cases even to celebrate programmes which some British and American critics (not limited to those contributing to this volume) firmly believe to be among the best and most interesting presently to be seen on either side of the Atlantic. The second is to stand back a little from such enthusiasms and to subject MTM itself and its reputation for 'quality' to critical analysis. What follows, therefore, takes the form of an investigation of the company's texts and televisual context, an investigation which examines both MTM's aesthetic and its industrial structures and strategies. Of the book's seven essays, three explore aspects of the company itself: its history as a production base and the specifics of its original formation and later diversification. Three discuss MTM's most celebrated series (*The Mary Tyler Moore Show*, *Lou Grant* and *Hill Street Blues*); and one attempts to combine textual and contextual analyses in an elaboration of MTM's 'house style'. A final section of the book, compiled and written by the three editors, records as comprehensive a list of MTM programmes as it proved possible to produce (working largely from Britain), complete with credits, synopses and critical commentary.

Clearly the choice of MTM as the focus for a book about American television was neither arbitrary nor innocent. MTM cannot be said to be typical or representative of the major independent production companies active in American television. Indeed, as indicated above, our very focus on MTM was in part predicated upon an enthusiasm for its products and a championing of their creative 'difference', their 'progressiveness', their 'reflexiveness'. But while recognising that 'difference' we would want to resist a view of MTM as the exception that proves the rule of American television. Clearly the company does serve something close to such a function inside the US television industry; equally clearly its apparent ability to make 'quality' pay makes MTM both typical and untypical: at once artistic and industrial, a veritable 'quality factory'.

Briefly, therefore, this book insists on MTM's specificity at the same time as stressing its very inextricability from the generalities of the American television industry. By replacing the company in its historical and institutional context it is to be hoped that both the particular conditions of its emergence and continued existence (the conditions which make 'quality' profitable) and the general workings of American television can be made more visible. And in parallel with this, by taking certain MTM texts out of their television context, by removing them from the flow, an attempt has been made to sketch out some of their characteristic features, in terms of differences from and similarities to the rest of 'popular' American programming.

JANE FEUER, PAUL KERR, TISE VAHIMAGI

MTM Enterprises: An Overview

Jane Feuer

BACKGROUND: AMERICAN NETWORK TELEVISION 1970

The Mary Tyler Moore Show, the 'flagship' programme of MTM Enterprises, premièred in the fall of 1970, at a time when the American television industry was undergoing extensive changes. MTM emerged as a force in an industry that was beginning to take on the structure that persists to this day. To understand MTM's role in the US television industry, one must first understand the economic and political underpinnings of that industry.[1] Theoretically, American television is based on a nationwide system of local stations each licensed to broadcast 'in the public interest' by the Federal Communications Commission (FCC). Each station is responsible for content, and under no legal obligation to broadcast national (network) television programming. In practice, however, local stations do very little programme production. The vast majority of day-time and prime-time[2] programming on the US airwaves is provided by three large corporate entities called networks, all of which have their corporate headquarters in New York but which since about 1960 have purchased programming from a handful of production companies all based in Los Angeles. The networks are also permitted five 'owned and operated' stations. Since these stations are in major markets, they reach at least 25% of the TV audience nationally, giving the networks a strong audience base even without the local 'affiliates'.

Although the exact distribution of these companies changed during the 1970s to favour the independents over the major studios, it has always been the case that the networks draw from a small pool of 'creative' sources. Local affiliates accept network domination because the networks make it profitable for them by paying 'station compensation' to broadcast network programming. The local stations are compensated for carrying national network advertising in the form of a small percentage of the network's advertising revenue for the programme. They also receive a few minutes of time in and between programmes to sell to local advertisers. The remaining 'local time' which, according to FCC regulations, must be programmed by local stations is largely taken up with syndicated programming.[3]

It is a truism in the industry that the purpose of commercial television is not to deliver programming to the people but rather to 'deliver' audiences to advertisers. Of course this mechanistic interpretation does not explain why some programmes succeed with the mass audience and others don't, a factor that the industry would dearly love to be able to predict. The television series is both commodity and text. Itself a commodity, the series acts as a magnet for the advertising of other consumer goods. Because it is an advertising medium, American network television differs both economically and aesthetically from its predecessor as a visual mass medium – the Hollywood studio film. In fact, American television has its roots in radio, inheriting from that medium many crucial practices. Like Hollywood studio films, television series are mass-produced by *genre*; however, the major television genres (the sitcom and action-adventure drama) take the form of series with recurring characters and situations. Both the sitcom and the adventure drama, with their segmented structures, lend themselves to the insertion of commercials, or to put it more accurately, these programme formats can be written *around* the commercial breaks. If indeed the programmes are there to attract viewers to the commercials, then the crucial determinant of the worth of a TV programme should be the 'numbers' it delivers to the advertisers. This emphasis on ratings (also called 'Nielsens' in honour of the company that provides them) makes for a much more swift and precise feedback process (overnight in the major markets) than Hollywood could ever hope to receive from box office reports. Even more significant than detailing the numbers of viewers for a particular programme, Nielsen could provide *demographics*, breaking down the audience by age, sex, urban or rural location, and educational level. Indeed it is possible to detail the history of American television according to the vicissitudes of network/sponsor relations.

In the 1950s, the most common practice was for advertisers and advertising agencies not only to sponsor complete programmes but to produce them as well. This gave advertisers direct control over programme content, with a single advertiser controlling each programme. In the 1960s, the networks moved toward greater control of the television schedule, presumably in order to abolish some of the abuses resulting from too much sponsor intervention, notably the quiz show scandal of 1959. In 1960, four out of five prime-time shows were licensed to the networks and sold to advertisers, reversing the previous trend.[4] This meant that the producers of television programmes were responsible, first of all, to the networks. The networks did not produce their own programming (two notable exceptions being news and afternoon soaps), especially after a 1972 antitrust suit, the imposition of consent decrees, and rules on financial interests and syndication prevented the networks from using their own facilities. In turn, the networks would sell advertising time to sponsors. During the 1960s there was a shift toward 'spot' advertising. Sponsors would purchase a certain number of thirty- or sixty-second spots on *specific programmes*, rather than sponsoring an entire programme. The higher the ratings on a particular programme, the more the networks could charge per spot. In this way, the popularity of a show determined its profitability.

The crucial change that began to occur around 1970 was a de-emphasis on numbers and a greater emphasis on 'demographics', i.e., directing television shows toward specific audience groups. The constitution of the audience had been a factor during the 1950s 'golden age' of TV drama, when 'upmarket' productions were used to entice the well-to-do to buy television receivers. However, during the 1960s the emphasis in ratings was on numbers alone. Without a shift toward 'demographic thinking', it is unlikely that MTM would ever have gotten off the ground. Today, the continued existence of MTM depends upon a notion of 'quality' demographics to an even greater extent than it did when the company was formed in 1970.

By 1969 the demographic approach had a strong advocate in Paul Klein, NBC's Vice-President in charge of 'audience measurement.'[5] During the 1970s, the crucial demographic variables were age and location. Specifically, it was discovered that young, urban adults (especially females) aged 18–49 were the prime consumers of the types of goods advertised on TV. Since Nielsen also conducts marketing research for products, sponsors can get matching 'ratings' on programmes and on their retail customers. According to Muriel Cantor, 'sponsorship became a matching exercise – the demographics of the audience against the demographics of the buyers of the products.'[6] The notion of demographics figured prominently in what Sally Bedell calls the 'sea change' in network television undergone in 1970 and what Les Brown refers to as a 'chaotic' twelve months [1970 calendar year] . . . 'full of change and portents of greater upheavals ahead – without doubt the harshest and most uncertain year in two decades of the Beautiful Business.'[7]

Based on numbers alone, CBS had led the ratings for 13 straight years when, in the 1968–9 season, NBC began to close in to 0.3 of a point behind in the ratings. The 1969–70 season consisted of a fierce ratings battle between CBS and NBC, since at the time ABC was considered a second-rate network with fewer affiliates and a predominantly youthful audience. In the winter and spring of 1970, chief programmer Michael Dann waged his 'Operation 100' campaign for dominance in the ratings.[8] Sally Bedell calls it 'the first flamboyantly public ratings battle in the annals of television.'[9] Dann programmed special events in an effort to catch up with NBC during the last 100 days of the ratings season. In retrospect, however, the crucial battle was not over ratings points but over different interpretations of the results. Although Dann claimed victory in terms of *numbers* of viewers, Klein at NBC claimed a *demographic* victory on the basis of a greater percentage of young adult viewers, the 'quality demographics'. Although CBS had the majority of the top ten rated shows, their appeal was primarily to a rural audience consisting of the undesirable populations of children and adults over 50. Moreover, CBS was losing out on the urban audience for its owned and operated stations.

Thus in programming the 1970–1 season, CBS accepted Klein's interpretation, replacing Dann as programming chief with the soon-to-be legendary Fred Silverman (though Silverman was appointed after the schedule had been chosen), a man who swore by demographics and audience measurement procedures. The philosophy behind the 1970–1 CBS programming strategy was to replace over a two-year period the CBS line-up of popular but demographically impoverished 'hayseed' shows (such as the rural sitcoms *The Beverly Hillbillies*, *Petticoat Junction* and *Green Acres*), and also many of its long-running and thus very costly series.[10] Although the 1970–1 season didn't yet signify a complete change, it did reflect the mania for young adult demographics in the form of a 'relevance' drive on all three networks, featuring 'now' programmes along the lines of ABC's already existing hit, *The Mod Squad*. For example, *Storefront Lawyers* featured idealistic young attorneys offering their services to the poor and oppressed. CBS used the slogan 'CBS is putting it all together' accompanied by rock music for its summer 1970 promotional campaign for the fall season. This 'young rebel' programming failed miserably, and by the 1971–2 season had been replaced by Silverman's less issue-oriented strategies. According to Les Brown:

> For all their genuflections toward social awareness, the networks' intent was not so much to involve themselves with the real issues of the day as patently to exploit them for purposes of delivering up to advertisers more of the young consumers than before, without alienating the older habitués of the medium . . . Relevance may have been the shortest programming cycle in the history of the medium.[11]

Nevertheless, out of the 'relevancy' craze were born the two most significant independent production companies of the 1970s: Norman Lear's Tandem Productions, producers of the controversial *All In The Family*, and the producers of *The Mary Tyler Moore Show*, MTM Enterprises.

FORMATION OF MTM

The relationship of *The Mary Tyler Moore Show* to the 'relevancy' programming of the fall 1970 season emerges only in retrospect. *The*

Mary Tyler Moore Show began, however, in a most conservative fashion out of CBS' desire for the 'star insurance' Mary Tyler Moore brought with her. Mary Tyler Moore had achieved minor video fame by playing Dick Van Dyke's scatterbrained wife throughout the 1961–6 run of the popular and celebrated *Dick Van Dyke Show*. In 1969, a CBS comedy special with Van Dyke (*Dick Van Dyke and the Other Woman*) earned high ratings. CBS asked Mary Tyler Moore to create her own show, guaranteeing thirteen episodes for the 1970 season. This was unusual, since most programmes at the time were developed into a pilot (test episode) before being given the go-ahead for a series. To produce Moore's new show, her husband Grant Tinker and her manager Arthur Price, along with Moore herself, formed a corporation called MTM Enterprises, a privately (and very tightly) held independent production company. Grant Tinker, President of MTM, was no prince consort. He had extensive industry experience, starting as a programming executive at McCann Erickson and then at Benton and Bowles (both are ad agencies) in the 1950s, and spending 1961 to 1967 as an NCB programmer before becoming an executive at Universal and 20th Century-Fox. Although Tinker claims not to have been directly involved during the first year of *The Mary Tyler Moore Show*[12] most sources agree that he made the crucial hiring decisions for the creators of the show and backed them up against network interference. Indeed Tinker would make his reputation as an executive noted for leaving the 'creative' side alone. Tinker was responsible for signing two 'hyphenates' – the industry term for writer/producers – to come up with a half-hour sitcom for Mary. James Brooks and Allan Burns would become the creative backbone of MTM over the next few years. At the time, however, CBS was dubious about their credentials.[13] Both had worked on the 1969 classroom comedy-drama *Room 222*, Burns as producer and Brooks as creator/writer; Burns had previously won an Emmy as a writer. Although they had never worked as a team, Tinker thought he saw in them, in the words of *Time* magazine, 'the aura of electronic Neil Simons'.[14] He gave them *carte blanche* to come up with a series.

The result – *The Mary Tyler Moore Show* – was just traditional enough and just innovative enough to inspire an odd assortment of opinions as to its status as one of the new 'relevant' programmes. Certainly Brooks and Burns were liberal thinkers.[15] However, whether their personal views may be found in *The Mary Tyler Moore Show* is another question entirely. Two reliable television journalists who have written books about this era – Sally Bedell and Les Brown – take different views as to just how innovative *The Mary Tyler Moore Show* really appeared in 1970. According to Bedell, the idea for a show about a thirty-year-old divorced woman working at a small TV station news department met with resistance from CBS executives, who saw it as breaking too many of the rules for a popular TV series, especially the received wisdom for female TV personalities.[16] In a much-quoted pronouncement (Brooks tells the story in all his interviews), one CBS executive said, 'There are four things Americans can't stand: Jews, men with moustaches, New Yorkers and divorced women.' The proposed sitcom featured a divorced woman with a New York Jewish sidekick. CBS objected to Mary's age, her divorced status and the Minneapolis location. (Although many sitcoms were set in fictitious small towns, it was unusual to locate one in a real city other than New York or Los Angeles.) Brooks and Burns compromised on Mary's marital status – they would have her unmarried and just ending a long relationship – but the basic idea for the show remained intact. In Program Analyser[17] results on the first show, the sample audience perceived Mary as a 'loser', Rhoda as 'too abrasive', and Phyllis as 'not believable'. Bedell asserts that if *The Mary Tyler Moore Show* had been a pilot, it probably would never have gotten on the air. Bedell's explanation of why Fred Silverman moved the programme from Tuesday night, where it was to have been stuck by Dann in a 'hammock' between *From Rome With Love* and *Hee Haw*, to Saturday (with *Arnie* – a contemporary comedy about the average man coping with the Establishment – as its lead-in), where it would at least be 'sampled' by its 'intended audience of young, urban viewers', places it with the 'relevancy' programmes of the season.[18] But Bedell also distinguishes *The Mary Tyler Moore Show* from the 'noisily relevant' fall 1970 lineup.

Bedell's version of the creation of *The Mary Tyler Moore Show* is a story of brave, original artists and their fearless leader Grant Tinker who went up against the bad guys at the network for the sake of quality programming. Because her book views Silverman as the Great Man of 1970s television, she has to portray him as the network redeemer figure, confident in his knowledge that – given the panacea of proper scheduling – the show would find its demographic spot in heaven.

Les Brown, on the other hand, sees the emergence of *The Mary Tyler Moore Show* as a much less radical occurrence, saying that it was not 'so fresh or distinguished a series that it could be said to have uplifted situation comedy as a form.'[19] Certainly *The Mary Tyler Moore Show* was never – as later MTM programmes *Lou Grant* and *Hill Street Blues* were to be – a ratings *failure* kept on the air for reasons of 'quality'. Although the trade journal *Broadcasting* predicted that *The Mary Tyler Moore Show* would fail, 'because her success came as a result of being tied to Dick Van Dyke's coat-tails,' as early as 21 December 1970 the same trade referred to *The Mary Tyler Moore Show* as one of the two new CBS shows that were 'standouts' in the ratings. At that time the show had a 35 share, meaning that of the sets tuned in during that time period, 35% were watching Mary's show.[20] At that time a 30 share was considered the cut-off for cancellation, with 35 quite a respectable figure for a new programme. *The Mary Tyler Moore Show* gradually climbed to number 22 in the ratings by the end of the season.

But it was through the impetus of another CBS sitcom – Norman Lear's *All In The Family* – that *The Mary Tyler Moore Show* became a genuine hit in 1971, remaining in or near the top ten for most of its seven-year run. Based on the BBC's *Till Death Us Do Part, All In The Family* appeared on CBS as a mid-season replacement show in January 1971; in the fall of 1971 Silverman moved it to the 8.00pm Saturday night spot at the head of a line-up of sitcoms. As the number one rated show, it boosted the ratings of all the CBS shows that followed. During the 1973–4 season, Silverman used a similar strategy, giving *M*A*S*H* a 'hammock' between *All In The Family* and *The Mary Tyler Moore Show* and creating what many consider to have been the most impressive evening of comedy ever to appear on any American television network with *All In The Family* at 8, *M*A*S*H* at 8.30, *The Mary Tyler Moore Show* at 9, and *The Bob Newhart Show* at 9.30. In both controversy and popularity, *All In The Family* overshadowed *The Mary Tyler Moore Show*; indeed there were scores of articles in the popular press on Lear's programme for every one on *The Mary Tyler Moore Show* during the early years of both programmes. The programming of the controversial *All In The Family* was, again, not necessarily a bold move toward innovative programming on the part of CBS; rather, it too was part of a calculated strategy to change the demographics of CBS and to establish the network as the leader in quality comedy with a broad popular appeal that would also capture the audience of young consumers, aged 18–34, that television had lost in the 1960s. As independents, Norman Lear and his partner Bud Yorkin had clout because they were not at that time regular suppliers of TV programming and did not depend on the networks for regular sales. Thus they could afford to hold firm on the language and sophistication of their programmes.[21] It seems unlikely that *All In The Family* would have made it on the network schedule through integrity alone, had it not been part of CBS president Robert Wood's strategy for the prestige and youth appeal of CBS in the coming decade. In fact, the pilot had been rejected by ABC as too controversial, since it tested low with sample audiences.

All In The Family, with its overtly political content, took the onus off the innovative aspects of *The Mary Tyler Moore Show,* but also allowed MTM to push a little harder in later seasons by breaking down some of the taboos that had existed at the time both shows went on the air. As James Brooks explained in a 1973 *TV Guide* article on the greater sexual explicitness of *The Mary Tyler Moore Show* in its third season, 'At the time we started in 1970, every other show was restricted to plastic, Protestant, virginal people.'[22] But *The Mary Tyler Moore Show* was also defined *against* the Lear comedies, as a show which dealt with 'reality' but not with explicitly political themes; CBS, says Bill Davidson, persisted in 'maintaining a fatherly distinction between Mary's show and the network's other more libertarian top-tenners.'[23]

The relationship between what were to become the two leading comedy producers of the early 1970s both was and was not one of competition, owing to the peculiar economic structure of the network system. In a sense both MTM and Tandem competed to sell programmes to CBS; when MTM's *Paul Sand in Friends and Lovers* was cancelled in 1974–5, it was replaced by Tandem's *The Jeffersons* in the spot on the Saturday night line-up after *All In The Family* and preceding *The Mary Tyler Moore Show*, representing a gain for Lear in the competition for the number of programmes on CBS. Yet by the mid-seventies, most sitcom slots on CBS were monopolised by the two companies in about equal numbers. Although neither had a contractual obligation to CBS, both Lear and Tinker felt comfortable with the network, and both appreciated the cross-promotion Silverman could give them by having all their programmes on the same network. Moreover, since all the sitcoms were on CBS, the Lear and MTM programmes did not compete directly against each other; quite the contrary, in the case described above, Lear's *All In The Family* actually pulled MTM shows up in the ratings. In a sense the Tandem and MTM sitcoms of the early 1970s represented a kind of brand differentiation within the same product line. Both represented the new wave of CBS comedy, but each in a different way – the Lear shows presented the issues; the MTM shows presented the 'feel' of a culture undergoing the upheavals of the decade.

At its peak in the 1975–6 TV season, MTM had six weekly series, running neck-in-neck with Tandem for domination of the television sitcom. MTM had become the queen of the sitcoms, a specialist 'indie prod' with a distinguishable product to sell. The following section discusses this period of MTM history up to the end of *The Mary Tyler Moore Show* in 1977, both in terms of programming and of MTM's corporate fortunes.

THE SITCOM FACTORY (1970–7)

The Rise of the Independent Producer

When MTM started out in 1970, conditions were ripe for the small independent production companies to rise to the forefront of the industry. In August 1970 *Variety* reported that the 'indies' were in better financial health than the major motion picture studios and their Telefilm divisions. According to *Variety*, independents could flourish for three reasons:

1. Since most of the new independents are based on the specialised creative and production talents of their principals, they are free from the large overhead expenses of the majors.

2. They film on location rather than the back lot.
3. Since they are not steeped in bureaucracy and decades of experience, they are better able to attempt new things, if only out of ignorance.[24]

All but the second reason (sitcoms were filmed in studios) explains the manner in which MTM was able to grow in the early 1970s. Although Tinker claims he started out with no plans beyond *The Mary Tyler Moore Show*,[25] by the 1975–6 season, MTM was the leading independent producer with six weekly series on CBS, surpassing even Norman Lear's operation.

Grant Tinker's goal of 'growing in a select, Tiffany manner'[26] began in the second year of *The Mary Tyler Moore Show*, when they attempted a 'spin-off' episode that failed. In 1972–3, MTM created a programme around another of Arthur Price's clients, comedian Bob Newhart. *The Bob Newhart Show* followed *The Mary Tyler Moore Show* on Saturday night throughout the existence of the latter show and continued for one year after it.[27] Also in 1972, *Mary Tyler Moore Show* producer Ed Weinberger created and wrote a pilot with John Ritter and Harold Gould (Rhoda's father) called *Bachelor at Law*. When CBS turned it down, Tinker began to think of selling to the other networks. For the 1974–5 season, MTM sold *The Texas Wheelers* to ABC and *Second Start*, aka *The Bob Crane Show*, to NBC. One source even claims that MTM went to ABC with the idea of *Rhoda*, but CBS 'got wind and wooed them back, agreeing to air *Rhoda* without even seeing a pilot.'[28] Ironically, the non-CBS shows failed while two new CBS shows for the 1974–5 season – *Rhoda* and *Paul Sand in Friends and Lovers* – thrived, the latter, however, only because it had *All In The Family*, the number 1 rated programme, as a lead-in. CBS worried as the audience fell off from *All In The Family* in increasingly large numbers, and eventually, *Friends and Lovers* was cancelled. Those who worked on it believe the programme never quite jelled artistically either. '*Paul Sand in Friends and Lovers* didn't die from lack of attention ... we just never quite got it,' Tinker commented. James Brooks explained that the 'brilliant' plot concerned a man and woman as each other's best friend, but that the leading actress was dropped and replaced by a series of girlfriends for Sand, and says 'we should have gone ahead with the original concept.'[29]

The CBS sitcoms bore a family resemblance. Both *Rhoda* and Paul Sand's show derived from *The Mary Tyler Moore Show* (Sand had played an income-tax auditor in one of the episodes) and used creative personnel from that show. In July 1974 the *Los Angeles Times* reported that MTM programmes were currently taking up all available stage space at CBS Cinema Center Complex in Studio City.

Different sources estimate that MTM employed anywhere from 2–500 people during this period.[30] Such was the company's success Burns

Mariette Hartley and Paul Sand appearing in *Paul Sand In Friends And Lovers*.

even joked that he was afraid to leave any scraps of paper on his desk for fear that Tinker would sell them to CBS.[31] Due in large part to the achievements of Tinker and Lear, by 1977 the independent producers had overtaken the majors in overall production of network series.[32] In 1974, the network programming chiefs had more half-hour comedy shows in development than ever before.[33] The early seventies were the heyday of the sophisticated sitcom. What enabled MTM and Tandem to produce so many successful programmes during this period was a system known as 'spinning off.'

Spin-offs

Briefly defined, a 'spin-off' is when a minor or supporting character from a successful programme becomes the star of his or her own show. Related to the spin-off proper, an actor may get his or her own show, playing a similar but not identical character. The MTM sitcom repertory of the early to mid-seventies was generated almost completely through this process. *The Mary Tyler Moore Show* alone generated *Friends and Lovers*, *Rhoda*, *Phyllis*, *The Betty White Show* and *Lou Grant*. *Rhoda* represented the greatest success story of the spin-off process. The première episode on Monday 9 September 1974 won first place in the

Nielsens against Monday-night football (often the highest rated programme on US TV). This was the only time in TV history that a new programme had accomplished such a feat. *Rhoda* outperformed the parent show in the first season ratings, peaking at a 35.1 rating with Rhoda's wedding episode.[34] Meanwhile *The Mary Tyler Moore Show* was down from the previous season's 23.1 average to 22.9.

The spin-off system, although it did not guarantee success, became a trend in the 1970s because of the ratings successes it generated for producers such as Tandem and MTM. In 1974 there were eight spun-off series in the top 30, including the *All In The Family* spin-offs *Maude* and *Good Times*; and *Rhoda*. Spin-offs were attractive to both producers and networks because they eliminated some of the financial and ratings risks of the costly pilot system of programme development. Developing characters from already existing series saved the cost of making a pilot episode, and also ensured, because of audience familiarity with the characters, higher initial ratings than a totally new show.[35]

The Syndication System

A long-running series such as *The Mary Tyler Moore Show* represents enormous profits to its producer not in terms of initial sales to the networks but because lucrative syndication sales require at least 100 episodes. This is because series re-runs, originally scheduled to air on a weekly basis, are shown daily in syndication. Prior to the 1970s, a season of a TV series consisted of approximately 39 new episodes per year, with the best selected for summer re-runs. In 1977, because of higher production costs, the average was 24, and some shows produced as few as 22 episodes. Thus a show which could have produced the requisite 100 episodes in 2½ years, now must run for nearly five years to become a good candidate for syndication (except for syndication abroad, where they may be aired weekly). A very successful series can, through syndication, earn a profit of $50 million or more; a less successful one from 10 to 20 million dollars, says Robin French, president of the syndication division of Norman Lear's TAT Communications Co.[36] On most stations, the main time periods for syndicated programmes are the 4–6.00pm block or the 7.30 slot after the evening news. Since these draw younger viewers, the situation comedies seem to do best in syndication. The all-time most successful syndicated sitcom is *I Love Lucy*, but *M*A*S*H* shows signs of becoming its successor. *M*A*S*H* plays three times a day in New York and Los Angeles because it can capture the 11.00pm adult audience *and* the young audience of early evening and later afternoon.[37] It was this possibility of future syndication profits that enabled MTM to operate at a deficit during its sitcom glory years.

In spite of its seeming success, during the years of MTM's sitcom pre-eminence Grant Tinker continually complained in the trades that the networks were not paying him enough to make a profit. In 1974, Tinker began to agitate for higher network fees to programme suppliers. According to *Broadcasting*:

> When Mr Tinker had only the Moore and Newhart shows to worry about, he didn't mind taking a loss at the end of each year because of the fat syndication fees he will be able to command when these successful series end their network runs.[38]

The article goes on to state that with three new shows, he was sustaining weekly losses. Tinker said he spent $130,000 for each episode of *The Mary Tyler Moore Show*, but that the network payments fell far short of that. He claimed that although MTM's gross income had reached the $20 million a year category, they wouldn't break even at the end of the season. In November 1974 Tinker told *Advertising Age* that MTM lost on all its shows and had been in the red for several years, complaining that he was 'working for nothing and going into debt doing it.'[39] According to Tinker, *The Mary Tyler Moore Show* didn't turn a profit until it went into syndication in 1977.

Tinker said that with network licensing fees[40] running from under $100,000 (for tape) to about $120,000 for prime-time half-hour shows, and from $200,000 to $240,000 for hour-long filmed shows, most producers now lose several thousand per series episode. Even Universal, the largest major, was losing, Tinker claimed. The networks responded by encouraging the use of videotape; however, MTM continued to film their existing sitcoms for artistic reasons.

Tinker's charges were corroborated by a 35-page report, 'The Television Programming Industry', distributed by a Wall Street firm. The report stated that most suppliers don't break even on network sales; rather they depend upon syndication for their profits. The report concluded that the networks needed to pay more, but also praised CBS for encouraging the independents, saying that 'CBS has done an excellent job of founding, developing and nurturing the independents.' According to the report, CBS had obtained 49% of its prime-time programming from the indies over the past four years. NBC tended to buy from the majors; and ABC to depend on theatrical motion pictures.[41]

Programming

Despite MTM's remarkable success, toward the middle of the 1970s the company also began to have its share of flops and marginal successes. The failures seemed in part to stem from a broadening of MTM's base beyond the solid core of Moore Show-trained writer-producers. In the first years, MTM employed the spin-off system not just for programmes but for creative personnel as well. During the first two years of *The*

Mary Tyler Moore Show, Brooks and Burns created jobs as line producer for David Davis and story consultant for Lorenzo Music. In the third season, Davis and Music left to create *The Bob Newhart Show*, Ed Weinberger then produced the Moore show for three seasons, joined by writer Stan Daniels for the 1974–5 season. Meanwhile, Brooks and Burns created *Rhoda* and *Friends and Lovers*, remaining as executive producers of the original programme. Ed Weinberger and Stan Daniels went on to create the sitcoms *Phyllis* and *Doc* in 1975. In 1976, Newhart producers Tom Patchett and Jay Tarses created *The Tony Randall Show*. One producer described MTM as a 'combination comedy club and Triple A baseball league ... We always hire our own successors here,' he concluded.[42]

Of the MTM comedies prior to 1977, only two were formed outside of this creative nucleus – the only two programmes not sold to CBS. *The Texas Wheelers*, referred to by the *Los Angeles Times* as an 'outside job', was brought to MTM by its creator, writer Dale McRaven, because he felt that Screen Gems – where he had been working on *The Partridge Family* – might not be able to handle its unorthodox elements. The article goes on to say that McRaven and producer Chris Hayward, while 'friends' with the rest of the MTM people, would probably keep their show separate from the others.[43] *The Texas Wheelers,* about a contemporary family of Texans, was a one-camera show that moved around a lot outside. Even the MTM kitten at the end was filmed against a real background rather than animated. The MTM sitcoms, by contrast, were three-camera shows filmed or videotaped in the studio in front of a live audience. *The Texas Wheelers*, although a critical success, was a ratings failure. 'It should have been an hour show,' Tinker said retrospectively, referring to the programme as 'a contemporary Waltons but harder. In its half-hour format, the audience expected hard comedy from the beginning. They didn't understand it.' Tinker takes personal responsibility for this, saying he was less in touch with *Wheelers* than with shows originating inside MTM.[44]

Second Start, created by Norman S. Powell for actor Bob Crane and written by Martin Cohen and Jim Allen, was another 'outside job'. MTM approached NBC with a premise involving short scenes with medical reality similar to *M*A*S*H*. NBC supplied Crane, who convinced MTM to do a show with longer scenes and more laughs. The combination never meshed, and the show was a critical and commercial failure. Tinker felt the show was 'ill-conceived and ill-fated from the beginning. It was not up to MTM standards. It deserved to fail.' Ironically, in 1975 Grant Tinker, a former NBC executive and future network Chairman, said that NBC was the network least likely to air an MTM programme.[45]

These early failures did not represent significant losses for MTM. *The Texas Wheelers*, cancelled after four episodes, represented a loss of only $150,000, according to Tinker. ABC had to pay MTM for nine shows already in the can.[46] The cancellation of *Friends and Lovers* was more significant because it represented the first failure of the in-house sitcom generating system. The new sitcoms generated inside MTM, for 1975–6 and 1976–7, while not outright failures, were only marginal successes compared to the earlier hits, *The Mary Tyler Moore Show, The Bob Newhart Show,* and *Rhoda. Doc, Phyllis* and *The Tony Randall Show* lasted two seasons each, the latter with a change of network (moving from ABC to CBS for its second season). But none would reap the profits of domestic syndication.

Even at its peak in the mid-seventies, the success of MTM was linked to its anchor, *The Mary Tyler Moore Show*, As a sitcom factory, MTM never really recovered from the self-imposed ending of *The Mary Tyler Moore Show* in 1977, and *The Bob Newhart Show* a year later. Even before this crucial turning point, MTM had begun to diversify its image as a comedy mill. By the end of the decade MTM would be primarily a producer of one-hour dramatic programmes.

DRAMA AND DECLINE 1977–81

For a number of reasons, MTM appeared to go into a decline after *The Mary Tyler Moore Show* ended: MTM could not come up with a hit sitcom of the magnitude of its previous hits; the 'Silverman era' of mindless sitcoms had commenced at ABC; key personnel left to form their own production companies; many series were cancelled and pilots did not sell; MTM programmes did not do as well in syndication as anticipated; and the diversification into drama and variety programming did not produce significant ratings successes. In September 1978 a two-part article in *TV Guide* (the largest circulation magazine in the US), which Grant Tinker later referred to as a 'hatchet job',[47] discussed the decline and fall of MTM. According to both *TV Guide* and Tinker, MTM's demise was reported around the industry. However, what appeared to be a decline might better be interpreted as a transitional period for MTM, in which the company diversified its 'product'. The company never collapsed financially, and, as the *TV Guide* article points out, 'MTM had actually experienced failure almost from the moment it expanded beyond its first two shows . . . and has still managed to come back and produce successes like *Rhoda* and *Lou Grant*.'[48]

The decision to end *The Mary Tyler Moore Show* in 1977, although justified as an artistic one, had good practical reasons as well. In the fall of 1975, *The Mary Tyler Moore Show* and *The Bob Newhart Show* dropped in the ratings, suffering from the removal of *All In The Family* at the head of the Saturday evening line-up and from Rhoda's departure to her own show. This indicated that it was time to go for the profits promised by syndication. However, in the ensuing years MTM could not come up with a hit sitcom to replace the old shows, and its remaining hit sitcom, *Rhoda*, also fell in the ratings when Rhoda and her husband separated in the third season. The sale of *The Mary Tyler Moore Show* and *Bob Newhart* by Viacom (a distributor) ensured MTM's economic survival, but the MTM type of programme seemed to have lost its popularity. As Grant Tinker told TV columnist Gary Deeb, 'The pendulum did swing away from our kind of programme. In fact, I'm not sure it'll ever swing all the way back. But our company certainly never was near death.'[49]

Ironically, the man in part responsible for the success of the MTM and Lear sitcoms – Fred Silverman – was also involved in their decline. Many attributed ABC's ascendency to the position of number one network after decades of being a poor relation to the programming 'genius' of Silverman, his ability to sense the mood of the times. If this was true, then the mood of the mid-to-late-seventies was one that demanded a new kind of sitcom – not the sophisticated 'adult' programming that MTM and Tandem had provided. The ABC sitcoms of this era – many produced by Garry Marshall – appealed to younger viewers and marked the end of the Norman Lear era of social relevance. Many of the hit ABC sitcoms were spun off from Marshall's 1950s nostalgia show, *Happy Days*. These included *Laverne and Shirley* and *Mork and Mindy*. The three top-rated programmes for 1977–8 were *Laverne and Shirley*, *Happy Days* and *Three's Company* – the latter specialising in none-too-subtle sexual innuendo – in that order. In 1978–9 it was *Laverne and Shirley*, *Three's Company* and *Mork and Mindy* in the top three slots. (*Happy Days* had been displaced to fifth place by *The Ropers*, a spin-off from *Three's Company*.) During this period, neither Lear nor MTM seemed able to come up with replacement hits for their successful shows.

Although the entire story of the rise of ABC during the 'Silverman Era' is not relevant to MTM, two crucial factors were: the increasing importance of 'youth' demographics and the FCC's designation of the early evening part of prime-time (8–9.00pm) as 'family viewing hour', effective in the 1975–6 season. Both of these developments aided ABC, which had always had a youthful audience, but both hurt MTM, a specialist in 'adult' programming. In the 1976–7 season, ABC finished an astonishing 3 points ahead of CBS, and 3.5 points ahead of NBC. At ABC during this period, Silverman developed a number of practices that went against MTM-style programming. Programmes were judged by immediate rating results and by extensive audience research, which meant that only those programmes with immediate appeal succeeded. Those which might take longer to catch on, or which tested poorly (as had *The Mary Tyler Moore Show* and *All In The Family*), tended not to make it on the air or to be subject to what Bedell calls 'the quick yank'.[50] A programme that failed in the ratings would now be cancelled immediately and another programme put in its place. Silverman would also change the programme's time period with what would in the early 1970s have appeared as careless abandon. By the fall of 1977, the schedule, especially at ABC, was chaotic.

Another Silverman speciality that eventually permeated all three networks was the 'promo' (promotional advertisement), which 'cross-plugged' other ABC shows by giving the viewing audience a peek at them through 5, 10, 20, or 30 second snippets. According to Sally Bedell, Silverman's 'block promotions' could consist of:

> a 'two-way twenty' (two ten-second messages), a 'four-way twenty' (four five-second messages), or most irritating of all, a 'five-way thirty' (five nerve jangling promos jammed into thirty seconds). Such blocks were designed to promote an entire evening's line-up of programmes, often by straining to link them with an overarching theme. Silverman commanded that these blocks be thrown into the middle of shows, in addition to the customary place at the beginning and end . . . the average prime-time programme came to resemble a gauntlet of carny barkers on a noisy, crowded midway.[51]

Bedell goes on to argue that the demands of these promos shaped the content of shows, favouring material such as 'one-liners, leers, wiggles, pratfalls, fistfights, explosions, and car chases.' The proliferation of promos was likely to affect the subtle, low-key atmosphere of the MTM style of comedy. Certainly the MTM programmes did not lend themselves to the Silverman style of promotion as well as did the ABC sitcoms which specialised in the material Bedell cites.

According to the *TV Guide* article, people at MTM felt that the success of the ABC sitcoms made the networks less interested in MTM and Lear types of comedy. In the article, Tinker describes the ABC-style comedies as 'witless . . . candy for the mind . . . tight leotards and short skirts.'[52] Tinker told both *TV Guide* and Gary Deeb that he felt he didn't belong in television any more, and that he'd be unable to produce the ABC style of comedy at MTM ('If things get really bad, I don't think I could start doing *Mork and Mindy* just to make a living. I might just find another line of work.').[53]

MTM 'hyphenates' Burns and Patchett deplored the return to a kind of comedy they were certain MTM had superseded. Patchett said that the 1978 shows would be even worse: 'you're going to see stuff so putrid you won't believe it.'[54] James L. Brooks, on the other hand, defended *Laverne and Shirley* to *TV Guide* as part of a normal cycle in viewer tastes. He also said that the success of *The Mary Tyler Moore Show* was more unusual than the failure of the other shows, especially since many of the writers had become producers. But by that time Brooks had already left MTM.

In early 1977, as *The Mary Tyler Moore Show* ended, ABC signed four veteran MTM producers – Brooks, Ed Weinberger, Stan Daniels, and David Davis – to turn out an MTM-style sitcom for ABC. Brooks told *TV Guide* that all the departing writers were tired of the half-hour sitcom format and that all wanted to write movie scripts. He said he left because ABC promised that he could create, write and produce three specials and two series without having to make pilots; and that Paramount would produce his motion picture scripts. The *TV Guide* article also insinuates that Brooks left because he felt the money men were taking over at MTM.[55] According to Bedell, Fred Silverman 'raided' the MTM organisation as part of an effort to tie 'talent' to exclusive contract agreements. She says that ABC guaranteed the four MTM writers two series and also theatrical movies through a shared agreement with Paramount pictures. The first series they produced was the top-ten hit *Taxi* for the 1978–9 season. For the 1979–80 season they produced *The Associates*, this time not a success but nevertheless resolutely within the MTM style.

In the understatement of the year, Tinker said that the talent raid 'did not do MTM any good. But we managed to survive.'[56] Increasingly the best MTM 'hyphenates' would leave to form their own production companies. Even Allan Burns, after creating *Lou Grant* with Brooks and Gene Reynolds, largely withdrew from MTM to write movie scripts, although both he and Brooks remained as consultants on *Lou Grant*.[57] (Both Burns and Reynolds would return to active duty around 1983.) The post-1978 'MTM-style' sitcoms were recognisable as such because they were often written and produced by MTM alumni. The four defectors went on to create the parody series *The Best of the West* in 1981–2. Weinberger and Daniels created *Mr Smith*, a short-lived sitcom about an ape who becomes a presidential advisor, for fall 1983. MTM director James Burrows and MTM 'hyphenates' Glen and Les Charles (all of *Taxi* fame) created *Cheers* in 1982–3. Also in the 1982–3 season, *Family Ties* was created by Gary David Goldberg, the MTM-bred writer who had produced *The Last Resort* for MTM in 1979. Tom Patchett, who with partner Jay Tarses had helped write and produce the original *Mary Tyler Moore Show*, *We've Got Each Other*, and the Randall and Newhart shows, and who had worked on Mary's 1978 variety show, created the sitcom *Open All Night* and the much acclaimed summer 1983 comedy *Buffalo Bill*. (When *Buffalo Bill* went on 'hiatus' prior to cancellation in the winter of 1984, its time slot was filled by Allan Burns' *The Duck Factory*, produced by MTM.) Most of these programmes were 'Quality Sitcoms' in the MTM-style; the difference was that MTM as a company did not produce them. MTM was changing from a sitcom factory to an academy for sitcom writer-producers, a prestigious and elite university to be sure, but one from which graduation seemed inevitable.

At the same time as ABC was dominating the ratings and MTM was losing its writers, the company was unable to come up with a sitcom hit to replace *The Mary Tyler Moore Show*. (Ironically, *Taxi*, formerly a top-ten hit on ABC, would, after a drop in ratings, move to NBC under Grant Tinker, where it failed to score in the ratings and was cancelled.) *Phyllis* and *Doc* lasted only two seasons; it was said because Doc was too likeable and Phyllis not likeable enough.[58] The other two-season failure of this period was *The Tony Randall Show*, which some MTM people claim failed because of poor scheduling but which Grant Tinker claims failed in the office-home balance that had long been part of the MTM formula, by not staying in the courtroom enough.[59] In the 1977–8 season, MTM's most significant attempt at a witty, sophisticated *Mary Tyler Moore Show* successor, *The Betty White Show*, bombed in the ratings. Betty White had debuted on *The Mary Tyler Moore Show* as 'the happy homemaker', Sue Ann Nivens, in a 1974 episode entitled 'The Lars Affair'. The sweet-mannered yet vicious-tongued cooking show hostess became a regular after Valerie Harper left to do *Rhoda*. On *The Betty White Show*, she played a similar character and had Georgia Engel (Ted's wife Georgette on the Moore show) as a sidekick besides. Nevertheless CBS cancelled the programme, symbolising the end of the *Mary Tyler Moore Show* bloodline at the same time as its creators left MTM. MTM producers believe the show would have found an audience if it had not been cancelled right away, as several other MTM productions which started with low ratings did – among them *Lou Grant* and *Hill Street Blues*.[60]

In the 1978–9 season, MTM found a sitcom hit with *WKRP in Cincinnati*, another programme that got off to a slow start, but one which CBS allowed to go off the air temporarily and revamp. The *TV Guide* exposé saw *WKRP* as a compromise with the Silverman era:

> MTM executives seem to be looking to *WKRP* to salvage their comedic reputation in much the same way the ravaged Republicans looked to Dwight Eisenhower in 1952 . . . to salvage their political reputation. Toward that end, *WKRP* is going after a broader, somewhat different audience. The rock milieu provides instant identification for young viewers, of course . . . but the most egregious accommodation is the casting of a stunningly sexy blonde . . . although the comedy is still rather sophisticated, compromises have clearly been made; no one ever acted – or looked – like that in the old MTM newsroom at WJM, Minneapolis. Tinker insists *WKRP* will have 'character development in the MTM vein,' but he readily acknowledges the show is 'our attempt to have it both ways – to do our kind of comedy but still get an audience in this new comedy cycle.'[61]

WKRP was MTM's only successful sitcom of the period and it did not spawn any spin-offs. Failures included *We've Got Each Other*, the same season as *The Betty White Show* and *The Last Resort* in 1979–80. *We've Got*

Each Other, a Patchett/Tarses product, had an unusual premise in being about two rather homely people with occupational role reversals. Tarses (no doubt with tongue in cheek) said about it, 'If I were a network executive, I wouldn't have bought the show in the first place. I'm not even sure I would have watched it myself if I wasn't involved with it. I have better things to do with my time.'[62] The show lasted only 13 weeks.

Into Syndication

According to the *TV Guide* article, the compromises MTM made on *WKRP* 'clearly show a strong corporate concern with the bottom line.' The article states that MTM had been operating at a steadily increasing budget deficit for five years, often reaching seven figures. However, the sales of the Moore and Newhart shows to syndication were expected to reverse the trend.[63] As it turned out, Viacom, the syndicator for the two sitcoms, received high prices for the 168 *Mary Tyler Moore Show* episodes, but the show did not do as well in syndication as anticipated. *The Mary Tyler Moore Show* was sold locally in fall 1978, before inflation hit the programme marketplace. It reportedly brought around $11,000 per episode in New York and Los Angeles. However, Viacom didn't get as high an asking price for *Newhart*.[64] Neither programme received very high ratings in the first year of syndication. 'Almost everybody who bought it was disappointed with it,' according to an independent source quoted in *Advertising Age*.[65]

However, Wall Street entertainment analyst Anthony Hoffman expected *The Mary Tyler Moore Show* to become a syndication classic, and for the price to go up at renewal time in 1983. Neither of the MTM programmes did as well as *M*A*S*H* in the ratings because they did not appeal to as broad an audience, and did not appeal as much to the young audience necessary for a syndication hit.

Diversification

For a number of reasons, MTM moved away from the sitcom in the latter part of the 1970s, and toward a more diversified product of dramas, variety and movies. According to Tinker, MTM went into drama because he found similarly creative people (to his stable of comedy writers). But he also cited the economic advantage of having backup shows: 'Having six shows is a very gossamer thing ... we could be sitting here with two or three shows in a few months.'[66] Diversification also represents a hedging of bets against a failure in any one 'product line', such as occurred with the MTM sitcom in the later 1970s.

MTM's first real foray into the one-hour dramatic series format occurred in 1975 with *Three for the Road*, a drama about a photographer father and his sons who travelled about in a Winnebago home. Its rapid cancellation may have been due in part to poor scheduling. CBS put it in a popular time slot for local news shows, and 53 CBS affiliates passed it up, with 35 others carrying it later in the week. For the 1977–8 season, MTM premièred its landmark drama *Lou Grant* along with another *Mary Tyler Moore Show* spin-off, *The Betty White Show*. Ultimately, *Lou Grant* bore little relationship to its parent show, but it would set the pattern for MTM in the future as a high-quality, one-hour drama with an ensemble cast and undertones of comedy. In the fall of 1977, both *Lou Grant* and *The Betty White Show* were low in the ratings. According to Sally Bedell, *Lou Grant* might not have survived the ratings if Ed Asner didn't have a firm talent commitment to CBS.[67] Another interpretation was that *Lou Grant* was perceived as a 'prestige' programme, whereas *The Betty White Show* was seen as just another sitcom and cancelled. For whatever reason, those working on *Lou Grant*, which had been created by Allan Burns, James Brooks and Gene Reynolds (of *M*A*S*H* fame), were pressured by CBS to make the show more commercial. Although some compromises were made, most of the CBS ideas were resisted, according to Reynolds. When, in the summer re-runs, the ratings picked up, *Lou Grant* finished frequently in the top ten and once even reached number 1. Later, there would be other kinds of pressure due to the political content of the show, and finally, in 1982, the programme was cancelled, some say because of Asner's liberal politics and the liberal slant the show took.

In a sense, *Lou Grant* was a transitional programme, the bridge between the Brooks-Burns era of sitcoms and the less comedic dramas to follow. The programme continued the ensemble approach popularised in the sitcoms, while diverging to introduce social issues. Another source for *Lou Grant* was the film *All The President's Men*, from which its visual style was derived and to whose approach to investigative reporting as drama the public had responded.

Lou Grant's success gave MTM credibility in the dramatic field, which they followed up with another series, *The White Shadow*, that CBS put on as a replacement in late November of the 1978–9 season. *The White Shadow* was about a professional basketball player, forced to retire, who became a coach at a largely black Los Angeles ghetto school, and built a team of rowdy teenagers into winners. Like *Lou Grant*, *The White Shadow* dealt with topical issues (VD, drugs, teenage pregnancy) as well as the inter-relationships of characters. However, *The White Shadow* was not part of the sitcom lineage at MTM. Its producer, Mark Tinker (son of Grant), along with executive producer Bruce Paltrow (who also created the programme), would later work on *St Elsewhere*.

MTM's third one-hour drama, *Paris*, premièred in the 1979–80 season and took the form of a cop show. In many ways it was a trial run for *Hill Street Blues*. Its developer, Steven Bochco, winner of two Emmies for *Columbo* scripts, joined MTM in March, 1978, having been assured the chance to develop his own shows and share in the profits.[68] Just prior to joining MTM, Bochco had written and produced *Delvecchio*, a cop series starring Judd Hirsch which ran for only one season but which received critical acclaim and industry respect. A specialist in cop shows, Bochco came up with the idea for a series in which acclaimed Broadway actor James Earl Jones would play a police detective. Tinker, in typical fashion, gave Bochco the freedom to develop the idea and CBS committed to a pilot if Bochco could deliver Jones. Because of MTM's reputation, CBS did not ask Bochco to produce a script prior to the pilot, as was customary at the time for programme development.

Although a fairly traditional police show, *Paris* showed a number of tendencies that would later emerge in *Hill Street.* The *Paris* pilot is peppered with writers, producers and actors who would later win fame on *Hill Street Blues* – it was produced by Gregory Hoblit, written by Bochco, and featured in various roles actors Michael Warren, Barbara Babcock, Kiel Martin, and Joe Spano. Paris was to be something of an intellectual, although tough and crafty. Paris would double as a university lecturer in criminology and would solve crimes through deduction and insight, somewhat as Columbo had. Although *Paris* was among the first network dramatic series to have a black leading actor, Bochco decided not to foreground the racial issue. In the pilot, Paris pursues a white politician, even though a black patrolman warns him it will make things difficult for other blacks on the force. Although human, Paris had a high level of integrity and a commitment to justice, resembling in these respects other MTM heroes Lou Grant and Capt. Furillo. Perhaps because it tried for an 'upmarket' appeal, yet appeared to be a garden-variety cop show, *Paris* lasted only one season. However, it brought some influential artists into the MTM workforce, and gave them a chance to practise their craft.

During this period, MTM made a number of dramatic pilots which did not sell to any network. *Arthur Among the Animals*, broadcast in May 1978, as *The Many Loves of Arthur*, was a bizarre story of a young veterinarian who related to animals better than he did to women, and who is eventually united with his lover through their shared joy at the birth of a baby hippo. Seemingly even less characteristic of MTM was a pilot developed in 1978 for PBS, *Going Home Again*, which Tinker envisioned as a fifteen-part mini-series in the manner of BBC serials.[69] The story of an eccentric writer and his family unfolded against the background of events in the 1960s and 1970s. In fact, the whole tone of the pilot was one of 'TV drama' rather than commercial entertainment, and the pilot could pass for a BBC dramatisation.

In 1980 nationally syndicated TV columnist Gary Deeb announced a CBS series produced by MTM's Gary David Goldberg, then a script consultant for *Lou Grant*, which was expected to air in 1980–1. *Bureau* dealt with wire service correspondents in Saigon during the Vietnam war, and began in 1966, during Lyndon Johnson's presidency. Tinker told Deeb that the programme would have 'a sense of quality and social responsibility', and that the show would progress into the 1970s with various reporters as leading characters.[70] Deeb quotes 'MTM officials' (clearly his sources were Tinker and Goldberg) expecting the series to demonstrate how the news media often were pressurised by the American military to 'put a happy face on the Vietnam War for the folks back stateside.' According to Deeb, the success of the film *The Deer Hunter* and of the TV docudrama *Friendly Fire* demonstrated the public's readiness to accept such a programme. However, Goldberg clashed with CBS over the pilot and it never made the schedule for fall, even after being revamped as a half-hour sitcom. Goldberg commented on the incident:

> It was a show like *Lou Grant* . . . high class and stylish, with political overtones. The pilot concerned military lying. That was our mistake. We picked a subject everybody at the network was afraid of . . . it was too political . . . we should have done *Herbie Loses His Briefcase in Hanoi*; maybe we would have gotten it on the air.[71]

Given Gitlin's account and Goldberg's subsequent willingness to compromise on the politics of *Family Ties*, this is no doubt a self-serving view; nevertheless it corroborates the existence of a *political* conception of 'quality' among the MTM creative staff. At the same time, MTM waged a constant battle with CBS over the controversial *Lou Grant*. According to Allan Burns, 'we fought over nuclear war, rape, industrial pollution, everything. Sometimes we won, sometimes we lost.'[72]

Another MTM attempt at diversification – into the area of musical variety – was equally damaging to the company, but this time not for political reasons. In 1976 MTM had produced a syndicated comedy/variety show entitled *The Lorenzo and Henrietta Music Show*, which was broadcast from 13 September 1976 to 15 October 1976 and involved music, interviews, songs and comedy sketches. In 1978–9 MTM attempted twice to succeed with a variety hour starring Mary Tyler Moore. Despite every effort on the part of MTM and CBS to make it go over, the programme failed in the ratings twice within six months, both in its original and its completely revamped versions. Finally, Grant Tinker and Mary Tyler Moore admitted defeat, realising the public would not accept Mary in a singing and dancing persona. Although Tinker promised a new half-hour comedy for Mary in the fall of 1980, it never materialised. Mary Tyler Moore went on to star in feature films, and MTM did not attempt another variety hour.

MTM also went into the movie business in the late 1970s. By 1978, MTM had made five movies for television, partly in order to keep their creative people happy and challenged. They also produced a theatrical release, *A Little Sex*, a contemporary romantic comedy, for Universal in

1981, directed by Bruce Paltrow, that was a critical and box office failure. MTM's most successful made-for-TV movie was the CBS *Something for Joey*, a tearjerker about an award winning athlete and his cancer-stricken younger brother, based on an actual story. In April 1977 *Joey* received a number 1 rating (31.5) and a remarkable 51 share. Other TV movies included *Nowhere to Run* in 1977; *First, You Cry*, another true-life cancer story, this time starring Mary Tyler Moore in 1978; and *The Critical List*, a medical mini-series, in 1978. 1979 TV movies included *Vampire* and *The Boy Who Drank Too Much*.

During the 1980–1 season, two events occurred that would represent yet another turning point for MTM. In January 1981 the innovative *Hill Street Blues* debuted on NBC. And in the summer of 1981, Grant Tinker left MTM to become Chairman of the Board and Chief Executive Officer of the NBC Television Network.

MTM TODAY

According to *Advertising Age*, Tinker left MTM 'at a time when its fortunes [were] ebbing.' MTM had sold no new network series for fall 1981, and MTM programmes were 'marginal' in syndication. Nevertheless, looking at the unrealised potential revenues of eight major MTM syndication properties, A. G. Becker analyst Anthony Hoffman estimated that MTM was worth a minimum of $300 million at the time of Tinker's departure.[73] Tinker's share of MTM was expected to be put in a blind trust as a step toward selling out his interest to his partners, his former wife, Mary Tyler Moore, and Arthur Price, now MTM president.[74]

Industry reactions to Tinker's appointment at the helm of the third-place network from which Silverman had just ignominiously departed referred repeatedly to the curious combination of traits that had always constituted Tinker's image. At the time of his appointment (July 1981) *Advertising Age* reported an 'overwhelmingly positive' reaction to Tinker in the advertising community, and said that he was noted for his financial and administrative savvy, and for a 'slim, trim, low-overhead philosophy.' He was also, said the article, noted for his 'classy' programming.[75] These were the twin and seemingly paradoxical components of Tinker's industry image – fiscal prudence and a nose for 'quality' – that were echoed in the many articles that appeared in the trade and popular press at the time of his move to NBC. For instance, *Variety* quotes one NBC affiliate calling Tinker a 'creative genius who belongs in the creative arena'. But the article also says that Thornton Bradshaw, chairman of the parent corporation RCA, hired Tinker for his reputation for astute financial management. At the time of Tinker's appointment, Bradshaw called him a 'skilled administrator, adept at motivating creative talent.' *Business Week* also quoted a former NBC official to the effect that 'Tinker has some sort of mystical effect on the creative side'; the article goes on to detail Tinker's development of *St Elsewhere* from scripts in order to save on costly pilots.[76]

As chairman of NBC, Tinker would pursue his MTM strategy of transforming 'quality' into profits, while also commissioning a more commercial line of programmes.[77] Although he divested his share in MTM, the fate of MTM remained tied to Tinker in his capacity as buyer of their programmes. At the time of Tinker's appointment, MTM had produced 14 series for CBS, three for ABC, and only two for NBC. Yet by the fall of 1982, MTM would have one show on CBS (the new *Newhart*) and its other three (*Remington Steele, St Elsewhere*, and *Hill Street Blues*) on NBC. Both of MTM's programmes for the 1983–4 season were sold to NBC: Steven Bochco's *Bay City Blues*, an ensemble large-cast show about a minor league baseball team; and Allan Burns' *The Duck Factory*, which found the MTM work-family in a cartoon production studio. Moreover, all of the MTM 'second generation' programmes would be on NBC: *Taxi* (having moved from ABC); and two new 'quality' sitcoms by former MTMers: *Family Ties* (Gary David Goldberg) and *Cheers* (James Burrows, Glen and Les Charles). In the fall of 1983 both *Buffalo Bill* and *Mr Smith* were NBC programmes. Michael Zinberg, a long-time MTM writer-producer, left to take charge of NBC's comedy development and helped to develop, among others, *Cheers*. For fall 1982, he produced an hour-long Texan serial, *The Yellow Rose*. Taken as a whole, the purchase of these 'quality' programmes for NBC represented Tinker's new strategy for the network, a strategy, curiously enough, that had begun with his predecessor, Fred Silverman.

At the time of his appointment to NBC, Tinker was reminded of his complaints about the networks forcing programme suppliers to go into deficit financing on first-run, prime-time series. Tinker replied that he still believed the networks should not expect producers to subsidise their night-time programming, but that 'everyone, including producers, is going to have to realise that television is a business and it must be run like a business.'[78] Tinker suggested that this may mean that the industry can no longer afford 'loss leaders' that don't pay off for producers. Yet at the end of the 1982–3 season, Tinker renewed MTM's *Remington Steele* and *St Elsewhere*, and the MTM-related *Cheers*, despite ratings so low they would have signified instant failure just a year previously and would not have lasted out the season, much less been renewed. The explanation for this apparently contradictory behaviour can be given in three little words: *Hill Street Blues*.

Given the structure of the American broadcasting industry discussed at the beginning of this article, a child could come to the conclusion that innovative programmes are not likely to emerge from it. But such a simplistic conclusion is misleading, even in the industry's own terms. For just as the system demands the repetition of previously successful formulas, it also reproduces itself on the basis of constant novelty and innovation. There is a parallel between the development of *The Mary Tyler Moore Show* and *All In The Family* at CBS in 1970; the rise of ABC to the leading position through Silverman's programming of 'kidvid' and 'T & A' in the mid-1970s; and the emergence of *Hill Street Blues* at NBC in 1981. In each case, a network experimented with new forms of programming in an effort to displace the currently-fashionable leader. In 1970 CBS was threatened for the first time by NBC. In pioneering the sophisticated 'adult' sitcom, CBS was attempting to be in the vanguard in the quest for the new demographic audience of young, urban adults. Similarly, ABC was able to rise on the basis of CBS being locked in to its schedule of MTM- and Tandem-produced sitcoms, as well as on its traditionally youthful urban audience.

In 1981 Silverman had been unable to rescue NBC from third place, and he was replaced by Tinker. However, a closer inspection reveals that Silverman actually began the programming strategy that Tinker would continue: the programming of 'quality' shows with low ratings in an effort to capture the urban, aged 18–49, high-income and well-educated audience which was threatening to defect to cable and pay-TV. Silverman was responsible for renewing *Hill Street Blues*, a dismal ratings failure in its first season which would become NBC's most important hit. NBC took a chance on *Hill Street*, in a sense, because it had nothing to lose; they renewed it in part because they had no backup potential hit show to replace it with.

According to several accounts, it was none other than Fred Silverman who came up with the idea for *Hill Street Blues*.[79] Steven Bochco and Michael Kozoll, who had worked together on *Delvecchio*, came to MTM to work on *Paris* with – between them – a speciality in the cop show genre that included *Quincy*, *McCloud*, *Switch*, *Kojak*, *The Name of the Game*, *Columbo*, and *McMillan and Wife*. Ironically, they were no longer interested in doing cop shows when they met with then NBC president Silverman to discuss his idea for a new kind of cop show, a comedy-drama, 'set in a neighbourhood with a heavy ethnic mix.' MTM alumnus Michael Zinberg, who was then vice-president for comedy development at NBC , had suggested MTM, Bochco, and Kozoll to Silverman and to NBC programming chief Brandon Tartikoff. Bochco and Kozoll agreed to do the pilot if they were given *carte blanche* from NBC programming executives and if Broadcast Standards (the network censor) agreed not to censor the show in advance. Tartikoff agreed to these demands, and after a number of skirmishes with the censors the pilot was created, tested and aired in January 1981. In typical MTM fashion, the pilot tested poorly, but with Silverman and Tartikoff pushing for it, it remained on the air long enough to become a hit. According to producer Gregory Hoblit, it was possibly the lowest-rated programme ever to be renewed, finishing its first season ranked 87th out of 96, having been shifted into five different time slots on four different nights, and averaging a 23 share (a 30 share had long been considered the minimum for renewal.) In exchange for renewal Silverman asked the producers to use a more conventional dramatic structure with some of the plot lines being tied up in a single episode. (In the first season, one of the most innovative elements was the serial-derived multiplication of plot lines, some of which would continue, others of which just trailed off, unresolved.) In what industry sources consider a miracle (though one we have seen MTM pull off a number of times), in its second season *Hill Street* became a genuine hit: NBC's leading show, number 16 in the ratings, and the leader in its time period (now stabilised on Thursday nights at 10), averaging a 34 share. Advertisers who had bought time on the show realised a bonanza. *Hill Street* also brought up the price for buying time on NBC in general, since advertisers who want to buy on the network hits have to take the flops also.

A variety of factors – other than the intrinsic appeal of the programme – converged to contribute to its success: it was nominated for a record 21 Emmys and won 8; *TV Guide* did a big piece on it; the network developed a strong promotional campaign in which each of the characters counted down the days to the second season, and the promos reached a large audience due to the baseball playoffs on NBC. However, as Michael Pollan explains in an insightful analysis of *Hill Street*'s meaning for NBC, '*Hill Street Blues* is not a run-of-the-mill prime-time hit; it is one of those landmark shows that announce the trend for a decade.'[80] Its demographics, he argues, are even more significant than its ratings would indicate:

> *Hill Street* attracts such large numbers of the young adults (18- to 49-year-olds) for whom advertisers pay a premium, that the show is worth more than a Top Ten hit with lesser demographics. Advertisers pay $15 per thousand for the prime consumer that *Hill Street* attracts (compared to less than $4 per thousand for the general viewer), making a 30-second spot in the programme worth more than $125,000.

Second, *Hill Street*'s 'post-liberal shading to neo-conservative' politics seem to fit the mood of the decade, just as the Lear and MTM socially relevant 'Realistic Liberal Sitcom' had captured the mood of the early 1970s. Third, the programme's innovative style may become 'the new paradigm for television.' Finally, and most significantly, *Hill Street*'s brand of success provided the strategy for Tinker's programming philosophy at NBC.[81]

In a sense, Tinker took his MTM production philosophy and transferred it to the network. That philosophy can be stated succinctly as 'quality makes money'. This is because, by programming 'quality shows', NBC, while not assured of a hit, is at least assured of a 'quality' audience to build on. At a time when that segment of the audience most beloved by advertisers no longer had to watch *any* network, such a strategy is more prudent than idealistic. Following the *Hill Street* paradigm, Tinker programmed a line-up of 'quality' shows – almost all MTM-generated – for 1982–3. NBC's promos for fall 1983 emphasised 'quality', making quite self-conscious references to the network's image as a 'quality' broadcaster. Thursday night was billed by NBC as 'the best night of television on television', with *Fame, Cheers, Taxi* and *Hill Street Blues*. In addition, NBC scheduled a Hill-street clone, *St Elsewhere*, and *Remington Steele*, both MTM. In spite of low ratings, Tinker renewed *Cheers, St Elsewhere*, and *Remington Steele*, seemingly going against his statement about 'loss leaders'. The catch is that, demographically speaking, none of these shows are losers. As Pollan points out, *Taxi* and *Cheers*, along with *Hill Street*, ranked most weeks in the top five programmes for 18–49 year olds. These programmes also did extremely well with urban viewers, which also increased the profits from NBC's owned and operated stations in major markets. WNBC, for instance, ran in first place in New York, despite the network's coming in a poor third nationally. In terms of audience measurement, these programmes also ranked high among the quality viewers, says Pollan. Tinker's 'new wave' shows have excellent 'Q' scores, he says. (This measures how much audiences actually like the shows they watch.) Another reason for keeping these programmes while cancelling popular appeal shows equally low in ratings is that the demographics offset the numbers. One of Pollan's sources reports that these programmes could be 'in clover' with only a 25 share. In the cases of *Cheers, Remington Steele, Family Ties* and *St Elsewhere*, the strategy paid off, since all gained in popularity during the 1983–4 season and were renewed for fall 1984. Yet the same strategy failed for the new 1983–4 programmes: *Bay City Blues* was cancelled after only a few episodes; *Mr Smith* failed early in the season, and *The Yellow Rose* was cancelled at the end of the season. Not one but *two* MTM-related programmes – *Buffalo Bill* and *The Duck Factory* – failed in the 9.30 'hammock' between *Cheers* and *Hill Street Blues* on Thursday nights, even after *Family Ties* was moved to the 8.30 slot. Columnist Gary Deeb reported that an 'alarmingly large percentage' of the audience was turning from *Cheers* to the last half of *Simon and Simon* on CBS. Then, 30 minutes later, they turned back to *Hill Street Blues*. Deeb concluded that millions of viewers were making 'a conscious effort' to avoid *Buffalo Bill*.[82] In the spring of 1984, *Buffalo Bill* was put 'on hiatus' and *The Duck Factory* also failed to sustain high ratings in the same time slot. Neither programme was renewed for fall 1984.

Pollan believes that Tinker is succeeding in his goal of increasing NBC's profits rather than concentrating on ratings numbers as Silverman had. In the era of pay-cable, Pollan observes, 'the network best able to keep a reign on these [affluent] viewers will have the least to fear from the new technologies.'[83] *Hill Street* and *Cheers*, he says, actually rate *higher* in homes with pay cable than in those without. A December 1983 Associated Press article corroborates Pollan's view, stating that 'most commercial buyers feel NBC is in better shape than its Nielsen numbers suggest.' The article goes on to say that NBC is going for the prestigious audience of big-city, wealthier and more discerning viewers, coming in number 2 with the 18–49 age group.[84] For all these reasons, NBC's future should remain tied to MTM and its alumni, who continue to provide most of its 'quality' programming.

However, according to a May 1983 *New York Times* article by Sally Bedell, MTM also has some less optimistic tendencies working against the companies' present and future success: 'spiralling production costs, impatient networks seeking short-term successes in the ratings as their share of the prime-time is eroded by cable television; and the prospect of changes in Federal Regulations that could make these independent producers, whose very existence is tethered to television, totally subservient to the networks – both financially and creatively.'[85] Under the leadership of Arthur Price, she reports, MTM has continued to operate as a 'quality' producer with the high costs that entails. Bedell cites as an example that in 1982 MTM agreed to let executive producer Bruce Paltrow re-shoot the première of *St Elsewhere* with a new cast and director for an extra $1 million, spending $2.5 million more than it received from NBC for the first season of that programme. *Remington Steele* was similarly in the red; and MTM projects that after five seasons the total deficit for *Hill Street Blues* will be well in excess of $6 million. According to Price, 'we are dealing with large amounts of cash and hoping for a payoff down the road.'

On top of this, says Bedell, if the Federal Communications Commission repeals its financial interest and syndication rules, which prevent the networks from selling programmes to individual stations and sharing in the profits of those sales, MTM will lose some of its lucrative syndication profits. MTM excutives argue that this would prevent them from risking innovative shows, since as an independent producer MTM has always relied upon its anticipated syndication profits in order to go into deficit financing for first-run programmes.

Both Price and Tinker (when at MTM) have said they will continue to make the kinds of programmes they themselves would like to watch, or else get out of the business. MTM has always occupied a maverick position in the television industry. It remains to be seen whether Pollan's optimistic predictions or Bedell's more cautious ones will prove to be accurate.

Notes

1. My sources for this section include: Erik Barnouw, *The Sponsor: Notes on a Modern Potentate* (Oxford and New York: Oxford University Press, 1978); Sally Bedell, *Up the Tube: Prime-Time TV and the Silverman Years* (New York: Viking Press, 1983); Les Brown, *Television: The Business Behind the Box* (New York: Harcourt Brace Jovanovich, 1971); Muriel Cantor, *Prime-Time Television: Content and Control* (Beverly Hills: Sage Publications, 1980); and Todd Gitlin, *Inside Prime Time* (New York: Pantheon Books, 1983).
2. The evening network viewing hours from 8–11.00pm EST, so called because they are the 'prime' viewing hours with the largest audiences and highest advertising rates.
3. Syndication refers to the practice of selling distribution rights to a programme to a syndicator who in turn handles the business of leasing re-runs to local TV stations on an individual basis. (It is also possible to syndicate first-run programmes.) The syndicator normally takes as a fee between 30–40% of the sales price. Actors, directors and writers get residual payments out of the remaining 60–70%, leaving the production company with little more than half the price paid by the station, a price that varies according to the length and potential popularity of a given show. Another factor is the number of viewers served by a given station. *Wall Street Journal*, 27 December 1977.
4. Barnouw, *The Sponsor*, op.cit., p. 58.
5. Bedell, op. cit., p. 34.
6. Cantor, op. cit., p. 77.
7. Bedell, p. 31; Brown, op. cit., p. viii.
8. Operation 100 is chronicled in Les Brown, op. cit.
9. Bedell, p. 24.
10. Long-running series are good for producers because of lowered overhead, lowered production costs and greater syndication revenues, but they can be costly for networks because of annual increases in salaries and other costs.
11. Brown, pp. 30–1.
12. 'MTM's Sitcoms Prove Well Worth a Tinker's Damn', *Broadcasting*, 14 October 1974, p. 28.
13. Bedell, p. 63.
14. 'Rhoda and Mary – Love and Laughs', *Time*, 28 October 1974, p. 60.
15. As confirmed by their opinions cited in Ben Stein's book on producers' world-views, *The View From Sunset Boulevard* (New York: Basic Books, 1979). In these pages we discover that Brooks and Burns love New York, think small towns lack intellectual stimulation, fear that American is self-righteous, condemn materialism and believe in the Constitution of the United States. See Gitlin, op. cit., for a critique of Stein's view that TV programmes express directly the producers' world views.
16. Bedell, pp. 63–5.
17. The Stanton-Lazarsfeld Program Analyser, the basis for CBS' in-house audience testing system, is described in Gitlin, pp. 32–6.
18. Bedell, p. 65.
19. Brown, p. 291.
20. *Broadcasting*, 13 April 1970, p. 2; and 21 December 1970, p. 45.
21. Brown, p. 137.
22. Bill Davidson, *TV Guide*, 19 May 1973, p. 33.
23. Ibid., p. 34.

24. 'Indie Video Firms in Upsurge...', *Variety*, 19 August 1970, p. 33.
25. 'MTM: Hottest Sitcom Factory in TV Industry', *Los Angeles Times*, 16 July 1974, section 4.
26. Ibid.
27. MTM produces the current *Newhart*, its only remaining CBS show, which began in 1982–3.
28. Rick Mitz, *The Great TV Sitcom Book* (New York: Richard Marek Publishers, 1980), p. 351.
29. 'MTM Enterprises: Top Dog and a Different Breed of Cat', *Washington Post*, 2 November 1975, sec. 4.
30. Information from *Los Angeles Times*, op. cit.; *Broadcasting*, 14 October 1974; and *Advertising Age*, 13 July 1981.
31. 'In the Future: "No Moore", But More MTM', *Los Angeles Times*, 9 November 1975.
32. According to Ben Stein, op. cit., p. 3, in summer of 1976 there were fewer than a dozen contractors of any size. In order of importance there were Universal, the television arm of MCA, which produced action-adventure programmes; the two 'comedy giants', MTM and Tandem; the TV Production divisions of the former major Hollywood motion picture studios: MGM, 20th Century-Fox, and Paramount; two smaller action adventure companies: Quinn Martin and Spelling/Goldberg, and several smaller comedy-productng outfits.
33. 'Net execs see comedy, half-hour format on rise', *Advertising Age*, 18 November 1974, p. 3.
34. A rating represents the percentage of all possible viewers tuned to a programme; a rating share represents the percentage of all TV sets that are *on* divided among the three networks, which is why ratings given in shares are larger.
35. 'Spinoff rating successes seen perpetuating trend', *Advertising Age*, 9 December 1974, p. 2.
36. 'TV Series Only Become Profitable for Producers Upon Syndication, Years After They Are Made', *Wall Street Journal*, 27 December 1977.
37. Earl C. Gottschalk, Jr., 'SMASH', *Channels*, 6 (February/March 1982), p. 48.
38. *Broadcasting*, 14 October 1974, p. 28.
39. 'Tinker says MTM, other TV producers in red, even with hits', *Advertising Age*, 11 November 1974, p. 2.
40. The money networks pay to producers for the right to broadcast their programmes.
41. 'Escalating costs putting squeeze on TV networks' program suppliers', *Broadcasting*, 13 January 1975.
42. *Los Angeles Times*, 17 July 1974.
43. Ibid.
44. *Washington Post*, 2 November 1975, sec. 4.
45. Ibid.
46. Information from *Los Angeles Times*, 17 July 1974; and *Time*, 26 October 1974.
47. Gary Deeb, 'MTM & Co.: Alive and doing well, though bruised', *Chicago Tribune*, 11 June 1979.
48. David Shaw, 'Give a little, take a little', *TV Guide*, 30 September 1978, pp. 33–4.
49. 'MTM & Co.', op. cit.

50. Bedell, p. 209.
51. Ibid., p. 144.
52. David Shaw, 'What Happened, Pussycat?', *TV Guide*, 23 September 1978, pp. 28–9.
53. 'MTM & Co.', op. cit.
54. Ibid.
55. Ibid., pp. 27–8.
56. Bedell, pp. 151–3.
57. Shaw, 'What Happened, Pussycat?', p. 28.
58. *Washington Post*, 9 November 1975.
59. Shaw, 'MTM & Co.', p. 36.
60. Ibid., p. 38.
61. Ibid.
62. Ibid.
63. Ibid.
64. *Broadcasting*, 10 January 1977, p. 34.
65. 'Leader Raised MTM on Talent', 13 July 1981, p. 80.
66. *Washington Post*, 9 November 1975.
67. Bedell, p. 210.
68. This account of the development of *Paris* is taken from Tom Buckley, 'Priming for Prime Time', *New York Times Magazine*, 9 September 1979, p. 60.
69. According to Shaw, op. cit., p. 28.
70. *Chicago Tribune*, 5 March 1980, sec. 6. A complete account of the *Bureau* fiasco is in Gitlin, op. cit.
71. Mary Murphy, 'Hollywood's Forbidden Subjects', *TV Guide*, 13 August 1983, p. 3.
72. Ibid.
73. 'Leader Raised MTM on Talent', *Advertising Age*, 13 July 1981, p. 3.
74. 'Tinker Likes Lineup', *Advertising Age*, 13 July 1981, p. 3.
75. 'Tinker Called Ideal for NBC Top Spot', *Advertising Age*, 6 July 1981, p. 70.
76. 'Bradshaw Tinkering With NBC's Future', *Variety*, 1 July 1981; 'NBC Affils. Want Take Charge Tinker', *Variety*, 27 January 1982; 'Lots of Tinkering at NBC', *Business Week*, 1 February 1982, p. 74.
77. See 'Dialogue on Film: Grant Tinker', *American Film*, (September 1983), pp. 23–5, for Tinker's own views of his attempts to merge 'quality' and high ratings at NBC.
78. 'Tinker Likes Lineup', op. cit.
79. My sources for the creation and renewal of *Hill Street Blues* include: Todd Gitlin, 'Make it Look Messy', *American Film*, September 1981; Bernice Kanner, 'How *Blues* Became a Hit', *New York*, 21 December 1981; and Michael J. Pollan, 'Can "Hill Street Blues" Rescue NBC?', *Channels*, March/April 1983. Gitlin describes the process in great detail in *Inside Prime Time*, op. cit.
80. Pollan, op. cit., p. 30.
81. Ibid.
82. Column syndicated in *Pittsburgh Post-Gazette*, 27 February 1984.
83. Pollan, p. 34.
84. 'Advertisers say NBC ratings have "quality" not quantity', *Pittsburgh Post-Gazette*, 17 December 1983.
85. This and remaining quotes from Sally Bedell Smith, 'As MTM Goes, So Goes Quality in TV Programming', *New York Times*, 22 May 1983, sec. 2.

The MTM Style

Jane Feuer

THE MTM IMAGE

The fact that MTM *has* a public image is significant in itself. Most TV production companies remain invisible to the public. When Norman Lear made an appearance on the last episode of the first season of *Mary Hartman, Mary Hartman,* it seemed to contradict ordinary US television practice. In fact, Lear had been unable to sell the controversial serial to any network and was syndicating it directly to local stations. But when, in 1983, Steven Bochco put in a plug for the new *Bay City Blues* ('by the producers of *Hill Street Blues*') it was on the NBC television network. Indeed it was largely through Grant Tinker's scheduling of MTM and MTM-related programming that NBC attempted to change its image from that of the 'losing' network to that of the 'quality' network, despite the network's continued low ratings. NBC's ad campaign for fall 1983 was based on a notion of 'quality' for which MTM programmes provided the model.

The image of MTM as the 'quality' production company extends to features about the company in the popular press: according to the *New York Times Magazine*, 'MTM has a reputation for fair dealing, and, by prime-time standards, high quality.'[1] Articles in the trades and in popular magazines and newspapers have demonstrated that MTM would spare no expense in the visual style of its programmes, putting 'quality' above financial considerations. Long after other sitcom producers had switched to videotape, MTM continued to seek the 'quality' look of film. And MTM hired a different breed of television actor, actors trained in the new style of improvisational comedy, such as Paul Sand, Valerie Harper, and Howard Hessemen, all of whom had their roots in improv companies such as The Second City and The Committee rather than in mainstream television acting.

Perhaps the central component in MTM's public image is its reputation for giving its creative staff an unusual amount of freedom. Article after article on MTM details the way in which Grant Tinker ran interference between his writer-producers and the network bureaucracy. According to the *Los Angeles Times*, 'sources in and out of MTM insist he gives producers the freest hand in the business.' According to the *Washington Post*, 'the consensus at MTM is that if there's a "Tinker touch", it's this harmony among Tinker and his employees.' James L. Brooks told *Time* magazine, 'Grant gave us blanket approval of anything we wanted to do, not just autonomy but support.' And Steven Bochco told the *New York Times Magazine*, 'he leaves you alone and lets you do what you can do.' Tinker himself, ever modest in interviews, has said, 'I see my prime role as being able to attract the right combinations of creative people and then staying out of their way ... what I do mostly is try to remove distractions which might interfere with their work.'[2]

To the student of cinema history, all of this sounds familiar. Much of the rhetoric of creative freedom within a system of constraints is reminiscent of *auteur* historians' claims for certain film directors. In particular, the notion of the producer as protector and organiser of creativity permeates accounts of the Freed Unit at MGM in the 1940s and 1950s.[3] In much the same manner as Tinker, Arthur Freed forged a unit of the best 'creative' talent in musical comedy. Their films are regarded as 'quality' commercial entertainment at its best. As did MTM, the Freed Unit operated under conditions of exceptional freedom in part because their concept of quality was not outside the boundaries of commercial success.

Indeed MTM might be conceptualised – as the Freed Unit has been – as a corporate 'author' in two senses and at two levels:

1. Conditions of creative freedom enabled MTM to develop an individualised 'quality' style.
2. A corporate 'signature' may be deciphered from the texts themselves.

According to Michel Foucault, 'the name of the author points to the existence of certain groups of discourse and refers to the status of this discourse within a society and culture ... [it] accompanies only certain texts to the exclusion of others.'[4] MTM's image as the quality producer serves to differentiate its programmes from the anonymous flow of television's discourse and to classify its texts as a unified body of work, two of the functions Foucault says the author's name serves.

As a specialist 'indie prod' MTM was both an exception to the operation of American television in the 1970s and typical of that operation: exceptional in that Grant Tinker fitted his company into the cracks in the system; typical in that MTM operated under the same economic constraints as everybody else. Regardless of quality, the kitten also had to serve the devil Nielsen. The previous chapter, a narrative in the industry's own terms of absolute success (high ratings) and absolute failure (cancellation), amply demonstrates both the freedom and the constraints. But establishing such a context does not explain the structure and effectivity of the programmes themselves. The relationship between commodity production and textual production is a thorny one to theorise. The usual solution is to consider each level separately, or else to argue that one level (commodity production) determines the other (textual production) in a directly causal manner. In film theory, the 'relative' autonomy of the text from its conditions of production is now taken for granted: it has become a truism that the kind of knowledge found in the previous chapter does not explain the conditions of reception of the texts, conditions that may not correspond to a diary of profits and losses, however meticulously detailed. But in stressing the 'autonomy' part of relative autonomy, one misses the distinction between 'relative' and 'absolute'. If the corporate structure of MTM does not directly *cause* the structure of the texts or determine their reception, neither is it true that there is *no* relationship between the two levels. There exist structural correspondences (homologies) between the two levels that may be encapsulated in the terms 'quality TV' and 'quality demographics'. MTM is in the business of exchanging 'quality TV' for 'quality demographics' but we need not view this process as a functionalist correspondence without contradiction. Contradictions abound even in Tinker's dualistic image in the industry as both hard-nosed executive and 'creative genius'.

This chapter will analyse the MTM style, a style which signifies 'regular TV' and 'quality TV' simultaneously. I will argue not so much that MTM should be *considered* an author as that MTM's authorial status in industry discourse bears a relationship to its concept of 'quality'.

THE STRUCTURE OF THE MTM SITCOM

MTM and Tandem are said to have transformed the situation comedy as a form. The MTM and Lear sitcoms, the story goes, took a mechanistic, simplistic framework for one-liners and sight gags and made it into something else: whether an instrument for social commentary (Lear) or a vehicle for 'character comedy' (MTM). In the handful of commentaries that have been written on the sitcom, this has become the orthodox view. Horace Newcomb, for example, sees the sitcom as the most elementary of TV formulas. Using *I Love Lucy* as an example, Newcomb describes the 'situation' as the funny thing that will happen this week, developing through complication and confusion without plot development or an exploration of ideas. The only movement he sees is toward the alleviation of the complication and the reduction of confusion. The audience, he says, is reassured by this problem/solution format, not challenged by choice or ambiguity or forced to examine its values. Newcomb goes so far as to put the MTM and Lear programmes outside the sitcom proper in the category of 'domestic comedy'. With domestic comedy, he says, we find a greater emphasis on persons than situations;

the problems are mental and emotional; there is a deep sense of personal love among members of the family and belief in the family as a supportive group. The form may be expanded when, as in the Lear comedies, the problems encountered by families become socially or politically significant.[5]

The critical view on the MTM sitcom supports Newcomb's description of domestic comedy as a transformation of the basic sitcom structure. According to one TV critic:

> In sitcoms, MTM's approach has always been quite specific, but its influence has also been so pervasive that it may be hard to remember what an innovation the style originally was. Before *The Mary Tyler Moore Show*, no one believed that a sitcom's foundation *had* to be in character ensembles, and humor wasn't even necessarily linked to motivation: on even the best pre-MTM sitcoms, with few exceptions, the personalities and interplay were machine-designed mostly to generate the maximum number of generic jokes – or, on family sitcoms, of generic parables ... After MTM made likability the key, even the most mechanical sitcoms had to pay lip service to the idea of the sitcom as a set of little epiphanies.[6]

'Character ensembles', 'motivation', 'a set of little epiphanies', have transformed the problem/solution format of the sitcom into a far more psychological and episodic formula in which – in the hand of MTM – the situation itself becomes a pretext for the revelation of character. The relative insignificance of the situation itself contrasts sharply with the Lear sitcom's significant issues. And yet one could argue that *All In The Family* actually retains the simplistic, insult-ridden, joke-machine apparatus to a far greater extent than did *The Mary Tyler Moore Show*. From the perspective of narrative and character, the MTM sitcoms are the more complex. A comparison between Tandem's *Maude* and MTM's *Rhoda* – two sitcoms from the same period and with aggressive female stars – illustrates this.

Maude is far more politically astute than Rhoda; she deals with controversial issues such as alcoholism and abortion; she is far more the 'liberated woman' than Rhoda aspires to be. Yet the show *Maude* is structurally simplistic: there is one important dilemma per week which is usually resolved at Maude's expense, the main comedy technique is the insult, and the characters are uni-dimensional and static. Even those episodes of *Maude* which announce their experimental quality – Maude's monologue to her therapist, Walter's bout with alcoholism –seem to thrust themselves upon the viewer. *Rhoda*, whose most controversial moment occurred when Rhoda divorced her husband, nevertheless took the sitcom in new directions, employing a variety of comic techniques, an evolving central character and, arguably, moving toward the comedy-drama blend that would become the MTM formula of the late 1970s. The MTM sitcoms inflected the form in the direction of 'quality TV', of complex characters, sophisticated dialogue, and identification. 'Character comedy' in the hands of MTM became synonymous with 'quality comedy'.

'Character' in Character Comedy

It is in its conception of character that MTM's central contribution to the sitcom form is said to have been made. If we employ the traditional literary distinction between 'round' and 'flat' characters, MTM emerges on the 'round' side of the sitcom form. Of course, the comic effect of feeling superior to a character depends upon a certain amount of stereotyping and a certain lack of depth. When, for example, Rhoda's response to her husband's departure became too serious and too psychologically 'realist' the programme departed the realm of comedy, if only for an instant, and entered into the genre referred to by the industry as 'warmedy', i.e., comedy overlayed with empathetic audience identification. When comic stereotyping occurred on *The Mary Tyler Moore Show* it was reserved for the secondary characters such as Ted and Sue Ann. Mary herself functioned as what Richard Corliss has called a 'benign identification figure', not herself the object of much comic attention or ridicule.[7] For the generation of women who came of age with Mary and Rhoda, these characters seemed 'real' in a way no other TV character ever had. Of course the 'realism' of any fictional character is an illusion of sorts. A round character seems more 'real' than a flat one simply because 'roundness' is produced by multiplying the number of traits ascribed to the character. A flat character has only a few traits, a process often referred to as 'stereotyping'. But what many in the 'quality' audience felt for Mary and Rhoda went beyond a mere quantitative depth. Their 'roundness' was also a cultural construct. The MTM women caught the cultural moment for the emerging 'new woman' in a way that provided a point of identification for the mass audience as well. The MTM women could be read as warm, lovable TV characters or as representations of a new kind of femininity. In retrospect, the fact that the early MTM sitcoms were popular successes seems astonishing, but MTM knew how to provide the right combination of warmth and sophistication.

It would appear that Brooks, Burns *et al.* arrived at the correct formula through a process of experimentation. The first episode of *The Mary Tyler Moore Show* ('Love is All Around', 1970), despite its sophisticated humour, has not advanced much beyond *The Dick Van Dyke Show* in its conception of character.[8] While Mary is already established as the nice but 'spunky' figure we will come to know and love, the secondary characters are heavily stereotyped. Rhoda is the obnoxious New York Jew who will do anything to keep Mary out of 'her' apartment. Lou is portrayed as the typical drunken newspaperman, even affecting slurred speech. ('Wanna drink?' he asks Mary.) The first episode is instructive because in its as yet undeveloped conceptions of Lou and Rhoda we can see what the MTM view of character added to the sitcom formula. From the standpoint of quality TV, the charge levelled against stereotyped characters has always been that they lack psychological realism and the potential for identification from the 'quality' audience. The sitcom remains forever on the far side of quality for this reason, since a certain amount of stereotyping is necessary to get laughs. Ted Baxter may have elicited this kind of comic laughter, but the MTM characters evoked another kind of laughter as well, which I will call 'empathetic laughter'. Empathetic laughter is what we feel for Rhoda when she takes a piece of candy and quips, 'I don't know why I'm putting this in my mouth – I should just apply it directly to my hips.' It's what we feel for middle-aged Lou Grant, bravely attempting to put on a happy face at his ex-wife's wedding.

Sometimes, we don't laugh at all. A supreme example of the ability of the MTM sitcom to skirt the boundary of melodrama occurred in an episode of *Rhoda* called 'The Separation' (written by Charlotte Brown, 1976). This unorthodox *Rhoda* episode shows us the MTM sitcom style pushed to the limits of pathos, exhibiting in extreme form MTM's conception of 'character comedy' and 'warmedy'. In typical MTM sitcom fashion, 'The Separation' follows an episodic plot structure divided into segments which are separated by commercial pauses or scene changes or both. Although the plot appears 'loose', a closer inspection reveals that it is actually tightly structured. We can divide the episode into segments and subsegments as follows:

1 Rhoda's apartment
a. Rhoda and Joe bargain for a house with a real estate agent. Joe subverts the offer.
b. Rhoda fights with Joe and locks him out on the balcony.
2 Brenda's apartment
a. Brenda and Ida Morgenstern discuss Ida's camping trip and her feeling that something is amiss with a family member.
b. Rhoda enters and fakes out Ida.
c. Rhoda discusses her marriage with Brenda.
3 Rhoda's apartment
a. Carlton the doorman hears Joe's screams and thinks it's the voice of God.
b. After a discussion, Joe leaves Rhoda.
4 Brenda's apartment
Rhoda discusses the separation with Brenda; Rhoda phones Joe.
5 Joe's Wrecking Company
Ida visits Joe at work and finds out the truth.
6 Rhoda's apartment
Ida and Rhoda talk.

The episode is structured around three scenes of unusual seriousness (segments 1b, 3b, and 6), evenly distributed throughout. Two of these segments are preceded by light comedy 'shticks' (segments 1a and 3a) involving stereotyped characters, an insincere real estate lady and Carlton the doorman in one of his set pieces. The final segment between Rhoda and her mother, however, contains only light humour and ends on a 'warm' moment. There is no comic 'tag' at the end. Almost all US sitcoms use the tag as a opportunity for one last laugh. Even some of the serious issue-oriented Lear episodes would use the tag to lighten things up before the final credits. The standard *Mary Tyler Moore Show* and *Rhoda* episode employed the tag to end on an 'upbeat'. For example, a quite sad episode of *The Mary Tyler Moore Show* features Jerry Van Dyke as the quintessential loser – a scriptwriter for Chuckles the Clown who aspires to be a standup comic. He is humiliated in front of the WJM family when it turns out that his first standup engagement is at a bowling alley lounge. After a touching scene between Mary and Lou (discussed below), we return for the tag to find the comedian standing at the mike in the deserted lounge, finishing up his routine for an appreciative Mary.[9] In 'The Separation', the absence of the tag emphasises the melodramatic nature of the ending.

A third type of segment in the *Rhoda* episode includes scenes between Rhoda and her sister (2c and 4); and scenes between Ida and Brenda, and Ida and Joe (2a and 5), symmetrically balanced around the major scene in which Rhoda's marriage collapses. In the world of the MTM sitcom, a couple's problems become the concern of the entire family, and any disruption of the extended family relationship is treated as seriously as a divorce. A good example of this pattern is *The Mary Tyler Moore Show* episode in which a disagreement between Mary and Rhoda involves all their friends and is eventually mediated by Georgette. Marriage is never privileged above friendship. Indeed it is arguable that the true 'epiphany' of the separation episode consists not in Joe's departure but in Ida's atypical understanding response to it. Joe, an outsider to the show's family structure, could be written out, but Ida and Brenda could not be removed without the entire edifice collapsing.

As the subdivision of the episode's neatly patterned narrative reveals, 'The Separation' moves back and forth between 'warm' and 'funny' moments to the point where the two blend into 'warmedy'. For example, the opening scene with the real estate agent is a typical MTM comic reversal; she tells Joe:

> Mr Girard, in all my years as a realtor, I have never been subjected to the shame, the humiliation, and the degradation that you put me through on that phone. Mr Girard, I have nothing but contempt for you – (cut to reverse reaction shot of Joe) – and if you're ever in the market for a house (cut back to shot of realtor) again – here's my card.

This very funny scene is followed by the quite serious confrontation between Rhoda and Joe, ending on Rhoda's hostile but comic gesture of locking him out. The following scene between Brenda and Ida is full of snappy one-liners:

> *Ida:* Your father and I are gonna just keep going until we stop having a good time.
> *Brenda:* I don't think you'll make it through the Holland tunnel.

This exchange is set up in typical MTM three-camera fashion. There is a cut to Brenda for her joke line, a cut to Ida's reaction and a re-establishing full shot for the next routine. In addition, Brenda has her typical, self-deprecating lines, the kind of lines they used to write for Rhoda before she spun off. For example, when Rhoda tells Brenda that she and Joe haven't had sex for seven weeks, Brenda whines, 'Please, don't make seven weeks sound like a long time to me.' But there are also touching, even sentimental moments between the sisters, as when, in the same scene, Rhoda tells Brenda, 'If it were nothing, you wouldn't have your arms around me.'

The 'big' scene between Rhoda and Joe has laugh lines too, but they are echoed by the nervous laughter of the studio audience. The scene shifts from anger to humour to pathos (as when Rhoda begs Joe, 'Don't do this to me'). It may be funny that Rhoda refuses to let Joe take his underwear, but her 'damn' at the end of the scene elicits empathy rather than laughter.

But the true 'epiphany' comes in the final scene of 'The Separation' as Ida Morgenstern confronts Rhoda with her knowledge. In her appearances on *The Mary Tyler Moore Show*, Ida functioned as a comic foil for Rhoda's neurotic behaviour. In the spin-off, however, she began to emerge as something other than a caricatured Jewish mother. In an early *Rhoda* episode, Ida went so far as to throw Rhoda out of her Bronx apartment when it became obvious that Rhoda was enjoying her reversion to dependency. This new concern for Rhoda's maturation culminates in a scene all the more touching for being many years in the making. 'Rhoda, I love you,' she says. 'Don't shut me out.' And Rhoda, herself coming of age, doesn't. In this final scene of 'The Separation', the long-time viewer is reminded of Ida's very first appearance on the parent show ('Support Your Local Mother', 1970) when Rhoda was so unable to cope with Ida's 'Bronx love' that she allowed her mother to spend three days in Mary's apartment. Now they move closer together. Ida offers to stay, then corrects herself, 'That would have been good for me, but it's not good for you.' She starts to leave. Rhoda, reduced to tears, has a reversal of her own. 'Ma,' she says, 'stick around.' They embrace, and the episode is over. There is no tag, no comic relief. The atypical poignancy of 'The Separation' stems from playing Ida against type far more than from Joe's desertion. (Indeed the pragmatic reason behind the separation was that the writers had trouble coming up with plots for the happily married couple and lines for Joe's wooden character.)

The *Rhoda* episode contradicts a commonly-held notion that the sitcom cannot allow for more than trivial character development. In fact, the MTM sitcom operates almost entirely at the level of character. It would be more accurate to say that the sitcom does not allow for complexity of *plot*. Watching MTM shows rerun, 'stripped' daily in syndication, one can view within an hour episodes from the first and last seasons of *The Mary Tyler Moore Show*. The situations are remarkably similar, even identical: Mary asks for a raise, Mary is offered a job by a competing station. But Mary herself has changed: she is more the career woman, less the daughter. This movement toward an expansion of character is arguably more an MTM than a Lear contribution to the sitcom. 'Character comedy' hinges upon the stability of the quasi-family structure, yet it permits individuals to grow within the family rather than by leaving home. Such growth should not be measured against traditional literary norms of 'recognition' and 'reversal', but rather in terms of the sitcom's internal history.

A look at MTM's approach to the opening credit sequence reveals the importance of character transformation to the MTM conception of character comedy. In the original *Rhoda* credits, a chronicle of Rhoda's life, she quips, 'I decided to move out of the house at the age of 24. My mother still refers to this as the time I ran away from home.' For the regular viewer, the change between this and Ida's incarnation in 'The Separation' is immense. Similarly, the title song of the first season of *The Mary Tyler Moore Show* begins by posing the question, 'How will you make it on your own?' In the ensuing seasons, the question has been dropped entirely. Presumably, Mary's survival on her own is no longer in question. Mary's evolution as a character represents an enormous change, not just for the static sitcom formula but for women historically as well. But critics whose conception of dramatic change can accommodate only earth-shattering moments of reversal are likely to overlook it entirely. Arguably, the viewer does not.

'Character comedy', with its emphasis on family ties (not coincidentally *Family Ties* is the title of a 1980s sitcom created by MTM alumnus Gary David Goldberg) and on identification with characters, also changed the nature of humour in the sitcom. If we accept the traditional notion that a comic effect is produced by *detachment* from character, what brand of comedy could the fetishisation of character produce?

'Comedy' in Character Comedy

Jim and Allan and I agree on the most important things. None of us would ever write in a gratuitous putdown just because it was funny or satirise something that was pathetic. The characters have a lot of affection for each other and we don't want to destroy that. (Treva Silverman, Senior Story Consultant, *The Mary Tyler Moore Show*)[10]

The MTM sitcom employs a range of comic devices to produce both laughter and the pathos of 'warmedy'. Although MTM might use similar comic techniques to Lear – the insult, a Lear staple, forms the basis for the interactions between Rhoda and Phyllis, Murray and Ted – they rarely have the same impact. The vast majority of laughs on the Lear sitcoms are produced by name-calling and shouting, or by the malapropisms for which Archie is famous. We laugh *at* Archie or Maude because they are self-deluded. The laugh track on Lear sitcoms is full of hoots, applause and condescending giggles, whereas the MTM audience produces little chuckles of identification more often than howls of derisive delight. Treva Silverman's remarks are clearly a slap at the Lear sitcom factory's attitude toward its characters.

In the MTM sitcom, laughter tends to be tempered by sympathy. Even the most stereotyped characters – Ted, Phyllis or Sue Ann – have their little moments of self-revelation: Ted when he meets up with the father who abandoned him as a child; Phyllis when her husband Lars has an affair with the Happy Homemaker; and Sue Ann herself when she admits to Mary that she's not attractive to men. The most ridiculous MTM characters – the group members and Howard on *The Bob Newhart Show*, for example – are rendered pathetic rather than thoroughly risible. Infantile, narcissistic characters are never expelled from the family: Ted remains on the air; Mr Carlin stays in the group; Carlton is rehired at Rhoda's request despite an astonishing lapse of 'professionalism' in his doorman duties (he has ushered in the burglars who strip Rhoda and Joe of their possessions). Yet the MTM sitcoms remain remarkably funny. This is because the comic devices employed produce the laughter of recognition, an identification that is especially acute for the 'sophisticated' audience.

Empathetic laughter transforms even the most primitive of sitcom devices: the sight gag. Every episode of *I Love Lucy* had at least one set piece of physical comedy. But they were rarely tied to character psychology. Surprisingly the sight gag turns up rather frequently on MTM sitcoms as well. Perhaps the funniest moment in 'The Separation' occurs when Ida visits Joe, unaware that he has left her daughter. After Ida insists that 'she can take it,' Joe announces, 'Rhoda and I are separated.' Ida proceeds to grab his face and pinch his cheeks with considerable force. 'Does Rhoda know?' she asks. Joe is unable to break her grip, but when he finally does, Ida claims she can behave with maturity, and then, as a parting thrust, zaps him with her handbag. This is a typical MTM situation: a character claims to be able to behave maturely, then proceeds to act childishly. A classic instance occurs on *The Mary Tyler Moore Show* when Mary, having been fired by Lou for writing with Rhoda a tongue-in-cheek obituary in the wee hours of the morning which Ted accidentally reads on the air, returns for a visit to WJM and finds another woman in her chair. In the midst of a polite visit to Lou Grant's inner sanctum, she becomes hysterical and sobs repeatedly, 'Oh Mr Grant, I want to come back.' She regains control, apologises, then lapses back into the same childish plaint. In both examples, the gag involves a set piece for the character – Mary's famous crying scenes or Ida's moments of fierce maternal protectiveness. And in each case, the motivation is familial love.

Another classic Ida Morgenstern sight gag occurs in 'Support Your Local Mother' when Ida and Mary race around Mary's sofa trying to stuff money in each other's bathrobe pocket. This hilarious scene reverberates at a number of levels. There is the obvious Bergsonian notion that humour stems from the human body being transformed into a machine. But there is also character comedy: Mary has refused to believe Rhoda's promise that Ida will drive her crazy with guilt. When Ida attempts to pay Mary hotel costs for sleeping on her sofa, she reduces Mary to the neurotic acting-out that is displayed in the physical gag.

Our response to MTM sight gags can even stem from pathos. In the Jerry Van Dyke episode, a moment of supreme embarrassment occurs when the comic is humiliated by having to deliver his standup routine to an audience of bored bowlers. In keeping with the MTM attitude toward characters, the routine is actually quite clever, which only increases our pity for the character. This reduces Mary to tears, and she flees to the ladies' room. To this point, the scene is embarrassing rather than funny. But Lou Grant, with typical paternal protectiveness, follows Mary into the ladies' room, much to the surprise of a woman who emerges from one of the stalls. As Lou attempts awkwardly to comfort Mary (herself a victim of over-identification with a friend's pain), another woman attempts twice to enter. 'Not now,' Lou growls at her. The culmination to this bizarre moment occurs as a visual joke, when Lou, trying to help Mary dry her tears, pulls out a towel from the dispenser. But it's on one of those circular rolls, and he winds up yanking the entire length of towel across the room, as the laugh track explodes with hilarity. We laugh in part at the notion of a machine not serving its proper function, in part at this bear of a man's very presence in the ladies' room, and in part at the genuine concern it takes for Lou to so abandon his macho decorum. Without the narrative context, the gag would seem only moderately funny, whereas most of Lucy's sight gags work perfectly well on their own.

But the tradition of physical comedy is not the essence of MTM character comedy; comic reversals of expectations are. Typically, an

MTM script will set us up for a sentimental moment and then puncture it by reversing the predictable sentimental response. On a *Mary Tyler Moore Show* episode, Sue Ann has lured the WJM family into her studio during a November blizzard to consume the food prepared for her 'Christmas Around the World' edition of 'The Happy Homemaker'. Prior to this, Mary and Murray were reduced to stony hostility over a disagreement as to whether Ted's new salutation should go 'news from around the corner and around the world' or 'news from around the world and around the corner'. Now they are trapped together by the blizzard. At the dinner table, Sue Ann has forced everyone to wear silly 'international' hats and sing 'A Partridge in a Pear Tree'. There is a moment of hostile silence, whereupon Georgette, ever the innocent peacemaker, begins to sing 'Silent Night' *a cappella*. This reduces Mary to sentimental guilt and she says 'Can anyone remember why we were angry with each other?', setting us up for a sentimental family reconciliation. But the reversal occurs when Murray grunts 'Yeah, I can remember' and Mary replies, 'Yeah, well, me too,' and the feud continues.

The most famous MTM comic reversal occurs in 'Chuckles Bites the Dust'.[11] Chuckles the Clown, dressed up as a peanut, comes to a tragic end when he is trampled by an elephant. Mary is outraged when Lou, Murray and Sue Ann persist in making jokes about it. But at Chuckle's funeral, in an atmosphere of hushed silence, Mary bursts into peals of laughter during the eulogy. The minister consoles the mortified Mary by telling her Chuckles loved to make people laugh. Mary, of course, promptly bursts into tears. Once again we have the puncturing of potential sentimentality but also empathetic laughter, since we too laughed at the jokes about Chuckles and at the very funny eulogy.

The reversal may operate in conjuction with another kind of MTM humour, the self-deprecating 'Jewish' humour of a Rhoda, a Brenda or a Bob Hartley. Most of Rhoda's laugh lines fall into this category, but this author's favourite self-deprecating reversal occurs in the scene between Ida and Brenda in 'The Separation'. Ida tells Brenda that she 'feels in her bones' that something is amiss with a family member. Brenda takes this as an opening and muses, 'I woke up this morning feeling very alone with this fear I'd never find anybody to love me. I would just be –' We cut to a reverse shot of Ida who interrupts, 'Oh, please, I don't mean the normal stuff.' It gets a big laugh, but also sympathy for poor Brenda whose neuroses are dismissed so lightly.

'Character comedy' reinforces MTM's emphasis on the familial and the interpersonal. It frequently verges on 'warmedy'. Since 'warmedy' itself frequently verges on sentimentality, the comic reversal also has its self-mocking aspect. The same sentimental moments are often played 'straight' in the MTM dramas later in the decade. However, overt satire and self-parody are rare in the early MTM sitcoms. To be sure, local TV news operations are made fun of repeatedly in the person of Ted Baxter; and Bob Hartley's therapy group reduced psychotherapy to psycho-comedy. But because of the sympathetic attitude toward character, the satire lacks bite. This begins to change in the mid-1970s. *The Betty White Show, Phyllis, Remington Steele* and the MTM-syle *Buffalo Bill* introduce self-satire into the MTM comic repertory. Yet self-reflexivity may be interpreted as yet another mark of 'quality'.

SELF-REFLEXIVITY AS 'QUALITY'

'Intertextuality', a literary term, refers in its broadest sense to the ways in which texts incorporate previous texts. Sometimes this takes the form of 'self-reflexivity', when a text refers in self-conscious fashion back to itself. Both terms have been associated with 'modernist' art: T. S. Eliot's *The Wasteland* operates intertextually, whereas Pirandello's *Six Characters in Search of an Author* exhibits self-reflexivity. It has been argued that these self-conscious strategies distinguish 'high-art' from the unselfconscious popular arts – such as TV series – and that even within high art, self-reflexivity distinguishes 'modernist' from 'classical' forms. Yet many popular forms are highly intertextual without being in a modernist vein.[12] In fact, the idea that within a form new works are created by recombining elements from previous texts in the same or different genres is crucial to an understanding both of Hollywood genre films and of TV series. The oft-accused lack of 'originality' of most TV series stems from this self-generating mode of construction. Intertextuality and self-reflexivity operate both as the normative way of creating new programmes *and* as a way of distinguishing the 'quality' from the everyday product. In aligning itself with the modernist self-conscious mode, the MTM style makes yet another claim to quality status. Within the MTM style, intertextual and self-reflexive references have both constructive and deconstructive purposes. When used constructively, these techniques renew and validate the style itself, as when new programmes spin off from old ones. But the same techniques may also be used so as to critique or *de*construct their own genre and style, as I will argue *Buffalo Bill* does in its commentary on *The Mary Tyler Moore Show*.

MTM's use of what Todd Gitlin calls 'recombination' places its style within the norms of textual construction in American television. As Gitlin and others have argued, even the 'innovative' *Hill Street Blues* recombines the conventions of the continuing serial melodrama with those of the cop show, adding a bit of cinéma vérité in the visual style.[13] Recombination continues from *Hill Street* with *St Elsewhere* and *Bay City Blues*. *St Elsewhere*, when it was being developed, was referred to around the shop as 'Hill Street in the hospital'. Its style is wholly derivative: the large ensemble cast, the blending of melodrama and comedy with the more or less 'realist' treatment of the medical series tradition and of controversial issues (AIDS, sex change operations), and in its use of the continuing serial narrative. *Bay City Blues* bore an even closer family resemblance to *Hill Street*, imitating even the dense image and sound track of the parent programme.

At a high enough level of abstraction, one could see the entire core of MTM programmes as a process of 'begats', with *The Mary Tyler Moore Show* as Abraham. The original programme (itself not without roots in the sitcom tradition) pioneered the ensemble cast of co-workers which would become an MTM trademark; it merged farce with forms of comedy based on empathy; it incorporated a literate style of writing in its dialogue. The sitcom spin-offs continued in this tradition with *Phyllis* and *The Betty White Show*, adding the elements of acerbic wit that would culminate in the MTM-related *Buffalo Bill*. The transition to the dramas occurred with *Lou Grant*, a programme poised midway between the sitcoms and the serial dramas. *Lou Grant* took the work-family concept from the sitcoms, added a heavier strain of drama and an emphasis on public issues, and began to expand the narrative beyond the 'series of little epiphanies' that had distinguished the sitcoms. The most issue-oriented of MTM programmes retained a focus on the personal dimension of public issues. Sometimes it seemed to stress the public dimension of personal issues as well, as when, in the final season, Billie Newman's agonised decision to remarry appeared to have cultural significance.

One can see in *Lou Grant* the beginnings of the multiple-plot line construction often claimed as one of *Hill Street*'s great innovations in prime-time drama. In an episode about child pornography, four different plots are interwoven. Already the TV convention of main plot and subplot is being deconstructed. In both the sitcom and drama, the subplot serves to 'lighten' the main plot. The Lear sitcoms would use this strategy in instances where the main plot was seen as too 'heavy'. In the *Lou Grant* episode, the two major subplots are also lighter, but they serve to reinforce the seriousness of the main plot, which concerns a young black female reporter named Sharon who gives confidentiality to a source. The conflict arises because her source is the mother of a young daughter who has allowed her child to appear in porno movies. Meanwhile, Donovan, a regular character, breaks his ankle after skydiving from a helicopter while covering a story on a mountain search and rescue team, in consequence failing to cover an important story for Lou. Both Sharon's and Donovan's commitment to getting the story at all costs alienates them from the 'Trib' family. In the end, both are accepted back into the family, with Donovan regretting his macho pride and Sharon feeling she would proceed differently in the future. In another comic subplot, a cub reporter named Lance finds out his ear problem will prevent him from achieving his goal of being the first reporter in space; this comic relief echoes the theme of risk-taking in the larger plotlines. Although the main plot/subplot division remains distinguishable, there is a thematic connection between them, and both take the form of the parable. The public issue of child pornography remains unresolved, but the familial conflicts are mediated. *Hill Street* would take the multiplication of plots one step further, reducing the sense of hierarchy to the point where the plot lines would take on nearly equal status, and rendering the sense of closure even more ambiguous.

The *Lou Grant* episode also moves toward the serial form in a discussion Sharon has with Rossi about the issue of confidentiality. Rossi refers to the time he went to jail for refusing to reveal a source. This had indeed occurred on an episode about pill pushers in a previous season. (Indeed Mary Richards had been the first MTM character to go to jail for refusing to reveal a source, so that there is a double level of historical reference operating.) Rossi recaps what had happened in the earlier episode but tells Sharon his case was different in that he wasn't protecting a criminal. The reference calls for the viewer to compare the issues involved. In this way, the series *Lou Grant* is seen as possessing a history, moving it away from the ahistorical sitcom genre and toward the continuing serial, as Rhoda's divorce had produced a series of interconnected episodes within the sitcom form. *Lou Grant*'s insistence on relating the private to the public sphere would continue in *The White Shadow* and in the serial dramas. Yet all would retain the MTM characteristic of focusing on the personal dimension of the public issue, never inverting that hierarchy as Lear had done, by using characters as stick figures in a political allegory.

In this way, intertextuality can be seen as the generator for the entire MTM output. Yet when self-referencing occurs, it tends to be constructive rather than critical of the MTM heritage. As an example of constructive reflexivity, no MTM programme is more significant than the company's excursion into musical-variety with the short-lived 1978 *Mary/The Mary Tyler Moore Hour.* The abysmal failure of Mary Tyler Moore's return to the small screen might make it appear that the programme was – like *The Texas Wheelers* or *Three for the Road* – foreign to the MTM style or aberrant in its generic uniqueness. Quite the contrary: the variety hour took the self-referencing of the MTM style to its furthest extreme in the constructive direction. A contemporary of *Lou Grant, The White Shadow, WKRP in Cincinnati* and *Taxi, Mary* faced many of the same problems as the other shows attempting to compete in the Silverman era, and in attempting to extend the MTM sitcom bloodline at a point where the blood was getting a bit tired.

Would the public accept Mary as a dancer and sketch comedienne, or would the memory of Mary Richards prevent such an acceptance? was the question the writers had to ask. Their solution was one encountered many times before in the movies and in television series:

rather than ignoring Mary's past incarnation, it would become the point of reference for her present one. In the first hour of *Mary*, Mary Tyler Moore addresses the live studio audience, asking them what they've been doing on Saturday nights. The first comedy routine has Mary looking back upon Ed Asner's audition for *The Mary Tyler Moore Show*. She then introduces the 'Ed Asner' dancers, and an ensemble of fat balding middle-aged men in Lou Grant outfits emerges dancing to a disco beat. Mary then introduces the 'family' of comedy players for the new programme by showing excerpts from their audition tapes, one of which consists of imitations of Mary's lines from the old show. Although it is primarily constructive, the new programme takes an ambivalent attitude towards the old show, on the one hand wanting to capitalise on its success and the audience's affection for Mary; on the other hand wanting to go off in a newer, more 'modernist' direction, derived from the late-night improvisational comedy tradition that was then emerging. (The idea of a pure construction is of course a theoretical fiction; there can be no construction without some element of deconstruction and vice versa.) The first episode is *self*-reflexive to an extreme. In addition to the audition tapes, it features a satire on television's self-congratulatory tendencies in a recapitulation of 'historic moments from the first 25 minutes of *Mary*'. And in a segment at the end of the hour, the cast members gather at a restaurant across the street to discuss the programme we've just viewed. They decide they really like Mary, but trash David Letterman who has appeared as an obnoxious member of the ensemble.

After the ratings failure of *Mary*, the show went on hiatus and returned in a revamped version, *The Mary Tyler Moore Hour*. Far from having disappeared, the intertextual references and self-reflexive moments were once again central to the show's format. Now the programme took on a backstage musical plot structure whereby Mary Tyler Moore played 'Mary McKinnon', a fictional character who just happened to have her own musical variety television show. Each week Mary McKinnon would deal with problems involving that week's guest star on the fictional programme. *The Mary Tyler Moore Hour* commenced with a re-arranged version of the old 'Love is All Around' theme song, and continued the references to Moore's previous television roles. Mary McKinnon seemed familiar; she was nice, spunky, and a pushover for manipulators. In an episode centering around Mary's fear of dancing with guest star Gene Kelly, her assistant answers the phone saying, 'She's exactly like she is on television', reinforcing our fondest desires about Mary Richards. Iris, Mary McKinnon's unglamorous female secretary, discusses Mary's weekend during which she attended a 'little' testimonial dinner in her own honour. It does not take us long to realise that Iris is a Rhoda-substitute. 'Iris, what do you want?' Mary inquires of her. 'I want your life,' Iris replies, in typical Rhoda fashion.

Not surprisingly, the new programme's only satirical comment on Mary's past involves not her sacred role of Mary Richards but her far more vulnerable stint as the feather-brained Laura Petrie on *The Dick Van Dyke Show*. Mary McKinnon's guest star is Dick Van Dyke, and the joke revolves around his never having met Mary McKinnon. The producer asks him, 'Don't you think Mary looks like the girl who played Laura Petrie?' Dick Van Dyke ponders for a moment and replies, 'No.' He goes into a flashback on the old *Dick Van Dyke Show* set, in which Laura has become a feminist, Richie a gay, etc. The skit plays the audience's recollection of their mutual video past against Van Dyke's claim never to have met 'Mary'. Finally they meet at the end of the hour. 'I auditioned for *The Dick Van Dyke Show*,' Mary McKinnon tells him. 'Rose Marie got the part.'

Although the variety hour took self-referencing to an extreme, other MTM programmes of the period also referred back to the MTM past, either directly or indirectly. A direct reference occurred on an episode of *Taxi*, the first programme produced by the MTM creative team after they left the company. In the fall 1982 première, Marcia Wallace, who had played Bob Newhart's secretary, is the guest star. In an odd play on the fictional status of a television character, Jim, one of the regular fictional characters on *Taxi*, is portrayed as idolising Marcia Wallace in her role as Carol, the secretary on *The Bob Newhart Show*. But Marcia Wallace plays 'herself'. The episode makes numerous references to Jim's memories of the older programme, culminating in a scene with all the fictional *Taxi* characters and the 'real' Marcia Wallace, in which Jim makes up a hymn of praise to the tune of the old Bob Newhart theme song. Although it is not unusual for actors to appear as 'themselves' in a fictional TV series (after all Henry Kissinger appeared as 'himself' on *Dynasty*), the complexity of the reference on *Taxi* puts it in a modernist vein, especially since the programme does not ordinarily use guest stars in this fashion. The *Taxi* episode plays on nostalgia for the earlier show, but also plays with the nature of the fictional enclosure, as does much modernist 'high art'. A similar play on the border between fiction and reality occurs in an uncharacteristic in-joke on a 1984 *St Elsewhere*. Dr Morrison goes on a tour of Boston, the locale for the hospital series, with his young son, Petey. Suddenly they pass by the 'fictional' bar, Cheers, and Dr Morrison asks Petey, 'Do you want to eat where everybody knows your name?' One expected them to go inside and chat with Sam and Diane, but the fiction of *St Elsewhere* was rapidly re-established. Nevertheless the MTM company family had asserted its intergenerational bonds, as well as acknowledging that the same 'quality' audience would watch both programmes.

Another late MTM programme which continually asserts a continuity with the modernist tradition as a claim to 'quality' is the detective show spoof, *Remington Steele*. The show displays its sophistication by having

Steele solve crimes by reference to plots from old Hollywood movies. Steele's relationship to the detective genre is entirely fictional. In this way the show includes the audience in its sophisticated circle of allusions. In the pilot, Steele, an ex-jewel thief, uses for his aliases character names from old Bogart movies. In the second episode, he watches *The Thin Man* and uses its plot to solve a crime. The second season of *Remington Steele* stakes a further claim to the modernist tradition. 'Small Town Steele' alludes to the Frank Capra tradition of small town populism as Steele and Laura visit a tiny burg named 'Da Nada'. But the townspeople are inhospitable and corrupt, and Steele is disillusioned. The first year credits had featured a first-person narration by Laura Holt of how she'd become a detective and had to invent Remington Steele. But the second season credits show Laura and Steele in a cinema, watching scenes from the first season. This self-reflexive vein culminates in an episode structured around dream sequences that Laura and Steele have about each other. The final dream involves Steele looking over a balcony from which Laura has fallen in the actual plot. He screams her name, and we cut to Laura in a hospital bed, having returned to 'reality'. The source of the final dream is never revealed to the audience.

If these stylistic touches link *Remington Steele* to modern art, its many media allusions place it firmly within a television tradition. Many American and British television programmes base their jokes and parodies on media references. This in itself does not necessarily entail a critical stance toward the television tradition, although it does reveal an awareness of television's status as 'low culture'. Most often, an appeal is made to a common media culture and a shared 'inside' knowledge among audience members. If you watch TV, you will get the joke; just as if you are an educated literary intellectual, you will 'get' the references in modernist poetry. Many MTM programmes seem to take this normative TV practice a bit further by being set in media institutions. WJM was always trying to improve its ratings, and many episodes showed these futile attempts in a humorous light. In one such episode, the WJM news team decides to broadcast from a singles bar. Mary's research goes well, but in the actual live broadcast, their sources panic in front of the cameras, and clam up, leaving Lou with egg on his face and Ted back in the studio with a lot of empty air time on his hands. MTM programmes not about media professionals often featured the media in a subsidiary way. *We've Got Each Other* had the female lead working as a photographer's assistant. Phyllis also went to work in a photography studio, allowing for jokes about advertising such as 'I backlit the sesame seeds.' This line exhibits more sophistication than the usual TV references to other programmes and stars because in order to laugh at it, you have to know what backlighting is, and you have to take an irreverent attitude towards advertising.

Remington Steele shows its sophistication in episodes where Remington Steele and Laura Holt investigate crimes occurring in media contexts. In one such episode, they visit the set of a frozen food commercial. 'Ah, commercials, the lynchpin of the television industry,' Laura observes. Although it is not uncommon for US TV shows to mock the ads that enable them to exist, such a literate analysis is characteristic of quality TV, especially since Laura is also mocking Steele's elevated style of speech. 'Television is so disillusioning,' says Mildred Krebs in the same episode, after discovering that the romantic TV stars featured in the boeuf bourguignon commercial actually hate each other.

When media references occur on US television, they rarely take up such a deconstructive position. Yet a number of MTM series episodes have tackled the nature of their own medium in a manner verging on the critical. Since presumably it's OK for the quality audience to hate TV, this practice should not be construed as subversive in any absolute sense. It does, however, exhibit MTM's 'quality' mode of satire. Another episode of *Remington Steele* involves a sustained sendup of local TV news operations far less affectionate than *The Mary Tyler Moore Show* ever was. Various members of the news team are being murdered on the set of the evening news. After a lengthy exposé of the idiocies of producing 'happy news', it is revealed that the culprit was a formerly respectable print journalist outraged at the way the news was being corrupted into entertainment. He delivers his confession on the air in the form of a *Network*-like diatribe against broadcast news.

The Betty White Show, the most brilliant and acerbic of the MTM 'failures', also had a quite reflexive format. White's character was a toned-down version of her Sue Ann Nivens, another acid-tongued television performer. The pilot episode begins with a show-within-the-show, a TV cop show called *Undercover Woman*. The camera pulls back to reveal Betty White as Joyce, watching the female cop show on her TV. We then see the credits for *The Betty White Show* itself. This is perhaps the only recorded instance of a TV pilot within a TV pilot, setting the self-reflexive tone for the sitcom which follows. The episode revolves around whether the network (actually called 'CBS') will buy the series Joyce makes under the direction of her much-loathed ex-husband. Such a situation provides many opportunities for media-related jokes, although in typical MTM fashion another focus for humour is Joyce's relationship to her ex. The CBS liason, Doug Porterfield, figures prominently in the pilot. His title is Vice-President in Charge of Prime-time Dramatic Development, but he tells Joyce, 'Yesterday I was working in the mailroom.' (This brand of satire is repeated in a later *Taxi* episode in which the spaced-out Jim reveals an uncanny ability to predict which network programmes will 'score' in a given time slot, and becomes a consultant to a juvenile network programming executive.) At the script reading, Porterfield tries to censor a scene in which the undercover woman is disguised as a nun. 'What do you suggest,' the director says, 'that we disguise her as an atheist?' Later Joyce asks her ex husband director, 'What is my motivation in the car chase?' Sight gags involve a burly stunt man emerging in Joyce's brief costume and a scene in which the entire set collapses when Joyce slams the door. At a cast party celebrating the network's acceptance of the programme, Doug Porterfield reads the network's report on the show: 'Lurid, the mentality of an eight year old ... they loved it.' The parody of the television industry combines with the show-within-a-show device to place *The Betty White Show* in the quality reflexive style. In mocking ordinary television, *The Betty White Show* exempts itself and claims quality status.

An episode of *The White Shadow* appears even more critically reflexive in that it sets up pointed parallels between a TV show within the show and *The White Shadow* itself. *The White Shadow* revolves around a white former basketball player who becomes the coach for a Los Angeles ghetto high school basketball team. Typically, the programme dealt with interpersonal conflict and social issues among the largely black, youthful cast. Unlike other MTM programmes involving media professionals, the incorporation of a parallel television programme within the programme does not evolve naturally from *The White Shadow*'s premise; the commentary in this case appears all the more overt. As did the *Betty White Show* pilot, this episode of *The White Shadow* commences directly with the internal programme. We are shown a typical TV drama series about a black kid with a drug problem, and the camera pulls back to reveal the film crew on a Los Angeles-based location accessible to the regular cast. The kids are critical of the TV show for its portrayal of blacks and for its lack of realism (all criticisms which might be levelled at *The White Shadow* itself). In the school corridors, the team members discuss this 'ridiculous' new TV show about a white principal in a black ghetto school who always gets involved in the kids' personal problems. 'Sounds like a lotta bull to me,' one of them says. At that point Reeves, the white coach, walks past and the kids do a double take, reminding us again of the parallels between the much-maligned internal show and the programme which contains it. While observing on the set, Warren Coolidge, a regular character, is invited to direct the TV episode, after he criticises its lack of realism. We then fade in to Coolidge *on* TV, in the role we saw at the beginning of the episode. He has just been cast in the lead, and the team is watching him at the coaches' home. (A third such pullback shot occurs later when it is revealed that the team is watching the internal show on a bank of TV monitors in a video shop; we always see the programme from their point of view as 'real' spectators.)

The remainder of the episode involves the problems that occur when Coolidge 'goes Hollywood', and his conflict with another team member, Hayward, who thinks the show puts black people down. The team visits Coolidge on the set and Hayward complains to the production staff that they are making blacks look like fools. Hayward's charges are corroborated in a scene in which the white director asks Coolidge to strut soulfully with a ghetto blaster. 'You don't dress like that,' Hayward tells him. 'It ain't supposed to be real,' Coolidge replies. A secondary satirical strain revolves around Coolidge's immersion in the Hollywood scene. He begins to pick up the lingo, saying that he and his girlfriend are 'on hiatus'. When they run into Ed Asner (playing himself) on the lot, Asner shakes hands with Coolidge and calls him by name. Both strains culminate when the team crashes a Hollywood party. Hayward argues with the white creative staff of 'Downtown High' who are exposed as hypocritical and more than a little racist. When Coolidge evicts them from the party, Hayward tells him he's 'developed a serious case of Oreo mentality.' Ultimately, Coolidge comes around to this point of view. He refuses to do a comic scene in which he shines a white man's shoes; the producer gives him an ultimatum and Coolidge quits, returning to the team. From this description, the episode would seem to be a scathing critique of the portrayal of blacks on American television, and possibly a self-criticism as well. Yet this latter aspect is never fully brought out. At the end, Coolidge tells the high school drama teacher that there was some good and some bad in his experience of the TV world. Moreover, the parodic exaggeration with which that world is portrayed tends to set up the team members as 'real blacks', in a sense congratulating *The White Shadow* for doing a better job than the programme portrayed within. Ultimately, the episode sets us up for a genuine self-criticism, then fails to deliver.

None of the examples discussed to this point has been wholly subversive of dominant television practices, nor have they invoked the MTM tradition in a critical manner. Indeed it could be argued that in their very 'modernism' and their satire of 'regular TV', they are further distinguishing the MTM 'quality' style. It took a non-MTM sitcom, yet one wholly within the MTM style, to take the parodic strain in this style beyond a mere 'quality' reflexivity. *Buffalo Bill* is the most subversively comic programme yet to emerge out of the MTM style. Earlier MTM sitcoms, *Phyllis* and *The Betty White Show*, had featured unpleasant lead figures and acerbic wit, but Bill Bittinger was as far as one could go from the benign identification figure that Mary Richards had epitomised. The programme received a lot of publicity, centering around the unqualified nastiness of its central character, which was seen as transgressive of television's 'likeability factor', a normative strategy central to the MTM style. The most subversive reading of *Buffalo Bill* would see it as a complete inversion of *The Mary Tyler Moore Show*. Its modernist style and use of the anti-hero makes it recuperable to the quality tradition, but it does not take a 'forced' reading to see that *Buffalo Bill* also subverts that tradition.

The inversion is accomplished by incorporating all the MTM traits and then playing them against themselves. Instead of the sympathetic Mary, we have a Ted Baxter as the main character but one without any of Ted's endearing child-like qualities nor his familial acceptance. Like Ted, Bill is wholly a television personality, a talk show host in Buffalo, New York. Unlike Ted, Bill is clever and manipulative, giving his immersion in the world of image-making a far less affectionate slant. He is a fool, but not, like Ted, an innocent fool. Instead of the gruff but kindly Lou Grant, we have Karl Schub, the ineffectual station manager whose repeated failed attempts to stand up to Bill render him a comic figure. In lieu of the naive Georgette, we have the beauteous Wendy, the show's researcher who, although a bit naive, is nevertheless committed to liberal social issues and aware of the exchange value of her good looks. The other characters are less obvious inversions of the old MTM show crew, but all lack the 'warmth' of the old characters, and lack as well much familial feeling toward Bill Bittinger. Woody, played by the same actor who had portrayed the henpecked Mr Petersen in Bob Newhart's therapy group, is Bill's devoted and self-effacing factotum and floor manager. He would thus seem to occupy the same comic space as his previous role. Yet Woody is allowed to comment on his persona in a way Mr Petersen never could. In a moment of revelation, he tells another character that he considers Bill to be his mission in life, that Bill is so despicable that he needs Woody's faith if he is ever to be redeemed. Similarly, the two black characters, Tony, the assistant director, and the 'uppity' make-up man, hold Bill to account for his racism, and make scathing comments on their boss's personality. The other major character is the female director of 'The Buffalo Bill Show', JoJo, who is also Bill's sometime lover. But she is no Mary Richards, eternally respectful of 'Mr Grant'. In a controversial two-part episode, JoJo even has an abortion, knowing that Bill could never be a suitable father.

The *Buffalo Bill* characters thus seem to serve as a commentary on the old *Mary Tyler Moore Show* Utopian family of co-workers. They are a family, but at best a neurotic and disturbed one, headed by a father who is also a child. This twist on the warmth of the MTM family is brought out in an episode in which an unctuous correspondent for the station's 'View on Buffalo' does a spot on 'The Buffalo Bill Show' staff. We see her interviewing the various family members, trying to get the dirt on Bill. Her interviews with the cast members are intercut with scenes of Bill in his dressing room, anxiously preparing for his own interview. In each of the staff interviews, Bill is damned with faint praise. 'I don't hate Bill Bittinger,' says Karl Schub, 'occasionally he's selfish . . . he can be cruel and vicious.' To JoJo the reporter says, 'It probably helps having a personal, intimate relationship.' She proceeds to read aloud a diary of Bill's sexist comments which JoJo is forced to corroborate. Even the benevolent Wendy is led to make unfavourable comments about Bill. 'Bill can be cruel and hateful,' she says, 'but lately he hardly ever tries to get me into bed.' Meanwhile, we view Bill alone in his dressing room, trying out different charming personae for the interview. As we keep returning to these monologues, Bill's narcissistic imagination runs wild. He becomes incensed by an imaginary scene in which the reporter seduces him and he tells her, 'I'm offended by your lack of journalistic ethics.' Bill proceeds to evict the 'View on Buffalo' crew, pulling open the door and shouting 'get out' only to return from his fantasy to discover they are waiting at the door to enter. In a typical face-saving manoeuvre, Bill has nothing but praise for his staff; as he tells them afterwards, 'Liane tried to get me to knock you guys.' He traps his guilty cohorts into coming to his flat to view the broadcast.

As everyone but Bill could have predicted, all of the scenes we have watched being taped are edited into a scathing exposé of Bill Bittinger. The staff's worst comments are selected and, with heavy irony, the segment ends with Bill himself speaking of 'warmth, family and love.' (A caustic echo of Mary Richard's speech on 'The Last Show'.) After the broadcast there is a deathly silence, with everyone looking for an escape hatch. Wendy begins to cry and Karl carries her out. JoJo tells Bill, 'I said things like that to your face, but to say it on television is inexcusable.' As the deeply ashamed group gathers in the corridor, Bill, isolated as ever, drags his immense TV set onto the balcony and starts to shove it over the edge. JoJo tries to stop him, at which point Bill delivers a speech about his relationship to the family which, although pathetic in its way, is a far cry from the typical MTM attitude of sentimental familial affection:

> Friendship happens to be a very overrated commodity ... I believe in me ... because I've been left too many times by too many people ... starting with my father ... friendship just slows me down ... [to be and stay on TV] you'd better learn to live by yourself ... for yourself ... I like living alone ... I may be the happiest person I know of ...

JoJo responds, 'Oh, Bill,' and as she starts to embrace him, they knock the TV set over the ledge. This undercuts any sympathy we may have felt for Bill. We return for the tag. Bill is yelling '$800 cash' while JoJo expresses concern that it might have killed someone below. 'Don't worry,' Bill tells her, 'nobody's down there ... except Karl, Wendy, Tony, Woody ...' and the episode ends. This is a far cry from the typical MTM pattern whereby family harmony is restored by the end of every episode. In the usual pattern, a violation of family harmony is seen as a breach that needs to be healed in order to restore the Utopian moment; in this case, the aberration is Bill's uncharacteristic moment of concern for the others, a moment which is itself rapidly undercut. As a character, Bill is compelling in his very narcissism and isolation, but he is not 'benign' and he is not an identification figure. We are more likely to identify with the other staff members and to laugh at Bill's pain, an inversion of the MTM pattern which produces a dark rather than light mode of comedy. The Buffalo Bill family is the MTM family viewed through dark glasses instead of the usual rose-coloured ones.

Even more subversive than its treatment of the work-family, is *Buffalo Bill*'s attitude toward television itself. *Buffalo Bill* directs its satire *at* television as an institution. Its critique of television does not occur on isolated episodes; it informs the very core of the programme's structure. The various broadcasts of 'The Buffalo Bill Show' take up far more time than Ted's bloopers ever did, and these on-air sequences are played off against Bill's off-camera hypocrisy. In addition, our view of the show is frequently from the inside of the control booth, so that we watch Bill's show on the various monitors and from the viewpoint of the production staff. Much of the satire is achieved through the staff's outraged reactions to Bill's on-camera antics. The 'inside' point of view is subversive as well as reflexive.

An especially blatant instance of *Buffalo Bill*'s critique of television occurs in the episode in which Bill invites an octogenerian former tap dancer on the programme. Bill coerces the old man, who has long been retired, to do a few steps on the air, during which the man has a heart attack and dies. At this point Bill goes berserk and addresses the studio audience directly. Quite like the anchorman on the *Remington Steele* episode, Bill's speech is a condemnation of television. In this case, however, the message is complicated by the fact that it was Bill himself who brought on the man's death. Bill refuses to allow JoJo to cut to a commercial. 'Television killed him,' he tells the audience, referring to it as 'the human sacrifice business.' He asks the audience to quit watching TV. Of course Bill's hypocrisy is revealed when a woman in the audience goes into labour and Bill turns it into melodrama with a 'miracle of life' speech. Then Bill runs out of steam with 51 minutes of air time left for the staff to fill. They go immediately to a pre-recorded 'Best of Bittinger'. In the tag, Bill has returned to normal, refusing to see the woman who has named her baby after him.

Buffalo Bill's critique of television is complex since the characters themselves have an ambivalent attitude toward the medium. 'The Buffalo Bill Show' is no respected Los Angeles daily; it is not even the second-rate but sincere WJM local news. The internal show is unlikely to be perceived as having any redeeming virtues, even if the programme as a whole may be read as an 'intelligent' criticism of the lowest form of television. If *The Mary Tyler Moore Show* was both regular TV and quality TV, *Buffalo Bill* was both 'quality TV' and 'radical TV'.

But the programme started no trend. *Buffalo Bill* was replaced in its time slot by Allan Burns' *The Duck Factory*, a virtual re-creation of *The Mary Tyler Moore Show* set in a cartoon factory, complete with warm, likeable characters and an identification figure even more benign than Mary Richards. It also failed in the ratings, indicating that even the orthodox MTM style of sitcom may have outlived its cultural moment.

CONCLUSION: THE POLITICS OF MTM

Quality TV is liberal TV. Given its institutional constraints and its entertainment function, one cannot expect American television to take self-criticism to the level of a Godard film. Yet both MTM and Godard gear their discourse to an assumed audience. Godard's extreme self-reflexivity appeals to the small audience of avant-garde intellectuals who pay to see his films. The appeal of an MTM programme must be double-edged. It must appeal both to the 'quality' audience, a liberal, sophisticated group of upwardly mobile professionals; and it must capture a large segment of the mass audience as well. Thus MTM programmes must be readable at a number of levels, as is true of most US television fare. MTM shows may be interpreted as warm, human comedies or dramas; or they may be interpreted as self-aware 'quality' texts. In this sense also, the MTM style is both typical and atypical. Its politics are seldom overt, yet the very concept of 'quality' is itself ideological. In interpreting an MTM programme as a quality programme, the quality audience is permitted to enjoy a form of television which is seen as more literate, more stylistically complex, and more psychologically 'deep' than ordinary TV fare. The quality audience gets to separate itself from the mass audience and can watch TV without guilt, and without realising that the double-edged discourse they are getting is also ordinary TV. Perhaps the best example of a programme that triumphed through this process of multiple readings is *Hill Street Blues*, the programme which marked MTM's transition to the quality demographic strategy.

This does not mean that the MTM style lacks progressive elements, only that, as with all forms of artistic production under capitalism, the progressive elements may be recuperable to an ideology of 'quality'. As an illustration of the politics of quality, I will take as an extended example one of the crucial innovations that MTM gave to the sitcom and the TV drama: the idea of the family of co-workers.

Every genre of American television is based on some kind of family structure. Even the personnel of the news programmes are presented to us as a 'family'; and until MTM came along, the nuclear family was the subject of most TV genres, as it was for the Lear sitcoms. At a time when the nuclear family was under attack outside the institution of television, MTM pioneered a different kind of family, one that retained certain residual ideologies of family life while doing away with the more oppressive aspects of the nuclear family. The MTM work family both reproduces the wholesome norms of family life on TV and presents us with a Utopian variation on the nuclear family more palatable to a new generation and to the quality audience.

Rhoda was the only successful MTM sitcom to centre on a nuclear family rather than a family bonded by work and freely chosen (even then, Rhoda didn't live at home and the Morgensterns weren't very wholesome). *The Bob Newhart Show* featured a married couple, but the family unit included Bob's co-workers and even his therapy group. Those MTM sitcoms which featured a traditional family structure – *The Texas Wheelers, Doc, The Bob Crane Show* – tended to use an extended family structure and, moreover, tended to be outside the MTM creative nucleus and outside the 'quality' style. Eventually the idea of the non-nuclear family became the television norm.

The MTM work-family is clearly a response to the breakdown of the nuclear family inside and outside of the television institution. But how are we to interpret the politics of that response? On the one hand, the work family can be seen as Utopian in a reactionary direction. It presents a view of work as a familial activity, a view far from a 'realistic' representation of the real world of work. And the work family portrayed may be seen as a conservative force, valuing stasis over change. Many episodes of *The Mary Tyler Moore Show* take for their situation an eruption of disharmony within the WJM family: Rhoda and Mary feud; Murray and Mary feud; Lou fires Mary; Mary is offered another job; Rhoda gets a chance to move back to New York (this last prior to her actual spinning-off). In every case and in traditional sitcom form, harmony is re-established by bringing the family back together at the cost of what, in another context, might be seen as change or growth. Nobody is ever permitted to leave home. As one critic has written, the MTM shows' 'standard moment of epiphany' occurs with the discovery 'that nothing ever changes and people always stay reassuringly the same'.[14] This ideology of family harmony permeates the dramas as well, the difference being that in the continuing serial format, the moments of harmony are brief. Even *Buffalo Bill* represents the unity of the work family as a positive goal; it is just that Bill's presence makes that goal an impossible one.

Many MTM programmes make explicit references to the idea of the work family. In 'The Last Show' of *The Mary Tyler Moore Show*, Mary makes a long, sentimental speech about having found a family in her friends at work. The idea of the work family as a reactionary concept is rendered explicit in an episode of *WKRP in Cincinnati*. The employees of WKRP are asked to join a union. When Travis, the 'benign identification figure' of the programme, refuses to grant a pay raise, Johnny Fever calls him 'a true crypto-fascist puppet of the managerial elite', thus exposing Travis' position seemingly on the side of the workers but really on the side of management. Yet the rest of the episode undercuts this explanation. Johnny only becomes interested in the union when he discovers he will be paid by seniority (he is the oldest living DJ). When he gets this information, he breaks into the song, 'Look for the union label', and the others join in. This song comes from an unusually proletarian advertisement widely shown on US TV in which members of the International Ladies Garment Workers Union stand in formation and sing for us to buy clothing with the union label. In invoking the advertisement, including its image of solidarity, *WKRP* mocks its message. After much discussion, the situation is resolved when Travis negotiates with the station owner. He forces her to give the employees a raise, and they 'freely' vote against the union. In this way, an opposition is set up *between* the union and the family of workers (deductively, their interests might be seen as similar, but the MTM concept of the work family is an individualistic one). The owner's son, the timid Carlson, says 'We're a *family* here. I'm not going to have outsiders telling us what to do.' Andy Travis says, 'Don't let this union business split us up.' Although management is portrayed unfavourably, the message is clear: the work family does not need to organise because it is already a democratic institution; all problems can be resolved within the family structure. A union would represent an intrusion from the real world of work into an already Utopian situation. This reading of the work family would view it as a reactionary force, in that it presents an unrealistically familial view of what we know to be an alienated labour process.

Yet such a reading of MTM's own discourse about the family of co-workers is only the most obvious interpretation of the Utopian dimension of the work family. For the MTM family also represents a positive alternative to the nuclear family that had for so long dominated representations of the family on American television. If nobody ever changes (a reading we have already shown to be dubious at best), if nobody ever has to leave home, perhaps it is because the MTM family is one in which it's possible to grow up. This more positive reading depends on the assumption that American network television never represents 'realistic' solutions to 'real' problems, but that, for this very reason, it is capable of showing us ideal solutions to mythicised versions of real problems. The work family is a solution to the problems of the nuclear family. It gives us a vision of that merger of work and love that Freud said was the ideal of mental, and that many would also see as the ideal of political, health. MTM shows us this ideal over and over again within what in reality are the most oppressive institutional contexts: the hospital, the police precinct, the TV station. Media institutions work especially well for an idealised vision of work, since we already have a mythology of 'creative' work as an ideal.

WKRP in Cincinnati: (l. to r.) Loni Anderson, Jan Smithers, Frank Bonner, Gary Sandy, Gordon Jump.

The WJM family is what Mary Richards left home for, and it fulfilled her expectations and ours. For women especially, the alternatives presented were ideal ones, not depictions of the reality of work but images of a liberated existence that could be taken as a goal to strive towards. Mary and Rhoda came to represent an ideal of female friendship, a relationship that, due to the redundancy of the sitcom form, could never be torn asunder by the marriage of either woman. Mary's romances never represented a serious threat to either her relationship with Rhoda or her family at work. If the work-family concept proved pleasureable and reproducible, perhaps it was because it provided a positive alternative for the families who watched Mary and Rhoda on their TVs.

It must be stressed that neither of these readings of the work-family concept is 'correct'. Both are possible, but only the latter can explain the pleasure the concept must have provided in order for the programmes to be popular. That pleasure can encompass both progressive longings for an alternative to the nuclear family, and 'reactionary' longings for a return to the presumed ideal family structures of the past. The liberal, quality structure of the programmes permits and encourages both kinds of pleasure.

Notes

1. 9 September 1979.
2. 16 July 1974; 2 November 1975; 13 July 1981; 9 September 1979; *Los Angeles Times,* 16 July 1974.
3. See, for example, Donald Knox, *The Magic Factory* (New York: Praeger, 1973); and Hugh Fordin, *The World of Entertainment* (Garden City, N.Y: Doubleday, 1975).
4. 'What is an Author?' *Screen,* 20 (Spring 1979), p. 19.
5. *TV: The Most Popular Art* (New York: Anchor Books, 1974).
6. Tom Carson, 'The Even Couple', *The Village Voice,* 3 May 1983, p. 59.
7. 'Happy Days are Here Again', *Film Comment*, vol, 15 no. 4 July/August 1979.
8. Described in detail in Rick Mitz, *The Great TV Sitcom Book* (New York: Richard Marek Publishers, 1980).
9. MTM also developed a 'tag' ending that would trail off in such a way that the conversation appears to continue after the programme ends; this produces a 'quality' effect by rendering the sense of closure less emphatic.
10. *New York Times Magazine,* 7 April 1974, p. 97.
11. Written by David Lloyd; described in Rick Mitz, op. cit.
12. I make this point at greater length in my book, *The Hollywood Musical* (London: Macmillan, 1982).
13. Todd Gitlin, *Inside Prime Time* (New York: Pantheon Books, 1983).
14. Tom Carson, 'Lame Duck', *The Village Voice,* 1 May 1984.

The Making of (The) MTM (Show)

Paul Kerr

To the casual observer, the success of a sitcom series featuring a small-screen star like Mary Tyler Moore might seem unsurprising and thus undeserving of analysis or explanation. Similarly, the emergence and expansion of one more independent production company in the billion dollar business that is American network television seems, on the surface at least, less than noteworthy. This essay, however, argues that the success of MTM Enterprises as a production company and of *The Mary Tyler Moore Show* as a television series were far from predictable and were indeed predicated on a coincidence of developments both inside the television industry and in the broader stream of American life. The aim of this article, therefore, is to replace both MTM and *The Mary Tyler Moore Show* in the historical context out of which they emerged in 1970. It attempts, in other words, to diagnose the conditions of existence of MTM and thus to try and unpack – without resort to either reflection theory or simple studio-as-auteurism – the relations between the mode and moment of production and the product.

In the 1960s Mary Tyler Moore had been a popular television performer, particularly well-loved for her role as Laura Petrie, the wife of the Dick Van Dyke character in *The Dick Van Dyke Show*, which she came to after a series of lesser late 50s roles (notably as 'sexy' secretary Sam in *Richard Diamond, Private Detective* – in which she only ever appeared from the waist down – and as Happy Hotpoint, an anthropomorphic advertising gimmick for a washing machine).

Then, in April 1969, CBS reunited her with Dick Van Dyke in a television special entitled *Dick Van Dyke and The Other Woman*. When the show garnered the kind of critical respect and audience approval that several recent Van Dyke vehicles had all too visibly lacked CBS seems to have concluded that perhaps *The Dick Van Dyke Show*'s prestige and popularity weren't entirely attributable to the talents of its male lead. In September 1969 Mary Tyler Moore was offered a multi-million dollar deal by CBS to star in a series of her choice of (initially) thirteen episodes. Furthermore, the network were willing to offer an on-air guarantee without benefit of pilot or pre-testing. Her manager, Arthur Price, and her then husband, Grant Tinker (at that time a programming executive at 20th Century-Fox-TV) were apparently pleased to be able to steer the star back to the medium where her talents were best appreciated and perhaps best suited. According to *Rolling Stone*:

> At Tinker's urging she went with the CBS offer which was a multi-million dollar deal that allowed them to set up their own company – MTM Enterprises – and retain partial ownership of this and subsequent productions as well as creative control.[1]

The precise details of this deal have never been made public – indeed, MTM remains a privately held company in every sense – but the general practice of network/independent production company relationships at this time was for the network to commission programmes from programme producers for an agreed licence fee. This licence fee was paid in return for a licence allowing the network to screen these programmes twice (i.e. to include repeat rights) and thus functioned as a sort of rental. The licence fee system originated as a way of ensuring that both networks and production companies profited, but by the beginning of the 1970s for reasons outlined below licence fees could no longer always be relied on even to cover production costs. While the networks could earn immediate return on the programmes they transmitted – via advertising revenue – the production companies had increasingly to wait for their series to enter syndication before real profits could be made. This system is referred to as 'deficit financing' in the television industry.

At this time CBS's sales arm was Viacom. According to *Variety*:

> ... the contract ... called for control by CBS of the worldwide syndication rights to *The Mary Tyler Moore Show* which harvested big bucks for Viacom.[2]

The other side of this deal was that CBS granted the new company and the proposed programme an unusual degree of creative autonomy, as we shall see. By October 1969 *Variety* was announcing CBS's signing of Mary Tyler Moore and confidently predicting its significance for the forthcoming season. Under the headline, in *Variety*'s very own vernacular, 'CBS Inking of 3 New (Old) Stars Seen As Tipoff That Rube Image May Be Shucked In Next 2 Years' was a detailed diagnosis of the network's present ills and presumed remedies:

> The batch of Nielsen-proof stars just locked up by CBS – Andy Griffith and Mary Tyler Moore for next season and Dick Van Dyke for '71–'72 – shapes as significant in several respects. One is that the

web is making fewer development pilots these days. Another is that, stemming from this, program development costs are trimmed. And third, if suspicions of some insiders turn out to hold water, could be that the new additions to its star stable could be the opening move in de-ruralizing the currently heavy down-on-the-farm flavor of its sitcom profile.[3]

The 'rube-shucking' strategy was a consequence of changes in audience measurement by the A. C. Nielsen Company which in turn were related to changes in the attitudes to consumers on the part of television advertisers (for whom, ultimately, the Nielsen ratings are measured). Traditionally, Nielsen ratings had been determined in a pretty strictly quantitative manner to indicate the size of an audience tuned in for (rather than actually watching) a particular network at a particular time. This figure, supplemented by audience 'diaries', is calculated on the basis of a random sample of 1200 homes which function as a 'cross-section' of TV viewers nationally. In the 1960s advertisers occasionally requested breakdowns by age and by sex but the data were interpreted and indeed intended for relatively straightforward quantitative calculations; slots were sold to advertisers on the basis of the size of audience anticipated to be watching at that time. At the end of the 1960s, however, the then trailing network, NBC, began stressing the importance of the demographic composition of the total and even argued that the demographic parts could, thus calculated, be more important than their aggregate sum. At NBC the champion of this new approach was Paul Klein, who was then the network's vice-president in charge of audience measurement.

The extent to which this represented a dramatic reversal of CBS's previous strategy can perhaps be illustrated by reference to one series. In April 1969, the same month that Dick Van Dyke and Mary Tyler Moore were reunited in a CBS special, CBS cancelled a series called *The Smothers Brothers Comedy Hour*. Far from being one of the rural-based sitcoms, however, this was a controversial series which seemed particularly able to attract just the sort of young, sophisticated, urban viewers which the new season rhetoric was already promising. Furthermore, it even contained 'relevant' material; too relevant as it turned out – the series' political satire over such issues as racism and the Vietnam war proved too much for the CBS corporate stomach.[4] It also shared with another contemporary comedy series, *Rowan and Martin's Laugh-In*, a cynical self-consciousness about television itself which was rapidly to become a prime-time staple. One critic, David Marc, has attributed the advent of this sort of humour in the late 60s to two factors.[5] First, the adulthood of the first generation of 'television babies'; and second, the impact on what he calls 'electric shadow memory comedy' of the escalation of alternative technologies to broadcasting; alternatives such as syndication, satellite, cable and cassettes, all of which would need stockpiles of such material to fill out their product but all of which would need to take a new attitude to such material in order to 'distinguish' themselves as 'alternatives'. Of course, the siting of *The Mary Tyler Moore Show* in a local TV station newsroom rarely availed itself of the opportunity to create comedy at real television's expense. Indeed, Grant Tinker once described the series as sharing the 'good old-fashioned virtues we find in *The Waltons*. . . . The show appears to be rather hip for TV, but in fact the characters in that show, forgetting their comic eccentricities, are all four-square people.'[6] Tinker's unmasking of the reality behind the 'relevance' cycle is intriguing in the light of MTM's later essays in televisual realism. For he goes on to attribute the failure of the 'relevance' series to their ambition to 'portray unsolvable problems' and noted that such shows were populated by 'protagonists who were social worker types. They were anti-heroes.'[7] Such a diagnosis is ironic in the light of MTM's later triumphs with such 'anti-heroic' social worker protagonists as Lou Grant and *Hill Street*'s Captain Furillo, both of whom, for all their efforts, were unable to 'solve' societal ills within the span of an episode. While later series like *Lou Grant* were at least able to admit to such problems, however, *The Smothers Brothers Comedy Hour* was simply smothered. One of its writers, Lorenzo Music, soon found his way into another CBS-associated production company, MTM.

Meanwhile, as the months of planning the 1970–1 season passed, a number of additional changes were taking place. And one of these was to sound one of the first warnings to the networks of the 'narrowcast' future which Marc was later to point to. Between the 3rd and the 8th April 1970, for instance, the annual convention of the National Association of Broadcasters was held in Chicago. 1970 was in fact the 50th anniversary of American broadcasting, but the anticipated celebrations were slightly marred by worries about the imminent destruction of network hegemony by the unleashing of a technological monster. Since the majority of NAB membership was made up of local station owners and operators and their staffs there was considerable concern over the potentially damaging inroads into their advertising revenues (and profits) which the new media might forge. According to industry critic Les Brown, the fear most commonly expressed at the conference was that cable in particular might prove itself capable of:

> fractionalizing the television audience. . . . Television had always had a horizontal audience, playing to what was considered to be the mass taste. Cable's deed might well turn out to be to turn the stations into vertical entities, each addressing itself to a specific audience, whether white-collar, blue-collar, ethnic, suburban, teenage, geriatric, or whatever.[8]

Here perhaps is one key to Paul Klein's shift from the rhetoric of 'mass taste' to that of 'quality demographics' and specifically addressed programming. Another, of course, was NBC's better standing in terms of the latter criteria than the former.

The following month another conference was held. The 16th annual CBS-TV Affiliates Conference took place on the weekend of 5–6 May. (Each of the three networks is affiliated to local stations across the States as well as being entitled by Federal Communications Commission regulations to own and operate five such stations of its own in the largest markets.) This year, CBS Network President Robert Wood was announcing a new strategy for the network in spite of its place at the head of the Nielsen ratings. Perhaps surprisingly, the network had taken the decision to drop six very popular and long-running series from their schedules for the 1970–1 season. Wood argued that the network saw no point in:

> . . . stringing along with those shows that might still deliver respectable ratings for another season even though we had concluded, reluctantly, that they had no long term future on our schedule. . . . Neither past performance nor present popularity is sufficient any longer to guarantee future pulling power. . . . The days are gone in programming when we can afford to be imitative rather than innovative. We have to hold the audiences we have; we have to broaden our base; we have to attract new viewers of every generation, reflecting the educated and sophisticated in American life, people who live in every part of the country. We are taking a young, fresh, new approach to programming, The rookies are going to be given their chance.[9]

Beneath the inflationary rhetoric a number of quite material changes were being hinted at here, confirming *Variety*'s predictions of the previous autumn. The following month Wood appointed Fred Silverman as Head of Programming at CBS and the latter swiftly learnt that the network was under intense pressure through their sales department from advertisers who wanted them to 'think demographically'. Wood himself had worked his way up in the CBS hierarchy after serving as a manager of a CBS owned and operated station and he knew that some of their top-rating series nationally actually performed poorly in the top urban markets where the O&OS were located. They decided to drop some of those series, since the large audiences they still undoubtedly attracted were simply top-heavy with viewers who had little disposable income or were too young, too old or too far from the cities to be able to spend it.

Underlining the link between this 'demographic' determinant and the network's obligation toward (exceptional instances of) innovation, sophistication and the 'public interest' was the Red Lion case, settled in the Supreme Court the previous year. Red Lion concerned the questionable right of the Federal Communications Commission to infringe the First Amendment and place stipulations on local stations in order to ensure that in America 'it is the right of the viewers and listeners, not the right of the broadcasters, which is paramount'. On 9 June 1969 the court ruled that broadcasters are indeed obliged to 'present those views and voices which are representative of [the] community and which otherwise, by necessity, [would] be barred . . .'[10] Like other contemporary debates about broadcasting, the focus of the case had been news, specifically the issue of editorial rights and responsibilities.

Meanwhile television advertising was itself changing radically. It was, after all, the advertisers who were behind the changes in the Nielsen demographic categories. And this in turn related to the demise of the sponsorship system in the 1960s. The end of the single sponsor per programme system and the advent of magazine style advertising on television returned television programming to the complete control of the networks. And this, in turn, reopened the networks to the possibility of anti-trust action. And, as the number and frequency of commercial interruptions increased almost exponentially, the very form of programming and particularly of programme flow began to change. Instead of making programmes which would complement particular products – and particular groups of consumers – magazine style advertising necessitated the selling of separate 'slots' and a number of critics perceived an accompanying 'overcommercialisation' of the programmes themselves.[11]

Meanwhile, after several years of heated debate, the FCC finally decided to ban cigarette advertising from the small screen from 1 January 1971. When this decision was announced in 1970 there was considerable panic inside the industry. The tobacco business brought television an estimated $220 million revenue in 1970 out of a gross income of $3 billion. In the following year, the three networks lost some 12% of their total advertising revenue as a result of this ban and, in order to readjust their profits, the networks extended their control over programming and froze their fees to independent producers.[12] But with 12% of their revenue to make up, the networks necessarily turned to new advertisers to fill their empty prime-time slots. At first they were simply forced to lower their rates. In the final three months of 1970 (the very months of *The Mary Tyler Moore Show*'s launch) the networks' advertising sales fell by nearly 4%. Total pre-tax profits for the three networks in 1970 were just over $50 million – $43 million less than the previous year.[13] CBS in particular were determined to cope with this crisis. Firstly they reduced their overall programming budget by 15% in February 1971 though this ploy was too late to have effected *The*

Mary Tyler Moore Show. Rather earlier, however, they decided to cut back on commissions – restricting first commitments to a maximum of thirteen episodes and, where possible, eliminating the pilot stage of series development. *The Mary Tyler Moore Show* was to benefit from both these economies. Indeed, the first thirteen episodes of the series were commissioned without pause for a pilot and a 24-episode season was eventually produced where in previous years 36 episodes had been the practice. With advertising revenue continuing to fall, CBS came up with an additional strategy in their bid to win new advertisers:

> To lure new customers, especially advertisers with small budgets, CBS cut the minimum amount of time they could buy from one minute to thirty seconds. ... By early March [1971] a herd of advertisers stampeded the networks. They spent more than 100 million dollars in a two week period, prompting ABC, CBS and NBC to raise their rates by 25%. And the enactment of the Prime Time Access Rule [see below] in the fall turned out to help rather than hinder this new network boom. In relinquishing sixty-three minutes of commercials each week to the local stations, the networks reduced their available spots in prime time. Advertisers clamored to buy in a climate of sudden scarcity, and prices climbed even higher . . .[14]

Taken together these developments in television advertising also had their effect on the formation and strategy of MTM. In response to (some would say recuperation of) the women's liberation movement the advertising world belatedly began to recognise the existence of working women, of women as consumers with disposable incomes, of women, that is, who weren't simply being perceived as 'housewives' (who were considered to be already well served by day-time soaps). And this recognition in turn revealed a new realm of the audience and of the advertising world for the networks. In 1971 CBS even issued a demographic breakdown to potential advertisers about their programmes, entitled 'Where The Girls Are':

> Its cover featured a revolving disk which would reveal at a glance the age distribution of retail buyers of 91 different products bought mainly by women. 'And the pages inside,' said the brochure 'show you how you can apply this handy information to Nielsen's new audience reports by age of lady viewer.'[15]

The relationship between the advertisers' newfound ambitions – and audiences – and the new CBS strategy should not be underestimated. In 1969 a Virginia Slims cigarette advertisement with the slogan 'You've Come A Long Way, Baby' was screened regularly in prime-time. In September 1970 an article with the same title appeared in *TV Guide* launching *The Mary Tyler Moore Show.*[16] The article's subtitle also reflected this attention to changes in advertising: 'Happy Hotpoint is now Mary Tyler Moviestar'. But 1970 was also the year that the FCC decided to ban cigarette advertising from television. And although the ban didn't actually come into force until 1 January 1971 the participating advertisers in the first episode of *The Mary Tyler Moore Show* included Proctor and Gamble and Miles Labs – just two of the firms previously primarily associated with day-time programming who were tempted into prime-time by the exile of cigarette ads, the consequent cheapness of commercial slots, and the new Nielsen-led demographic emphasis on target audiences, specifically women aged 18–49.

All these factors reinforced the networks in their decision literally to disenfranchise one section of its audience to the benefit of another. And the disenfranchised sector was composed, predictably enough, of very young viewers, older viewers and viewers who were either too poor or too rural to be considered a priority by the advertisers. Ironically, they were doing just that in order to be able to produce programmes which could boast some sort of 'relevance', some sort of relationship to the real world and its social problems – the kind of problems, in other words, experienced by the very young, the old, the poor and the unprivileged.

Much of this change was due to an inbuilt contradiction between the economic interests of the networks and those of their owned and operated stations. Since Robert Wood's background was in running CBS local stations he may have understood rather better than some of his peers in the industry just how important they were and furthermore just how different they were (demographically and in terms of programme discrimination) from some of the networks' smaller stations. In 1970, fifteen O&Os held by CBS, NBC and ABC accounted for fully 70% of total pretax network earnings. Robert Wood had described the situation as it was in 1969:

> We operated stations in New York, Chicago, Los Angeles, Philadelphia and St Louis. Except for St Louis, these were large, urban and, I guess, to some degree urbane centers in the United States. And while the network was number one, it was number one largely because of the strength it drew in the C & D counties [industry shorthand for the less populated areas]. Moreover, the audience that was the most loyal to CBS was, by and large, the post-fifty-year-old group. I complained of the paradox that the network could on the one hand be the leading national network, and on the other hand CBS could own stations in major cities that weren't competitive. Because the programming that made the network number one was making our stations in the large markets number two or number three.[17]

When Wood was appointed CBS President in early 1970 he was swift to act against that paradox. Since the 1969–70 season was already decided, the earliest opportunity he had to act on his hunch was in his scheduling of the 1970–1 season. One series already pencilled in was *The Mary Tyler Moore Show*.

Meanwhile, in May 1970, the very same weekend that the CBS Affiliates Conference was taking place, the FCC announced a new set of rules. Of these rules, the Financial Interest Rule and the Syndication Rule barred the networks from benefiting from or partaking in the profits made by programmes in domestic syndication or foreign distribution and prohibited them from owning or even part-owning programmes made by the independent producers or the Hollywood majors for network television. In addition, the Prime Time Access Rule restricted the networks to three hours of prime-time programming per night, obliging the local stations (both the O&OS and the affiliates) to fill the other hour in the 7.00–11.00pm schedule. The FFC's apparent intention with these rules was to break up the duopoly of the networks and the Hollywood majors and encourage the formation of new and diversified sources of programme supply, since it had concluded that the television market was 'seriously unbalanced to the disadvantage of the independent producers'.[18]

Gary Edgerton and Cathy Pratt have detailed the place and purpose of the Prime Time Access Rule:

> The rule was part of the FCC's 1970 Report and Order on Network Television Broadcasting, and culminated more than a decade of research and investigation by the Commission. In 1957 the FCC was initially alarmed to find out that such a high percentage of prime-time programming, 28.7%, was solely produced by the networks. In 1968, this figure would drop to 19.6%, but the Commission determined that during this same time span the networks actually increased their control over the domain of prime-time by expanding their joint production arrangements from 38.5% to 75%. Corresponding to these percentages were figures indicating that independently produced, prime-time programming dropped by 32.8% in 1957 to 5.4% in 1968.[19]

Other sources differ on this. *Hollywood Reporter*, for instance, suggests that over the last 20 years the number of independent production companies has steadily increased, as follows: December 1953 – 25; December 1958 – 41; December 1963 – 29; December 1968 – 29; December 1973 – 87; December 1978 – 147; December 1983 – 199. An increasing number of production companies, however, does not guarantee more airtime allocated to those companies; rather the result may well have been a spreading of commissioning to more sources of supply, each of which may well have actually had a decreased number of programmes. Furthermore, the only substantial increase in exponential terms appears to be between 1968 and 1973 – the period of the implementation of the rules and of the emergence of MTM.

The Prime Time Access Rule was published on 4 May 1970 and went into effect on 1 September 1971. Along with the Financial Interest and Syndication Rules the FCC decisions caused consternation in the industry. The networks themselves, the existing major programme suppliers and the local stations (most of which had neither the resources nor the inclination to produce their own programmes) were all opposed to such 'restraint of trade'. In spite of their opposition, however, the Financial Interest Rule and the Syndication Rule became law in 1970, the former becoming effective in 1972 and the latter in 1973. Meanwhile, the trade press echoed the industry's insecurities about the future with articles entitled 'Where to find all these new shows?' and 'The Coming Upheaval in Programming'.[20] For all this furore there was no shortage of applicants for the new programme-making opportunities. In the decade since the rules were passed the number of independent producers providing prime-time programming has apparently quadrupled.[21]

Opposition to the rules was not only unsuccessful, however, it was also shortlived. Very rapidly the networks discovered that since the 7.00–7.30pm slot would probably continue to be occupied on most local stations by newscasts, only thirty minutes per evening were effectively being eroded. And this in turn allowed the networks to escalate their advertising rates and to shed six half hours that were least successful. CBS, the then leading network in the Nielsen ratings battle, stood to lose least in this erosion of airtime since it effectively enabled the network to drop its least popular – or, demographically speaking, least profitable – programmes without having to go to the expense of coming up with replacements. Hence the six sitcoms dropped by the network before the start of the 1970–1 season. What had been intended, in part at least, as an anti-trust measure against the networks was actually working out in their, and specifically CBS's, favour.

While the FCC was finding itself unable to effectively reduce network power, however, another attempt was being prepared to use anti-trust legislation to limit network autonomy. Edgerton and Pratt cite an October 1969 memo from the Department of Justice under Nixon's Attorney General John Mitchell. The memo was written by Presidential aide Jeb Magruder to H. R. Haldeman about 'unfair' journalistic coverage of the Nixon presidency and of the war in Vietnam:

> The real problem that faces this administration is to get this unfair coverage in such a way that we make a major impact on a basis in

which the networks, newspapers and Congress will react to and begin to look at this somewhat differently ... [We can] utilize the antitrust division to investigate various media relating to antitrust violation. Even the possible threat of antitrust action, I think, would be effective in changing their views in the above matter.[22]

On 13 November 1969 Vice-President Spiro Agnew made a speech whose invective against network monopoly made the FCC's criticisms seem positively mild by comparison. In the wake of what Nixon and his advisers clearly considered to be virtually treasonable broadcast coverage Agnew specifically denounced network news. His speech began thus:

> The purpose of my remarks tonight is to focus your attention on this little group of men who not only enjoy a right of instant rebuttal to every presidential address, but, more importantly, wield a free hand in selecting, presenting and interpreting the great issues of our nation. ... Is it not fair and relevant to question [the] concentration [of power] in the hands of a tiny, enclosed fraternity of privileged men elected by no one and enjoying a monopoly sanctioned and licensed by government?[23]

Brown notes that Agnew's speech appeared to indemnify the local stations, reserving its full venom for the networks and for New York.[24] Erik Barnouw, the eminent historian of American television, has also commented on this aspect of Agnew's strategy:

> A striking aspect of the Agnew attack was that it echoed liberal complaints against the monopolistic nature of the industry. Yet the target of the attack was one small segment of television – the news segment – that was not wholly submerged in the monopoly atmosphere, and was occasionally at odds with military-industrial views. The thrust of the speech was to smother this segment. Thus it sought to establish precisely the concentration of power it pretended to abhor.[25]

If this seems rather a long way away from the genesis of *The Mary Tyler Moore Show* (though perhaps not so unlike the rhetoric surrounding the cancellation of *Lou Grant*) Mary Tyler Moore has herself identified Agnew as one source of the series' premise:

> As for the idea of a TV newsroom, that came about at least partly from Spiro Agnew, of all people. We really have to give him some of the credit. When television news came under Agnew's scrutiny, suddenly everyone became aware of the people involved.[26]

The US Department of Justice, meanwhile, had not given up its assault on the networks. Between 1970 and 1972 it prepared antitrust actions against all three networks. On 14 April 1972 the Department of Justice, acting on orders from John Ehrlichman, filed antitrust suits against ABC, CBS and NBC for violation of the Sherman Anti-Trust Act. When the networks responded that these suits were politically rather than legally based, the Department issued a statement that news and non-fiction programming were exempted from the action, thus implying that political disagreements over news coverage were in no way connected with the suits. This was, however, an election year, and when Nixon was returned to the White House the suits were pressed forward with renewed energy. When Nixon was forced to resign, the political atmosphere changed, albeit briefly. In November 1974 the suits were finally dismissed from the court as politically motivated. On 10 December 1974, however, the Department of Justice filed further suits; in 1976 NBC signed a consent decree; CBS and ABC finally signed separate agreements in 1980.

Ten years earlier, the network newsman who most angered Agnew was CBS' own correspondent, the venerable Walter Cronkite. On 6 May 1970, the very same weekend of the CBS-TV Affiliates Conference and the FCC Rulings, Cronkite introduced a news report from Vietnam which included interviews with several very visibly reluctant American servicemen. Following the broadcast a number of CBS affiliate staffers attending the conference expressed their patriotic disapproval of what they considered 'slanted' news. Cronkite responded:

> ... with a strong defense of network news practices, pointing out that whatever is news has to be reported whether or not it fits anyone's preconceived notions of what the news should be.[27]

In spite of the liberal tautology here – a preconceived notion of what news is or what the networks consider news to be is indeed a necessary prerequisite of being able to report 'whatever is news' – Cronkite's defence was warmly received. Indeed, according to *Broadcasting*, of all the CBS stars in attendance at the Conference (including Ed Sullivan, Lucille Ball, Fred MacMurray, Doris Day, Andy Griffith and Glen Campbell) 'newsman Walter Cronkite received the loudest and most sustained applause, a standing ovation that lasted for several minutes.'[28]

CREATING THE SHOW

The Mary Tyler Moore Show evolved from a deal between CBS and Mary Tyler Moore. The deal was made, or at least announced, in September 1969. The first episode of the series was transmitted in September the following year. In that twelve-month period the series developed through a number of concepts to a treatment and then to a first draft and ultimately final draft script. The central characters were also fleshed out in this period. But at the same time as this process was taking place, as WJM Minneapolis was becoming a palpable fiction, so too was MTM Enterprises becoming a material fact. In September 1969, the same month that the CBS-Mary Tyler Moore deal was announced, 20th Century-Fox launched a new series entitled *Room 222* which went on to win an Emmy as Outstanding New Series at the end of its first season. *Room 222* was produced by Gene Reynolds (who was later to become co-creator of *Lou Grant*), created by James L. Brooks and scripted by Brooks and another young writer, Allan Burns. If this article has avoided attributing authorial responsibility for the series until now that is only a consequence of how often the prevailing conditions of the industry (and of America) in 1969–70 have been written out of the account of the series' genesis. There can be no doubt that between them Brooks and Burns were crucial to the creation of *The Mary Tyler Moore Show* and thus to the existence of MTM Enterprises. Nor, however, can there be any doubt that without MTM Brooks and Burns would probably never have produced work of the durability they did.

James Brooks had been working in television since 1964. His first job there had been as a writer for CBS News which he remembers very warmly:

> It was like being a kid in a toystore. There was no caste system, no bureaucracy in the newsroom. Everybody shared their feelings with everybody else.[29]

(It is surprising, to say the least, to find this apparently 'autobiographical' element in the origins of *The Mary Tyler Moore Show*.) After a period scripting documentaries for David Wolper (of *Roots* fame) he had written a few sitcom episodes and then received his first 'Created by' credit for *Room 222*. Allan Burns' career in television began rather differently in animation series like *The Bullwinkle Show* in the early 60s. Later, with his then partner Chris Hayward, Burns wrote for *Get Smart*, the spoof spy series, and *He and She*, a shortlived but sophisticated romantic comedy whose hero was a successful TV cartoonist and whose heroine had been a social worker. Whilst admiring *He and She* several critics commented that it 'bore more than a passing resemblance to the classic *Dick Van Dyke Show*'.[30] Finally, Brooks and Burns teamed up on *Room 222*, for 20th Century-Fox. Also at Fox at this time was Grant Tinker, who had left NBC and after a stint at Universal was working as a programming executive for the studio.

Tinker, Price and Moore together decided to invite Brooks and Burns to come up with a series concept for them:

All I had to start them off was the premise of Mary being single and 30 and living in Minneapolis – which on the face of it is a pretty dull thought. I just told them to go away and create.[31]

The combination of experiences which the two writers brought with them to this 'creation' clearly contributed to *The Mary Tyler Moore Show*. The latter has *He and She*'s TV show situation for its comedy as well as that series' focus on a professional female protagonist. It also echoed *Room 222*'s combination of humour with concern for topical and even occasionally controversial issues. Meanwhile, Brooks' background in a TV newsroom may well have contributed to the stealing of Agnew's thunder. Furthermore, there were at least as many examples of conscious and conscientious divergence from extant conventions as there were of accordance with them. Thus, for instance, Burns has recalled that they soon 'realized that first of all we couldn't possibly have her married, because that would bear too strong a resemblance to the *Van Dyke Show*.'[32] Nor, however, could she play a widow, since that would invite comparison with *The Doris Day Show*, one of the very series which was already identified with too rural and elderly an audience.

At this stage, according to Burns:

We hadn't even met Mary yet. What trust she had in Grant to let him put two total strangers in sole charge of re-launching her career. A good thing she wasn't in on some of our first sessions. Boy, did we come up with some lousy ideas. Like Mary was going to be a leg person for a gossip columnist. Mary was going to play the field dating two guys simultaneously – which one will get her? Then we latched on to Divorce and we knew we had a winner. Every writer in town had a divorce story on the drawing board. But we had the lady it would work with.[33]

Elsewhere Burns has described in rather more detail the process by which they came up with the concept which they took back to Tinker, Price and Moore and, ultimately, CBS:

It's a very mild idea: a single girl working in a television newsroom in Minnesota doesn't sound too scintillating and it was not our original concept. Our original idea, frankly, I thought was better than that, at least to get us going. It had been our observation, and not ours alone, that a divorce on TV was something that should be done. Up to then it hadn't been. . . . We thought it was damn well time to do it. We backed it up with lots of reasons and Mary liked the idea. We did not have the TV newsroom concept at the time. We had her working at a newspaper as a stringer for a columnist. We were really centering on the idea of divorce as being something that was

> interesting. This was just on the cusp of the women's movement, it not having become really full-blown yet. We might not feel it necessary today to explain why a woman at age thirty-one is not married but at that time ... we thought it was necessary to explain. We didn't want to make her one of those girls like Doris Day who didn't seem to have any age.[34]

Burns has elsewhere admitted that:

> It tells you a little bit about our own lack of awareness of the women's movement at that time, which was just starting, but our feeling was that if a girl was over thirty and unmarried there had to be an explanation for such a freak of nature as that.[35]

CBS rejected the divorce premise, and, having failed to persuade MTM to sack Brooks and Burns, the latter were granted extra time to come up with a rewrite. The new concept had Mary Richards as an unmarried, thirtyish, career woman on the rebound from a failed four-year affair. Perhaps significantly for debates about 'authorship' and 'creativity' in television the network's request for a rewrite had positively propelled Brooks and Burns toward the premise for which they became famous. As Allan Burns has put it, 'As it turns out a career woman of thirty is a more radical concept than a divorcee.'[36] Furthermore, the revision encouraged Brooks and Burns to extend their focus from Mary Richards herself (her personal life as a divorcee on the one hand, her isolated professional life as a stringer for a gossip columnist on the other) to two specific situations – one her apartment, the other an office. And this, in turn, led to the integration of Mary into a much larger than originally anticipated ensemble cast. Finally, the necessity to replace the 'relevant' issue of divorce with another fashionably topical situation may well have contributed to the dropping of the stringer concept and its replacement with that of a television newsroom which could capitalise on both Brooks' own experiences in a TV newsroom and on the continuing controversies about news practices during the Nixon presidency: 'We wanted to do something that seemed like it was the real world.' This 'realism' was reflected elsewhere in the series' specificity about the heroine's age and the show's location. Mary Tyler Moore herself has described how, 'At first people said "Why Minneapolis?" Why not Minneapolis? It's a sophisticated city and it's certainly something new on the tube. It's not Anyplace, USA and it's not Los Angeles ... Actually, it's a refreshing change – people in a TV comedy wearing galoshes and overcoats and sweaters and talking about the snow and sleet. Just having the four seasons on a show is refreshing. Very un-Southern California.'[37]

The new premise for the series, therefore, had Mary Richards living in Minneapolis. The first episode dramatised her 'backstory', her move from small-town Minnesota, the break up of her affair, and the search for a new apartment and a new job in a new city. The apartment is in a boarding house run by Phyllis Lindstrom, but another tenant, Rhoda Morgenstern, also wants it. Thus two of the series' running characters are swiftly introduced. Mary then hurries off to an interview with a TV newsroom editor, Lou Grant, for a job which she gets. The episode ends with the former fiancé, a medical intern, arriving to try and tempt Mary back to him, but his entreaties are interrupted by a drunk Lou Grant stumbling into her apartment.

Once the new outline was agreed MTM could, literally, go into business. Brooks and Burns were left not only to script the series but also to set up the company. As James Brooks has described it:

> In television I was really lucky because at the time that I was coming in they were beginning to give the inmates the run of the asylum and writers were getting control of their shows and being called executive producers and having total control and I was the beneficiary of that. At MTM this really flowered because when we started at MTM – Allan Burns and myself – we hired the businessmen, we hired the accountants. I don't think that's happened before or since, where writers call an accountant and interview them.[38]

Elsewhere, Brooks has explained how they proceeded:

> We hired a secretary, who became one of our best friends, and a writer. We hired a best friend we had in common for our first producer, Dave Davis. And then we hired the business people. The business people did everything we said because Grant Tinker said 'Do what they say.' We decided to make it a writers' shop and a place where writers would have a lot of say-so, so our friends who are writers came in and they felt good.[39]

Both Burns and Tinker point to the series' status as three-camera comedy (shot on film not tape but recorded with three cameras in front of a live audience and subsequently edited down to a fluid master) as being responsible for the decision to hire writer-producer teams at MTM. According to Burns:

> It was Tinker's idea to make us a team. I think that doing that kind of show, a three-camera show, is so demanding, that teams are almost a necessity; it's just tremendously hard to do them alone.[40]

Tinker agrees:

> MTM was founded on writers, Brooks and Burns being the first two,

and then others joined us later and these people became writer-producers. It's particularly important in three-camera comedy, which is evolutionary, from the Monday script read round the table till the Friday night we shoot it, that the people who are involved should all be writers. That's what they are doing all week, re-writing the show as things don't work, or they see they can improve it.[41]

This goes some way to explain the existence of the writer-producer hyphenate in American television and its particular prominence at MTM and the other independent companies specialising in sitcom launched at the same time. Unlike American cinema where, for all the debates about authorship, directors can exercise a considerable degree of creative autonomy, American television belongs to the producer.

Allan Burns has explained why this is the case and how precisely it inflected the structure and strategy of (The) MTM (Show). Burns argues that because, in television, the producer's authority is total and because it is writers who conceive projects rather than directors, the nature of network assembly lines makes the writer-producer a particularly privileged executive. Although writer-producers had existed in the 50s and 60s, they really only came of age in the industry in 1970 when the FCC's Financial Interest ruling and Department of Justice anti-trust action against the networks accelerated the emergence of small independent production companies – several of which were actually spun off from the networks. Burns is convinced that the continued presence of one writer-producer throughout a series elevates them above the roles of directors and individual episode writers, both of whom are usually only freelance, and so devolves to them, if only by default, the creative control of programme production.[42]

Nevertheless, Brooks, Burns and the series itself needed a director. Indeed, without one they couldn't even begin to cast the series. Jay Sandrich, the son of RKO director Mark Sandrich, had previously worked on such successful series as *I Love Lucy*, *The Danny Thomas Show*, *The Dick Van Dyke Show*, *Get Smart* and *He and She* in a career which involved a gradual climb from second assistant to director, with a brief but frustrating detour as a producer. Jay Sandrich takes up the story:

I got a call from Grant Tinker who I had known peripherally when I was doing *The Dick Van Dyke Show* and they were starting a new show called *The Mary Tyler Moore Show* and they were looking for a director. They had talked to a few other directors and for one reason or another they were not available. Grant and Mary had liked *He and She* and they offered me the show. At this point there was no cast and there was only an idea for the show – there wasn't even a script. I had met Jim and Allan and they seemed like really nice gentlemen. I said to Grant 'I do not want to commit myself to one series and then have it cancelled (as *He and She* had been) and all those heartaches, so I'll do the first three shows and if I like it I'll come back.' By that time I'd seen three or four of the scripts and I was reading writing the like of which I'd never seen. It was different, it was situational, it was not jokey as I had been used to. None of us were sure how it was going to work. Until we found the actors the characters were very hard to imagine. Well, it took a while to put that cast together and I was involved in the casting process – we had a lot of time to cast and we read literally hundreds of people. Eventually, though, it wasn't far from the production date and we really had nobody. One day this young, new actress to town came in, Valerie Harper. The part of Rhoda was written for essentially a very heavy, unattractive, New York Jewish woman. Valerie was not heavy, was not unattractive, was not New York and was not Jewish, but she read that part and we knew we had found that person. We would have to change our concept slightly – Valerie was a little overweight but far from unattractive. But she felt that she understood Rhoda. She felt that she was heavy, that she could really relate to Rhoda. And so Valerie was cast as Rhoda. We started to feel pretty good about that – Mary came in and read with her. We got Ted [Knight, who plays Ted Baxter] fairly late in the process. Chloris [Leachman, who plays Phyllis] came in after Rhoda was cast and we were about a week from starting production and had nobody for Lou Grant. I was off doing another show and I got a call from Jim and Allan that Grant Tinker had worked with somebody called Ed Asner, he'd not done a lot of comedy but we were going to go with him, and that's how the cast was formed – they liked him and there really was nobody else. Somewhere in the middle of rehearsals we realized that what we were doing was a cut above what was on television. We also heard rumours that CBS thought the show was being written off, in spite of their commitment to thirteen shows. We did the first 'pilot' in front of an audience four days before we were going to film it, and it was a disaster, the cast wasn't quite ready, the scenes that should have played didn't play, the audience didn't laugh. Test audiences sometimes are very misleading, they don't really know that they're supposed to laugh, they just sit there and enjoy it. None of us were prepared for the bad reaction because we thought we had a really good show. The strength of Grant and Mary is that they didn't panic. We sat there that night and discussed some of the things that we all felt should be changed but basically we said this is the show we're gonna go with. I said the acting pushed a little – everybody was worried that they weren't getting the laughs – and it was played a little too high, but we shouldn't really change anything. We did a very minor rewrite. We went back four nights later and filmed it and it was one of the great nights of my life because it was a really wonderful, wonderful show, beautifully acted and it was an exciting thing to be part of. We showed that show to CBS who had just restructured – Fred Silverman had come in as Head of Programming and Bob Wood had become President of the network. Although neither of them were the gentlemen responsible for buying [i.e. commissioning] the show they saw it and loved it and reslotted it on Saturday night and the rest is fairly well known. The show went on the first year – did not get great ratings but good enough ratings and people liked it though it did not test well. I left after doing the first three shows and after the second one I said to Grant, 'I love it, I'll come back and do as many as you want.' I ended up doing 16 out of 24 the first season and that's what I did every season for the next seven years ... [43]

As Sandrich points out, the first episode did not test well with audiences and, in the absence of an on-air commitment from CBS, it seems likely that the series would never have got on the air. Sally Bedell quotes some of the sample audience's responses to the first episode in her book *Up The Tube*. Apparently the Mary Richards character was perceived as something of 'a loser', Rhoda was considered 'too abrasive' and Phyllis was simply condemned as 'not believable'. When Mike Dann was replaced by Fred Silverman as Head of Programming *The Mary Tyler Moore Show* was hastily rescheduled from its initial slot on Tuesdays just before the rural comedy *Hee Haw* to a Saturday night slot previously occupied by the hayseed series *Green Acres*. This time it was scheduled immediately after another new series, *Arnie*, a blue collar comedy about an ethnic worker suddenly promoted to an executive position – both symptom and symbol of the overall CBS strategy. The following January (1971) another series, Normal Lear's *All In The Family*, was launched and when it too transferred to Saturday night CBS's schedule was secure for the new look: 8.00: *All In The Family*; 8.30: *Funny Face*; 9.00: *The New Dick Van Dyke Show*; 9.30: *The Mary Tyler Moore Show*. *Funny Face* was a sitcom which borrowed more than a little from the success of *The Mary Tyler Moore Show*, its single working woman protagonist also working in TV, this time in commercials. *The New Dick Van Dyke Show*, similarly, returned its star to a TV setting, this time in the guise of a talk show host for a local station in Phoenix, Arizona.

Where *Arnie*, *Funny Face* and even *The New Dick Van Dyke Show* differed from *The Mary Tyler Moore Show* was, among other things, in the latter's emphasis on the ensemble nature of the comedy and its consequent unwillingness to elevate Mary Richards into the only area of interest. (This in turn was to pay off later for MTM when they were able to spin off characters from the show into their own series.) Grant

Tinker has described the series, somewhat incompletely, as being 'about a single woman getting along by herself and for herself in our society'.[44] But in fact, by the late 60s successful series were rarely if ever 'about' single individuals in this way. Just as the Western at the end of that decade had developed a ranch family variant of its traditional lone gunslinger format, so too sitcoms had found families a useful way of spreading the workload and multiplying potential protagonists, thus increasing the identification figures for a show at the same time as hedging its demographic bets. As Grant Tinker puts it:

> At one time in television Jackie Gleason could sit out there and practically do it all by himself. But by the 1970s the attention span of the viewers had shortened. They were spoiled. You had to come at them from all directions to keep their attention. An ensemble could do that.[45]

Whether or not we accept Tinker's verdict that the move to ensemble was simply a response to the audience's shrinking attention span, the character ingredients of *The Mary Tyler Moore Show* are illuminating, both as textual difference and as demographic bait. Mary, Rhoda, Phyllis and Lou – to name only the most familiar characters from the series – all offered specific pleasures as distinctive personalities, specific images as identification figures, or comic butts; together they 'represented' network demographics in the new Nielsen categories.

In fact, much of *The Mary Tyler Moore Show*'s success has been attributed to its coincidence with the crisis of the nuclear family and the impact of the women's movement, in much the same way that *All In The Family* has been associated with changing liberal attitudes toward race and racial equality. But then that 'coincidence', after all, was very much intended by CBS and by the independent production companies they commissioned to fill the ideological vacuum they perceived. *The Mary Tyler Moore Show*, for instance, was a dramatic departure from the three female stereotypes that dominated prime-time comedy programming in 1970. The three dominant types were the zany incompetent, immortalised by Lucille Ball; the passive housewife, personified by Donna Reed and in her previous prime-time role Mary Tyler Moore herself as Laura Petrie; and the dumb blondes and brunettes that accompanied the male stars of some of the older shows, like Ellie May in *The Beverly Hillbillies*. (In film studies these three stereotypes have been 'fleshed out' theoretically as the screwball, the virgin mother and the eroticised/exoticised sex object.) If the screwball was the most obvious option for a sitcom it was by no means an easy identity to write in to the new 'realist' comedy. And Mary Tyler Moore had herself already played the other two roles on television – as Happy Hotpoint the housewife's friend, as husky-voiced, long-legged but head- and body-less Sam, and, of course, as Laura Petrie – perfect wife and mother. In a way, though, it was Mary Tyler Moore's association with such stereotyped roles that enabled the Mary Richards character to appear so utterly and dramatically to escape them and to evolve as a 'real' woman. Though she had a screwball side, she was never as nuts as Rhoda or Phyllis; though she was attractive and interested in men she was never as man-hungry as Rhoda, as faddish as Phyllis or as sex-obsessive as Sue Anne Nevins, WJM-TV's Happy Homemaker (a mockery of the Hotpoint role?). In fact, she had a rather straight-laced and conventional set of values.

The strategy of the series, then, was to steer a middle way between the 'thoughtless' acceptance of the conventional female role and the equally 'thoughtless' rejection of it. But if, in the real world beyond the small screen, this seems no more than a hedge-sitting compromise, on television itself it meant a great deal more. As Brooks remembers it:

> We began with the character, Mary Richards, who believed *Father Knows Best*. She was brought up in middle America, had done everything right and had not been prepared for an adulthood where there would be problems. Mary began to evolve almost immediately. I mean our timing was very fortunate, the way the women's movement started to evolve. So not only our ideas, but what was happening in society began to appear in the show.[46]

While Arthur Price looked after Miss Moore's interests, Miss Moore in her own words kept MTM at arm's length while remaining nominally in the chair. As late as 1978 she was quoted as saying, 'I'm always annoyed when people give me the credit for developing our company . . . Grant Tinker built the company and he runs it. I don't. I have no more to do with it than any other wife who might offer a suggestion about her husband's business.'[47] In 1980 *Rolling Stone* quoted her as admitting that 'In much the same way as you name a boat after your wife, he named the company after me, but that's the end of my involvement.'[48] If Mary Tyler Moore's involvement with MTM has been little more than nominal – except, of course, as an actress – Grant Tinker's involvement has also been presented as unusually 'passive'. In an article in *TV Guide* Tinker described himself as 'a first class delegator' and the same article notes that in the entrance to his office at NBC (where he now works, having left MTM in 1982) there is a blown-up dictionary definition of a tinker which explains that as a noun it means 'an unskilful or clumsy worker' and as a verb it refers to the activity 'to busy oneself without useful results'.[49]

Tinker's strategy at MTM, similarly, was to leave the creation of product to the creative teams hired for that purpose and to function as a protective shield between those teams and the network. Brooks has described Tinker's function as 'running interference' for his writer-producers. Tinker's role involved repelling network interference and at the same time attracting creative talent. Between them, Tinker and Arthur Price combined a background in production, the networks, advertising and talent management and this too may have contributed to MTM's apparent ability to gauge the market and at the same time stretch its possibilities. Even the initial deal with CBS seems to have been unusually liberal in conceding creative control to the production company. In spite of that liberality, except for the first two years of MTM's *The Mary Tyler Moore Show* the company's series have all operated in the red as a direct consequence of the deficit financing arrangements outlined above. There was therefore a painful hiatus before first *The Mary Tyler Moore Show* and then *The Bob Newhart Show* entered syndication and ploughed considerable amounts back into the company as well as, via residuals, to the cast and crew. Because MTM's contract with CBS stipulated that CBS held syndication rights (the deal preceded the FCC Rules on Syndication) the first two years of *The Mary Tyler Moore Show* were, rather ironically, the only ones in which MTM was operating in profit. All other MTM series, because they were made after the signing of the Syndication Rule, were probably granted smaller licence fees in proportion to production costs to enable the networks to compensate for lost profits in the area of syndication.

Because of the high status of the writer at MTM and American network television's elevation of the producer, MTM's writer-producer hyphenates were from the start both very privileged and immensely pressurised. The more successful a series becomes the more work there is to do and the more pressure for the company to expand. At MTM, at least initially, this meant inviting more writer-producers to join the company. According to James Brooks:

> When you start off you are basically producing the show and you are called executive producer. As you get into the second and third season you start backing away. . . . And then the line producers become more and more prominent.[50]

But because these line producers were also Brooks' and Burns' writer-friends they too began contributing scripts to the series and later coming up with series ideas of their own. Once *The Mary Tyler Moore Show* was no longer just an on-air commitment by CBS to thirteen episodes but twenty four episodes a season the pressure was on for a tactical withdrawal; no longer could Brooks and Burns attend every reading, every rehearsal, every recording.[51] And this policy, adopted for one series, became the model for many. For both Brooks and Burns it was crucial that the interlocking chain of writer-producers they hired at MTM to continue their work were also part of another interlocking chain – of friendships:

> We were all friends in the early days. . . . Even when we had a lot of shows going, Dave Davis and Lorenzo Music, who created the *Newhart* show, had been our producers on *Mary* the first year and we had known them for a long time. They just sort of slid over and did that series and then Tom Patchett and Jay Tarses came in to produce after them and then they did *Tony Randall*. We were very close with all of them. Then Ed Weinberger and Stan Daniels did *Phyllis*. It was sort of like The Begats, very much that; interlocking friendships over many years.[52]

This process, of course, finds its reflection in the spin-off strategy and stylistic signature at MTM. Brooks' account is similar. Having appointed Dave Davis, an old friend, as their first producer and after a couple of very successful seasons of *The Mary Tyler Moore Show*:

> Dave had an idea to do a show for Bob Newhart, and we began. Then we had two shows, and that was terrific. Both shows were doing well and then there were three. Then at a certain point the idea of giving the creative part of the staff that kind of autonomy became completely impossible for business reasons.[53]

Whether or not we accept this sort of account of the company, however, it is clear that before that chain of 'interlocking friendships' was finally broken by the inexorable logic of 'business reasons', before the atmosphere of 'creative autonomy' was forever eroded by economic expansion and the consequent privileging of profitability over either personnel or programmes, the 'MTM style' – both as a business and as an aesthetic – had been set. I will return to the family resemblances which have been identified across the range of MTM's output toward the end of this article. For the moment, though, I would like to examine those 'interlocking friendships', the very 'familiarity' that characterises the reminiscences of and rhetoric about the emergence of the company and those initially associated with it; the creative staff in general and the writer-producer lineage of MTM in particular. Very briefly – and without benefit of either corporate records or complete credit lists – the writer-producer lineage of MTM would look something like the following.

Mary Tyler Moore, her husband Grant Tinker and her manager Arthur Price hired two writer-producers, James Brooks and Allan Burns, to create a situation comedy vehicle for Miss Moore's return to CBS prime-time in 1970. With Brooks' and Burns' friends David Davis and Lorenzo Music as its producers, *The Mary Tyler Moore Show* went into the schedules and, somewhat later, the Nielsen ratings. With their first series a success, MTM were willing to expand the family a little and Tom Patchett and Jay Tarses were invited to take over the reins of *The Mary Tyler Moore Show*, freeing Davis and Music to create their own series, *The Bob Newhart Show* – a vehicle for another of Arthur Price's clients. Then, in 1973, an outsider, Ed Weinberger, wrote and produced MTM's first pilot, *Bachelor At Law*, and convinced the company that he was well worth hiring. Two years later, Weinberger and his partner Stan Daniels had created *Phyllis*, a series spun off from *The Mary Tyler Moore Show*, as well as an original if shorter-lived show, *Doc*. Meanwhile, in 1974, Brooks, Burns, Davis and Music had spun-off their own far more successful series, *Rhoda* (in the famous first episode of which Mary Tyler Moore waves goodbye while Patchett and Tarses attempt to prevent Rhoda from leaving). That same year Brooks and Burns also created a new series for another actor who had appeared in *The Mary Tyler Moore Show*, Paul Sand. That role had been written for Bob Newhart but with Newhart already committed to his own MTM show Sand had got the job and, eventually, a series of his own, *Paul Sand In Friends And Lovers*. In 1975 MTM commissioned an outside writer-producer, Jerry McNeeley, to create a show for the company and MTM's first drama series, *Three For The Road*, was the result. Although the series proved unsuccessful McNeely remained at MTM for a number of years, writing and/or producing three TV movies for the company as well as MTM's only mini-series, *The Critical List*. In 1976, Patchett and Tarses began to distance themselves from *The Mary Tyler Moore Show* and took over *The Bob Newhart Show* from Davis and Music as well as creating a series of their own, *The Tony Randall Show*. Meanwhile, another pair of writer-producers, Glen and Les Charles, whose first relationship with MTM had been sending scripts for *The Mary Tyler Moore Show* on spec, became staff writers on *Phyllis*.

Then, in 1977, *The Mary Tyler Moore Show* came to a voluntary end. What had happened? At the very simplest level, the MTM family had moved on to other things. While both Brooks and Burns were enthusiastic to work in features, the series' other writer-producers were already more committed to new projects of their own, albeit under the auspices of MTM. Meanwhile, 'sophisticated' situation comedies were being edged out of prime-time from two sides at once. From one side, a new 'generation' of sitcoms, aimed at an adolescent audience and focusing on teenage protagonists, were dominating the ratings. In 1975 *All In The Family* had been moved out of its key role in the CBS Saturday evening schedule and scheduled on Monday, immediately following *Rhoda* and *Phyllis*. That season, *The Mary Tyler Moore Show*'s lead-in was incalculably weakened and the combination of *The Jeffersons* and *Doc* could hardly compensate. The 1975 season ratings showed *All In The*

Family in first place, *Phyllis* sixth, *Rhoda* eighth and *The Mary Tyler Moore Show* 19th. After the shift of *All In The Family* in 1976, that series dropped to twelfth place and for two years no MTM series appeared in the annual top twenty-five listings. In their place, though, a new network and a new production company was dominating prime-time. The company was Paramount and the network was ABC. Ironically, it was to ABC that Fred Silverman had gone in 1975 when he left CBS; in 1977 it was to be a deal with ABC and Paramount that attracted Brooks, Weinberger and Daniels into leaving MTM altogether. The 1976–7 ratings listed *Happy Days* starring Henry Winkler in first place, and the *Happy Days* spin-off *Laverne and Shirley* in second. (Winkler's earliest TV roles had included small parts in MTM sitcoms; Penny Marshall, who played Laverne, had made her television name as Paul Sand's sister-in-law in *Paul Sand In Friends and Lovers*.) But the move toward such teenage fare was not merely the consequence of a cyclical shift in television's trends. Rather it resulted from very material changes, specifically the networks' imposition of 'Family Hour' and FCC's Access III ruling in the autumn of 1975. Access I, passed by the FCC in 1970 – and described in some detail above – had embarrassed the Commission considerably when it became clear that the lack of specificity about the kind of independently produced programming they were encouraging had resulted in little more than a flurry of further quiz shows, chat shows and variety specials, with 'quality' series like *The Mary Tyler Moore Show* very much the exception. And so, in January 1974 the FCC announced a second Access rule to become effective that autumn.[54] This time the rule was intentionally more specific: two hours per week, currently programmed by local stations (7.00pm – 8.00pm on Saturdays and Sundays), would be returned to the networks on the strict condition that those hours were wholly given over to FCC approved programming – current affairs and children's series in particular. The networks agreed to these stipulations, but the independent producers were more reluctant to accept what they saw as yet another constraint on their 'independence'. Furthermore, they felt, quite understandably, that the implementation period – the new rule was due to take effect that autumn – was far too short. In June 1974 a US District Court decided in favour of the producers' complaint and Access II was declared illegal. This left the networks little time to rejig their schedules and jettison their respective two hours of new programming, as Access I was reactivated. One of the casualties was an MTM sitcom, *The Bob Crane Show*.

Refusing to give up the legislative ghost, however, the FCC announced a third Access rule in the autumn of 1975. Access III laid down that an additional hour of prime-time be allocated to children's programming every week. Much more significant, though, was the networks' own decision to designate the hour between 8.00 and 9.00pm every evening as 'Family Hour'. Like the FCC's latest ruling, 'Family Hour' was a self-defensive manouevre on the part of the industry, reeling under the impact of a new moral panic aroused by court-room claims about outbreaks of imitative violence based on the controversial TV movie, *Born Innocent*. The networks' new code stipulated that 'Family Hour' should be free of 'programming inappropriate for viewing by a family audience' and of material which might be 'disturbing to significant segments of the audience'. When 'Family Hour' was finally applauded by both the FCC and the National Association of Broadcasters, the demographic shifts in the definition of 'significant segments of the audience' effected by the events of the early 1970s were all but overturned. But 'Family Hour' was not accepted without a fight. The Writers Guild, the Directors Guild, the Screen Actors Guild and several top independent producers, including Norman Lear, filed a suit against the networks for infringing freedoms guaranteed under the First Amendment. In November 1976, Judge Warren J. Ferguson ruled that 'Family Hour' did indeed infringe the independents' rights to 'free speech' but refrained from outlawing the code since it was a 'voluntary' measure of self-censorship rather than censorship itself. Ironically, it was CBS, foremost amongst the networks in drafting and drumming up support for 'Family Hour', which was to suffer most from it. For it was CBS which had led the field with MTM, Norman Lear and *M*A*S*H* in its adult, sophisticated programming – the very material which was now under attack. ABC, on the other hand, already boasted a predominantly adolescent audience and was more than ready to capitalise on the trend away from 'relevance' and toward 'kidvid'.

The effects of 'Family Hour' on *Rhoda* and *Phyllis* are detailed in the section on MTM series at the end of this book: language was toned down; once acceptable subjects became taboo; frankness was replaced by allusion and double entendre. *The Mary Tyler Moore Show*, already suffering from the removal of two of its best-loved regulars – Rhoda and Phyllis – was perhaps least able or willing to adapt to the new atmosphere. After half a decade its creative staff were themselves loathe to start indulging in self-censorship of the kind that would constrain the very characteristics – characteral growth, verbal jousting, a grappling with 'real' issues – which were the series' strengths. Instead of continuing the show until CBS itself began to consider whether it had run out of steam, MTM took the decision to put an elegant end to their first and still most successful series. Thus it was that in 1977 *The Mary Tyler Moore Show* came to the end of its seven season run, and MTM began to look around for new ideas and different directions. With a new set of obstacles to the 'adult' situation comedy in prime-time, alternative modes of independently produced programming were becoming increasingly attractive options. Mary Tyler Moore herself was keen to try out her talents in TV movies and television variety specials and MTM began to assemble the creative and administrative staff to facilitate such new directions. Meanwhile, two more of *The Mary Tyler Moore Show*'s co-stars, Ed Asner and Betty White, were rewarded with vehicles of their own to continue their paths in prime-time. Ed Asner resumed the role of Lou Grant he had played for so long in the original sitcom, this time in a sixty-minute dramatic format. And *The Betty White Show* retained the sitcom mode of its parent show, but aimed its comedy at the hour-long cop shows which were increasingly evident in prime-time.

Finally, while prime-time programming seemed to be closing off the spaces for 'realistic' situation comedies in which women, for the first time on American television, had been represented as other than sexual objects, screwball incompetents or sexless mother-figures, MTM's new ventures could claim to be taking their revenge. The ratings were dominated by examples of what were known inside the industry as 'T & A programming', 'candy-for-the-eyes' and 'jiggle television' – in all of which young women in minimal underwear were given equally minimal narrative motivation for parading their bodies before the cameras. But *The Betty White Show*'s actress heroine undercut the sexist heroics epitomised by *Charlie's Angels*, *Police Woman* and *Bionic Woman* by focusing on the behind-the-scenes comedy of a TV series about an undercover policewoman. And *Lou Grant* featured a young (divorced) female reporter, Billie Newman, whose character was an update of the original outline for Mary Richards, but whose abilities were never the subject of comedy.

THE MTM HOUSE-STYLE

The moment and manner of (The) MTM (Show)'s emergence – the political, economic and ideological conditions of its existence, including the televisual conditions – has clearly left its mark on subsequent structures and strategies, both economic and aesthetic. As Edward Buscombe has noted in an essay on Warner Brothers in the 1940s, 'studio style is a term which occasionally crops up in film criticism, but in a loose kind of way.'[55] In television criticism, whether journalistic or academic, it crops up even less often and even more loosely. Nevertheless, Buscombe's conclusions about the applicability of the 'studio style' approach to American cinema seem equally pertinent to the analysis of American network television. Buscombe makes two general observations about the concept of studio style. First, he argues that within the studio system that obtained in Hollywood in the 1940s (and still obtains in television) 'stars and genre ... were mutually reinforcing'; and second, he suggests that 'class' on the screen is in some sense related to class off it (in terms of staff origins and attitudes). His most substantive point, however, is that, as far as extant analyses of studio style are concerned:

> What seems to be lacking is any conception of the relations between the economic structure of a studio, its particular organization and the kinds of films it produced. For if there is such a thing as studio style it should be possible to provide some explanation of how it was formed.[56]

Before going on to try and provide some explanation of my own, it is necessary to ask whether such a style is indeed discernible across the relatively broad range of MTM's output and over the decade and a half of the company's history.

Journalistically (both in the trade press and among critical periodicals) and among MTM staffers themselves there certainly seems to be an assumption that MTM has a house style and that that style is comedy. Thus Howard Rosenberg described MTM as the 'House That Comedy Built'.[57] And thus, in 1977, MTM's then president, Grant Tinker, admitted 'We're sort of typecast. Our label is comedy.'[58] But 1977, as outlined in my chapter on *Lou Grant* and *Hill Street Blues*, was a watershed year for the company and indeed, by 1980, Tinker was announcing ' . . . we've begun to get rid of that label of comedy and do other things.'[59] The 'other things' that Tinker had in mind were not only non-comic series (like *Lou Grant, The White Shadow,* and later *Hill Street Blues*) but also TV movies, mini-series, variety specials. And it was in 1977 that MTM set up a subsidiary, MTM-AM, to develop day-time programming.

Furthermore, even the sitcoms themselves resist easy categorising. While television comedy since the 60s at least has tended to be bracketed under the umbrella of 'sitcom' Brooks, Burns and Tinker have refused that term, preferring to describe (The) MTM (Show) style as 'character comedy'. In a recent interview in *Film Comment*, James Brooks noted that, 'When somebody called *Mary* a sitcom, we'd be furious. We weren't doing sitcom. We knew what sitcom was. We had done sitcom. We were doing character comedy.'[60] Similarly, when quizzed about MTM's stylistic specialisation Grant Tinker responded:

> I think of it as character comedy. In the case of *Lou Grant* and to a somewhat lesser extent *White Shadow* and *Hill Street*, it is character drama. You are telling a story, for sure. That's important, but the shows are peopled by characters who are credible and carefully developed, and whose interrelationships are valid and consistent.[61]

In an interview for this book, Jay Sandrich offered his own brief definition of the MTM style:

> The MTM style is essentially good writing, sophisticated writing, and trying to present adult fare. Casting actors who could do comedy rather than comedians. Trying to maintain a certain reality.[62]

Writer-producer Jerry McNeely, who was recruited into MTM's creative stable in the mid-70s, echoes Sandrich's verdict on the company's preferred aesthetic mode – realism, sophistication, 'quality' – all, of course, arguable terms. But McNeely goes on to attribute their presence in MTM programmes to a particular industrial strategy:

> MTM is a company that was built on Grant Tinker's determination to let creative people have some freedom. Now of course that freedom was limited to what MTM wanted to have their company name connected with [but] I never experienced any serious resistance to things I wanted to do, certainly nothing I would call interference. MTM is a quality company – they want to do good television and they're willing to take some chances . . .[63]

It is the slippage here between 'quality company' and 'good television' that seems to point to a link between the MTM style as a business and the style associated with its programmes. Elsewhere in this volume Jane Feuer addresses the stylistic characteristics that are embedded in the texts themselves; here, however, I will concentrate on those perceived by MTM's own staff and by industry critics. Mary Tyler Moore's modest remark that 'I'm not a comedienne, I react funny' connects not only with the critical rhetoric about MTM's 'comic realism' and 'character comedy' but also with the comic style adopted by successive stars in the company's comedy series throughout the seventies. Of course, the 'quality' of the acting and the writing – so often applauded by those inside and outside of MTM – are 'mutually reinforcing'. Because the scripts are good, MTM is able to attract some of television's most talented performers to their shows, and because those performers are series regulars, the company can continue to attract top writers. Ironically, however, these very qualities (so reminiscent of the alleged strengths of British television), both of which contribute so much to what MTM refer to as 'character comedy' (and, later, 'character drama') have led to a stylistic quality which is often considered to be the antithesis of well-written, well-acted TV – its status as tele*vision*. For while an emphasis on 'realistic' character rather than on silly situations necessitates skilled performances and well-crafted, witty scripts – where sitcoms could rely on slapstick and farce – it also led to a character-motivated rather than just-another-part of-the-furniture role for the camera. Freed from the limited visual grammar of the studio, the MTM style would eventually include the employment of fluid tracks and long takes that would be the envy of many theatrical films (and which, ironically, were entirely absent from MTM's one feature film to date, *A Little Sex*, whose sitcom characters simply failed to motivate any motion pictures).

To a certain extent, of course, such 'quality' is always in the eye of the beholder. In another sense, though, it is also a marketable commodity, a hallmark or corporate calling card which helps to distinguish MTM product from its competitors for the benefit of networks, advertisers, critics and audiences alike. And while there is undoubtedly a rhetoric related to this quality there is also a very real ambition to aim higher than other independent producers in the television marketplace. MTM, in other words, has often aimed to ensure that its 'beholders' have higher levels of disposable income than many other sectors of the audience and many other companies. Thus Grant Tinker's suggestion that 'I think there's a connection between how high you set your sights and the resultant programs';[64] and thus the conclusion of sociologist Paul Espinosa, who sat in on early script conferences of *Lou Grant*:

> The producers of the *Lou Grant* show see themselves as producing a different kind of product; this notion of differentiation is a major motif in the discourse of production. From top management down to members of the crew, the show is talked about as though it were different from, superior to, better than, and more intelligent than other television shows.[65]

And once again, the cast and crew of *Hill Street Blues* – which at the end of its first season won more Emmys than any other weekly series in American television history – have often been quoted as determined to end the series if they felt that its quality was slipping. Robert Wood, one-time CBS President and now an independent producer in his own right, has said of MTM:

> They're not slicing bologna over there. Damn it, they're class, real craftsmen. Pound for pound there's no company better than MTM. I think they'd rather fold up than put on a piece of crap.'[66]

The criterion of 'class' echoes Buscombe's formulation and functions as a reminder of the company's status among the aristocracy of American TV.

MTM AND THE NETWORKS

MTM was set up in 1970 as the result of a unique agreement with CBS, who commissioned a sitcom series to star Mary Tyler Moore on the strength of her one-off reunion with Dick Van Dyke in *Dick Van Dyke and The Other Woman*. Both *The Dick Van Dyke Show* and this special reunion were CBS programmes and, when *The Mary Tyler Moore Show* proved itself a popular and prestigious success, Fred Silverman, then CBS President, encouraged the company – and the series – to groom possible spin-off material for the network. In an article in *Emmy*, Howard Rosenberg has described MTM's almost 'monogamous attachment to CBS' and quoted writer Gary Goldberg's comment that 'I felt that if I'd gone to another network it would have been like having an affair.'[67] Rosenberg also interviewed Grant Tinker on the subject, who expressed some worry about being taken too much for granted by the network:

> You do get sort of comfortable in one place. But it's not good to have all your eggs in one network basket. For one thing, it's as if they owned you, and there's no urgency to their buying from you. They don't have the feeling that you'll go across the street ... I think they've almost used [that loyalty] against us. We get a reception at CBS and they listen, but I think they may take us for granted a little bit. They know if they deny us today, we'll be back tomorrow.[68]

Rosenberg also cites CBS-TV president B. Donald Grant's conviction that without CBS, MTM would be considerably worse off: 'He [Tinker] has had long-running shows on CBS. He has not had quite as much luck on the other networks.'[69]

It may be significant, therefore, that MTM's first 'flirtation' with another network seems to have been the shortlived *The Texas Wheelers* and *The Tony Randall Show* for ABC, and the even less successful *Bob Crane Show* on NBC. Of these shows, only the Randall series was created by 'in-house' MTM staff and only the Randall show survived longer than one season; indeed, when ABC cancelled *The Tony Randall Show* it was acquired by and returned to prime-time on CBS. When Fred Silverman left CBS for ABC in 1975 he was soon followed (in 1977) by three of MTM's top writer-producers, Brooks, Weinberger and Daniels, in a deal to produce for that network at Paramount. Ironically, Silverman's reign at ABC was to prove particularly unreceptive to MTM's programming.[70] When Silverman left ABC for NBC, however, MTM won an open pilot commitment with that network for its writer-producer Steven Bochco (late of Universal, NBC's traditional source of supply for film drama programming), a commitment which eventually resulted in *Hill Street Blues*. Thus, when MTM came up with a medical series in the familiar *Hill Street* style, *St Elsewhere*, NBC bought that too and the network also leapt at *Remington Steele* – a private-eye series co-created by Robert Butler, the director who had contributed so much to the *Hill Street* visual style. Of course, this new relationship with NBC may in part have been the result of MTM's pleasure at that network's faith in *Hill Street Blues*, which had survived such disastrous ratings in its first season.

The following spring, while MTM celebrated the Emmys accumulated by its new flagship series, CBS cancelled both *WKRP In Cincinnati* and *Lou Grant*, two long-running MTM shows, both of which were higher-rated than the recently renewed *Hill Street Blues*.

The relationship between production companies and networks can also have consequences on 'house style'. CBS, for instance, in commissioning further series from MTM is unlikely to have expected anything too dramatically dissimilar from *The Mary Tyler Moore Show*. And such similarities, of course, can be at least partially vouchsafed by the employment of the same team of creative personnel, the same writer-producers. On the other hand, CBS may also have needed new series which could attract more of the same sorts of viewers – and advertisers – as their first series. To build on this house style the networks would actually schedule series from one company across an evening vertically (in what is known as 'blocks') or across the week horizontally (in what are called 'strips') in the same time slot on several different evenings. The intention of this procedure is to alert audiences to the 'sameness' of product in 'similar' slots and to be able to rely on attracting a specific demographic slice of the total audience to a certain sort of programming because of that time-slotting.[71] Thus the MTM shows on CBS were almost all to be found on Saturday nights at first, and later the MTM empire spread to Monday evenings. At NBC, on the other hand, most MTM programmes have been scheduled at 10.00pm although on different nights of the week. Grant Tinker, once he left MTM for the presidency of NBC, has even introduced what he calls 'the best night of television on television' by scheduling an evening (or block of shows) which includes *Hill Street Blues*, *Taxi* and *Cheers*.[72] While *Hill Street* may be the only MTM series in this block, both *Taxi* and *Cheers* are made by MTM alumni (the former was created by Brooks, Weinberger and Daniels, the latter by Glen and Les Charles). It seems likely that CBS had some sort of (perhaps unwritten) agreement with MTM during the early seventies of the kind that ABC has with another production company, that of Aaron Spelling, today.

MTM: 'THE QUALITY FACTORY'

In spite of such changes of personnel and of programme strategy over the years, MTM retains its reputation as a reliable supplier of quality product. Indeed, industry commentators who have worked at MTM or with MTM all appear to agree on the company's superiority to the competition both as a producer and, more simply, as a place to work, a company, an ensemble of its own. James Brooks, for instance, has described MTM as a Shangri-La;[73] Robert Wood – ex-CBS executive and now an independent producer in his own right – has called it the Tiffany's of television,[74] while Jay Tarses compared it to an Algonquin

Round Table.[75] This reputation rests in turn on a tradition of attracting and not interfering with top creative talent but instead making them their own producers. Thus Brooks described MTM as 'a writers' shop' and Tinker himself termed it 'an artists' company':[76] 'People do the shows without edict from us ... The kind of people we like to attract wouldn't come here if we tried to legislate.'[77]

The 'relative autonomy' afforded creative personnel at MTM seems to be based on and secured by the smallness of the company. Indeed, one aspect of MTM in which the economic and organisational structures of the company clearly intersect with each other (as well as with its aesthetic structures) is in MTM's size. At the time of Rosenberg's profile of the company in 1981 the full-time staff was estimated at no more than twenty and Tinker was quoted as admitting:

> We're wilfully small. There is a kind of optimum level at which we run best and at which I feel connected to things, and that's about where we are now. If we have four shows on all the time, that is optimum. Five is okay, even six may be okay but beyond that it might feel too impersonal, and I wouldn't feel connected. And below four, you begin to lose people you don't want to lose.[78]

By 1983, however, the *New York Times* could comment that:

> The company now has 300 full time employees scattered through four buildings on the CBS-20th Century-Fox studio complex. Where there were three vice-presidents five years ago, there are now nine.[79]

What had happened? It is difficult to judge just how important Tinker's departure – to head NBC – and his replacement by Arthur Price has been. Certainly, the shift towards drama series with 60-minute episodes shot on film and the move away from 30-minute sitcoms often made on tape took place in this period. Thus it is that while to the staff members who had worked with the company since its beginnings – predominantly in sitcoms – MTM appeared to have grown too large, to others it still seemed to offer just the right intimate, friendly atmosphere it had been championed for in the early 70s. James Brooks, for instance, has recalled that:

> In [those] days MTM was small, especially in relation to what it is now. I had real control over my work as producer ... I left MTM when its size precluded the luxury of intimacy in work ...[80] ... at a certain point the idea of giving the creative part of the staff that kind of autonomy became absolutely impossible for business reasons.[81] It went from intimate to large to very big. The Shangri-La had to end at a certain size. Going from three shows to four shows makes a

difference. Suddenly cost control becomes very important. [And this, in turn, leads to] a subtle shift from creative people to business people.[82]

Brooks' feelings about this shift are echoed by director Jay Sandrich in an intervew recorded for this book:

As the studio grew bigger and bigger they started doing more and more shows and what happened to MTM from the creative people's point of view was that the businessmen started taking over. What made it worthwhile for all of us was Grant Tinker – probably the best executive I've ever worked with – he always had an open door for those of us who started with him, always sided with the creative people; never said: 'the network wants', always said 'what do you want?' Unfortunately, from my point of view, Jim's point of view and Ed and Stan's point of view, a man who was essentially the production manager started getting too much authority, because when you are that large an organization you sometimes will make compromises for money and it was no longer the same family operation it had been.[83]

Jay Tarses, who left MTM with his partner Tom Patchett in 1980, seconds Sandrich's verdict: 'It's changed from a good solid mom-and pop company where everyone knows everyone to a factory. It started to get huge, out of hand.'[84] Even Allan Burns, the only one of the first writer-producers still at MTM, admits to these changes with some nostalgia: 'We were all friends in the early days, but now there are so many faces I don't recognize.'[85] Tinker himself, however, disagrees with this diagnosis strongly:

If you visited *Hill Street* and spent a little time hanging around the set, you would have a feeling of 'Boy, these people are really loving what they're doing.' They have that same sense of excitement and pride that the people who did [*The*] *Mary* [*Tyler Moore Show*] had several years ago, because they know they're doing something that is superior to most other television.[86]

Tinker's perspective is reinforced by Steven Bochco, *Hill Street Blues*' creator, who has compared MTM with the much larger Universal television production company where he worked for more than a decade:

They're not evil. They're just bigger – and there are certain inherent problems with being big. Because they deal in volume, they make volume decisions. It's the difference between factory-made goods

> and handmade goods. It doesn't mean the handmade good is always going to be better, but you're probably going to enjoy making it a lot more.[87]

Bochco has even compared the difference between MTM and Universal to:

> The difference between a Rolls Royce and a Chevy. That doesn't mean that a Rolls is a better product. At Universal there is more back-up and depth, and producing is quite simple, an assembly line, real smooth. Over here, there is an opportunity to handicraft.[88]

The recurrent complaints about the alleged erosion of a 'good solid mom-and-pop company where everyone knows everyone' and its replacement by a faceless corporation may or may not paint an accurate picture of the changes that have taken place at MTM since 1970. More interestingly perhaps, they illuminate the importance which the ideology of 'the family business' seems to have played in the minds of MTM's creative personnel. Similarly, rhetoric about the 'handicraft' nature of production (in some cases only nostalgia for those comedies recorded in front of an audience in an era now dominated by location film drama) and the creative community of 'interlocking friendships' which MTM-alumni so cherish seems curiously consistent with the settings of a number of their shows, each with its own real and/or surrogate work-family. Indeed, the characteristic MTM mixture of professionalism, ethics and either domestic life or a domesticated public sphere seem not only to apply to *The Mary Tyler Moore Show* but also to such later series as *Lou Grant* and *Hill Street Blues*.

Complaints like those reprinted above reiterate the familiar litany of criticisms levelled at the culture industry and at attempts to produce art on an assembly line. Such critics argue – and have done since Adorno – that industrial production and aesthetic production, art and business, are quite simply incompatible. If this is an unexceptionable argument to come across in the work of the Frankfurt School, however, it is rather more surprising to find it expressed quite so regularly and eloquently by those who work in the heart of the culture industry, American network television. And this illuminates how MTM's own compromise between 'family business' and multi-media corporation is not a concealment of the latter under the ideology of the former but rather a very material compromise between the two, a compromise which provided the space within which (The) MTM (Show) could function and even flourish – both as a business and as a series of fictions. Just as *The Mary Tyler Moore Show* is a product not only of the creative talents of Brooks, Burns, Sandrich and Mary Tyler Moore and her co-stars but also of MTM, so MTM itself is a product not just of the combined talents of Miss Moore, Arthur Price and Grant Tinker but of a moment in American television history. And that moment has exercised its own momentum on the 'television formation' of MTM, both as a 'house' and as a 'style'.

Notes

1. Michael Varmeulen, 'Mary Tyler Moore', *Rolling Stone*, 13 November 1980, p. 50.
2. *Variety*, 19 October 1983, p. 68.
3. *Variety*, 1 October 1969, p. 35.
4. Bert Spector, 'A Clash of Cultures: The Smothers Brothers vs CBS Television', in John E. O'Connor (ed.), *American History/American Television* (New York: Frederick Ungar, 1983).
5. David Marc, *Demographic Vistas* (Philadelphia: University of Pennsylvania Press, 1984), p. 165.
6. Edith Effron, 'What Makes A Hit?', *TV Guide*, 27 April 1974, p. 4.
7. Ibid.
8. Les Brown, *Television: The Business Behind The Box* (New York: Harcourt Brace Jovanovich, 1971) pp. 161–3.
9. 'CBS-TV affiliates strike a harmonious chord', *Broadcasting*, 11 May 1970. This speech is reprinted with some slight changes in Les Brown, op. cit.
10. Fred Friendly, *The Good Guys, the Bad Guys and the First Amendment* (New York: Vintage Books, 1977).
11. For a fuller discussion of this system see Les Brown, op. cit., p. 65. For a book length study of the subject see Erik Barnouw, *The Sponsor: Notes on a Modern Potentate* (New York: OUP, 1978).
12. For an excellent account of network reaction to losses in advertising revenue and the threat of anti-trust actions, see Gary Edgerton and Cathy Pratt, 'The Influence of the Paramount Decision on Network Television in America', *Quarterly Review of Film Studies* vol. 8 no. 3, Summer 1983.
13. Sally Bedell, *Up The Tube* (New York: Viking Press, 1981), p. 51.
14. Bedell, p. 54.
15. Barnouw, p. 71.
16. *TV Guide*, 19 September 1970, p. 34. The article's 'Happy Hotpoint' subtitle referred back to the eras of sponsorship and sexism as if they were both things of the past. *The Mary Tyler Moore Show* was to create its own equivalent, The Happy Homemaker, and later MTM was to begin to court corporate sponsors back into prime-time.
17. Todd Gitlin, *Inside Prime Time* (New York: Pantheon Books, 1983), p. 207.
18. Arnold J. Friedman, 'An Overnight Revolution', *TV World*, February 1983.
19. Edgerton and Pratt, p. 13.
20. 'Where to find all these new shows?', *Broadcasting*, 30 March 1970; 'The coming upheaval in programming', *Broadcasting*, 27 April 1970.
21. Friedman, op. cit., says, 'In the decade since they were passed the number of independent television stations has doubled; the number of independent producers providing prime-time programming has quadrupled; the

number of prime-time access program producers has increased by 26% and the number of syndicated program suppliers has increased by 51%.'
22. Edgerton and Pratt, p. 15.
23. Brown, p. 228.
24. Brown, p. 229.
25. Erik Barnouw, *Tube of Plenty* (New York: OUP, 1975), p. 444.
26. Don Freeman, 'Mary Tyler Moore; "I'm Not a Comedienne; I React Funny"', *Show*, October 1972.
27. Brown, p. 226.
28. *Broadcasting*, 22 May 1970.
29. *TV Guide*, 8 February 1975, pp. 31–2.
30. Tim Brooks and Earl Marsh, *The Complete Directory to Prime Time Network Television* (New York: Ballantine, 1979), p. 256.
31. *TV Guide*, 8 February 1975, p. 32.
32. Gitlin, p. 214.
33. *TV Guide*, 8 February 1975, p. 32.
34. Horace Newcomb and Robert S. Alley, *The Producer's Medium* (New York: OUP, 1983), p. 220.
35. Gitlin, p. 214. Eventually, *The Mary Tyler Moore Show* was to involve Lou Grant's divorce from his wife Edie. Later, *Rhoda* dramatised the divorce of its protagonist from her husband Joe, and the female reporter in *Lou Grant*, Billie Newman, was also a divorcee. Furillo, the lieutenant at the centre of *Hill Street Blues*, was already divorced from his wife Fay at the outset of the series.
36. Newcomb and Alley, p. 198.
37. Freeman, p. 40.
38. Unpublished interview with Sheila Johnstone in London, 13 March 1984
39. 'Dialogue on Film', *American Film*, June 1980.
40. Newcomb and Alley, p. 213.
41. Newcomb and Alley, p. 226.
42. Newcomb and Alley, p. 209.
43. Interview with Jay Sandrich conducted for this book in 1983.
44. Bedell, p. 66.
45. Ibid.
46. Newcomb and Alley, p. 219.
47. Cecil Smith, 'MTM on MTM', in Judy Fireman (ed.), *TV Book* (New York: Workman Publishing, 1977), p. 185.
48. *Rolling Stone*, 13 November 1980, p. 50.
49. *TV Guide*, 14 August 1982, p. 27.
50. Newcomb and Alley, p. 212.
51. Ibid.
52. Newcomb and Alley, p. 211.
53. *American Film*, June 1980.
54. Harry Castleman and Walter J. Podrazik, *Watching TV: Four Decades of American Television* (New York: McGraw-Hill, 1982), p. 263. The account of Access II and III is drawn from this book.
55. Edward Buscombe, 'Walsh and Warner Brothers', in Phil Hardy (ed.), *Raoul Walsh* (Edinburgh: Edinburgh Film Festival, 1974).
56. Buscombe, p. 52.
57. Howard Rosenberg, 'Above The Crowd: Grant Tinker's MTM', *Emmy*, Spring 1981.

58. Robert Sklar, *Prime Time America* (New York: OUP, 1980), p. 86.
59. Rosenberg, p. 24.
60. Kenneth Turan, 'On His Own Terms', *Film Comment,* April 1984.
61. Newcomb and Alley, p. 227.
62. Interview with Jay Sandrich conducted for this book by Tise Vahimagi.
63. Interview with Jerry McNeely conducted for this book by Tise Vahimagi.
64. Newcomb and Alley, p. 226.
65. Paul Espinosa, 'The Audience in the Text: Ethnographic Observations of a Hollywood Story Conference', *Media, Culture and Society* vol. 4 no. 1, January 1982.
66. Rosenberg, p. 24.
67. Ibid.
68. Ibid.
69. Ibid.
70. Sklar, p. 85.
71. Ibid. Sklar also notes that one of MTM's new ideas for the 1978 season was 'a family saga serial program that would be offered for late-night viewing, from 11.30pm to midnight, Monday through Friday.' When this idea was received unenthusiastically by the networks, Tinker took it to PBS and even made a pilot, though by this time the project had been modified to a proposed fifteen episodes. The pilot, *Going Home Again,* seems never to have been aired, though a copy is preserved at the Wisconsin Center for Film and Theater Research.
72. Sklar. p. 85. In his interview with Sklar, Tinker had suggested that 'Television would be better if it were only on Wednesday nights.'
73. James Brooks, 'Dialogue on Film', *American Film,* June 1980.
74. Rosenberg, p. 24.
75. Rosenberg, p. 25.
76. Ibid.
77. Ibid.
78. Rosenberg, p. 29.
79. *New York Times,* 22 May 1983.
80. Newcomb and Alley, p. 208.
81. *American Film,* June 1980.
82. Rosenberg, p. 29.
83. Jay Sandrich interview with Tise Vahimagi.
84. Rosenberg, p. 29.
85. Newcomb and Alley, p. 211.
86. Newcomb and Alley, p. 227
87. Gitlin, p. 278.
88. Rosenberg, p. 29.

The Mary Tyler Moore Show: Women at Home and at Work

Serafina Bathrick

Situation comedy situates us. More than any other television genre, it provides us, as viewers whose everyday experience may be shaped by TV's presence and programming, with a powerful model for private life in the age of broadcast culture. Sitcom humours us with its comic portrayals of the collisions which characterise our conflicting attitudes towards technology. By personalising the tensions that exist between our real needs as human beings and the dictates of a highly rationalised society, these comedies encourage us to 'fit in' and even to enjoy our efforts at doing so. But we may also continue to feel a sense of regret as we organise our lives around the televised image of the everyday. And although the representation of life at home has changed since the early years of television, we are confronted with our own loss of experience as we watch situation comedy. For while the video image seeks to be ever-relevant so as to integrate and ingratiate itself into our present lives through its visual style and narrative conventions, it also confronts us with what we have lost historically since the arrival of industrially produced culture.

By the mid-19th century a systematically cultivated ideology of the nuclear family compensated for the dissolution of community. A belief in individualism replaced the needs for collectivity, and rigidly imposed sex-gender differences helped explain the schism between private and public life. At this time the birth of a culture industry which printed and circulated the facts and fictions of this new era became essential to the shaping of a modern consciousness. In the mid-20th century, with the advent of a mass medium that brought a constant flow of images and information into the very centre of private life, the focus on the bourgeois family ideal gave way to an ideology of the familial. The old opposition between family and society had begun to collapse. Contemporary sociologists Michèle Barrett and Mary McIntosh describe this phenomenon:

Just as the family has been socially constructed, so society has been familialised. Indeed it can be argued that in contemporary capitalist society one dominant set of social meanings is precisely an ideology of familialism. The meaning of family life extends far beyond the walls of concrete households in which proverbial 'co-residing close kin' go about their business of marrying and raising children.[1]

Social and economic factors thus widened the gap between the promise and the reality of family life. In this way the ideology of the familial may be viewed as a new effort to salvage what is most positive about family-as-community, while at the same time it is used to reinforce some of the conservatism associated with gender and family hierarchy. Pivotal to this ideological shift is the changed position of the middle-class woman: from domestic True Woman in the nineteenth-century family idyll to the career True Woman in the twentieth-century familial workplace.

It is woman who provides situation comedy with its capacity to mediate historical change through its representation of both the family and the familial. This tendency began with the ideology of the nineteenth-century True Woman who was worshipped as she was assigned the role of family maintenance-expert. Ever devoted to her home and family, she was estheticised by the mass media as fragile and feminine while she was in fact asked to function as the powerful preserver of individualism in a newly competitive industrial society. Monumentalised as one who could 'uphold the pillars of the temple with her frail white hand', the True Woman functioned as an essential ally-and-invention of the culture industry.[2] Above all, she was to preserve her home as a refuge from the marketplace, while at the same time she would grow increasingly dependent on that marketplace for its goods and services. Thus many of the values which she maintained as alternatives to the rationalised work sphere were eroded by the invasion of consumer culture into the home. By the 1950s the arrival of television insured an almost complete 'occupation' of the private by the public. For the True Woman, there was surely the experience of seeing her own family replaced by the TV family. But there was also the new economic reality that confronted Americans in the post-World War II era: middle-class women, wives and mothers were entering the labour force as never before. Between 1950 and 1970 the number of married women who worked doubled, and the percentage of women who made up the workforce grew from 34% to 43%.[3]

When TV sought legitimacy as a made-for-the-family product during its first decade, situation comedy and nostalgic drama combined in popularity to recall a previous time in history when the nuclear family was in mother's keeping. The reality of the working housewife was denied completely as old-fashioned mothers on TV spoke family-wisdom to America's new postwar mothers. There were real married couples who played comic married couple routines for newly weds who were learning to stay home with their TVs. Because family 'togetherness' was synonymous with Americanism in the 1950s, the middle class who could afford the first televisions co-operated in front of their screens, their couches and chairs lined up as if to mirror the living-room sets in domestic dramas and sitcoms like *I Love Lucy* and *Ozzie And Harriet*. They rearranged their dinnertimes to allow for watching the dining-room-table-as-family-forum in *I Remember Mama*. That San Francisco-based Norwegian mother and her New York Jewish immigrant counterpart Mrs Goldberg wanted nothing more than to stay home. Lucy always complained that she wanted to be in show business, and we knew Lucille Ball was a powerful entrepreneur, but as Ricky's dizzy wife she too stayed home and had babies. (More people tuned in to the birth of little Ricky on *I Love Lucy* than to Eisenhower's inauguration spectacle: Americans were increasingly familiar with the television family.) Ozzie and Harriet, another married couple who performed as a TV family, provided broadcast fans with a continuous and seamless family-album as they moved from radio to television, bringing their sons into the picture when they were old enough to take on public personalities. All of these series preserved the mythic nuclear family ideal for postwar audiences.

Mary Richards and her working women friends appear in 1970 as television's first serious concession to a changed world where middle-class daughters leave home, earn their living, and remain single. This new image emerged at first quite tentatively. *TV Guide* presented Mary Tyler Moore the actress and Mary Richards the central character on *The Mary Tyler Moore Show* to a first season audience as if they had both been helped substantially in their efforts to perform as modern women by the television industry itself. The rhetoric of a September 1970 article in *TV Guide* describes the star's capacity as a television actress, and maintains its own self-promotional interests by presenting Mary Tyler Moore as an 'instinctual' performer who has 'never had a lesson in her life', and who is thus a natural 'fit' for the medium that seeks to validate daily life as sitcom. Not a professional who had made it on stage or in the movies, this star is quoted in an article entitled 'You've Come A Long Way, Baby': 'I'm not an actress who can create character. I play *me*. I was scared if I tampered with it I might ruin it.' As if to suggest that the television medium is best for the untrained but trusting neophyte, Mary Tyler Moore is also credited with having grown up to success as 'middle-class America's zingiest housewife' on *The Dick Van Dyke Show* from 1961–6.[4] As is characteristic of *TV Guide* and of television culture, this actress' inability to succeed in any other of the performing arts of mass media is attributed to her own gender-determined priorities: she has a private life and works to protect a happy marriage to her business partner. All of these points are made as preface to the season's new show – about a single career woman of thirty. Surely such a mixture of self-congratulatory praise for television and for the inherently home-loving nature of this star must remind us that *The Mary Tyler Moore Show* stepped cautiously into the American living-room.

Soon after *The Mary Tyler Moore Show* had become a successful Saturday night prime-time programme *TV Guide* published a second kind of commentary which dealt with women who sought jobs in TV production, and women's roles in current TV series. Much like the self-aggrandising prose that had previously hyped the responsibility of the industry as it 'looked after' its female star, these articles promote an image of a responsive medium that is granting women opportunities to work behind the scenes. In both instances, the sexism is blatant: the female star who appears on screen is a virtuous homebody, while the working woman who produces is revealed as a pin-up on the job in articles entitled 'The Writer Wore Hotpants' and 'Cameraperson in Hotpants'.[5] It is in this context that *TV Guide* readers encountered a number of serious attacks by feminist journalists who were finally voicing and publishing their outrage about TV roles for women. Early in 1971, Caroline Bird, author of *Born Female*, reviewed the roles played by women in the so-called 'relevant' shows of the recent seasons. In an essay entitled 'What's Television Doing for 50% of Americans?', Bird asserts that working women portrayed on TV are never granted private lives and that mothers are denied any relationship to the workplace. The few 'shadowy' female characters who exist as independent women in responsible jobs take no initiative within the narratives, and frequently disappear for weeks at a time. Caroline Bird sees and names covert hostility on the part of network television towards working women, claiming that 'None of these shows is challenging the family system, demanding a new kind of sexual relationship or a new division of labour in the home.'[6]

Diane Rosen contributed an attack on 'TV and the Single Girl', in another 1971 *TV Guide* article, where she remarks that fifteen years have passed since *Father Knows Best*, and yet, 'I, a single 27-year old living alone in New York City, can no longer find a reflection of my life anywhere on commercial television.' She points out that for five years (1966–71) Marlo Thomas' portrayal of *That Girl* simply reinforced the idea that a single woman is endearing only insofar as she is incompetent. Marlo Thomas' role is that of a dizzy aspiring actress who depends on her father and her boyfriend for all advice and affection. Rosen credits this actress with having struggled with ABC executives for permission to play the part of a single woman who lived alone, and even implies that she may have helped *The Mary Tyler Moore Show* to appear in 1970. While this article emphasises the miraculous arrival of two unattached thirty-year-old working women in Mary and Rhoda, the author suggests that shows about single women remain rare and necessarily tokens to the modern woman's experience. Rosen notes that neither Sandy Duncan in *Funny Face* or Shirley MacLaine in *Shirley's World*, both from the 1971 season, present unmarried women in convincing contexts. In fact neither of these shows lasted out the season, a further indication that *The Mary Tyler Moore Show* succeeded in part because it was the only one of its kind.[7]

In another *TV Guide* article that appeared in late 1973, Letty Cottin Pogrebin, a feminist columnist and author of *How To Make it in a Man's World*, writes an introductory essay to an upcoming ABC documentary entitled *Woman's Place*. Like Bird and Rosen, Progrebin reinforces the feminist claim that 'the personal is political', in a recollection of how television betrayed her as she was growing up in the 1950s. She develops a powerful argument for how she learned to lie as she became a well-socialised girl during this decade, and cites the many self-demeaning steps she took in an effort to imitate television's teenagers and to obey television's mothers. Pogrebin shows how the mass media, specifically TV, aligns itself with the interests of the nineteenth-century bourgeois family. Thus women continue to uphold the myth of the patriarch. 'In the constant search for male approval we were willing to lose ourselves,' she laments. Her argument suggests that middle-class mothers who were learning to shape family life around the TV family in the 1950s saw themselves idealised by the medium, and from that private bond created between mothering and televised representations of mothers, Pogrebin adds that as teenage daughters, 'We never knew a girl had any other choice.' Finally, the article exonerates network TV, for it turns the reader's attention to the possibilities within contemporary documentary to explore woman's place in American society. And insofar as 'unlearning the lie' means rejecting the early decades of family-focused sitcom, her final lines affirm a determination apparently shared by television itself: 'Now we are teaching the truth to our daughters so that growing up female can mean growing up free.'[8]

It is interesting to note that in some of the same ways that *TV Guide* sought to reassure its viewer-readers that the network's new career woman show was really another, albeit more 'responsive', commitment to family values, the determination of its co-producers Allan Burns and James Brooks to avoid social issues complemented what the publicity branch of the industry was promising. Burns and Brooks have recently been interviewed in *The Producer's Medium* and both make clear their commitment to 'character comedy' rather than Lear-style comedy with its political tendency. When asked whether he felt that *The Mary Tyler Moore Show* addressed the question of women's rights, Brooks attributes to 'good timing' the relationship that is established. Mary Richard's character and the women's movement 'evolved' simultaneously, he claims, 'but we did not espouse women's rights, we sought to show someone from Mary Richard's background being in a world where

The Mary Tyler Moore Show (from bottom left, clockwise): Betty White, Ted Knight, Gavin MacLeod, Ed Asner, Mary Tyler Moore, Georgia Engel

women's rights were being talked about and it was having an impact.'[9]

But while these producers may have viewed the women's movement as 'background' to their series, it is essential to note that they did hire women scriptwriters for *The Mary Tyler Moore Show*. The fact that Burns and Brooks bought more material from women writers than any other TV producers at that time is noted by Ellen Sherman in a 1974 *MS Magazine* article on the long history of discrimination against women scriptwriters in the medium. Sherman remarks that it is one of *The*

Mary Tyler Moore Show regulars, Gail Parent, who along with Renee Taylor, became the first woman to win an Emmy in 1973. In 1974 there were eight women awarded Emmys for a variety of categories in TV production, among them Treva Silverman, who received an award for Best Comedy Series Writer for *The Mary Tyler Moore Show.* Silverman, Parent, the team of Barbara Gallagher and Sybil Adelman, as well as Karyl Geld, all worked for Burns and Brooks. In 1974 Silverman, then the only female head story editor in television, is quoted by Sherman: 'Women on *The Mary Tyler Moore Show* are allowed to have a sense of their own intelligence. It's only then that the real breakthroughs for women can be made in television.' The *MS* article mentions that 50% of the scripts accepted by the MTM producer team in 1973 were written by women, way above the typical percentages for other shows. During that same year, Sherman attests: 'out of 63 series on television, 36 employed no women writers whatsoever.'[10]

It remains important to explore how Burns' and Brooks' commitment to character rather than social comedy occasionally collided with the political interests of female writers who had struggled for work in a sexist culture industry. What these producers say about politics as 'background' and the ways in which they defend the primacy of individual characters as the basis for comedy confirm what we have seen as the historical and ideological mandate for keeping the familial intact through the presence in the workplace of the humane and accessible woman. There is surely a move away from domestic sitcom where a private house provides the stage for all problem-solving, but whether the TV newsroom as workplace marks a new environment for a new kind of women's work remains to be considered. Just as television audiences were comforted in the 1950s by the mirroring of their own lives in the screen's surface imagery of home spaces, it is arguable that the 1970s audience was wholly familiar with the look of a 'newsroom-family', and so was receptive to the position of the career woman in this context. The emphasis on character remains a powerful reminder of how the appeal of the familial includes its expansion at various times in history to encompass the sanctity and significance of human relationships in all aspects of daily life. And while there is an important concession to woman's new place in the postwar economy, we must also ask to what extent Mary Richards remains separated from the powers of authorship in the newsroom and from the policy-making work that is involved in editing and shaping television news.

THE MISE-EN-SCÈNES OF HOME AND WORK ON THE 'MARY TYLER MOORE SHOW'

The continuity which is achieved by character comedy is heightened by the use of limited sets and locations; we quickly learn to associate the three men and the three women who play major roles on *The Mary Tyler Moore Show* with specific rooms, doorways and furniture. The men function primarily in the WJM newsroom where each occupies a designated desk or separate office. The women who are Mary Richards' neighbours meet in her apartment where they situate themselves in different areas, depending on whether they have been invited or have simply dropped in. Domestic and work spaces are thus quite rigidly distinguished, and are marked according to gender by the kinds of social interactions which take place in each. Because we do not know what goes on between these two worlds, we are further reinforced in our perceptions about separate spheres. While Mary alone is consistently comfortable in occupying both places, we never see her commuting between the two. And aside from the opening montage sequence which accompanies the titles for every episode, there is no city, no suburb and no transportation to connect them. We thus view Mary's privileged role in both spheres as uniquely hers, perhaps coming to believe that she is afforded this mobility largely because others remain in their gender-determined places. Although there are significant instances when a woman from her house appears in the newsroom or when a newsman visits her apartment, these events mark irregularities in the narrative, small transgressions often associated with personal crises or more specifically with the needs of individuals to seek out Mary at such times.

The two principal interior sets provide contrasing *mise-en-scènes*, although they are similar in their obvious staginess and so remind us that both exist for a live studio audience as well as for us as home-viewers. As a TV audience we are established in relation to the live performance by the use of an editing pattern that cuts from full stage shots to tight shots on individuals or pairs. There are two long shots that recur: one of the whole set that is Mary's apartment and one that encompasses the entire newsroom. Both of these camera positions provide us with a strong sense of accessible space – space that may mirror or simply come to feel as familiar as the place of the viewer her/himself. Above all, there is a symmetry in the composition of these two establishing shots. They function in similar ways to return us to 'normal', a well-tried technique in sitcom. From having been moved about and around the verbally conflicting and sometimes physically colliding characters as they break from their places with such inevitable rhythms throughout any episode, these shots return us to a calm associated with spectator privilege but more importantly they affirm our belief that resolution involves people-in-their-proper-roles-and-places. They also affirm Mary Richard's power to mediate, so that a return to a full stage shot heightens our awareness of and even our investment in her social skills. Thus the *mise-en-scène* of her apartment and that of her workplace gain a particular significance in relation to that True-Womanly aspect of her character. We see that she shapes and guides the interactions in both places, insuring that each remains separate but connected, by her own presence.

From the first episode ('Love is All Around', 1970), a number of clues to Mary's personality and to her social role are established by her relationship to her private living space. Some of the same efforts to legitimate modern womanhood by recalling old female attributes are intact through the very architecture of her home.[11] As she moves into a one-room 'studio' apartment, from the quaint interior details and from an exterior shot that introduces the first scene as she arrives in the Minneapolis suburb, we also learn that Mary lives in a big Victorian house. Subdivided now for the modern one-child family or the 'single' adult, the turreted mansion recalls an age when an extended family lived there with servants to care for its three generations of inhabitants. Its present state also reminds the audience of war-time changes and postwar realities: the middle-class family can no longer aspire to such palatial housing, and by the 1950s the surburban tract-home became the model for a more efficient nuclear family that could not afford to hire domestic help. Mary's apartment house thus represents the entire history of the American middle-class family home, and we are alerted to the ways in which she herself might embody one hundred years of good housekeeping. It will be her task to ensure that yesterday's family becomes today's familial. When Mary first enters the modernised space that will be hers, it is the empty but potential stage that will contain all her private life encounters for the first five years of the show. (Mary moves to a downtown highrise apartment towards the end of the series.) As an audience we are asked to identify with this moment of arriving and moving-in, and while her first encounters at home and at her job all take place on Mary's first day in this new city, each meeting provides us with a brief dramatic introduction to the five characters who will become her familial-friends and co-workers.

Phyllis Lindstrom is Mary's married friend from the past who lives on the first floor with her daughter Bess and husband Lars. She is landlady for the house and is the one who introduces Mary to her new apartment. While boasting about the clean paint and the new wall-to-wall carpet, Phyllis leads Mary towards the closed curtains, as if finally to display a view of suburbia through the three-part Victorian windows. She opens them with a dramatic gesture and what is revealed instead of the wooded landscape is the dark figure of a woman washing the windows from the outside ledge. Shrouded in an old-world kerchief and a big black coat is Rhoda, the other woman with whom Mary will share this house. She is disdained by Phyllis, and the reason for their animosity seems instantly apparent: Rhoda has challenged her neighbour's would-be gentility as hostess and even Phyllis' right to rent the apartment to Mary. As though from another world (and indeed as a

Jew from the Bronx she is an invader to Mary and Phyllis' midwestern idyll) Rhoda enters her new neighbour's space through a window. She is dark and comical next to Phyllis Lindstrom, a recalcitrant city woman who transforms a polite discussion of decor to talk of salaries and property and upward mobility. Rhoda claims she put a whole month's paycheck into the new carpet because she planned to move from her upstairs garret into this more airy space. Phyllis characteristically runs for help from the building's owner and returns with the authority to 'tell on' Rhoda and to inform Mary that she is lying. Mary registers shock at her crass invader: 'You lied to me,' she says to Rhoda, who answers with perfect equilibrium: 'You betcha'. Mary Richards must learn to mediate. From the first encounter with her opposing women neighbours, one from upstairs and one from downstairs, we find her in the middle, bending to negotiate the differences between an aggressive single working woman and a passive-aggressive married one. Throughout *The Mary Tyler Moore Show* she will bring Rhoda and Phyllis together, thus finding within herself and within her living space, the room for difference. Mary's true work as mediator will depend very much on her apartment, situated as it is between these opposites and in a house that once contained a family. We will ask, throughout the series, as if to rework the words of day-time radio programmes: 'Can Mary Richards, girl-next-door, learn to live with and let live, her antagonistic neighbours?'

There are three important parts to the set that is Mary's living space, and each area provides for different kinds of interactions between the residents of the big house and others who visit her there. At the extreme stage right is a door to the hallway on the second floor. This is Mary's front door, but it is also the meeting place for Phyllis and Rhoda, who frequently collide at this half-way point between their own apartments. They are always seeking out Mary's capacities to find equilibrium and often they want both her spiritual and material provisions. This doorway also serves as a mini-stage for numerous goodnight kisses that become awkward goodbyes because just as things get serious in Mary's private life, one of her 'family' members rings the bell or just walks in. Mary's boyfriends become strangers when Lou, Murray or Ted appear at her door. There is a passageway that leads from the door behind the sunken living-room centre of the stage to the kitchen on the extreme left. This allows the characters who know and need Mary to proceed directly to her food supply or to her round dining table. It also distinguishes them from the 'guests', outsiders who are motioned to the couch and stuffed chairs that consitute a 'parlour'. Because this more formal space often appears to dictate where people should sit and even what they should say, it functions to remind us of the differences between an old-fashioned hostess and a modern friend. Sometimes an establishing shot of the whole set reveals an agonised group staring out at us as though obedient to some decorous ideal that went out with horsehair furniture. But Mary's apartment as a whole does not have that kind of formality. Neither a fireplace nor a TV set provides a focus for her visitors. As a result it is Mary herself who is a centre. Sometimes still and attentive with one other person, sometimes moving skilfully between several people, her apartment appears to facilitate her social skills.

Mary can stride like a long-legged runner across the span of her apartment in order to answer the doorbell, and she can provide for close community needs by settling people at her dining table, the third important area in her place. Innermost, and closest to the kitchen that is every True Woman's heartland, this space recalls the round-table togetherness that included the Nelsons, the Goldbergs and Mama's Norwegian family in the early years of TV. Mary gathers her feuding neighbours there for quiet meals, serves coffee and cookies to the newsmen who visit, and reminds us that she can still bring everyone together in old-fashioned ways. We also learn in the first episode that Mary's 'open-house' modern lifestyle corresponds to the same lack of privacy which characterises life in an old family house. In the first episode when Rhoda returns for the tag to commiserate with Mary about the final visit and departure of her two-year-long 'relationship', Mary marvels that her crass neighbour could be so attuned to her feelings of regret and resignation. The house itself provides an answer to this bond among sensitive women: Rhoda points to a low place on the wall near Mary's door and says, '*I've* got this tremendous intuition and *you've* got this heating duct that goes all the way up to my apartment.' The script and the *mise-en-scène* thus confirm that both women's language and listening skills are dependent on their home-lives. Here is the origin of the communications skills which Mary will take into the workplace.

In the WJM newsroom, Mary's desk situates her in a fixed position at the very centre of the set. Her desk is next to Murray's, and their names and places suggest that 'Mur' and 'Mair' provide the newsroom 'family' with its twins: the associate producer and the newswriter. The narrow space between their desks serves as a median-line in the composition of the whole, with an entry door on the extreme right, a path across the open space behind Mary and Murray, and on the extreme left, usually off-screen (like Mary's kitchen), the private office of the boss, Lou Grant. Ted Baxter, the newscaster, appears frequently coming out of his dressing room or from the broadcast booth where he has been on-camera. The booth is behind a curtained wall at the back of the set, placed in a relationship to the room that is similar to that of Mary's windows in her apartment. But the newsroom is painted blue and grey, and what is warm and colourful about Mary's room is cold and efficient here. While we look directly out of Mary's big windows to see nature's changing seasons, the curtains to the broadcast booth are never opened, and the windowless newsroom is related to an outside world only by multiple clocks, wire-service machines, telephones, typewriters and television sets. The lack of visual stimulation tells us that this is a 'man's world', a bastion where man-made machines send and receive man-made information. There are large grey panels that make up the walls of the newsroom. They look as if they could be moved and resituated to provide for more efficient space-modules as new machines replace the few humans that are left. We learn that Mary works here and that she is a central character among the men at WJM, but we also see that she will never conform to this space, never disappear into its hard surfaces.

Mary's clothes (she never appears in the same outfit on different shows, perhaps to suggest that because we only see her once a week, unlike her co-workers, we miss some aspects of her everyday presence) frequently provide a dazzling contrast to the grey neutrality of the newsroom. And in conjunction with her animated gestures, the higher pitch of her voice, and her capacities to move speedily from her desk to her boss's door, these brightly coloured costumes mark her feminine presence at all times. Sometimes too, Mary and Murray both dress in bright colours, as if bonded in an effort to be inconsistent in a consistently rationalised atmosphere. When these two match it is often because their allegiance as teamworkers is emphasised, or because Lou Grant's patriarchal postures make their tie more urgent. The self-serving vanity of Ted Baxter is also made obvious by occasional outrageously loud ties and handkerchiefs, and these function to keep him the ready-target of his boss's anger. There are occasions when Ted's red ties seem to stimulate Lou's bullish disposition, confirming for us the differences between an old time shirt-sleeves-rolled-up newsman and a foppish anchor-man.

Above all, the newsroom is a divided place. Unlike Mary's apartment it does not allow for the easy flow of people nor does it provide access and intimacy. Its different parts suggest hierarchy among workers and competition between men and machines. In particular Lou Grant's office is a sealed-off glassed-in private space where loud confrontations are audible only to specific victims on the inside, but are visible to those who are on the outside. The ritual of knocking and waiting outside this door provides a vivid contrast to the way that people are welcomed into Mary's apartment. And because Lou's office corresponds to the space that is Mary's kitchen on that set, we also experience the sharp differences between her boss's desk-drawer liquor supply and Mary's kitchen coffee. When she is first interviewed for the job, Lou barks an invitation to her, hoping he has found a drinking partner. She completely misses his meaning, asks for a Brandy Alexander, and watches in silence as he drops his whiskey bottle back into his filing cabinet. Its metallic clank punctuates a meeting which is not what this newsman had expected from an office buddy. But Lou Grant remains intrigued by Mary, aware of a new kind of energy brought into his daily routine. In a three-part shot-reverse-shot sequence, he barks at her: 'You know what? You've got spunk.' Mary responds with a smile, and we cut to another medium close-up of her future boss: 'I *hate* spunk.' This non-conversation is followed by another in which the older man closes their deal: 'If I don't like you, I'll fire you. If you don't like me, I'll fire you.' Are these the words that men in power speak to women who have none? Mary listens. We listen. In this way and in many others she will provide this workplace with some humorous alternatives to its own deadlines and its own division of labour. She brings with her the playful flexibility of a modern woman and the sensitivities of a True Woman. Both are qualities much needed in an atmosphere where communication depends more on machines than people.

To what extent, we must now ask, does Mary's presence in these two locations grant *The Mary Tyler Moore Show* a critique of woman's place? The answer to this question will emerge in relation to the concept of family that is developed throughout the series. There are two directions in which these characters are pulled by Mary as a family-minded single woman. One is in the direction of community and co-operation, and the other is in the direction of a rigid social order that keeps men's and women's roles organised around opposing values and modes of behaviour. This comedy series takes us both ways. We have observed how the *mise-en-scènes* of home and work mark the differences between these two aspects of the familial. And we have noted how it is Mary's capacity to move between the two spheres which keeps the comedy intact. On the one hand, she can go beyond her nineteenth-century domestic model to accept and combine all kinds of single and often separated characters in her one-room apartment, and similarly can enter the workplace to encourage more collectivity. On the other hand, Mary often appears to mediate between widely different people in order to send them all back into their narrowly-defined roles as men and women who seem unchanged by and unable to challenge the social constraints that surround them.

RELATIONSHIPS AND ROLES AT HOME AND WORK

Three kinds of relationships that have been the focus of much feminist debate provide *The Mary Tyler Moore Show* and *Rhoda* with some of their central themes and incidents. The first is mother-daughter relationships. There is perhaps no subject of more significance to the women's movement than this one: it raises historically and psychologically important questions about both kinds of women's roles, and more importantly about the kinds of family bonds that are traditionally maintained through these relationships. Mary Richards has left her mother, but is placed decisively in the middle of Rhoda's relationship to her mother and Phyllis' relationship to her daughter. Second, we will look at a related matter: how does 'sisterhood' become a new source of strength and community for women who seek alternatives to marriage and family-defined roles? The importance of Mary's familial friendships with Rhoda and Phyllis are central to her own show, and remain intact throughout both of these characters' spin-off series. These three women are bonded initially as neighbours, but also because they are engaged in finding careers *and* male lovers, a combination long considered transgressive, if not impossible. Lastly, this study will explore some of the issues raised on *The Mary Tyler Moore Show* around women and work, more specifically Mary's relationships to both the men and the job in the TV newsroom. Feminist critics have long noted that women in journalism are frequently isolated or infantilised by their all-male co-workers, and it is most important to observe the ways in which Mary as a writer-producer appears to be a source for constant jokes, while as a smoothing force of mediation within the newsroom, she is a serious, if not central character at WJM.

While Mary has left her small Minnesota town to come to the big city (we see her making this break, with flowers and goodbyes, during the opening montage sequences that accompany the titles of each episode for the first two seasons), she remains a midwestern middle-class woman who lives alone on the middle floor of her apartment house. Separated from her parents, who occasionally visit in an episode, Mary appears to be a well-adjusted daughter who has successfully internalised her mother's homemaking and interpersonal skills, while having also moved towards the world of the father where there is financial autonomy and a public presence. Her separation from the mother recalls Pogrebin's article on 'Woman's Place' in a *TV Guide* from the early years of *The Mary Tyler Moore Show*. It was this feminist's argument that she could not separate from a web of girlhood lies until her father intervened to unfasten the glue that attached her own mother to the TV Mother of the 1950s, and that had thus entrapped the adolescent author in the feminine mystique. Mary Richards does not discuss her own parenting, but her move from a small home town mirrors Mary Tyler Moore's own move from *The Dick Van Dyke Show* where she played a perfect wife and young mother from 1961-6. When Mary meets Lou Grant in the first episode of *The Mary Tyler Moore Show*, he affirms this many-levelled act of separation for her: he is the father-like boss who will take her away from her family past and will give her a job in the WJM newsroom. In this sense Mary Richards is beyond *her* family, but is still linked to familial needs and concerns. There is a marked difference between biological mother-daughter relationships in *The Mary Tyler Moore Show* and Mary's more mediated position as sisterly or daughterly in her friendships with women at home and men at work. Both Rhoda and Phyllis are still caught in mother-daughter dependencies, and it is Mary's task and trial to listen and often negotiate for her two best friends: one a daughter and one a mother.

Rhoda's relationship to her mother Ida is the central one in her life. While she has moved to Minneapolis to work, it is immediately clear that Rhoda has not separated from her mother in any way but geographically. She enjoys some respite from Ida's Jewish mothering because, she tells Mary, talking on the telephone is less taxing: 'I like her better person to person than in person.' Later she will cling to the distance that the intercom provides when she is back in New York dealing with Ida on the *Rhoda* show in 1974. Rhoda refers to the double difficulty of meeting her mother after a long commute; 'Ma and jet lag' seem an awful combination. In short, there is no separating from this kind of mother, and in addition to the temporary relief that Rhoda may find from short and long distance communication systems, she depends primarily on Mary's capacities to mediate when Ida is a visitor to Minneapolis. In the first two years of *The Mary Tyler Moore Show*, there are at least two such occasions: one episode in 1970 when Ida arrives with an immense present for Rhoda, with which she will attempt to guilt-trip her daughter, and another in 1971 when she will try to establish a 'modern' mother-daughter bond around look-alike outfits. In both of these shows, Mary rescues Rhoda from two oppressive kinds of mothering: one Ida's own Jewish version, in which the note on the present says 'No one in the world will ever love you as much as I do', and the second in which mothering as friendship is challenged as a miserable alternative to the first.

In both of these episodes, Rhoda clarifies for Mary the profound problems that are associated with Ida's mothering. In the first ('Support Your Local Mother', 1970), as Mary goes to read the card on what she sees as a most generous gift from mother to daughter, Rhoda cracks: 'It's not a card, it's a curse.' She can feel the ways that this attachment is not love, but *need*, and yet she cannot escape it. Mary must listen to her friend: 'You're talking about midwestern love, I'm talking about Bronx love . . . My mother wants the people she loves to feel guilty.' But it is not until she agrees to let Ida stay with her that Mary recognises the no-win situation that Rhoda is in. In one of the more physical comic scenes between women, Mary and Ida chase each other around Mary's sofa trying to grab and give back the money which Rhoda's mother pretends-and-insists she wants to pay for her stay. Mary is exhausted and even frightened by this acted-out game, so that the next day when Ida moves to another level, demanding to be called 'Mama', she becomes more determined to reunite Ida with her own daughter. We view Rhoda in the window of Hemple's department store fussing with a bridal couple, mannequins who are perfectly placed and dressed for the very event that Rhoda herself longingly anticipates. With the appearance of her mother outside the store window, and Mary on the inside urging her friend to talk with Ida, Rhoda is caught. As the unhappy daughter is reunited with her mother in a resigned embrace, we cut to Mary still standing in the store window. As if she wishes to be invisible, she assumes the pose of a mannequin well-wisher at the wedding. The comedy is thick with something serious, if not tragic, about Rhoda's life. While we may laugh to see the topic of predatory mothering as something that well-adjusted, midwestern Mary has to confront, at another level it is an essential part of every woman's experience in this culture. Feminist scholars have long noted the implications of women's tendencies to merge, relating them frequently to mother-daughter bonds. Questions of women's relationships to men and to work are skilfully integrated in this script, where Rhoda's mother is a deterrent to the sense of self that is required for both. It is in this way that we come to understand Mary's critical role for Rhoda, as a separated 'sister' and a midwestern friend.

In 'A Girl's Best Mother is not her Friend', from the 1971 season, Ida visits and attempts to imitate Phyllis' relationship to her daughter, Bess. Because we know that Phyllis is a follower of trends and a consumer-wife and mother, her inane claim that mother-daughter matching dresses are a sign of 'an easy, open relationship' falls into the comic realm of her character-type. It is only when Ida hears this that it becomes the primary theme for this episode. This sometimes cruel mother has already, upon her arrival at the house in Minneapolis, begun to insult her daughter by comparing her to Mary: 'Mary, you look so slim and trim, and Rhoda, you . . . ' This comment is based on a sight-gag created by a cut from the three women in a long shot to Ida's point-of-view shot of Rhoda's bottom as she bends over to pick something up. Mother's critical gaze thus becomes an invitation, if not an insistence, that the TV audience participate in the competitive exchange. Now we know that Ida is in control, and will attempt to build a faddish mother-daughter friendship with the vulnerable Rhoda. Phyllis, the 'expert' in this context, offers to lend Ida the books she has bought on the subject. The episode culminates with the unexpected appearance of Ida and Rhoda in the WJM newsroom, holding hands as they stand together in matching dresses. Ida's foolish plan has now become a comical performance for Mary and the newsmen. In a previous scene Murray, the father of two, had responded to Mary's worried account of the mother-daughter plan: 'Kids don't need parents for friends.' So that when the two look-alikes arrive, Ida's misconceived notion of modern mothering has been partially corrected by

Murray's paternal wisdom to Mary. Now the dynamic shifts, and in the next scene Ida, Rhoda and Mary are eating dinner at Mary's table. We learn that Ida is taking some desperate steps to identify with her daughter, and has decided to stop wearing a bra in order to be 'with it'. Rhoda responds succinctly: 'Ma, you're not "with it", you're "without it".' By the end of this episode, perhaps because Mary has learned and mediated Murray's position and because Mary's table provides the necessary forum for exchange and clarification, Rhoda says to her mother: 'You've been a swell friend, but I need a mother.' This brief moment of equilibrium is soon lost, however, and in the tag we see Mary standing guard between mother and daughter. The feuding pair speak to each other through Mary: 'Will you tell her . . . ,' 'Will you tell her . . .' Mary mediates as the scene fades to black.

In this episode, there is a clear mockery of consumer-defined relationships between mothers and daughters, and of that post-war domestic ideal that implies that consuming is mothering and that shopping for matched outfits insures 'togetherness'. But at a deeper level, the attachment between Ida and Rhoda is also represented as a genuine longing on the older woman's part to be close to a 'younger self'. Even this sentiment is related to a critique that runs throughout *The Mary Tyler Moore Show* and *Rhoda*, of the many ways that our culture privileges youth just as it idealises motherhood and marriage. Perhaps Rhoda's constant talk of diets and make-up serve as reminders of how mothers' criticisms feed a marketplace that in turn profits from daughters' low esteem.

It is evident throughout the MTM shows that while character comedy remains foregrounded, what co-producers Brooks and Burns call 'fortunate timing' in relation to the women's movement served script-writers, directors and actors well. And while social issues surface largely through personality and family interactions, the critique – in this case of mother-daughter bonding – resonates with feminist concerns. As we have seen in other contexts, family relationships are often depicted as rigid and even harmful. Neither Ida nor Rhoda can separate enough to accept each other as different people. It is noteworthy, however, that these series do leave room for personal growth and change. In this way, there is an apparent response to some of the utopian aspects of feminism, and beyond providing 'background' for static or stereotypic characters, there is movement implied by some developments in Ida and Rhoda's relationship. The *Rhoda* show continues to explore this same mother-daughter dynamic in considerably more detail, and while the gags about fat and age provide the necessary character-based continuity with *The Mary Tyler Moore Show*, the two women gain a new understanding of themselves as they become more separated. When Rhoda leaves her marriage to Joe after one year, Ida works through something for the first time: 'In my day,' she tells her newly separated daughter, 'my mother would have said, "make any adjustment to save the marriage . . . ;" that doesn't go now, does it?' ('The Separation', 1976) Also for the first time in this episode, Ida realises that while she would like to stay with Rhoda to comfort her at this lonely time, 'That would have been good for me, but not for you, huh?' At this moment Rhoda can accept her mother's concern, and says 'stick around, Ma'. For viewers who have followed this painfully routinised relationship from its first appearance on *The Mary Tyler Moore Show* in 1970, to the moment when Ida in her old-world kerchief can listen to and embrace her daughter in the final seconds of the episode, this change has historical meaning. It is not that all family relationships are hopelessly entrenched, or that we can only sit back and laugh at the status-quo. It is also that alternatives surface in these women-oriented comedies, and that the possibilities for new relationships among women seem to emerge, even within families, when there are possibilities for relationships between women and work.

In the case of Phyllis' relationship to her pre-teenage child, Bess, a very different dynamic is brought to light. Like Ida, Phyllis is a home-bound parent, infantilised by Lars in the way that Ida is 'taken care of' by Martin. Both women appear determined to prove their capacities for full-time mothering, whether in an up-to-date mode or in a traditional sense. Phyllis has clearly read the latest literature, and she and Bess are on a first-name basis. Bess has been encouraged to regard the All-American family mythos with distaste and to make precocious comments whenever possible. The basis for comedy in this mother-daughter relationship lies in the fact that Phyllis herself is deeply committed to most of the conventions and values upheld by the bourgeois family, and perpetuates myths about the 'creativity' of housework, a 'pleasurable' marriage to Lars, and a 'rewarding' and 'open' relationship to Bess. From the moment when she introduces Bess to her 'Aunt Mary', and is unmasked for such family-mindedness when Bess calls her antagonist 'Aunt Rhoda', we know that Mary Richards will be caught in many years of mediating another mother-daughter conflict. Her rapport with Bess will be built on the fact that, for different reasons, both have accepted family-togetherness as something of the past, perhaps as mass media hype. In 'Baby Sit-Com' (1971) Lou Grant is asked by Mary to take care of Bess one night when Phyllis and Lars are away and when Mary wants to go out on a date. The young girl and the older man get along fine; she makes cookies and he gets drunk. They end the evening playing poker with the cookies, having decided that there was nothing worth watching on TV, once Lou's much anticipated prizefight was over after a few seconds. Bess makes it clear that she has better things to do than to watch *The Clancy Clan,* where 'They have all these kids, and everyone laughs a lot because they have all these kids.' She is, like Mary, one of the single female characters on *The Mary Tyler Moore Show* and on its spin-offs, who understands that family no longer means the redundant comedy generated by two parents and a lot of children. Her thinly veiled reference to *The Brady Bunch* (1969–74), an ABC programme about the marriage of two widowed parents with three children each, functions to provide *The Mary Tyler Moore Show* viewer with some added encouragement to question that older model. Treva Silverman is the scriptwriter for this episode and her efforts to place this series outside the family sitcom involve her pointed use of Bess, the wise only child who 'knows best' that friendship is more enduring than family, and whose 'old man' is too loaded to disagree.

In another episode scripted by Silverman ('The Birds and-um-the Bees', 1971), a different kind of commentary on family-ideology emerges. In the central plot Phyllis begs Mary to tell Bess the facts of life. This plan has been triggered by a subplot about a TV programme that Mary has produced, entitled: 'What's Your Sexual I.Q.?' While Phyllis found the documentary 'informative, enlightening and mature' ('in other words, boring,' says Rhoda), she does not feel like enough of an expert to tell Bess about such matters. When Mary asks if perhaps Bess' father Lars, a doctor, could do so, Phyllis notes that because he slept through the programme, he would do the same while talking about sex to his daughter. Rhoda supports Phyllis in this one instance, and asks Mary to speak to Bess, recalling the absurdities of her own mother's explanation of the facts of life: 'I thought I had to swim up the Columbia River.' But before Mary agrees, she tries one more possible source of fatherly advice, for herself in this instance. She speaks to Lou Grant at the office, who explains to her that it was 'perfectly natural' to educate his three daughters; he had simply told them that their mother had something to say to them about sex. After this extended buck-passing, itself a gentle mockery of how unmodern modern parents really are and of how much they may need to rely on a non-parent for this kind of interchange, Bess and Mary do begin to talk. Predictably, Bess takes over: 'Are you leading up to telling me about love . . .?' but unpredictably adds 'I already know about sex.' Their conversation uncovers the greatest of family myths, and Bess asks for clarity: 'Love and sex go together, right? So if you love someone, do you . . .?' Mary is cornered as the only expert, a single woman and a TV producer-expert who must play the role of a parent. But she is honest and acknowledges to Bess that there is a difference. Perhaps for censorship reasons it is Rhoda who calls out her gratitude from the armchair where she has been listening in: 'Thanks Mary, separating love and sex has changed my life.' The tag supplies this episode with a last stab at family-based morality. Phyllis re-enters Mary's apartment to try to talk to Bess on her own, now that Mary has done the real work: 'I'll make it sound spiritual and ethical . . . almost true.' Silverman's script explores the comic side to the ways in which mothering means lying, and as is frequently the case, it is Mary's task to provide an alternative to that kind of female socialisation.

The need to bypass and seek alternatives to family-defined relationships is nowhere more obvious than when we look at the ways in which Mary's female friendships are privileged in this series. Most particularly in the first four seasons, before Rhoda moves to New York and begins her spin-off in 1974 and Phyllis moves to San Francisco for her own show in the next year, these two neighbours are the subjects of every episode, central friendships in Mary's daily life as a career woman. We find that Phyllis and Rhoda provide her with more interesting interactions, conversations and comradeship than do most of the dates with whom Mary shares some of her private life. While often these boyfriends are buffoons who make brief comic appearances, they also disrupt the primacy of her friendships at home and at work. The WJM newsmen are often depicted as jealous and petty about any 'outside' man in Mary's life, and similarly her women friends are shown to be occasionally jealous but more often hurt when she ignores them for a stranger. While we are encouraged to admire Mary's capacities to keep everyone feeling cared-for, so that she can freely pursue her romantic interests, *The Mary Tyler Moore Show* is largely about the vitality of her friendships at home and at work. We too learn to take lightly the intruders. We are involved with Mary's own determination to live and work alone, among friends. Phyllis and Rhoda provide particularly significant alternatives to romantic or marital relations, and seem to affirm the feminist slogan of the period: 'Sisterhood is Powerful'.

By the early 1970s consciousness-raising groups had begun to politicise many middle-class feminists. In these contexts they could practise another basic tenet of the women's movement: 'The personal is political'. Such groups allowed participants to acknowledge the isolation of their lives at home as well as the inadequacies of their social lives, where in 'mixed company' they were isolated by gender. CR groups challenged the claim that women's talk was trivial, for they provided the safety wherein women could discuss both personal and political issues. Above all, women could come to understand that these two spheres are related, and that there are similar needs for collectivity at home and at work. *The Mary Tyler Moore Show* reinforces the importance of women's talk by presenting small gatherings at Mary's apartment as a daily event in the lives of Mary, Rhoda and Phyllis. In some ways, the old ideal of women's community in pre-industrial times was behind the structuring of modern CR groups: women had met regularly to talk, quilt, and share meals. At Mary's, women convene spontaneously for coffee, or to talk about problems associated with not-eating. The simple repetitions of Rhoda's and Phyllis' entrances and exits reinforce for us the interconnectedness of their lives. In addition to these regulars, Mary is also visited by Ida and Bess and, after the *Rhoda* and *Phyllis* spin-offs, by Georgette and Sue Ann, her two other friends whom she knows through connections at WJM. But all of these encounters, and the fluidity with which they occur, are associated with Mary's position as a single woman, and all of them serve to remind us that women's talk is neither trivial nor peripheral to women's lives. It is interesting to note that while Mary and her friends are often lured into alternative communities where lonely people meet, these excursions prove to be inadequate, if not farcical. There is no place like Mary's apartment where her circle of women friends feel at home.

Early in the first season of *The Mary Tyler Moore Show*, in a script written by Treva Silverman ('Divorce Isn't Everything', 1970), Mary and Rhoda are seen exercising together in Mary's apartment. The two seem aligned in their commitment to the new cult of aerobics, but only Mary is really moving her body. Rhoda stands still and waves her hands, for she is more interested in talking about joining the 'Better Luck Next Time Club', where newly-divorced people meet. She asks if Mary is often questioned about being single. Mary stops jogging in place and gathers herself to answer in her most elegant way: 'I could discover the secret of immortality, and still they'd say, "look at that single girl, discovering the secret of immortality".' With this comment, Mary focuses the entire episode on this absurd and painful truth about women's lives when they remain unmarried. She first suggests that singles are forever 'girls', a word which a woman scriptwriter was surely sensitive to, and that no effort of imagination or humane work can provide a meaningful identity in the face of this *lack*. It is with this admission of anger that Mary is convinced to join Rhoda for an evening among the divorcees. While Rhoda is usually willing to lie her way into such situations, Mary is humiliated into this activity. The group is pathetic and Mary is approached by a strange dentist who falls for her teeth. There is some irony here, since of all the characteristics that make Mary insecure about her appearance, her teeth are often the subject of comic exchange and some mockery about how her eager smile makes her 'likeable'. Her encounter at the divorcees' club results in Mary's being elected vice-president, at which point she admits that she has never been married. Rhoda confesses at the same time, and so do all the people assembled. All of them are single, and all of them live with the awareness of what Mary had said about the onus of not being married.

In *Rhoda* there are many incidents devoted to similar efforts by the women characters to join 'groups' which provide encouragement and company for the lonely and the overweight. In 'An Elephant Never Forgets' (1976), Rhoda and her sister Brenda, both single at this point, go to a 'weight control centre' in an effort to find a way out of the fat-and-therefore-lonely rut they share. The first segment of this episode is devoted to several comic exchanges between the instructor and the participants. Miss Fiske is thin and snippy, and we laugh at her claim to control the situation with scales. The room is filled with men and women who lie and confess, each with a mother-food story or a secret spaghetti-popsicle recipe. The scene culminates with a physical fight between Rhoda and Miss Fiske over Rhoda's weight. Each woman accuses the other of 'jiggling the beam' on the scales, and Rhoda takes most of her clothes off in an effort to 'win'. But the lesson learned in this case is only presented after the sisters have gone home (they share the same apartment building in much the way that Mary, Rhoda and Phyllis had on *The Mary Tyler Moore Show*), and Brenda is approached by a handsome male neighbour who 'sees' her now that she is thinner. He brings her flowers, but she is troubled: 'Would you go out with me today if I were fat?' she asks. He answers 'no,' and asks her, 'Would you go out with me if I were ugly?' To this she answers 'yes,' and sends him on his way. 'You're the best-looking guy I ever rejected ... You're also the *only* guy I ever rejected.' In each of these episodes the ways in which American culture conflates singleness and loneliness are articulated. So too the ways in which marketing and promotion benefit from this pro-family tendency within the society become the basis for many comic incidents.

But the most important critique of pro-family ideology is shaped by Mary and her woman friends whose meetings prove essential to the problem-solving that brings comic possibilities and calming resolution to every episode. In 'Father's Day' (1973), the central plot revolves around a reunion between Ted and his long-separated father. Ted's anxiety about this encounter immediately involves Mary – for her own distance from family matters and for her compassion towards others who are less reconciled. She sympathises with Ted's fears, and like his wife Georgette, who cares for him at home, Mary accepts this vain and infantile man in the workplace. With both women's encouragement Ted is finally on his own, alone with his father, and we watch the two exchange life-experiences: those of a pompous anchorman and those of a humble laundromat owner. It is Mary's clear-thinking that enables Ted to meet his father, and as he does so we also recognise something that Mary seems to know about Ted's unformed sense of self: there may be a connection between Ted's perpetual childishness and his unresolved status as a son without a father. Following the scene in which the two men talk in Ted's dressing-room at WJM, we see Mary alone in her apartment cooking. Rhoda enters saying that she is bored, and Mary replies, 'Tell him to go home.' Rhoda responds, 'Tell who? I'm alone.' Mary concedes that she is also bored and the two sit down to share Mary's meal, as if to acknowledge that their friendship is an essential antidote to being bored with a man or by oneself. At this point, Ted and Georgette enter and Ted's proud reunion with his father is the subject: 'Someday I'm going to look that way, like that little bald old man with a laundromat.' Ted has agreed to loan his father the money he'd asked for, and Mary and Rhoda approve as he goes off to take the older man to the bus station. Thus while families can pose problems for almost all the characters on *The Mary Tyler Moore Show*, Mary's single status and the alternative to parenting that she provides keeps her capable of helping others while she enjoys the friendships that they provide for her.

While Mary and Rhoda may complain about being bored and alone, the ways in which they consistently find each other and affirm their positions as single women is an important concession to the historical changes that have been shaping women's lives since the 1950s. Middle-class women in the 1970s are marrying later, and are doing so after they have established careers. As we have observed in this discussion of *The Mary Tyler Moore Show*, the extent to which the single career woman can provide the centre to a circle of people at home and at work is dependent on the fact that she cares for and mediates between people who are either married or are involved with family relationships. Mary does not proselytise against those who have families, but as an outsider to their worlds she can offer and sometimes advocate the new familial way of life. In a last example of how she recalls for us both the resilience of women's collectivity and the needs for people to make family-like commitments, we find that Mary promotes the more utopian aspects of the familial as she cultivates her dependencies on women friends. In 'The Square-Shaped Room' (1971), written by Susan Silver, Mary, Phyllis and Rhoda form a chain of interdependence as they appear to perpetuate the borrowing and returning of advice and things among themselves. At the outset of this episode Mary is alone in her apartment talking with Phyllis about her latest problem: how to help Lou Grant choose the new decor for his house. Surprisingly, Phyllis recommends Rhoda's skills, perhaps because Rhoda is not present, but at this moment her sometimes adversary enters and good-heartedly suggests that Phyllis' talents be involved. Mary's feuding neighbours meet and co-operate to help her help her boss, but at another level they affirm a female pattern of sharing as they exchange suggestions. Rhoda's pretence for coming down to see Mary is to borrow an egg. Mary gives one to Rhoda who then gives the same egg to Phyllis from whom she had originally borrowed one. Phyllis recalls that she owes Mary an egg, and so gives it back to her. This circular game accompanies their three-way conversation about Lou's decorating problem, and through such co-operative words and gestures there is suggested a modern quilting bee. In the tradition of naming patterns for their specific documentary functions, this visual counterpart might have been called 'Sister's Choice', or 'Robbing Mary to Pay Rhoda'. At Mary's there is affirmed both the place for familial trust and the mutual exchange that has always characterised the daily lives of women. Theirs is not a competitive but a co-operative relationship, as long as Mary is in the middle. While some older gender-defined topics are central to this conversation, these women appear to be making and affirming a network for modern life where being single can still mean belonging.

When Rhoda and Phyllis leave *The Mary Tyler Moore Show* in 1974 and 1975, there is a shift in Mary's focus away from her women friends. In part because the two women who remain on the show are directly related to Mary's work life at WJM, and in part because there is no longer a communal house where Rhoda and Phyllis surround her, Mary's relationships with Sue Ann and Georgette are less integral to her daily life. These two have been peripheral characters from early on in the series, but after the departure of Mary's neighbours for opposite coasts in spin-off shows of their own, these two women are included in almost every episode. But they are profoundly different from the two women friends whom they replace. While Rhoda and Phyllis had been somewhat rounded characters whom we knew to be engaged in their mother-daughter involvements and in their efforts to be separate people, Sue Ann and Georgette are caricatures of the male-defined woman. Perhaps because narrative continuity dictates, and because it is fully in keeping with Mary's character, these women also gain Mary's respect and acceptance. She establishes an allegiance to both the naive newly-wed Georgette and the seasoned marriage-wrecker Sue Ann. These two function in a different way from Mary's earlier friendships, and while they do not offer the same circle of trust and commitment that Phyllis and Rhoda had provided, by comic contrasts to Mary's stability, Sue Ann and Georgette depend on and thus further motivate Mary's single lifestyle.

Georgette is helped by Mary in her efforts to marry Ted (these two characters' off-screen names are Georgia Engel and Ted Knight – surely another effort to integrate life and TV and a 'perfect' marriage for Mary to mediate), and is counselled early on in *The Mary Tyler Moore Show* by both Rhoda and Mary to quit doing Ted's laundry and acting like a 'professional victim'. On 'The Georgette Story' (1972), they teach Georgette to have some self-esteem. 'Say something positive about yourself', Mary demands of the fluffy blonde dressed in pink. Georgette's response reveals her willingness to learn, an attribute that will soften her child-bride stereotype. 'I have good handwriting and I like animals. I like to think I'm a nice person. Very Nice. Damn nice!' Throughout the series Georgette will accompany her saccharine baby-talk with tough-talk, perhaps the vestiges of what she learned from the old days with Rhoda and Mary. We know from this episode on that

Ted will not change and will remain a sexist, but that Mary's concern for and advice to Georgette will lead to their happy marriage. Ted tells Mary how pleased he is with Georgette's new self-esteem: 'It's like being with a different woman. It's like being equal. I understand you're responsible. As long as I live, I'll never forgive you.' This exchange characterises Mary's friendship with Georgette; they will never be women who share the same commitment to a career and a single life, but Mary does not condemn Georgette, and operates as a caring counsellor to her throughout the show, finally even playing, with Lou Grant presiding, hostess and midwife at the birth of Georgette's and Ted's daughter, born during a party in Mary's apartment.

Sue Ann is Georgette's opposite, a bawdy TV personality who calls herself 'The Happy Homemaker', while behind the scenes she is an outrageous vamp. Competitive and quick witted, Sue Ann needs Mary for some very different reasons. She is often led astray by men whom she believes that she has captivated, and because we see her almost exclusively in the WJM newsroom, on frequent breaks from her own show, Mary's role as Sue Anne's rescuer is also cultivated by Lou Grant's advice and fatherly concerns. Sue Ann is one of the family in this context, and when a seductive but deceitful woodsman seeks to enter into a business deal with her, it is Lou's request to Mary that she save Sue Ann from this fate. As they hug each other in a ladies' room, Sue Ann softens and admits to Mary: 'I feel so alone.' It is Mary's capacity to be alone that allows others to accept similar feelings. And even though she has lost her two best friends, both of whom are capable of living alone, Mary's continued bonding with Georgette and Sue Ann recalls for us that in being alone she is not a lonely woman.

Mary's relationship to the men at WJM confirms the pattern that we have seen emerging. Friendship is *the* enduring social bond, and as a single woman Mary is the one who demonstrates and teaches this truth. But while she seems to form a centre for her closest women friends, Mary's work-related friendships with men are less convincingly 'modern'. It is in this sphere that far more rigid familial roles operate, and Mary seems to play the female parts necessary to maintain a traditional dynamic. Her same capacities to listen and mediate in this context are less directed towards a larger critique of woman's place in the society, and are consistently associated with her obedient 'daughterly', admiring 'sisterly', and her accepting 'motherly' qualities. That is, the social model for the newsroom maintains the conservativism of the nuclear family, and some of Mary's resistant impulses that are shared with Phyllis and Rhoda are lost in this context. It is ironic, but perhaps historically predictable, that as we find her a competent career women in an all-male office (and a largely male profession), we also find her limited to female family-stereotypes. We must ask if this is because our society has deeply cultivated a belief that women can only be mothers *or* whores, a dichotomy that leaves no place for a 'good' career woman? Or does this tendency simply reflect ways in which patriarchy is the basis for institutional relationships that endure under capitalism, even when the traditional family has been challenged by women's new social and economic needs? A last consideration must include the fact that until Mary arrives WJM is a motherless-daughterless family, and that as Mary becomes an integral part of that group, she ultimately reveals her male co-workers as somewhat trapped in their own patriarchal world, and clearly lacking some of the qualities and skills that are limited to women's roles in this culture. If there is a critique implicit in this aspect of the series, it lies in the fact that we see all three newsmen grow increasingly dependent on Mary in ways that they cannot admit or consciously accept.

In a 1976 episode entitled 'Mary's Three Husbands', the fantasy lives of Lou, Ted and Murray are enacted as 'dreams' when each imagines his own version of a marriage to WJM's associate producer. The narrative begins as the three men sit in Lou's office drinking late into the night. Mary is conspicuously absent, on a date, and the somewhat inebriated men acknowledge their desires to possess her as a wife. Each one focuses on an aspect of Mary's personality and each reveals his own specific need to move her from the familial to the family – where his control is unchallenged. Murray's dream is the first: he situates himself as a struggling creative writer, impoverished but adored for his genius by his wife Mary. In this fantasy Mary appears as a flower-child bride, pregnant and absolutely selfless as she waits on Murray. When she feels the pains of labour, rather than disturb him, she retires quietly to a back room to give birth. Mary Richards' qualities of caring and competence are recognisable in Murray's imagining, as are her few familiar shouts of 'Oh Boy!' as she ackowledges some pain. When she returns within seconds to show Murray the new baby, he looks up in awe and says 'What a woman' as his dream fades out. It is fitting to find that Murray, father of three and the newsroom's family-man, sees a magic mommy in his co-worker, but as viewers we have come to know and accept Mary's decision *not* to marry and mother. Thus Murray's comical fantasy reveals a conflict that men cannot easily acknowledge but must feel as they learn to work with career women whose encouraging ways they need but whose lives they cannot control.

In the next sequence, Ted's dream envisions Mary as his new bride as they enter a lush honeymoon hotel suite. 'You're mine,' he tells her, and she answers, 'Ted, darling, let's never leave this room.' But as he sits on the bed's satin sheets and removes his shirt, his undershirt has an image of his own face on it. Trouble. Mary appears in a baby-doll nightie, and Ted says, adoringly, 'You're even more beautiful than I am.' Ted's cliché-ridden mind can find no more alluring way to imagine a wedding night with Mary, but what transpires is indicative of how truly limited this man really is, even in his own unconscious. Ted's Mary has no intention of being 'his', and she tells him so as she leaves the room: 'I will not get into that bed with you. Bye.' Ted blubbers on alone until his fantasy with Mary fades. This man is such a narcissist that it is only in his dreams that he can picture Mary as anything but his mother. The role she plays with him in the newsroom is indeed that of a tolerant and often nurturant parent, who works to keep Ted's fragile ego intact when Murray and Lou cannot stop themselves from mocking him outright. That his dream should bring him close to a sexual relationship with this unconditional provider, a woman who gives him her home-made fried chicken for his office lunches, is indeed a comment on Ted's confused sense of self.

But it is Lou's fantasy about a marriage to Mary that shapes our final understanding of her role in the newsroom. In his dream, Lou and Mary have been married for fifty years. They are an old white-haired couple who are still putting the news together for Ted Baxter, an aged anchorman who cannot even remember his name. An old mustachioed Murray accuses Ted of being 'as senile as you were 50 years ago', and Ted simply says 'thanks', as he would have 50 years ago. But the comic sameness that Lou's dream implies shifts when Mary calls after her ancient boss and husband: 'Mr Grant, it's time we consummated our marriage.' To this Lou replies from his beloved off-screen office: 'Now you have to ruin it.' But Mary demands an explanation in this flash forward, and Lou tells her: 'When we were first married you were like a daughter to me, and it seemed unthinkable. Then you were like my sister, and now you're like my mother.' At this point Mary Richards, done up in a white wig, unpins her hair and lets it fall to her shoulders, bats her eyes at Lou and waits for him to call her into his office. The dream fades to black and we return to the three newsmen, now quite drunk and tired from their story-telling. In the tag, Mary comes into the newsroom, late in the evening and finds her three colleagues muttering to her about some future marriage. Each one gives her advice that is related to his own dream of desire, and as they leave her puzzled and alone, she stands for a minute, lifts the empty whiskey bottle and looks into it.

This curious episode is as tasteless as it is mythic, a script that seems not to fit the pattern of this series. But what it does do, is to reveal in perhaps the only way that is possible for such comedy, the underlying dynamics that operate to keep Mary in her job. 'Mary's Three Husbands' touches on the nature of her relationship to the newsmen, and makes an awkward effort to comment on the incest taboo that keeps this news-family in working-order.

There are numerous routines that occur frequently throughout *The Mary Tyler Moore Show* which further contribute to our understanding of this traditional family model. In the final pages of this discussion, let us turn to an examination of how this dynamic functions to keep Mary Richard's career as a newswoman in the shadow of her family-dictated role. There are several instances where Mary's efforts to define her job as a journalist conspire to humiliate her, in most cases returning her to the work she does as Lou's assistant, a role that suggests she is more secretary than producer.

From the first episode when Mary arrives in the WJM newsroom to be interviewed for what she believes to be a secretarial job, there is the lurking possibility that this is what she has been hired to do. Murray calls out to Mary as she crosses the newsroom for the first time: 'We've already hired a secretary', but when Lou Grants meets her in his office, Mary impresses him as someone whom he needs around. He negotiates with her for the salary and the title she will have: as associate producer he will be able to pay her ten dollars less per week than a secretary. She says that she cannot afford to be a producer when he goes on to offer that job for fifteen dollars less than a secretary per week. This comic exchange terminates when Mary delightedly agrees to be hired as an associate producer, but as she reaches across her boss' desk to shake hands, he doesn't budge, so she recovers in her most gesturally creative way, and simply waves goodbye – like a little girl. In seven years, Mary will never call this man Lou, or only when she is angry. In one instance, she defends her need to call him Mr Grant. It is in her character to do so: 'I call him Mr Grant because I want to, not because I feel I have to. I started calling him Mr Grant six years ago. It was comfortable then. It's comfortable now. It's what I want to call him. It's what I'm going to call him.' Mary's history at WJM is the history of every woman who works in an all-male office. From the first day, they all call her Mary, and from the first day, she calls her boss Mr Grant. This deference may be explained as part of Mary's nature, but it is also a feature of her job and of the hierarchy that remains intact through such means.

Mary asks for a raise on 'Good Time News' (1972), and the central plot revolves around whether or not Lou Grant will agree to giving her the fifty dollars more per week that she has found her male predecessor received. Before this issue surfaces, in a discussion at home with Rhoda, there are several indications that Mary is resentful of this and other inequities. She and Rhoda discuss the latter's recent date with a 'stewardess'. Mary corrects Rhoda, 'They're called "stewards"' and Rhoda responds, 'I'm no sexist'. Mary is working late a lot at the newsroom and in the same conversation with Rhoda, she explains that she feels burdened by her token position. '*This* is our woman executive,' Mary quotes as she describes the way in which she is presented by the station managers. Following this exchange at home, Mary complains to Lou about her needs for a higher salary. He brushes off her request as 'one of those woman things', and until the end of the episode there is no more mention of Mary's right to equal pay. But it is the way in which she is finally granted this raise that is suspect from a feminist perspective, for Mary is 'rewarded' by Lou mainly because she talks back to Ted Baxter while he is acting like an arrogant fool on the news show. Because he does not want to share the camera with anyone else, and because Lou has been told to add some 'entertainment values' to help boost his ratings, it is Mary's responsibility to break Ted into this new format that will involve several different newscasters on each programme. She does Lou's work for him, and in one of the few ways that an expressive and angry woman can be useful to a news producer. Because Ted actually interrupts Mary's editorial commentary while she is on the air, she shouts at him: 'Shut up, Ted'. This is Lou's own style, and he is delighted to see Mary on the screen doing what he could not do to humiliate Ted in public. It is a gesture that is not characteristic of Mary's way in the newsroom, but she is given her raise for this outburst. The question of equal pay for women is thus subverted by an interaction that ultimately reflects the boss' needs and his own power to get what he wants from his workers.

It is possible that the sexist nature of Mary's work as a producer of feature stories is occasionally mocked by a scriptwriter who titles her documentaries to suggest that she is stuck in the soft-news ghetto that is woman's place in journalism. There are some references to the names of her productions which perhaps serve as commentary on this phenomenon: 'Chimps and What They Teach Us', or 'Know Your Sexual I.Q.' But the most explicit instances where Mary's opportunities as a journalist are shown to be limited are in the episodes where she attempts to become a writer, and fails each time. In 'Room 223' (1971), by Susan Silver, Mary's lack of experience is first revealed when she must take over for Murray, and finds she cannot write up the fire story that comes over the wires. Lou hovers authoritatively over her as she tries to type this in time for the evening news, loses patience with Mary's bungling efforts and writes the story himself in a few seconds. Mary is hurt by this incident, and in the next scene she, Rhoda and Phyllis are found sitting in her apartment talking about what she should do. Phyllis suggests a college journalism course, which is what Mary tries. But the central plot in this episode soon forms around her relationship to her male professor, who is instantly both attracted to Mary and anxious about her authority as a full-time news producer. The conflict over her work-related skills and authorship thus becomes a romantic problem, somewhat complicated by the fact that Lou Grant is jealous of Mary's new-found authority figure. When Mary receives a C+ on her first assignment, she is reassured by her arrogant professor that he has 'gone out with "C" students before'. She wonders why he gave her a 'plus' since his comments had harshly criticised her writing for being too 'flowery' and feminine, to which he quips: 'I couldn't keep my personal feelings entirely out of it.' Discouraged, Mary shows her first effort to Murray, her best-brotherly fan, and he is predictably enthusiastic about her work, calling it 'terrific'. Mary is caught between three men-who-write in this episode. She cannot get either genuine encouragement or fair criticism from any one of them, and this is because she is a woman. The issue of authority is here explicitly related to authorship, and Susan Silver's script seems to suggest that within the institution of journalism, a woman may mediate but not make the news.

In 'Mary the Writer' (1976) she tries to affirm her skills as a journalist by producing a personal reminiscence about her grandfather. Once again, automatically Murray likes her work, and once again Lou does not even want to read it. She begs for his response, however, and after reading it he tells her, 'It stinks.' She stands tentatively in his office while he rants on about 'what good writing is', and finally reads her a passage from Raymond Chandler. The prose is 'masculine', a classic description of Los Angeles-style anxiety: 'It was one of those hot dry Santa Anas that come down from the mountains and curl your hair and make your nerves jump.' Lou Grant's effort to demonstrate 'good writing' to Mary is obviously unrelated to her preferred subject or style. But she puts her boss and his favourite mystery author in their places with a deft and backhanded compliment: 'He writes well about the weather.' And from this brief rallying point she goes on to insist that her idea for a story is valid too: 'Most people love reading about delightful, warm-hearted old men ...' We respect Mary for her tenacity, but the battle is lost. Mr Grant is no sentimentalist, and in this context 'father knows best'. Later in this same episode Mary again challenges him for his tough-mindedness and his refusal to compliment her on her writing efforts. She compares herself to Ted, saying that Lou Grant never treats him so meanly for his miserable writing skills. At this point her boss explains: 'I respected *you* enough to tell the truth,' and thus reveals to Mary his fatherly concern that she learn the trade like a 'real man'. What he cannot concede is that as a woman she might choose to write a different kind of prose, perhaps challenging the myth of objectivity that informs the form and content of news journalism. But the legitimacy of her position is completely eroded by the end of the episode and although Lou Grant may be learning to be more sensitive to the feelings of a new writer, Mary's impulse is to retreat from the confrontation, having begged her boss to lie to her about the quality of her prose. Like a daughter who was briefly treated as a son, Mary recovers her girlishness as if to keep the familial order intact. As we have seen in other instances, an episode which begins by opening up a series of questions about authorship and authority ends with the recuperation of inter-familial relations and roles. In the context of the workplace this tendency preserves the division between the sexes for the sake of the traditional division of labour. Mary will type the words and thoughts of the men who write the news at WJM.

CONCLUSION

In 'The Last Show' (1977) a final goodbye scene takes place in the WJM newsroom where a sobbing, clinging collective of the three newsmen, Mary, Georgette and Sue Ann bunch together in an enormous hug. With their arms intertwined they pass around a box of tissues for their tears, and move in unison towards the office door for the last time. The station manager has fired everyone but Ted, who never produced the news and who will remain behind as a showbiz personality, perhaps a last comment on the priorities of modern broadcast executives. Implied is the fact that an old-style journalist like Mr Grant is no longer relevant for the production of today's TV news-as-entertainment. As this nostalgic group gropes its way across the floor, Mary steps aside to make her own farewell statement. As much as the past seven years may mark the end of an era for broadcast news, for Mary Richards they allowed a beginning and a new way to see herself as a working woman:

> I just wanted you to know that sometimes I get concerned about being a career woman. I get to thinking my job is too important, and I tell myself that the people I work with are just the people I work with, and not my family. And last night I thought, 'What is a family anyway? They're just people who make you feel less alone and really loved.' And that's what you've done for me. Thank you for being my family.

It is this message which explains in personal terms what is historically regressive about *The Mary Tyler Moore Show*, as well as indicating its innovative dimensions. In its seven years the heroine, Mary Richards, remains separate from her own family, their small town, and the 1950s TV-idyll in which women married and stayed home to raise big families. She continues throughout the series to grow up as a single woman, occasionally mentioning her age as if to remind us of her special authority and her increasing confidence that living alone is not lonely. Her friends at home and at work are her 'family', she says, and we have seen how these dependencies provide the basis for what is most positive about family trust and co-operation and what is most confining about family roles and hierarchy.

In a brief but significant scene during 'The Last Show', Mary is reunited with Rhoda and Phyllis. Lou Grant has arranged for them to surprise her with a visit to her apartment, and they arrive from opposite coasts to support and cajole their old friend as she adjusts to the loss of her job at WJM. It is reassuring and comical to see that Mary is still the stable centre for these two who scrap over which one she will visit and which one she will sit nearest to as they talk. All three women are single now, with Rhoda's divorce in the past and Phyllis recently widowed. Their appearance functions in part to recall for us the feminist concerns and hopes that had for so many years connected them as neighbours. During the first half of the series these three shared lives that provided an alternative to family life, and Mary played an important part as she encouraged Rhoda and Phyllis to struggle within their individual families. Most particularly, she was a role model for these two friends as they sought to separate from a mother and a daughter. They also questioned consumer values and the place of woman as buyer and believer in the myths of transformation. And above all, these women affirmed the interdependence and compatibility of a daily life that combined home and work. Thus Mary, Phyllis and Rhoda formed a familial group, sustained by what is most necessary to modern life: community and critique.

What is clearly a more patriarchal notion of family relations appears to have shaped Mary's role among the newsmen and the nature of her work at WJM. In this sphere the problems raised around sex-roles and the division of labour provide the basis for much comic conflict between the men and Mary, but narrative closure in each episode involves the return to a 'working order' that affirms traditional family hierarchy. Problem-solving in this context requires that Mary mediate less as a single woman friend and more as a daughter, sister or mother – and sometimes even as a forbidden wife-lover. In playing these roles Mary functions as a nineteenth-century True Woman, this time 'upholding the pillars' of the workplace with her willing hand. But while she thus humanises the newsroom, we see that in many ways she must deny her role as a producer in that context. Like her counterpart from a previous era when middle-class women were the angels of the home, Mary sacrifices with a smile at WJM, granting her co-workers a sense of individual worth and the capacity to form a caring collective. The increasingly rationalised and highly technical aspects of TV news production are thereby slowed for a resistant moment – those seven mythic years when Mary Richards brought her familial skills into the workplace.

Notes

1. Michèle Barrett and Mary McIntosh, *The Anti-Social Family* (London: 1982), p. 31.
2. Barbara Welter, 'The Cult of True Womanhood: 1820–60', *American Quarterly* vol. 18, no. 162 (1966), p. 152.

3. Fabian Linden, *Women: A Demographic Social and Economic Presentation* (New York: 1973), pp. 22–3.
4. Dwight Whitney, 'You've Come A Long Way, Baby: Happy Hotpoint is now Mary Tyler Moviestar', *TV Guide*, 19 September 1970, p. 34.
5. Dick Adler, 'The Writer Wore Hotpants', *TV Guide*, 15 July 1972; Joseph Finnigan, 'Cameraperson in Hotpants', *TV Guide*, 9 September 1972.
6. Caroline Bird, 'What's Television Doing for 50% of Americans?', *TV Guide*, 27 February 1971.
7. Diane Rosen, 'TV and the Single Girl', *TV Guide*, 6 November 1971, p. 12.
8. Letty Cottin Pogrebin, 'Woman's Place: A Personal View of What It's Like To Grow Up Female', *TV Guide*, 1 September 1973.
9. Horace Newcomb and Robert S. Alley (eds.), *The Producer's Medium: Conversations With Creators of American TV* (New York: OUP, 1983), p. 216.
10. Ellen Sherman, 'Femme Scribes Cop Top Jobs', *Ms Magazine*, December 1974.
11. Most of the episodes cited in this essay are from the collection that was donated to the Wisconsin Center for Film and Theater Research in Madison, Wisconsin. I am grateful for the permission granted to study these tapes and films, and thank Ms Lynn Dietrich at MTM Enterprises. I am also most grateful to Ms Maxine Fleckner, the director of the Wisconsin Film Archive, for her resourcefulness and guidance. The episodes are titled in the MTM collection and I have used these throughout the essay. But the reader may note that these titles do not appear in *TV Guide* for the weekly listings, and are not included in the credits of the shows as televised.

Drama at MTM: *Lou Grant* and *Hill Street Blues*

Paul Kerr

If the first seven years of MTM's existence were inevitably dominated by *The Mary Tyler Moore Show* and its sitcom spin-offs, the second seven years can best be characterised by two drama series, *Lou Grant* and *Hill Street Blues*. For, by 1977, American television had changed profoundly and MTM, in order to ensure its own survival, had to change with it. This essay attempts to detail the strategy it elected to follow in negotiating the new era of broad-and-narrow-casting, of cable and cassettes, superstations and satellites. That strategy, however, was to prove double-edged, for it depended on the tempting not only of 'quality' audiences back into prime-time but also of major corporate sponsors in order to secure the spaces, the relative autonomy that only non-network corporate capital could acquire. But at the same time it necessitated granting those same corporations considerable power over their product – the power to advertise or not. The controversial history and eventual cancellation of *Lou Grant* and the equally renowned creation and amply celebrated survival of *Hill Street Blues* testify to the existence of spaces for such 'difference' at the same time as evidencing their very precariousness. Certainly, corporate capital has 'bought' MTM Enterprises the space for 'contradiction' and 'quality' in prime-time; equally certainly, the price exacted in return for that space can be inflated at any time to enforce the incorporation of such contradictions either literally, via the acquisition of MTM by a major studio, or metaphorically, via acquiesence to an at best ambivalent, at worst anodyne, aesthetic.

When, in 1982, CBS announced the cancellation of *Lou Grant* it was abandoning the then longest-running fictional character on prime-time television. Lou Grant, played by actor Ed Asner, had first appeared on the small screen in 1970 as Mary Richards' irascible boss in the TV newsroom setting of WJM Minneapolis in *The Mary Tyler Moore Show*. Indeed, Lou Grant as a character and as a series had only been spun off from its parent show when MTM decided in 1977 to wind up its first and oldest series while it was still a major success. With a self-consciousness that was already an MTM trademark, the final episode of *The Mary Tyler Moore Show* involved the acquisition of WJM by a cut-throat competitor whose first action as new owner was to sack the entire newsroom staff – with the exception of the monumentally incompetent Ted Baxter – in an abortive attempt to improve flagging ratings. While *The Mary Tyler Moore Show* was sold off into syndication and perpetual re-runs, *Lou Grant* was created by MTM on the basis of a CBS commitment to actor Ed Asner, on whose already familiar face, and on whose already popular persona as Mr Grant, the network felt they could capitalise. But *Lou Grant* was always much more than a mere sequel to its prestigious predecessor. It was not a 30-minute comedy but a 60-minute drama and, according to sociologist Paul Espinosa who sat in on some of the early story conferences, there was an ambition for and an atmosphere of confident distinction and distinctiveness about the series:

> The producers of the *Lou Grant* show see themselves as producing a different kind of product ... From top management down to members of the crew, the show is talked about as though it were different from, superior to, better than, and more intelligent than other television shows ... The *Lou Grant* show is an odd hybrid of television genres. As an hour long show it has the form of the dramatic show, as opposed to the situation comedy show, variety show, game show, etc. Nevertheless, what is peculiar to the *Lou Grant* show is that the central character, Lou Grant, is a spin-off character from a situation comedy, another distinctive genre. From the start, the show's executive producers, all veterans of the situation comedy genre, intended to blend comedy and drama in the show, recognizing that they were switching genres. One of the early promos the producers wrote for the show reflected this split: '*Lou Grant*. It's drama. It's comedy. It's new and different.'[1]

This 'difference', this distinctiveness, was a consequence of a desire to differentiate MTM's new series not only from its competitors but also from the MTM house style itself. And this desire is realised in both the move to a 60-minute dramatic series format and the hybridisation of genres. For MTM in 1977 was in the thrall of a major attempt to diversify its product. From its origins as a sitcom (or character comedy) company, MTM determined in 1977 to move into a variety of other fields. That year the company set up a subsidiary MTM-AM, to make day-time programmes such as soaps and game shows, and also produced the company's first mini-series, TV movies, specials and so on. A brief glance at the section of this book devoted to pilots reveals the extent to which this trend away from sitcoms had effected MTM by 1977. Two years earlier they had set up an unpublicised subsidiary to develop quiz shows[2] and, when that proved unsuccessful, MTM made its first – and to date only – series directly for first-run syndication, *The Lorenzo and Henrietta Music Show*. All these attempts to diversify related to the expansion of MTM from what had once been a 'family' firm specialising in character comedy to a 'faceless' corporation; as James Brooks put it, 'at a certain point the idea of giving the creative part of the staff that kind of autonomy became completely impossible for business reasons'.[3]

Certainly the company needed to diversify. Equally certainly it lacked both the creative staff and the resources to do so. New writer-producers were required if MTM was to be able to conceive the sorts of TV movies, mini-series and specials that the new era of programming apparently demanded. Gene Reynolds, who had worked with Brooks and Burns on *Room 222* and who had since been at work on CBS' *M*A*S*H*, was attracted to MTM on the strength of a part in developing *Lou Grant*. Patchett and Tarses were persuaded to stay by being given the opportunity to oversee an hour-long variety show, *Mary*, for the 1978 season. Writer-producer (and sometime director) Bruce Paltrow was hired to create *The White Shadow*, which was produced by Grant Tinker's son Mark (who had previously worked on such series as *Three For The Road*, *The Bob Newhart Show* and the pilot *Royce*). Also involved in *The White Shadow*, which was another hour-long drama series, were the writers Joshua Brand, John Falsey and John Masius. Together with Paltrow and Mark Tinker they remained with that series and, after it was cancelled, reunited to create *St Elsewhere* in 1981. In the meantime, Steven Bochco, a writer-producer MTM hired away from Universal, had overseen several pilots for MTM including *Operating Room* (with Bruce Paltrow – seeds of the later successful series *St Elsewhere*?), *Every Stray Dog and Kid* and *Vampire* (which was screened as a TV movie). On *Vampire* and the shortlived series *Paris*, Bochco was teamed up with another writer from the Universal lot, Michael Kozoll, who had already contributed to *Three For The Road* as a freelance. When *Paris* was cancelled in 1980 Bochco and Kozoll, in collaboration with director Robert Butler, came up with a new series, *Hill Street Blues*, the unprecedented success of which encouraged NBC to acquire another *Hill Street*-style series from MTM, *St Elsewhere*. Also in 1982, Robert Butler co-created another crime series for MTM, *Remington Steele*, and the following season Bochco and *Hill Street*'s Greg Hoblit co-created *Bay City Blues*, an unsuccessful baseball variation on the police precinct original. Like *The White Shadow* and two of MTM's TV movies, *Fighting Back* and *Something For Joey*, this was another sports-based fiction, which attempted to transfer the dense texture of *Hill Street Blues* to yet another fictional site. 1984 saw only one new MTM series on the schedules; *The Duck Factory* was created by Gene Reynolds and Allan Burns, the only one of MTM's writer-producers who has stayed with the company since its beginnings. It concerns, appropriately enough, the employees of an independent production company producing (animated) programmes for television. (This combines an homage to Burns' background as a TV cartoonist with a reflexive focus on an 'indie'.) *The Duck Factory* shares with MTM's most recent pilot, *Bliss*, a factory setting (the latter concerned the owner of a chocolate factory), an interesting departure from the familiarly intimate environs characteristic of earlier MTM fictions. Perhaps product here was simply reflecting the changes undergone by the production company itself, from a family business to a considerable corporation.

From the late 70s to the early 80s, MTM's full-time staff rose from about twenty to about 300 employees; its three vice presidents escalated to nine. Some of this expansion, of course, is no more than a necessary consequence of diversifying from 30-minute sitcoms to 60-minute dramas. But in the course of its first decade as a production company it did grow from a single-series firm to one of the largest independents in Hollywood. One consequence of this expansion was that the cost of production escalated enormously. It was not simply that deficit financing was still a drain on resources; rather, MTM was willing to invest larger amounts of money in its products than almost any of its competitors. This was the price of quality, after all. But the other side of the quality coin was the attractiveness of such series for luring back to prime-time the large corporations which had left network television in the 1960s. One pointer to this change was the fact that it was not a network series which won the most Emmys in the mid-seventies but PBS' import *Upstairs, Downstairs*, which went out in the corporate-sponsored anthology slot 'Masterpiece Theatre'.

CBS' series commitment for an MTM-produced package starring Ed Asner – once again an agreement which did not oblige MTM to make a pilot or involve them granting the network story-approval rights – freed MTM to try out several ideas. But because the Asner/Grant persona was so well-known and because its past associations with 'news' offered such natural opportunities for the sort of topical and/or relevant fictions which were an MTM trademark, they stayed with the idea of a newsroom, this time in the world not of television but of the press. A newspaper setting had, in fact, been among the original concepts for *The Mary Tyler Moore Show*, in which the Mary Richards character was to have worked as the stringer for a gossip columnist. Also in that series, Lou Grant had occasionally harked back to his apprentice years in the newspaper business (just as in *Lou Grant* he would occasionally reminisce about his time at WJM Minneapolis). Thus Brooks, Burns and Gene Reynolds became convinced that a newspaper setting was perfect for the new series. But if the setting was, in part, a legacy of Lou Grant's past life in *The Mary Tyler Moore Show* (and a 'realistic' continuation of that life story) it also provided a comfortably familiar but credibly facilitating site from which to launch and in which to anchor pointed fictions about the real world.

Grant Tinker once described the 1977–8 season – the season of *Lou Grant*'s launch – as 'the year of the stewardess'. He did so while taking part in a PBS station discussion about the networks entitled 'The Realities of Commercial Television Production'.[4] In that programme, Tinker proposed that network television could be considerably improved if it readopted the sponsorship system which obtained in the 50s and early 60s. (The programme was made and transmitted by the Los Angeles PBS station KCET-LA, which in 1982 was to broadcast a documentary anthology series entitled *Independent Eye*, all of whose 'presentation costs' were underwritten by MTM.)[5] Also in that programme Tinker took the opportunity to attack the network's current obsession with ratings, arguing that under a renewed sponsorship system there need be no more of such hysterical competition or of its concomitant lowest common denominator programming. As if to illustrate the depths of his frustration with the networks – and with the advertisers – Tinker took the opportunity to announce MTM's completion of a pilot for PBS for a fifteen part series entitled *Going Home Again.* As it turns out, the pilot never seems to have been developed into the hoped-for series, though whether this is due to the decision of MTM itself, PBS or simply the (ironic) absence of corporate sponsors for the series is unknown. However, it should be noted that it was precisely the success of *Lou Grant* in attracting major corporate advertisers to regularly advertise in its slots which was to facilitate the sponsor blacklist that came into operation in 1982. For in fact, *Lou Grant* was to suffer from almost exactly the same sort of advertiser interference, outrage and eventual blacklisting which characterised the sponsorship era of the 50s and 60s and which Erik Barnouw has described in such detail in his book, *The Sponsor.*[6] The only obvious difference is that with *Lou Grant* the interference was retrospective (i.e. it either occurred at the time of re-runs or, finally, after rather than before a 'controversial' statement, by Asner himself as well as by the series). The final irony, therefore, is that if *Lou Grant*'s eventual cancellation can in some senses be laid at the door of the political timidity of corporate sponsors (or advertisers) its very success as a series and, indeed, MTM's own economic upturn in the 1980s is equally attributable to those large corporations which were explicity wooed to advertise in such series as a result of their 'quality' audiences.

Lou Grant was created by Brooks, Burns and an outsider, Gene Reynolds, who, before co-creating *M*A*S*H* in 1972, had worked with both of them on *Room 222*. At first, there seems to have been some difference of opinion within MTM about the extent to which the series should and could concern itself with 'real' issues. There was also a simultaneous and in some ways analogous reluctance among some of those involved to privilege drama over and above comedy. That these differences within the production team didn't result in disastrous compromises is probably at least partly due to the series' newspaper setting. This enabled the series to 'naturalise' those concerns by transforming them into the day-to-day business of the reporter protagonists. From the very beginning, however, *Lou Grant* ran into difficulties with CBS, who considered it too upmarket for its audience and advertisers and not heroic enough. At the beginning of the première season CBS executives told the series producers, 'Fellas, fellas, what you're giving us is the *New York Times* and what people read is the *Daily News*.' Another executive added that, 'Ed is a loser. He's not heroic enough.'[7] Apparently they wanted a crimefighter, not another newspaperman; 'They wanted Kojak.' But MTM, as if to snub and at the same time console CBS, came up with a story for the very first episode of the series set in a police station, 'Cophouse'. While CBS were eventually satisfied, first by the series' accumulation of Emmys and later by its steadily increasing audience, the advertisers were always sensitive. In 1982 a *Lou Grant* episode entitled 'Blacklist' prefigured the series' own eventual end by doing a story about a moral majority campaign to dissuade corporate advertisers from using the 'Tribune' (*Lou Grant*'s fictional paper) because of its sex column. MTM being MTM, in fact, the company's house-style hybrid between 'realism' and 'self-consciousness' was illustrated in the very first episode of the series, in which the Grant character berated his ultimate boss, the owner Mrs Pynchon, with the words 'You hired me for being a man of strong opinions. You didn't tell me they had to be yours.' It was a remark that could be repeated with multiple ironies in 1982.

From its inception and as a direct result of its ambitions the creative team behind *Lou Grant* were committed to – and proud of – their achievement. And that pride, that commitment, that ambition was both a consequence of and a contributor to the series' identification with the real world of reporting. In this identification, as much as in the association between actor and role (Asner was later accused of thinking he was Grant), some of the seeds of the controversial cancellation of *Lou Grant* were sown. Certainly, Ed Asner was often quoted about his own pre-acting ambitions to be a reporter. And two of the three creators of the series stressed the importance of rigorous research. James Brooks had actually begun his career in television as a CBS newswriter, an academic researcher Michele Gallery was hired to check the 'accuracy' of the series stories, while Gene Reynolds was well known for arguing that television fiction can and should disseminate ideas as well as entertainment. Reynolds also noted some surprising similarities between actors and reporters:

> Reporters are very much like actors. That's the last thing a reporter would like to hear – but they have these things in common, a sense of craft, great identification with their work, caring a great deal about

their work. There's a certain amount of their work under the control of somebody else, like a director or an editor. They want to get credit for what they're doing. Most of all, they're very sensitive people. . . .[8]

Seth Freeman, another of the *Lou Grant* creative team, has added another parallel. 'Episodic television is a weekly thing – which can be like having your own newspaper column.'[9] Allan Burns has also noted the function of the newspaper setting to 'naturalise' a certain style of topical story-telling, more in tune and intertwined with the real world than *The Mary Tyler Moore Show*:

> In *Lou Grant* we are into larger issues because of the newspaper setting. Newspapers deal with large issues as well as small ones. I'm uncomfortable with *Lou Grant* sometimes because I think some of the subject matter leads us into polemic. I think our most successful shows are the ones that deal more with people and less with issues. *Lou Grant* has very much taken on the character of Gene Reynolds, who is executive producer. Gene, having come off *M*A*S*H*, I think saw an opportunity to say some things he felt needed airing. When we all (Jim, Gene and I) did *Room 222* together Gene would want to get into issues. Gene is a very concerned individual, more than I am on a day-to-day basis. Gene really pays his dues. He does a lot of research and goes to a lot of conferences and he especially wants to impart his knowledge to other people, to share it ... Nobody would deny that *Lou* has a liberal slant, but then most newspapers have a liberal slant. Most reporters are liberal. Most management is not. So we try to show that, too.[10]

Burns' discomfort with the liberal polemic of *Lou Grant* is shared by Jim Brooks, who left MTM after co-creating the series:

> I think you can mark it as becoming more and more issue-oriented, and I think brilliantly so, but I was less and less involved as that was happening. If I were active with *Lou Grant* right now [1981] it would be less involved with issues ... [11]

The ways in which such 'issues' are dealt with and dramatised in *Lou Grant* is described elsewhere in this book. Paul Espinosa's account of the early story conferences of the series also sheds some light on the manner adopted by the series' creators of dramatising such issues without transgressing the 'acceptable levels' of their assumed audience or advertisers or CBS Standards and Practices department.[12]

Perhaps significantly, however, Tinker himself while stressing the importance of balance seems more sympathetic to *Lou Grant*'s topicality and polemicism than two of its creators:

> What we do is open up the mind a little bit. I think we shouldn't take a strong position, though I guess you can't not seem to be on the side of God and motherhood and what's right, but if we just get people thinking about things, talking to each other, I think then that's about all that you can expect to do. If you just do personal stuff, then it doesn't have any great value: if you just have Linda and Bobby and Ed relating to each other, I think that wouldn't last too long. I think the glue is that it's about something.[13]

Allan Burns attributed both *Lou Grant*'s basis in issues and its ambitions for balance and avoidance of bias to Gene Reynolds:

> The *Mary [Tyler Moore] Show* couldn't be accused of having a political bias, I don't think. Where I think you see it is in *Lou Grant*, but there is an attempt, and Gene is really scrupulous in this, to try to balance everything. He thinks we should always keep a point of view but that you should try to show the other side too.[14]

I will return to Reynolds' contribution to *Lou Grant* and to the wider MTM strategy in the late 70s later in this article.

The combination of assumed determinants here, from authorial creativity to character continuity, to realism about the newspaper business and about newspaper reporters are all deeply embedded with liberalism. But they are also all symptomatic of several broader changes both at MTM in particular and across the entire television industry in 1977. Indeed, 1977 was proving a watershed year for the industry. In particular, ABC, which was challenging CBS for the ratings lead, was championing a new form of programming and scheduling with a succession of specials and big events culminating in the mini-series *Roots*. In fact, 1977 was the year in which the networks belatedly discovered that long-form programming (in 60, 90 and even 120 minute slices) could be even more popular – and profitable – than 30-minute sitcoms.[15] But while 'event' scheduling was making headlines, so too was a shortlived trend toward topical 'issue-oriented' content-based drama. Thus it was, that when David Wolper (Brooks' old boss) produced *Roots*, which was transmitted in a week-long strip in January 1977, 130 million Americans were watching. That same year (6–11 September), Paramount produced a mini-series 'faction' about Watergate entitled *Washington: Behind Closed Doors*. James Brooks has denied that *Lou Grant* was created on the crest of the Woodward and Bernstein wave (the film *All The President's Men* had been released in 1976): 'We were not doing Woodward and Bernstein like everyone else was doing.'[16] But several critics have noted some similarities, not surprisingly, to the film, the book on which it was based and to the crusading reporter mood which Watergate and its fictional reproductions brought into being.

If the success of *Roots* in particular and the mini-series and TV movie balloon inflated at that time had any influence at all on MTM, one aspect of that influence may have been at the level of casting. *Roots* was transmitted while MTM and CBS were discussing the format for Ed Asner's new series and the casting of Asner in a straight role in *Roots* (for which he won an Emmy) may well have encouraged MTM to attempt a dramatic rather than comedic vehicle this time. More certainly, the casting in *Roots II: The Next Generations* in 1979 of James Earl Jones as Alex Haley and Lee Chamberlain as his wife was replicated in MTM's *Paris*, which reunited Jones and Chamberlain as husband and wife in a detective series. And *Paris*, in its turn, was to sow the seeds for *Hill Street Blues*.

Some critics have attributed the liberalism of *Lou Grant* to the period of its emergence, that of the Carter presidency (1976–80). Others have seen it as the ironic result of that period's very illiberalism in television, when the imposition of the Family Hour forced sitcoms like MTM's out of prime-time and away from their audience, hence accelerating their move toward later slots in the schedule and more 'serious' modes like drama. Either way, it's a happy irony that during the Carter presidency MTM's Lou Grant could have his revenge on behalf of all reporters on Nixon and Agnew and the American right for their attack on press freedom a decade earlier.

In 1978 *Lou Grant* did an episode based on the so-called Love Canal incident in which most of Michigan's cattle were poisoned as the result of a toxic fire-retardant chemical in their fodder, PBB. This episode, 'Slaughter', was initially scheduled for transmission on the night before the 1978 Michigan gubernatorial primary in which the incumbent's candidature was being challenged on the grounds that he had not acted swiftly enough to avert the catastrophe. The episode proved so topical – and so sensitive – that its transmission was postponed until the following week when the election would be over. Grant Tinker has commented on the sort of interference such topicality aroused:

> On *Lou Grant* we had a kind of Love Canal show, and the network made us put in a speech that one character makes, saying, 'Well, not all chemical companies do this.' Even though we were telling the story about a fictional chemical company that was polluting, consciously, and that seemed believable enough, the network didn't want to suggest that all chemical companies were that way. I guess that saves them a lot of grief.[17]

Network sensitivity over such issues is often a consequence of actual or potential offence to programme sponsors or regular advertisers. 'Home', a 1979 episode, portrayed a fictional home in which Billie went undercover to investigate complaints about ill-treatment, and was attacked by the American Health Care Association for 'distortions and lies'. When this episode was re-run on 27 August 1979 the AHCA persuaded Prudential, Kelloggs, General Foods and Oscar Meyer to withdraw their commercials, while the American Association of Retired Persons and the National Retired Teachers Association urged their members to tune in. So *Lou Grant* had experienced some considerable trouble with both CBS and its advertisers long before 1982. Indeed it is to the series' and to MTM's credit that it sustained its critical edge for so long rather than blunting it against network and corporate inertia. Tinker defended the series' topicality against objections that recall critical complaints in Britain about the politics of plays like *Scum*, in which specific fictions have been mistaken for journalism.[18]

> We did an episode ... about nursing care, and there was an organization that started a letter-writing campaign not just to CBS, but to the sponsors. I got a lot of it here. And people do pay attention. In that case, even though in the body of the show there were the same 'Not all nursing homes' kind of speeches, they just don't hear those, they just see you doing a story about inadequate or bad care and they take offense at that. That's what I love about the *Lou Grant* show, its topicality. The fact that more often than not what you see on Monday night was in the papers yesterday or will be tomorrow.[19]

This topicality, which had been a factor in MTM's 'house-style' since the company's inception, was perhaps both *Lou Grant*'s finest attribute and one of its final assassins. Certainly Tinker's claim for the series' topicality is easy to substantiate. The first episode of its second season, 'Pills', concerned Rossi's right to protect a news source (Mary Richards had gone to jail for the same thing in *The Mary Tyler Moore Show*). This episode was transmitted in 1978 while a *New York Times* reporter, Myron Farber, was fighting a contempt of court violation for exercising just such a journalistic right. Similarly, the second episode of that season, 'Prisoner', dealt with allegations of torture in a fictional Latin American dictatorship, 'Malagua', and this while in Managua and the rest of Nicaragua the Sandinistas were fighting Somoza's (CIA-backed) army.

Such issues and the confusions between fact and fiction, between characters and performers were to have repercussions on *Lou Grant*. Indeed it was, ironically, to be Asner's comments in a private capacity about another Latin American regime and its American allies which were finally to contribute to the cancellation. In 1979 the Los Angeles chapter of the American Civil Liberties Union gave actor Ed Asner its Bill of Rights Award for his character's contribution to civil libertarian causes. Ramona Ripston of the ACLU explained that the award was for 'the kind of topics his show had devoted itself to. It raised important issues in a popular way for large audiences.'[20]

The following year the entire *Lou Grant* cast were invited to a Press Meets Press briefing on the then imminent Screen Actors Guild strike. During the strike which followed – and which postponed production of *Lou Grant* and other MTM series – MTM's president Grant Tinker condemned Asner for 'talking with Lou Grant's credibility' but 'thinking with Ed Asner's judgement'.[21] *Lou Grant*, which had dominated the Emmy nominations in 1979, also dominated the awards in 1980, winning five Emmys including Best Drama Series. Ed Asner, one of the leaders of the strike, did not attend the ceremony; nor did Nancy Marchand (Mrs Pynchon), who won a Best Actress award. In November of 1981, Asner was elected President of the Screen Actors Guild. Within six months *Lou Grant* had been cancelled.

One of SAG's discussions in the winter of 1981–2 concerned the proposal to give the Guild's annual award to ex-SAG president Ronald Reagan. Reagan was rejected as the preferred recipient of the award, however, on the grounds of his harshly anti-union stance. (In the deciding vote, Asner abstained.) The relationship between Asner, SAG and the campaign against them both by the new American right has been described elsewhere. Suffice it to say that SAG's liberal attitudes to such foreign issues as Apartheid, Solidarity and, crucially, Latin America, as well as numerous domestic issues such as the Equal Rights Amendment, unemployment and union mergers proved increasingly provocative to the 'moral majority'.

On 15 February 1982 Asner gave a Washington press conference on behalf of Medical Aid for El Salvador. At the same time he signed a mailout appeal for the same organisation which began with the words 'My name is Ed Asner. I play Lou Grant on television . . .' Almost overnight a campaign was organised against Asner and subsequently against the series he starred in. Another ex-SAG president, Charlton Heston, was one of the right's spokespersons and he was quick to warn Asner to dissociate himself in his personal pronouncements from both his prime-time persona and his union function: 'He should remember that he is Ed Asner, president of of the Screen Actors Guild, not Lou Grant the crusading editor.'[22]

Allan Burns has described the campaign against Asner as: 'swift, continuous and excessive . . . I've never seen anybody transformed so quickly from being everyone's favourite uncle to a Communist swine.'[23]

On 25 February the *New York Times* announced the plans of the newly formed Congress of Conservative Contributors, a right-wing campaign against sponsors of liberal TV shows, set up to 'urge a boycott of advertisers on the *Lou Grant* television series'.[24]

Lou Grant was one of prime-time's most prestigious programmes and consequently its advertising slots sold at a premium. But that very virtue had its own drawbacks; its regular advertisers included some of America's major corporations and their spots on *Lou Grant* were very visible. On 1 March immediately preceding that evening's transmission of *Lou Grant* John Amos, the Chief Executive Officer of a television organisation called American Family Corporation's Broadcast Division went on air on his own stations (which were CBS affiliates) in Georgia, Missouri, Alabama and Iowa condemning Asner for assuming the role of a 'self-appointed Secretary of State' and accusing him of seeking to influence the beliefs of his audience.[25] On 10 March Joseph Solomon, the president of Vidal Sassoon Inc., a regular *Lou Grant* advertiser, wrote to CBS president William Paley expressing his own concern:

> Please find attached to this letter copies of letters we have received from viewers who have taken exception with Ed Asner using his position for political purposes. As the sponsors of the Ed Asner show we are indeed concerned. We, by sponsoring the show, did not wish to embroil ourselves in a political controversy. We do not feel that we should be pressured into withdrawing our sponsorship, but on the other hand, we do not wish to have our products suffer because of an unfortunate association with a political issue. Please advise us how this matter should be handled. We are very concerned about our company image and the image of our products, and we therefore look to you for a solution to this unfortunate situation.[26]

Sassoons were obviously very sensitive; according to Gitlin even by as late as early June they had still only received 13 letters complaining about Asner's political exploits. Nevertheless, CBS President Thomas Wynan felt obliged to reply and on 5 April CBS stressed their absolute unwillingness to interfere in matters of privately held beliefs.[27]

By mid-March another *Lou Grant* 'sponsor', Kimberly-Clark, the makers of Kleenex, were said to be sending out explanatory letters to 'worried' customers about their withdrawal of advertising spots from the series. Their letter read:

> Thank you for writing to us about your objections to Ed Asner's recent statement on El Salvador. We appreciate the opportunity to tell you that we have discontinued all advertising on the *Lou Grant* television programme[28]

Since several sources reprint an anecdote about one of the first recipients of this 'withdrawal' letter having in fact written to Kimberly-Clark congratulating them for their sponsorship of the series, since CBS denied that Kimberly-Clark had any ads to withdraw from the series and were thus in no sense a 'sponsor' and since Kimberly-

Clark had two paper plants of their own in El Salvador and were a fervent supporter of the regime there, their attack on Asner and *Lou Grant* must be treated with some caution.

On 19 March Jerry Falwell sent out a direct mail letter about Asner/Grant's threats to civilisation as we know it to members of the moral majority movement, which had been one of the prime movers behind Reagan's electoral victory. Falwell's letter alleged that:

> Ed Asner says President Reagan's Communist enemies are his friends. Are we to stand idly by while ultra-liberal actors like Ed Asner arrogantly insult the president of the United States?[29]

Other mailings soon followed Falwell's. On 22 April the Council for Inter-American Security, a right-wing think-tank specialising in propaganda about Latin America, sent out a direct mailing to an estimated 50,000 sympathisers. This letter, which enclosed a pre-addressed, pre-written postcard to CBS Chairman Paley, encouraged recipients to join a nationwide boycott of eight *Lou Grant* sponsors' products (excluding, significantly, Kimberly-Clark and Sassoons) with the words:

> If you liked Jane Fonda you'll love Ed Asner . . . If Ed Asner says he has the freedom to do what he wants, then you and I have the freedom to refuse to buy his sponsor's products.[30]

By the end of April Peter Paul-Cadbury and Estee Lauder were also reputedly considering withdrawing their sponsorship of the series. Then, on 3 May, an episode of *Lou Grant* entitled 'Unthinkable' about the lead up to a nuclear crisis was aired. The series' ratings had been dropping all season; this episode, though, was the lowest-rated in the series' history. As always in television, simple explanations are seductive but suspect. The campaign against *Lou Grant* and Asner was clearly important but whether or not it was decisive is hard to say. Asner may have become just too familiar a face – by 1982 he had been playing Lou Grant for twelve years – and since his election to the SAG presidency he had made numerous television appearances in that capacity too. Meanwhile CBS series were slipping in the Nielsens right across prime-time schedules and *Lou Grant* was by no means their worst-rated show. Others, including some MTM insiders, have suggested that the series itself may have been slipping; CBS to avoid attracting criticism may have been down-playing the series in their on-air promotions; furthermore, the NBC and ABC counter-programming against *Lou Grant* was particularly tough in the 1981–2 season with Monday night football and expensive specials proving hard to equal in the ratings. Finally, on 6 May CBS announced that both *Lou Grant* and another MTM series, *WKRP In Cincinnati*, would not be renewed for the following season. *WKRP* had also, in its own way, been a controversial series, if only in its 'counter-cultural' protagonists and its (characteristic MTM) media setting, a rock and roll radio station.[31] That both these series were made by MTM is perhaps less a consequence of an explicitly 'political' strategy on MTM's part than a symptom of the company's creation in 1969–70 in a political climate which positively encouraged the incorporation of counter-cultural rhetoric, if only in order to tempt back young, urban consumers into the thrall of prime-time.

In the immediate aftermath of the cancellation Ed Asner was apparently given only 48 hours to clear his office in the CBS building. MTM were treated little better by CBS: 'The producers learned of the show's cancellation only two hours before the public did.'[32] On 8 May the *Chicago Daily News* reported that CBS had imposed a virtual blackout on material poking fun at the White House.[33] (*Lou Grant* and *The Mary Tyler Moore Show* had had more amicable relations with Reagan's Republican predecessor, Gerald Ford, whose wife Betty made guest appearances on both series.) On the same day, moral majority leader Jerry Falwell was quoted in the *New York Times* as saying 'I have absolutely nothing to do with the cancellation of the series.'[34]

On 10 May, a Monday night, at the regular time of *Lou Grant* screenings, opponents of the cancellation held a large demonstration outside CBS. Similar demonstrations took place on 17 and 24 May. Meanwhile, numerous contradictory accounts of the events leading up to the cancellation were beginning to emerge. In some accounts the 'political' explanation dominates; in others the economic explanation is privileged; others still like MTM's Michele Gallery opt for combinations of the two (arguing, for instance, that disenchantment with Asner's politics aroused by moral majority propaganda caused fewer people to tune in to the series and the ratings to drop to a level where cancellation was 'naturally' on the cards).

As early as 7 May James H. Rosenfield, executive vice-president of CBS Broadcast group, was quoted in the *Wall Street Journal* as declaring that 'Politics had nothing to do with this. There's one reason and one reason only that we made this decision – the ratings were on the decline.'[35] As late as July, Rosenfield was still sticking to his apolitical guns, telling *TV Guide* that ' ... emotionally we wanted to keep it on ... [but] the audience was eroding. *Lou Grant* was five years old, and that's when series begin to show wear and tear ... There was no political pressure or political complaints.'[36] At least one American magazine, however, cited an unnamed CBS official as admitting that 'When Asner made his comments [about El Salvador] it became inevitable the network would have to cancel the show. He left us no choice.'[37] Similarly, Arnold Becker, CBS vice-president for National Television Research, admitted that ever since his election to the SAG presidency 'Ed Asner was perceived as a pain in the ass' and added that 'the best we could expect would be another marginal year. No one thought there was any chance of turning it around.'[38] Tinker himself had expressed a similar view about Asner's political judgement during the strike and this too may have made MTM uncertain how to react to the cancellation. An additional – but unquantifiable – factor is the fact that being deficit-financed *Lou Grant*, like other MTM series, would only go into profit when it was sold into syndication and, ironically, while some local station operators like John Amos were in favour of the cancellation and loathed *Lou Grant* others were willing to offer large amounts for the series.

While MTM declined to comment, Michele Gallery, a writer on the series and its one-time creative consultant, has suggested a number of contributory factors:

> My guess is that network research indicated that the show was not getting stronger, it was getting weaker. The ratings evidence indicated that it was a show that nobody in the network was going to lose a job keeping on the air. I also think nobody in the network was going to lose a job by cancelling the show. *Lou Grant* definitely fell in a grey area. CBS had been strong in the last several years and therefore could afford to cancel marginal shows, in the way NBC in the last couple of years held on to marginal shows – like *Hill Street Blues*. I think the audience had seen a lot of Ed Asner. Lou Grant existed seven years before the show and so I think the desire to watch what that character was doing had diminished a bit. I think we tended to have a sharper audience than many shows on television. And I think for some reason we weren't meeting those demands. I think many people saw a lot of Ed Asner on the news – and not just with El Salvador, but also doing public service announcements. People saw a lot of him and that might have had some influence on whether or not they might have wanted to see him on a Monday night. There's some difference of opinion in the office. I think I subscribe to the political theory of the cancellation less than the people in the office. Some people, and their arguments are pretty persuasive, think that the network jumped at the opportunity to cancel *Lou Grant* because it was a political hot potato.[39]

The ratings explanation seems the weakest of all. As *Media Reporter* has revealed, the ratings at the end of *Lou Grant*'s 1982 season were running at about a 27% share, which is by no means low enough to automatically lead to cancellation.[40]

Allan Burns, the only one of the original *Mary Tyler Moore Show* creative team still at MTM, has commented on the company's and its première series' defining characteristics in a manner that reflects on the demise of *Lou Grant* and the success of *Hill Street Blues*. Describing the differences between the MTM approach and that of their rival Norman Lear, Burns suggested that:

> He deals with controversy; we are subtler about it. We were more content to take on small issues, the day-to-day issues of living, of just getting through the day, of interpersonal relationships and heartbreak and disappointment and hopes and small dreams and big ones. We dealt with problems, the day-to-day stuff that ordinary people go through as opposed to big themes that Norman would take on: birth control and abortion. Our issues were the small ones. I find those frankly more interesting for myself ... that's why I like *M*A*S*H*. Despite the fact that there is a large war going on, basically those are people just trying to get through the day.[41]

Here Burns seems to be both describing his own disenchantment with *Lou Grant* and at the same time announcing his preference for a series such as *Hill Street Blues*, which would adapt the MTM house-style to the everyday lives of people in a tough situation just trying to make it through the day, while around them in the ghetto a kind of war rages.

Rosenfield commented simply that: 'The mood of the country may have shifted away from the topical subjects handled in *Lou Grant* and toward lighter, more fantasy and more comedy-type escape entertainment.'[42] Rosenfield was right; the mood of America (its president and network presidents included) was changing. CBS, for instance, no longer wanted to be identified as the network that brought its audiences *Lou Grant*; it wanted to be known for *Dallas*. At NBC, there was a similar move 'downmarket' toward traditional genre television and, interestingly enough, re-elevating female viewers. For this was the season of *Flamingo Road*, *The Gangster Chronicles* and *Hill Street Blues*.

In 1977–8, 1978–9 and 1979–80 *Lou Grant*, like its parent series, won copious critical acclaim and ultimately numerous Emmys. But at the end of the 1980–1 season another MTM series had taken its place in the limelight; that series was *Hill Street Blues*. Indeed, at the end of its very first season *Hill Street* won more Emmys and Emmy nominations than any other weekly series in American television history. Ironically, MTM by producing a series even more prestigious than *Lou Grant* was stealing both its thunder – and its umbrella – as the quality show of the year. From then on the defence from prestige for *Lou Grant* was much harder to make. Back in 1977 when *Lou Grant* was first aired, *Hill Street Blues* wasn't even on the horizon. There were, however, signs of things to come. One was a pilot made by MTM for NBC which was known in production as *Doctors And Nurses* but was eventually broadcast, in 1978, as *Operating Room*. It was created by Steven Bochco and Bruce Paltrow, co-creators respectively of *Hill Street Blues* and *St Elsewhere*, and it starred, among others, *Hill Street*'s Barbara Babcock. *Variety* noted a resemblance to *M*A*S*H*. While *Operating Room* was in production, PBS transmitted a video vérité documentary entitled *The Police Tapes*. The impact this documentary made is important; extracts were run on ABC News and an edited version became the first PBS documentary ever to be broadcast by one of the networks. In 1979 Ed Asner, with time on his hands before throwing himself into the SAG strike and later the SAG presidency, was cast in a feature film about the same police precinct which *The Police Tapes* had been about. The film was called *Fort Apache, The Bronx*. That same season Fred Silverman (who had just moved from ABC to NBC) decided that what his new network needed was an updated, ethnic gritty cross between a precinct sitcom and procedural drama. Whether or not Silverman remembered *The Police Tapes* from his ABC days, the formula he gave to Michael Zinberg, an ex-MTM director/producer now an NBC vice-president for comedy development, encouraged Zinberg to recommend MTM and two of its in-house writer-producers Steven Bochco and Michael Kozoll. Between them Bochco and Kozoll had clocked up credits on such series as *The Name Of The Game*, *MacMillan And Wife*, *Columbo*, *Richie Brockelman–Private Eye*, *Quincy*, *McCloud*, *Switch*, *Kojak*, *The Six Million Dollar Man*, *Delvecchio* and *Paris*.

The meeting between Bochco, Kozoll and NBC's top brass has become almost legendary. The sort of mixture that Silverman and his fellow executives had in mind included such ingredients as the films *Hospital*, for its ragged style and generic parody, *M*A*S*H*, for its tragicomic tone, and *Fort Apache*, *The Bronx* for its ghetto precinct settings and protagonists. Also mentioned were such series as *Police Story* for its focus on the private lives of its police protagonists and on the consequences of their professional public duties on those lives, *Barney Miller*, for its ethnic mix and precinct comedy, and the TV spin-off series *M*A*S*H* for its televisual version of a cinematic style.

MTM, of course, had already essayed its own generic parody of police series with the show-within-a-show conceit of *The Betty White Show*, and while the prospect of another crime series seemed uninviting, the promise of unusual licence in the conception and creation of a pilot proved irresistible. Initially, however, Bochco and Kozoll were cautious about what sounded to them like just another example of Silverman's notorious affection for spin-offs and clones (ironically perfected while he was at CBS when among the beneficiaries of his style of programming was MTM itself). It was Gene Reynolds who brought to MTM *M*A*S*H*'s multi-character, multi-narrative blend of comedic and tragic elements, as well as an indebtedness to the visual style of the feature film of the same name which had been directed by Robert Altman with much fluid use of telephoto lens, eight-track sound and hand-held camera. Up until then, however, this style was unique to

*M*A*S*H* on television (for all its overuse in cinema) and *M*A*S*H* itself employed it only very sparingly. *Hill Street Blues*, on the other hand, partly because of its nature as a generic hybrid (fusing crime series, sitcom, soap opera and cine-vérité), could accommodate such devices in considerably more prominence. For by virtue of encompassing all of these tele-genres at once *Hill Street* could lay claim to being ruled by the conventions of none of them and this simultaneity of 'similarities' produced a 'difference' all *Hill Street*'s own, licensing MTM to infringe (within a rigidly restricted range) some of prime-time's – and network standards and practices' – own aesthetic law and order.

Gene Reynolds' experience on *M*A*S*H* may well have been decisive. While that series was set during the Korean war (among a medical team) it was screened during the Vietnam war and it regularly echoed that contemporary conflict in its storylines. On *Lou Grant* Vietnam reappeared on numerous occasions, from the second episode of the first series, 'Hostage', to a second season episode entitled 'Vet', in which we learn that *Lou Grant* regular, Animal, is a Vietnam veteran, to a final season story, 'Immigrants', in which the 'Trib' hires a Vietnamese photographer. One of the series writers, Gary David Goldberg, was encouraged by MTM and CBS to attempt to create a series about journalists under fire in Vietnam, under the title *Bureau*. Eventually, after two unsuccessful pilots had been made (the first was a 30-minute sitcom, the second a 60-minute drama, though neither of them was ever transmitted) the idea was dropped. But the Reynolds influence was not restricted to *Lou Grant* or its offshoot, *Bureau*. *Hill Street Blues* not only continued *M*A*S*H*'s grim combination of comedy and tragedy but also, by going back to the latter series' cinematic source, introduced an 'Altmanesque' style to television filming, a style that later was also borrowed for *St Elsewhere* where it was returned to its original medical environs.

Before *Hill Street Blues*, the most recent development in the police series genre to have received critical acclaim of any kind had been liberal, 'realistic', anti-heroic series like *Police Story* and *The Blue Knight*, both of which were based on the stories of Joseph Wambaugh. *Police Story* had run on NBC from 1973–7 and Ed Asner had appeared in the TV movie pilot that launched it. Because its format had been that of an anthology drama series with new characters and situations every week it was unable to adapt to the melodrama-led move to continuing series of the second half of the 70s, spearheaded by series like *Dallas*. On the other hand, however, it was in a sense a precursor of the TV movie and mini-series trend toward 'issue-based' stories epitomised by *Roots*. In 1973, Wambaugh's novel *The Blue Knight* provided the basis for one of television's first mini-series. It was directed by Robert Butler. In 1975 a second *Blue Knight* TV movie was made as the pilot for a series that ran on CBS through the 1975–6 season.

Meanwhile at MTM the success of *Lou Grant* both with audiences and critics alike encouraged them to try and come up with additional drama series. *The White Shadow* and *Paris* are discussed briefly elsewhere in this volume, but one side-effect of this decision was the need to attract further writer-producers to the MTM stable. One such recruit was Steven Bochco, who had been writing crime series for Universal for several years and was grateful for Tinker's offer to come up with pilots for the studio. Aside from the already mentioned casting coup of re-uniting *Roots II*'s combination of James Earl Jones and Lee Chamberlain, *Paris* also afforded Bochco the opportunity to build up a veritable repertory company of performers who he would return to for *Hill Street Blues*. It brought together Michael Warren, Joe Spano, Keil Martin and Michael Conrad. Conrad and Martin had also appeared in Bochco's last series for Universal, *Delvecchio*, alongside Charles Haid. Bruce Weitz had played an eccentric cop in *Every Stray Dog And Kid*. Between them, the *Hill Street* cast had also appeared in a number of feature film adaptations of Wambaugh's multi-character procedural novels: Charles Haid in *The Choirboys*, James B. Sikking in *The New Centurions*, and Barbara Bosson in *The Black Marble*. Other cast members had long track records with MTM; Taurean Blacque, for instance, had appeared as a guest in *The Tony Randall Show, The Bob Newhart Show, Paris* and *The White Shadow*.

Hill Street Blues emerged out of a complex intersection of forces in late 1970s American television – and, of course, American culture generally – including the advent of prime-time soaps like *Dallas* with their large casts and multi-layered storylines; the move toward mini-series and TV movies and 60-minute long-form drama series; the return to prime-time – and to American political life – of (the Reaganite rhetoric of) law and order; NBC's shortlived but decisive strategy to sidestep Nielsen aggregates by buying 'high quality' consumers via 'quality' programmes; MTM's attempt to sustain its demographically targetted product by transforming itself from a provider of character comedies with ensemble casts into the supplier of character drama, with work-based situations, synthesising comedy, drama, topicality and a reflexiveness about genre rare in prime-time but not at MTM.

Since it eschews the issue-based approach of *Lou Grant, Hill Street Blues* has been the subject of considerable political debate. Some critics on the left, for instance, have argued that the series offers an aestheticised – or even anaesthetised – image of the operation, and the operators, of law and order in 80s America.[43] Such critics suggest that the series' very 'realism' about the apparent insolubility of social problems, about the difficult job done in impossible conditions by all too human police officers, personalises and depoliticises one of the most urgent issues on the lips of the Reagan rhetoricians. One – perhaps the only – defence against such charges is implicit in Bochco's boast that

Michael Warren and Joe Spano in *Hill Street Blues*

Hill Street is 'an equal opportunities offender'. The series, and MTM itself, have evolved a strategy for eluding network censors and eliding prime-time conventions by building such densely constructed shows (dense, at least, in terms of the accustomed conventions of most American television if not necessarily in those of classic Hollywood, let alone European art cinemas) with such a dexterously handled orchestration of tone, such a panorama of points of view, so many characters, so much over-lapping dialogue, so many intricate – and yet integrated – storylines that it is, ironically, a difficult series to police. Testing this hypothesis out in an interview with actor Joe Spano, who plays the liberal Lt Goldblume in the series, I suggested that beneath the surface chaos lurked a layer of quite conventional narrative and characteral strategies epitomised, for example, in the counterbalancing roles of Goldblume and the station's SWAT (in the series it's called EAT) team leader, Howard Hunter. Spano rejected my suggestion that the series had seen a very visible diminution in the right-wing rhetoric of Hunter (making the character more conventionally likeable, more of an MTM character and less a Lear type). When I proposed that as Hunter's politics were blunted so Goldblume's liberalism was necessarily weakened to maintain 'balance', Spano responded that 'Perhaps Howard Hunter seems to have softened simply because of our increasing familiarity with the character', adding that Goldblume's retreating liberalism might equally derive from a realistic acknowledgement of the effect of several years in a tough spot 'on ideals that may just not be operable there'.[44] While we are not obliged to accept Spano's analysis and its 'realism' it is tempting to apply the same terms to *Hill Street Blues* itself, which has exhibited a very markedly diminished 'difference' from the rest of prime-time programming and, indeed, from its own original style after its four seasons.

Certainly the sophistication of its narrative and stylistic strategies remains very different from the relatively simpler structures of *Lou Grant*, for all the latter's own departure from conventions, its unresolved plots and filmic fluidity. Barbara Bosson, a *Hill Street Blues* regular, has noted that while *Lou Grant* aimed for an issue-oriented approach: 'What is typical about *Hill Street* is that we are not issue oriented. And by that same token we often help the issues.'[45]

Steven Bochco, interviewed at the same time, used the example of an episode in which a brutal policeman is posted to the precinct to illustrate the pitfalls of a content-based approach to scripting:

> You see that is the trap. That is where you become pedantic ... Those episodes weren't about police brutality – they were about a man under crippling stress and that is all ... and there's actually no conclusion that we tried to draw from that story and, boy, I tell you, anytime anybody starts talking to me about message or soap box politics I start running.[46]

The 'liberalism' implicit in these remarks – the emphasis on individual cases and extenuating circumstances – apart, there is also a hint of the ways in which *Hill Street* has indeed at its best avoided being 'about' social problems and has instead dealt with them indirectly. Instead of making racism an 'issue' as perhaps *Lou Grant* would have done, *Hill Street Blues* actually wrote racists and anti-racists into its continuing characters in the precinct. In an interview with the cast in *Playboy*, the Howard Hunter character is described as 'our Archie Bunker' and the Renko character is identified as a redneck racist.[47] By integrating characters like this into the series as regulars, by including arguments about urban policing and positive discrimination among the running conversations of the characters, the partisanship of the series is difficult to identify but equally difficult to legislate against. Bochco defends this strategy in a discussion of NBC's Broadcast Standards Department and their incessant demands for 'balance':

> The moment they demand balance, you're dead in the water, because it takes away from your opportunity to say anything. So they give with one hand and wind up taking away with the other. You're

never going to get a balance in terms of demographic equality. Our feeling is that over the long haul, it all balances out. You are going to see many sides of every question in the process.[48]

It is interesting to speculate where *Hill Street*'s licence to supersede such 'balance within each episode' strictures originated. Several factors seem crucial. First, the series emerged from an arrangement with NBC which guaranteed no network interference with storylines. Furthermore, the pilot of the series was actually written and shot on the clear-cut assumption that it was extremely unlikely ever to go to series. Before writing the pilot script, therefore, Bochco and Kozoll demanded an unusual preliminary meeting with Broadcast Standards to ascertain what kind of 'liberties' they were able to take and to what extent the imprimatur of Fred Silverman would carry over such obstacles. According to Kozoll:

> Fred Silverman wanted to make a cop show and Steven Bochco and I were invited to do it. I didn't particularly want to do it. I owed a favour to MTM because I had spent a year there in 'Development' not agreeing with anybody and consequently not developing anything. And since they're nice people I thought I'd oblige them with a pilot. Because I was given autonomy to do what I wanted to do and because I didn't care about the show getting on the air I wrote something that I had some feeling for and that's how *Hill Street Blues* came into being.[49]

Bochco's account of Broadcast Standard's responses to the pilot script's provocations is similar:

> Broadcast Standards loves to demand kind of equal time in all areas. They always want to be able when they get the angry letter to point to something which is its opposite number in terms of balance. And we maintained that there would be no balance. I mean the thing that I began jokingly to say and which became less and less of a joke is that we were equal opportunities offenders.[50]

Indeed it even seems possible that the strengths of the series owe less to Bochco and Kozoll's 'inspired creativity' than to their very disenchantment with the project as just another cop show pilot. According to Kozoll:

> No matter how well intentioned you are when you go out to do a cop show it's almost impossible not to end up with a bag of shit afterward. Because we've all done those boring, heroic, tired, tired shows, and you're going to kill yourself and the public doesn't want to watch them any more and they really don't address a serious issue . . .[51]

But while Broadcast Standards at NBC could certainly legislate forcibly on the series' use of language and on 'explicit' violence and sex, it was considerably harder to coerce MTM into employing the conventions and character types characteristic of the classic realist text. Bochco and Kozoll claim that perhaps because *Hill Street Blues* 'raised unanswerable questions' they and their series were 'unfashionably liberal', 'a little out of fashion with the rest of the country'.[52] Arguably, however, the very success of the series is predicated less on its casting, craft or 'chemistry' than on that very ambivalence, that very avoidance of overtly visible partisanship, of one sort of solution over another. Todd Gitlin has elaborated this approach succinctly:

> . . . it spoke to and for a particular cultural and political moment. *Hill Street* worked in part because it immersed itself in major popular crosscurrents – far more than the law and order shows that hit the airwaves at the same moment. The energy swimming through in *Hill Street* was the energy of American liberal-middle class ideology turned on itself, at a loss for direction, Bochco and Kozoll had floated into a maelstrom point of popular consciousness.[53]

That this success is therefore not entirely attributable to authorial talent (Kozoll, for instance, attributed the series to 'a long series of flukes') is evident in the history of the series' title. Far from it being the result of an inspired moment among the creators of the series it came up out of an argument with NBC's Fred Silverman. The pilot had originally been called *Hill Street Station* but NBC was apparently unhappy with this. Silverman, to Bochco and Kozoll's despair, came up with *The Blue Zoo* as an alternative. Incensed at its racism but unable to think up an alternative they were relieved when an NBC staffer in Business Affairs came up with *Hill Street Blues*, economically combining connotations of police uniforms with a melancholy which was later amplified by Mike Post's theme music.

Bochco's own diagnosis of the series' political project and subsequent popularity is suggestive:

> We don't answer questions that people desperately want answered simplistically. The appeal of Ronald Reagan . . . has always been solid, simple answers to very complex questions. I think what Michael means when he says that we are unfashionably liberal is in our perception that those simple, easy answers don't yield results.[54]

Elsewhere Gitlin mentions an episode in which the murderer of a prostitute turned out to be the self-righteous city-councillor – a clumsily predictable 'surprise' denouement. Bochco commented, 'Every time we get neat we make mistakes.'[55] When NBC began to demand a little more 'neatness' in the second season by obliging MTM to tie up at least one story-line per episode, the tendency to opt for this sort of narrative strategy was increased and the series suffered as a result.

Perhaps, therefore, the role of Furillo, balancing between his duty to the streets his precinct oversees, the police station and its officers and to his bureaucratic superiors, can be compared to the roles of Bochco and Kozoll themselves, who are also balanced, between networks, advertisers and sponsors, up-market audiences and ambitious but constrained regular members of cast and crew. If this is the case, it may also be significant that, in Bochco's words:

> Furillo is a pragmatist. Furillo is very rooted in the real world . . . he understands that he's not going to solve crime. By and large that's not what he's there for. He negotiates truces; he keeps the peace to some extent. He negotiates survival on the hill.[56]

Elsewhere Bochco has described the precinct as 'a holding operation' and this is ironic in that Hoblit, by the beginning of the third season, and in the wake of some inescapable creative retreats, was admitting of the series itself – rather than of the fiction – 'What we're up to now is a highly paid maintenance operation.'[57] Certainly, since the now legendary first series there have been a number of modifications and softenings of the original structure and style. At the end of the first series Kozoll withdrew from his role as co-executive producer and co-writer to become creative consultant, composing storylines with Bochco but otherwise having almost no further involvement. By the end of the second series he was gone. Meanwhile, NBC imposed their compulsory narrative wrap-up on MTM for at least one major storyline per episode for the second season and thereafter. In 1982, a Writers Guild Strike postponed the season start but still meant that the backlog of *Hill Street* scripts was severely reduced and writing schedules were drastically cut back to one week per script. Previously writers had enjoyed a fortnight or more full-time writing on each episode. Hoblit began monitoring the average number of stunts employed per episode and noted that the second season exhibited an acceleration in the show's reliance on fights, shoot-outs, car-wrecks and chases in what amounted to an attempt to conceal diminished creativity and complexity in the scripts. Hoblit's figures showed that the stunt factor had risen from an average of 0.8 in the first season to an average of 2.4 in the second. And, to make matters worse, these stunts took their own toll on production; they were more expensive and exhausting to shoot than the sort of 'character drama' dialogue sequences which they were replacing and which had characterised the series.

How then has *Hill Street Blues* been able to survive where *Lou Grant* finally proved so vulnerable? One answer seems to be in its very ambivalence. Where *Lou Grant* tackled issues and, its creators ambitions toward 'balance' notwithstanding, often pointed to the perpetrators of some of America's social ills, *Hill Street* tackles consequences not causes. (It may be significant here that MTM's follow up to *Hill Street, St Elsewhere,* is set in a hospital, which almost guarantees a focus on victims rather than perpetrators, as well, of course, as naturalising those social 'ills'.) Grant Tinker has been quoted as admitting that *The White Shadow* ran into problems because it was 'about real and frequently unresolvable problems and situations'.[58] *Hill Street*'s televisual solution to this apparent impasse is, quite simply, to delete the 'about' and turn its predecessor's subjects into its own backdrop. Thus Tinker could say of *The White Shadow*, 'We and CBS decided inner-city problems that didn't have solutions and therefore couldn't be wrapped up neatly and happily at the end were depressing people . . . '[59] *Hill Street* was not about such problems, it was simply set amongst them. If the advantage of this strategy was the ability to continue smuggling 'the real' into prime-time programming whilst simultaneously avoiding the issue-based and occasionally crusading rhetoric of *Lou Grant*, the disadvantage was an erosion of any attitude at all to those 'problems' and a consequent pessimism.

One aspect of this 'ambivalence' finds its form in the generic mix of the series between character drama, (sit)comedy, crime series, prime-time serial melodrama and, of course, documentary – its style borrowed from, indeed based on, *The Police Tapes*. In *Emmy*, Tinker defined the MTM style as evidenced in *The Mary Tyler Moore Show* as 'more steak than sizzle. There was a beginning, a middle and an end. You sort of had to pay attention.'[60] *Hill Street*'s beginning, middle and end – though each episode is always apparently chronological – is much harder to describe in such linear terms. And both sympathetic and unsympathetic critics agreed that you had to watch carefully. A third ambivalence is its politics. One simple example will suffice. In the 1970s the critical debate par excellence was about the inherent liberalism – or otherwise – of *All In The Family*'s protagonist Archie Bunker, whose reactionary attitudes were the object of the series' 'ironic' humour. There was to be no really right-wing regular character in an MTM series until the advent of Howard Hunter and *Hill Street Blues*. Hunter, the foil for Goldblume's liberalism, also provided a target for the writers' assumption about the inadequacy of conventional 'simple' solutions. By the second season, Hunter's reactionary rhetoric had been visibly reduced and Henry Goldblume too was less the precinct's token liberal.

The complexity that these characteristics lend the series has contributed to what is often described as its 'quality' and this in turn has been seen as responsible for its comparable longevity. In the year before *Lou Grant*'s assassination at the hands of network indifference and moral majority interference Tinker suggested:

I think if you set your sights high enough, these problems that perturb Donald Wildman and Jerry Falwell will largely go away, or be significantly reduced. I don't mean they won't have some problems – for instance, on Wildman's hit list is *Hill Street Blues*, because he sees it as violent, and I guess, maybe, sexy. The reason that the Wildmans of this world don't bother me, and that I don't think they ever will become any kind of a major factor in terms of influence, is because he's crazy to pick a show like *Hill Street*. It is a legitimate entry in the mix of network television: I think a rather responsibly made show with good values.[61]

Hill Street's high sights and good values have paid off magnificently for NBC and, in the long term, should do the same for MTM. One NBC vice-president has been quoted as admitting that *Hill Street* is of incalculable value to the network since it successfully attracts those all-important young urban adults in the 18–49 age range which advertisers are willing to pay the highest premiums for. Indeed, NBC can charge more for *Hill Street Blues* than for top ten hits considerably better rated generally for just this reason.[62]

Mercedes-Benz – a rare presence in prime-time – became a regular *Hill Street* advertiser in 1983, continuing a tradition of major corporate sponsorship of MTM programmes comparable to PBS. (*Just An Old Sweet Song* was a General Electric presentation; *Something For Joey* was sponsored by IBM; *The Boy Who Drank Too Much* was sponsored by Xerox.) And the reason for this attractiveness to advertisers is, quite simply, demographic, itself the very raison d'être of MTM's emergence. Thus *Hill Street Blues*, for all its relatively low status in the overall ratings, actually rates first among men of all prime-time programmes in the crucial consumer category of 18–49 year-olds, as well as rating third among women in the same age group. Pollan also points out that *Hill Street*, alongside some of NBC's other 'quality' series, actually proves:

exceptionally popular with urban viewers, which is why NBC's prime-time ratings in the large urban markets belie its poor national showing. This bodes well, not just because most advertisers want the urban viewer, but because NBC's five owned stations are in the big cities: New York, Los Angeles, Chicago, Washington and Cleveland. Collectively, the stations are having an exceptional year. And most significant of all, in the face of NBC's bleak national Nielsen returns week after week, the flagship station, WNBC – TV, has been running first in prime-time this season in New York City, the nation's largest and richest market.'[63]

This recalls – and neatly reverses – Robert Wood's verdict in 1970 on CBS, which was winning the nationwide Nielsens but faring far worse in its owned and operated stations. It was WNBC–TV, ironically, which was the New York station re-running the made-for-CBS series *The Mary Tyler Moore Show* in late night slots in 1984 to high ratings.

That the success of MTM is perhaps less a consequence of the quantity of ratings its programmes accumulate than with the 'quality' (i.e. disposable incomes) of the demographics of the specific audience they attract is discussed elsewhere in this volume by Jane Feuer. But that that connection may itself be a consequence of the company's origins in 1970 when the networks were finally prohibited from profiting from syndication, and were worried about what Les Brown described as the future fractionalising of the audience into demographically distinct and differentially addressable 'vertical' sectors, is intriguing.[64] When the Nielsen company in 1982 did a survey of television usage in homes receiving pay cable, most prime-time programmes were rated lower in cable households but *Hill Street Blues* accumulated even larger shares of the audience in such homes.[65]

It is, therefore, perhaps equally unsurprising that it was *Hill Street Blues*' commercial breaks which were chosen by the sales department of Thorn-EMI as the site of the first advertisements for video software on American network television.[66] Similarly, computer owners subscribing to a computer information service called The Source were able, in 1981–2, to tap in their responses to the series in a scheme in which *Hill Street*'s producers apparently co-operated. The Source, owned by The Reader's Digest Association, had some 17,000 subscribers by this time and in a pilot scheme they invited them to input their responses to two television series, *Simon And Simon* and *Hill Street Blues*. Though the initiative was launched by the executive producer of *Simon And Simon*, that was soon cancelled by the network and *Hill Street Blues*' producers were left to monitor the results of this electronic 'Points of View'.[67] Elsewhere, one of the series' producers, Gregory Hoblit, has described the show's regular viewers as 'college educated and middle class' noting that they often 'pride themselves on their selective viewing'.[68] The obvious attractions of such an audience in an age when the networks are worried about the impact of video and cable and their value in attracting corporate sponsors rarely seen in prime-time may also have nurtured MTM's relationship with public broadcasting.

In this respect, it is useful to remember that Grank Tinker urged the return of the sponsorship system in a 1978 speech, in which he urged that network television would be better under the old system.[69] (By 1978, of course, only PBS remained, rather ironically, as a network largely funded by corporate sponsors.) As we have seen, these remarks were made in the course of a PBS local station programme entitled 'The Realities of Commercial Television Production', which was broadcast in September 1978, and during the programme, Tinker announced the completion of an MTM pilot for PBS called *Going Home Again*. He argued that corporate sponsors were more public spirited than they had been in the 50s and 60s and that a consequence of a return to a sponsorship system would be an end to the obsession with ratings that characterises network competition.

On that same programme, Lee Rich, president of Lorimar (the independent production company which produces *Dallas*) was complaining that the networks were finding ways around the FCC regulations prohibiting financial interest. Rich charged the networks with: 'setting up .... indie producers or going out and tying talent to a web on an exclusive basis and then laying them off to an outside production company ... '[70] That, of course, was precisely what Fred Silverman had done to MTM in tempting away Brooks, Weinberger and Daniels in a deal with ABC and Paramount the previous year.

That same season, in an interview with Robert Sklar, Tinker was more ambivalent about support for further anti-trust action against the networks.

> A lot of the producers think it's time to move in and attack through the Justice Department a lot of the practices the networks have been getting away with for years. All of those things that work to make theirs a good business and ours not so good. My fear is that we might be out of business ourselves. The networks act as policemen in our forest, and without them there might be anarchy. Universal might come in and gobble us little guys up. I'd like to see the law of supply and demand work a little better. I don't want to see it change that much.[71]

In 1980, when ABC became the last of the three networks to sign consent decrees with the Justice Department over the Syndication and Financial Interest Rules, numerous independent production companies expressed their disappointment at the weakness of the conditions.[72] Tinker, however, was almost indifferent to the decision: 'The whole thing seems much ado about little. There are only three networks and there is nothing anyone can do about it. You can't expect them to allow people to run across the street to sell spin-offs.'[73] Then, in 1980, the FCC published a report which argued that the Financial Interest, Syndication and Prime-Time Access Rules were inefficient and obstructive to the operation of the forces of the free market. In general, therefore, it concluded that network television should be shaped 'by impersonal marketplace forces rather than by the desires of a centralized government agency'. (*New Television Networks: Entry, Jurisdiction, Ownership and Regulation; Final Report.* October 1980, Federal Communications Commission.)[74] In 1983 the FCC expressed its ambition to deregulate

American television. In November President Reagan advised the FCC that a two-year moratorium on the subject would be beneficial to all interested parties. In March 1984 a group of fifteen senators led by Barry Goldwater wrote to the FCC chairman recommending the Commission's agreement to such a moratorium. At the time of writing that moratorium holds. Nevertheless, throughout 1983 and into 1984 there was considerable concern in the industry about the possible repeal of the FCC rules, particularly those which in 1970 had helped to bring many of the independent companies, MTM included, into existence. *Variety* commented that free of FCC restraint the networks could lure independent producers away from the majors:

> And that situation could deal a crushing financial blow to the TV divisions of the six major studios (Universal, Paramount, 20th Century-Fox, Warner Bros, MGM/UA and Columbia) and a possible knockout blow to Embassy, MTM and Lorimar.[75]

The FCC Rules, according to *Variety*, had 'helped these three companies to become giants by permitting them to own the worldwide syndication rights to all of the series they produced subsequently.'[76]

In response to the proposal to repeal the rules an opposition caucus within the industry was promptly set up; MTM was one of the first members of this Committee For Prudent Deregulation.[77] At a press conference held by the Committee in Los Angeles, Mel Blumenthal, an executive vice-president at the company, argued that independent producers feared that the networks would be freed by repeal to 'warehouse' shows until they finished their first runs rather than allowing them to be sold off more swiftly into syndication, where the independents made their profits. Blumenthal alleged that the network efforts to repeal the Financial Interest and Syndication Rules were an attempt to put a stop to the increasing share of the audience which was being taken by the local independent stations:

> I don't believe what the networks say about their problems being pay-TV. The problem is that the independent stations are making inroads. The networks want to keep them down ... Without the expectation of selling a successful show into syndication, there will be no incentive on the part of the producers. We won't have the ability to take financial risks. MTM would not be able to do such programmes as *Hill Street Blues* or *St Elsewhere*, where the deficits are enormous.[78]

Interestingly enough, Viacom International, the syndication company that was spun off from CBS in the early 1970s (as Worldvision was from ABC) as a direct result of the FI & S Rules, was also expressly opposed to repeal. Viacom's chairman, Ralph M. Baruch, has been quoted as follows:

> Networks do not want programmes which are successful to compete with them; they do not want strong independent stations made stronger and more competitive through programming. Networks, if allowed to do so, will totally control software ... If the networks were to take over programme ownership and syndication, competition would certainly be decreased. A producer trying to get his show on the networks will give up everything to the networks just to get his show on the air. Without that airing, the show has no value. So when the networks take over ownership and distribution, the smaller distributors, like Victory Television, distributing programmes for Mary Tyler Moore Productions such as *WKRP* and *White Shadow*, tell us they have to go out of business.[79]

CBS responded to fears about the potential increase in network monopoly over independent producers in a post-repeal industry by placing an advertisement in the trade press which 'conjured up for the independent producer a land of opportunity post-repeal.'[80] *Variety* also quotes CBS vice-president for corporate affairs, Bill Lilley, who had devised the ad, arguing that:

> The ad is a rebuttal to the hyperbolic charges of network monopoly by the six major studios and the three big independents. From that charge you'd think the networks have a secret agenda to crush independent producers and make all of them nothing more than employees of the networks. None of that is true. We have no plan to start up any in-house production. We want more independent producers submitting ideas to us, not fewer. In the 10 years since the FCC established the rules, the number of producers has decreased by 40%.[81]

Whether one believes that the networks want an increase in the number of independent producers in order to diversify their sources of supply and the sort of programmes supplied as a result, or whether one concludes that their goal was more probably a weakening in the bargaining power of the existing suppliers (a sort of diversify and conquer strategy) is hard to decide. *Variety*, though, points out that while CBS effectively financed the three largest independents in the early seventies by commissioning *All In The Family* from Norman Lear, *The Waltons* from Lorimar and *The Mary Tyler Moore Show* from MTM, both Lear's company Embassy and MTM itself are rather reluctant about expressing their gratitude.

Thus, *Variety* concludes:

> . . . it's ironic that CBS is using *All In The Family* and the *Moore* show as examples of why independent producers should be happy about repeal of the rules, because both companies are convinced they were taken to the cleaners by CBS in the deals for those shows.[82]

Norman Lear even launched a major law suit against CBS – which he eventually lost – in his attempt to wrest the syndication rights for *All In The Family* away from Viacom, while: 'MTM made no secret of its unhappiness with the contract that called for control by CBS of the worldwide syndication rights to *The Mary Tyler Moore Show* which harvested big bucks for Viacom.'[83] In the spring of 1983 the *New York Times* noted that *Hill Street Blues* was costing some 65,000 dollars an episode more than the 800,000 dollars licence fee being paid for it by NBC. By the end of that series' fifth season MTM expects it to have run up a total deficit of well in excess of 6 million dollars. Arthur Price, president of MTM, is quoted as saying that: 'We are dealing with large amounts of money and hoping for a payoff down the road.'[84]

The prospective repeal of the FCC Financial Interest and Syndication Rules has obliged MTM therefore to explore other options than those offered by traditional networking. According to the *New York Times* article: 'Mr Price is not especially interested in producing mini-series or made-for-TV-movies for the networks but he is looking seriously at feature films.'[85] After the critical and commercial failure of *A Little Sex*, MTM appointed a new vice-president for Feature Films, and spent thousands of dollars developing scripts as well as reserving 10 million dollars to make two features. As early as 1981, however, MTM had launched a feature arm to develop two projects: *Finnegan Begin Again* and *Prisoners*. At that time Mary Tyler Moore, who was to star in both films, said: 'We [MTM] will develop them and take them to a major to coproduce.'[86] In the event, *Prisoners* has still to surface while *Finnegan* is presently being made as a co-production by several companies, including Home Box Office and Central TV's film subsidiary Zenith, as a TV movie to star Miss Moore but without MTM involvement. James Brooks, writer-producer of the Oscar-laden and hugely successful *Terms Of Endearment*, was initially unable to raise enough money until his agent thought of going to MTM for the rest. Brooks is quoted in *Film Comment* as admitting that Price: 'said to me later that his associates told him he was crazy to make the investment, and he said, "I don't expect to make money, but I think it'll do well enough where I'll break even . . ."'[87] MTM has also recently appointed Harlan Kleiman, formerly of HBO, to explore the possibilities of producing for cable:

> Irrespective of what I may feel about the movie business, we have to

be out there to participate in the pay and cable business. Producing for cable is not economically viable yet, but it is going to be and we might as well grow with it. The company has to grow. It can't stand still. I don't think the industry can allow MTM to exist anymore the way Grant and I were running it.[88]

At the time of writing, though, MTM still seems not to have entered these new markets. Meanwhile, although MTM's only feature film to date, *A Little Sex*, was a critical and commercial failure, James Brooks' *Terms Of Endearment* proved a triumph and Hugh (*WKRP In Cincinnati*) Wilson's *Police Academy* broke box office records. There had, briefly, been plans to spin off a cinematic feature from *Hill Street Blues*; Steven Bochco, for instance, had at one time been keen to 'explore the feasibility of making a feature' version but as Barbara Bosson pointed out the idea begged the question, 'Why anyone would pay money to see something that they could see on television for free?' MTM decided not to develop the idea and it remained stillborn, just as they rejected NBC requests to spin-off a series featuring the characters of Hill and Renko.

Notes

1. Paul Espinosa, 'The Audience in the Text: Ethnographic Observations of a Hollywood Story Conference', *Media, Culture and Society* vol. 4 no. 1, January 1982.
2. The formation of these two subsidiaries, both of which appear to be inoperative, was reported in the *Los Angeles Times*, 5 June 1977.
3. 'Dialogue on Film', *American Film*, June 1980.
4. See *Variety*, 27 September 1978, pp. 41 and 78 for a detailed discussion of this programme.
5. For further information about MTM's arrangement with KCET-LA see *Variety*, 5 May 1982.
6. Erik Barnouw, *The Sponsor: Notes on a Modern Potentate* (New York: OUP, 1978).
7. Quoted in Todd Gitlin, *Inside Prime Time* (New York: Pantheon Books, 1983), p. 219. Gitlin's book begins with a prologue about the cancellation of *Lou Grant* and his penultimate chapter devotes more than fifty pages to *Hill Street Blues*.
8. Quoted in Christopher Wicking, *Time Out* no. 524, 2–8 May 1980.
9. Ibid.
10. Horace Newcomb and Robert S. Alley, *The Producer's Medium* (New York: OUP, 1983), p. 218.
11. Ibid.
12. Espinosa, op. cit.
13. Newcomb and Alley, p. 228.
14. Newcomb and Alley, p. 218.
15. For a short introduction to the advent of mini-series and specials, see Paul Kerr, 'The Origins of the Mini-series', *Broadcast* no. 998, 12 March 1979.

16. Newcomb and Alley, p. 217.
17. Newcomb and Alley, p. 228.
18. See, for comparison, Andrew Goodman, Paul Kerr, Ian Macdonald, *Drama-Documentary*, BFI Dossier no. 19 (London: British Film Institute, 1983).
19. Newcomb and Alley, p. 228.
20. Susan Heeger, ' "Ed Asner" Starring Lou Grant', *Channels of Communication*, April/May 1979.
21. Ibid., p. 40.
22. Ibid., p. 60.
23. *Mother Jones*, August 1982, p. 6.
24. *Media Reporter*, Autumn 1982, p. 15.
25. Ibid.
26. Gitlin, p. 5.
27. *Media Reporter*, Autumn 1982, p. 15.
28. *Media Reporter*, op. cit., p. 16.
29. *Mother Jones*, op. cit., p. 10.
30. *Media Reporter*, op. cit., pp. 14–15.
31. Gitlin, p. 4. While *Lou Grant* seems to have been deemed too sensitive for swift syndication, *WKRP In Cincinnati* was speedily sold off to 'superstations'. See the entry for *WKRP* under 'MTM Series' in this book.
32. *Media Reporter*, op. cit., p. 16.
33. *Media Reporter*, p. 16.
34. Ibid.
35. *Media Reporter*. p. 15.
36. *TV Guide*, 24 July 1982.
37. *Mother Jones*, op. cit., p. 11.
38. Gitlin, p. 4.
39. Michele Gallery interviewed by Stephen Dark in 1982.
40. *Media Reporter*, op. cit., p. 16.
41. Newcomb and Alley, p. 215.
42. *Media Reporter*, op. cit., p. 16.
43. For a discussion of the history of the American TV crime series, see Paul Kerr, 'Watching the Detectives', *Primetime* vol. 1 no. 1. For an attempt to place *Hill Street Blues* in the context of critical debates about the politics of police series, see 'The Bad Stuff', *City Limits*, 27 April 1984.
44. *City Limits*, op. cit., p. 21.
45. Stephen Woolley and Stephen Dark, 'Catching Light in a Bottle', *Primetime* vol. 1 no. 4.
46. Ibid.
47. *Playboy*, October 1983.
48. *Playboy*, op. cit., p. 152.
49. In an interview with Tise Vahimagi in 1983.
50. In an interview with Paul Taylor and Martyn Auty in 1982.
51. Gitlin, pp. 279–80.
52. Gitlin, p. 304.
53. Gitlin, p. 303.
54. Gitlin, p. 306.
55. Ibid.
56. Gitlin, p. 310.
57. Gitlin, p. 322.

58. Newcomb and Alley, p. 225.
59. Howard Rosenberg, 'Grant Tinker's MTM', *Emmy*, Spring 1981.
60. Rosenberg, p. 25.
61. Newcomb and Alley, p. 227.
62. Michael Pollan, 'Can *Hill Street Blues* Rescue NBC?', *Channels of Communication*, March/April 1983.
63. Pollan, p. 34.
64. Les Brown, *Television: The Business Behind The Box* (New York: Harcourt Brace Jovanovich, 1971).
65. Pollan, p. 34.
66. *Variety*, 20 October 1982.
67. *American Film*, June 1982.
68. *American Film*, July/August 1982.
69. *Variety*, 27 September 1978.
70. *Variety*, op. cit., p. 41.
71. Robert Sklar, *Prime Time America* (New York: OUP, 1980), p. 83.
72. *Variety*, 27 July 1980.
73. *Variety* op. cit., p. 62.
74. See Thomas Streeter, 'Policy Discourse and Broadcast Practice', *Media, Culture and Society*, vol. 5 no. 1.
75. *Variety*, 19 October 1983.
76. *Variety*, op. cit., p. 68.
77. *TV World*, February 1983.
78. *TV World*, op. cit., p. 54.
79. *Screen International*, 15 January 1983.
80. *Variety*, 19 October 1983.
81. *Variety*, op. cit., pp. 40 and 68.
82. *Variety*, op. cit., p. 68.
83. Ibid.
84. *New York Times*, 22 May 1983.
85. Ibid.
86. *Daily Variety*, 14 August 1981.
87. *Film Comment*, April 1984.
88. *New York Times*, 22 May 1983.

Lou Grant

Christopher Wicking

In the beginning there was 'Lou Grant' – a running character as Mary's boss and producer/news director of WJM-TV for the whole of *The Mary Tyler Moore Show*'s seven year tenure. Like most of the news crew, Lou was fired in the final episode of the series when new management took over the station. In the normal course of TV history, that might have well been that. But some four months later, at the opening of the 1977–8 season, Lou and Edward Asner, the actor who portrayed the character, were back on the air in a spin-off series bearing his name, *Lou Grant*.

Such developments are quite common TV events, and the audience would have taken it in its stride. After all, two previous series – *Rhoda* and *Phyllis* – had spun-off from *The Mary Tyler Moore Show*. What more natural than a new series about a 50 year old divorced and unemployed news director going it alone? The difference, however, was striking. *The Mary Tyler Moore Show*, *Rhoda* and *Phyllis* were all 30-minute situation comedies (their creators prefer the phrase 'character comedies', and quite right too) with audience laugh tracks. *Lou Grant* was an hour-long show, with no laugh track. Indeed, apart from a vein of naturalistic wit, it wasn't a comedy at all. It was a dramatic series, relocating 'Lou Grant' in California, where he was starting a new job as city editor of the daily newspaper 'The Los Angeles Tribune' ('The Trib'), returning to his roots in journalism after many years away.

It probably took some adjustment for the audience to relate to the 'new' Lou and a framework dealing with heavyweight social issues such as the American Nazi party, senile Superior Court judges, mental hospitals, wife-beating, football scandals, cult religions, radioactive contamination and other such subjects which the Trib investigated in its first season. In the event, *Lou Grant* proved more successful than anybody at MTM could have hoped for. Five seasons and over 100 episodes later, *Lou Grant* went off the air amid fierce controversy – cancelled, said the CBS network, because of falling ratings; cancelled, said outraged supporters of the series, because actor (and Screen Actors Guild president) Asner's political activities and outspokenness had riled right-wing sponsors who had threatened retaliatory action against CBS if the show remained on the air.

But by then, MTM had become as renowned for its production of innovative, prestigious and award-winning drama as it had previously been for its comedy output. Arguably, without *Lou Grant*, MTM would never have achieved such a pre-eminent position. How ironic then that, without Asner, *Lou Grant* might not have happened at all. As co-creator James L. Brooks recounts: 'Allan Burns and I were given an on-the-air commitment by CBS to come up with a show starring Ed Asner. We were going to make him something else, and Ed said to us, "Just in terms of your thinking, I love the character [of Lou]. Do what you want, but I love the guy." We asked ourselves, "when is a spin-off not a spin-off?", and that's when you spin off into another form, you take a comedy character and you go into a dramatic form. And that's what we did.'[1]

In its first season, *Lou Grant* quickly established itself as the best 'serious' series on the networks – indeed it was just about the *only* one that didn't depend on the genre frameworks of cop show, soap opera or sitcom (though, in a way, it blended all three). To be sure, 'the reporter' had long been a hero-character in movies and on TV, but by the mid-1970s had generally gone out of fashion in favour of the visual media (the trend already evident in *The Mary Tyler Moore Show*'s situation – ex-print editor Grant as news director on TV). But *All The President's Men* the previous year had made reporters – and newspapers – 'sexy' on the movie screen again, excellent timing for Brooks and Burns with their 'Lou Grant' spin-off problem. What better than to take Lou back to his professional roots in journalism, and be 'inspired' by *All The President's Men?* Consciously or unconsciously (for a lot of original research went into the creation of the series) *Lou Grant* owes a heavy debt to *All The President's Men.* The movie posters bore the catchline 'The most devastating detective story of this century' – and allowing for Hollywood hyperbole, the detective aspect is a crucial one, for *Lou Grant's* investigative journalism is closely related to the process of detection. The film also provided a 'look' for the Trib's vast newsroom set; a model for a new generation of committed journalists; a female publisher/owner and a team of editors concerned as much about printing 'the truth' as they were about the moral and social repercussions of doing so (or of *not* doing so).

In itself, it is perhaps doubtful that these and other ingredients would have been enough to make *Lou Grant* successful. For the TV audience is in many respects a quite different one from the movie audience, with a loyalty to and a preference for its own stars and their fictional incarnations. The renewed public interest in newspapers and crusading reporters was a timely element for the series itself – but what *Lou Grant* had going for it in the first instance was good old 'Lou Grant', and a small-screen favourite for seven years already in the role – Edward Asner.

Thus the *character*'s proven popularity – and Asner's identification with the role – gave the new series a standing start and doubtless also made it easier to sell the liberal, socio-political framework which it used; ironically, again, in the light of the controversy to come, when Asner's very identification with the role, and his other public persona as President of the Screen Actors Guild, were to conflict with his individual citizen's rights to hold – and freely practise – his political beliefs.

The most initially startling aspect of *Lou Grant* was its willingness to confront important social and political issues of the day. Where once American television had its 'Golden Age' of TV drama, and subsequently produced *East Side, West Side* (social workers), *The Defenders* (the legal system), *Slattery's People* (the legislature), *For The People* (the Public Defender's office) and other dramatic series in the 1960s which took their impetus from the world around them, by the 70s such series had all but disappeared from the screen. By then, the 'made-for-TV' feature had become an established part of the medium and provided a framework for the film equivalent of 'Golden Age' anthology drama, although such works as *Green Eyes, The Death of Richie, The Deadliest Season, The Amazing Howard Hughes* and *Red Alert* (all from the 1976–7 season preceding *Lou Grant*'s debut) were very much the exception to genre and action-adventure dominance. In that same 1976–7 season, *Police Story* and *Family* (the one a cop show, the other a soap opera) were the only series dedicated in their own ways to looking at the deeper issues of modern life.

This is not necessarily to condemn the other, more 'escapist' series, for American film/TV has always used the concept of genre in a distinctively creative way. Nevertheless, when *Lou Grant* arrived on the air it was received with gratitude and surprise by most media observers starved of intelligent, non-genre episodic TV, and the series was quickly picking up a loyal and ever-growing audience along with major awards.

When *Lou Grant* first opened in London, this viewer at least had no strong recollection of Lou's previous life at WJM-TV. The opening episode, 'Cophouse', seemed in no way really remarkable, dealing with Lou's problems in settling into the new job, having a conflict with young hotshot reporter Joe Rossi as the major dramatic hook and an investigation into alleged police corruption as its main 'story'. Most remarkable was the disparity between Edward Asner's performance – broad and blustery – and the 'naturalistic' style of the rest of the cast. Retrospectively of course, Asner was finding it difficult to adjust from 'sitcom' to 'drama'. From just this one episode, *Lou Grant* seemed a cut above the then-average TV episode, but little more.

The main titles to the series, however, were intriguing, and in marked contrast to any others currently on the air. A bird trills in a tree, a power saw cuts the tree down, it's stripped and sliced in a mill, is converted to paper, wrapped round a printing press drum and becomes 'The Los Angeles Tribune'. A newsboy tosses one copy into a puddle near a front stoop, a second up onto a shingle roof, a safely-delivered copy gets read at breakfast and, when finished, gets slid onto the floor of a birdcage, whose occupant trills as unconcernedly as his cousin in the opening shot. (For the second and subsequent seasons the credit sequence was of a more conventional kind, introducing the regular cast at work in the Trib office.)

There's a nice, dry humour here and a wry acceptance of the transience of a newspaper's life, a far cry from the frenzy of *The Front Page*, or the acerbity of *Ace In The Hole* in the big screen newspaper genre. So it shouldn't have been surprising, really, that the second *Lou Grant* episode, 'Hostage', was so good.

A young man, played by John Rubenstein, bursts into the city room at gunpoint and holds the staff hostage – in order to get a story printed in the Trib. A store owner – a disabled war veteran – has shot a young man who was attempting to rob him and this has been reported. But Rubenstein, the brother of the young man, wants the 'real' story to be reported: that his brother worked at the store, had been fired, was owed $148.50 and was trying to recover the debt. He wasn't 'shot', says Rubenstein, he was 'killed' . . .

While a S.W.A.T. team lurk outside (presented as trigger-happy louts, frustrated because they can't use their weapons in the situation), the Trib's personnel debate what can be done, with the dramatic shape of the narrative inspired by 'The Stockholm Syndrome' (victims getting to like their kidnapper). By the time the episode ends ('reason' having prevailed, a compromise reached), we have experienced a lively and (in the context of American prime-time television, 1977) a most surprisingly literate and intelligent presentation about the moral and social responsibilities of a newspaper's role in society, enlivened by sharp writing, deft characterisation, low-key, unsensationalised *mise-en-scène*. The various narrative and character threads interweave richly, there is no formulaic 'suspense' nor last-minute 'rescue'. The whole thing has the complexity of a minor-league *Rashomon*. New-name-to-me writer Seth Freeman being credited as the series story-editor seemed to bode well for the future – and indeed, 'Hostage' proved to be a *Lou Grant* 'norm'.

Lou Grant works on a very intelligent double level, which is mirrored in the overall shape of the series. As Horace Newcomb remarks in his book *Television: The Most Popular Art*, 'the regular and respected appearance of a continuing group of characters is one of [TV's] strongest techniques for the development of rich and textured dramatic presentations.' As with the baldest soap opera, we're drawn into the lives of the *Lou Grant* regulars so that we 'care' what happens to them

Ed Asner in *Lou Grant*

each week. Lou himself is bluff, gruff, somewhat old-fashioned, but an old-fashioned liberal. Very much the boss to his staff, he is just as much an 'employee' to his own bosses, widowed owner/publisher of the Trib Margaret Pynchon (Nancy Marchand) and managing editor Charlie Hume (Mason Adams). Lou's team is the younger generation: reporters Billie Newman (Linda Kelsey), the model of the 'new' independent career girl, and Joe Rossi (Robert Walden), brash, aggressive and vain. Assistant editor Art Donovan (Jack Bannon) is the cool, cynical 'dandy' of the office, while Dennis Price, known as 'Animal' (Daryl Anderson), is a loping, neo-hippie photographer.

This group (along with a handful of other 'irregular' regulars, such as Adam Wilson (Allen Williams), financial correspondent, and, in the final season, Lance Richarky (Lance Guest), the new trainee, is very much the archetypal surrogate TV 'family', a cross-section of types and ages corresponding to the main audience groups and containing underlying father/mother/children/lover relationships on a symbolic level. Yet their stories are not what animate the series the way inter-personal intrigues push *Dallas* and its clones to near stream-of-consciousness proportions. Instead the *Lou Grant* 'family' is closer to the Howard Hawks-type team of professionals, about whom we're curious the way we are about friends and colleagues, wishing to 'understand' them as they go about their work, but not living/loving/hating vicariously, which is the required response of the soap opera.

The family's work – news-gathering, reporting, bringing out a daily newspaper – is what propels *Lou Grant*'s second, parallel level: the 'story of the week', usually a contemporary social issue of great public concern, less often more 'timeless' issues such as the inevitability of old age and its problems, indeed the process of dying itself. The way the personal and investigative stories interweave, sometimes kaleidoscopically, is one of *Lou Grant*'s great accomplishments on a creative level.

Take, for example, a splendid, *tour de force* episode titled 'Marathon' (from the second season), which is the apotheosis of this kaleidoscopic style. Reminiscent of Jack Webb's feature film *-30-* (aka *Deadline Midnight*), it is set almost entirely in the newsroom (most other episodes go with the reporters as they trail their stories) from 9.00am one morning to 2.00am the following day, as a cave-in out at Chatsworth dominates the news. Skilfully creating concern for those trapped, the course of the rescue attempts create the main dramatic tension, along with the Trib's deadly rivalry with TV coverage and its on-the-spot immediacy (eventually the rescue breakthrough is made around midnight, when TV news is over – meaning that it will be a scoop for the print media). Also, there's the story behind the story; was negligence on the part of the construction company the reason for the cave-in?

But also packed into a 47-minute running time are the following themes and stories: will Donovan resign as Lou's assistant to take a job as press secretary to the Governor in Sacramento, causing Charlie Hume to put pressure on Lou to soften his criticism of Donovan (their occasional rivalry being a key reason why Donovan wants to go)?; another continuing story of a human fly climbing the outside of a building in the city; the progress of a new intern from USC on a three-month gig with the Trib (chiefly because he's heard that it would be good training for a TV career); a return visit from an earlier episode of a crank who regularly reports extra-terrestrial visitations from Andromeda (the next one's due at the end of the month at Burbank Airport; there will be a press reception held for the visitors after they land at the Baden-Baden Hofbrau downtown); a team of Swedish businessmen and their interpreter touring the building; a running joke about the TV reporter (the TV coverage of the cave-in is naturally scrutinised thoroughly by the Trib's team) and will someone get him a warm coat before the next telecast, it having started out a warm day, with nobody anticipating how long it would take to effect a rescue (he doesn't get the coat; on the next telecast, 'This is Ken Burgell *freezing* in Chatsworth'); Mrs Pynchon's weekly lunch with some of the staff; and probably other little nuts and bolts which I have now forgotten. As the evening comes round, and the day staff stay on in the newsroom, both to help the night staff and because of their own concern about the events in Chatsworth, the Hawksian 'professional' ethic referred to earlier is exemplified.

An episode like 'Marathon', though exceptional in terms of its self-imposed strictures of form, the claustrophobic concentration on events as they unfold in the newsroom, is a *Lou Grant* norm in terms of the series' attempts to be continually different, to push the conventions of the episodic series. The writer of 'Marathon' was Gene Reynolds, co-creator of the series with Brooks and Burns. He was also executive producer of the entire series, produced the first season, wrote four other episodes and directed eleven more. He was a newcomer to the MTM set-up, though he had worked with Brooks and Burns before, and there was even a Grant Tinker connection with all three before MTM was ever conceived.

It was Grant Tinker, then a television programming executive at 20th Century-Fox, who put the team of Brooks and Burns together to develop what became *The Mary Tyler Moore Show*. And it was under Tinker at 20th Century-Fox, where he was a contract producer/director, that Gene Reynolds first worked with Brooks, on the development and production of the series *Room 222*, which sounds very much like an MTM show in embryo. It's described in *The Complete Directory of Prime-Time Network Television* as a 'School room drama about Pete Dixon, a black history teacher in an integrated big-city high school. The programme was highly regarded for tackling current problems relevant to today's youth (prejudice, drugs, dropping-out, etc.) and it received many awards and commendations from educational and civil rights groups.'

'At the time,' said Reynolds, 'there was the black revolution in America, along with the youth revolution and a kind of explosion of ideas in education. *Room 222* was a successful show – and quite a unique one in its time – kind of a comedy drama. I was on it for a couple of years before I got into a quarrel with the ABC network, because they kept saying "make it more of a sitcom, make it *funnier*." I got bounced off the show at the end of the second year. Then Fox asked me to develop the pilot for *M*A*S*H*. There's a lot of "story" in *M*A*S*H*. Sometimes we had three themes in one show. Like in *Lou Grant*, where we also have parallel stories. Sometimes there's no connection, sometimes they mirror each other, there's a counterpoint. I like that way of working. It gives the story a tremendous amount of *motion*. You work on one area, one theme, one story, then – we call it a Double Curve – you pick up another story and when you come back to the first one you'll have finessed some of the less interesting transitions and intervals in between. The story has progressed. Both stories are developing as you bounce back and forth. It's actually a form of cutting which is just a variation on what D. W. Griffith discovered in parallel cutting. The fact that there's sometimes a harmonic between the two stories gives them a certain amount of weight, and gives the audience something that they have to reach for which is always desirable. Make them reach for it, don't lay it right out in front of them.' (From an interview with the author in 1980)

Hence, an episode like 'Home' (a gimmick of the series is that all the episode titles consist of just one word). Old age is the theme; a corrupt nursing home the focus of the Trib's investigation; Lou's relationship with an elderly jogging partner (played by the wonderful Jack Gilford) the parallel story. A report comes in of an 80 year-old lady who had been wheeled into the county medical office by the nursing home owner because, through a computer foul-up, $5000 of state funds have not been paid into the home for patient upkeep. The opening shot of the episode is the bewildered but compliant old lady being wheeled into and left in the office, staring out of the window at a brick wall. She dies. A telling first sequence to hook, and outrage, the audience. Reporter Billie Newman goes 'undercover' to work at the home as a night nurse, and through her eyes we see the apathy and callousness of the place. Meantime, Joe Rossi follows up on general stories about 'old age', and his investigations bring forth a myriad of views from, among others, representatives of the Grey Panthers. Meantime, Gilford, who has been in happy retirement but is now feeling bored and useless, is trying to find a job, gets mugged by some youths, is rejected by an employment agency, and begins to lose hope, feeling like 'a bum', until he learns of a job agency specifically for senior citizens, and gets work as a 'grandpa' in a children's playground. In between times, Lou and Charlie talk about getting old themselves, retirement, and one way or another just about every aspect of 'the problem' is discussed – but in an organic, logical way, arising either out of the investigation or the natural conversation of the characters.

While the episode is didactic to a degree, it is never a sermon. And as the 'problem' is not a 'criminal' one, the investigation and the ideas discussed are by turns reflective, discursive, enthralling. And while each of the main stories is resolved 'happily', this seems emotionally justified when so much bitterness and hopelessness has been revealed (which, we know, *won't* be quickly alleviated, if ever). Thus, such an episode comes across to the viewer more like a magazine feature than a newspaper story.

The teamwork of the Trib's staff in an episode like 'Home', and exemplified in 'Marathon', is paralleled by the teamwork of the *Lou Grant* personnel, which is probably the main reason for the series' success. The five seasons of 113 episodes used only 28 writers and 29 directors. Fourteen directors did one episode each, five others did two each. On the other hand, Alexander Singer directed eighteen, Burt Brinckerhoff and Roger Young thirteen each, Gene Reynolds eleven,

Peter Levin ten and Mel Damski three. This pattern is repeated with the writers: – Seth Freeman, twenty-one episodes; Michele Gallery, seventeen; Steve Kline, eleven; April Smith, ten; Bud Freeman and Leon Tokatyan, six each; Gene Reynolds, four.

Part of a 'Directors' Roundtable' discussion from the Summer 1979 *Emmy* magazine will give some idea of the creative atmosphere that permeated the *Lou Grant* unit. Alexander Singer is talking:

> There is a situation that I've been involved in for a couple of seasons that represents a unique combination of elements from a director's viewpoint, and it exists on an episodic show called *Lou Grant*. A group of factors exists in making that show very close to unique in my experience. First of all, the producer – Gene Reynolds – is himself a director, which may be both a curse and a blessing. In most cases, I found it a blessing because of his understanding of the director's problems – a craft understanding.
>
> There are two producers working under Gene, both of whom are writers: Seth Freeman and Gary Goldberg. There's a story editor named Michele Gallery who was a researcher the first season and became the story editor the second season. All four of them supply scripts to the series. Now, they have an executive story editor named Leon Tokatyan who is a very gifted, very talented guy, and very frequently they have an executive consultant named Allan Burns sitting in, who is himself a first-rate screenwriter. I have sat on a one-hour episodic show with all of these people working as hard on improving the script and attending to my questions and my inquiries and my criticisms as if it were the most important thing in the world.
>
> There is a cast reading, which for an episodic dramatic show is very unusual. Out of the cast reading there proceeds a series of intense story sessions in which the director's viewpoints are so seriously paid attention to they will literally rewrite at your request. And they will continue to work on the show up to the moment of shooting on the set.
>
> I am treated – all the directors are treated – as if my needs and opinions were of such a serious order that they will move almost anything they can.

'What happens at other companies? What's the difference?' *Emmy* asks. 'The difference is the difference between life and death,' Singer replies.

Singer's delight as expressed above is more than reflected in his work on the series. The previously-discussed 'Marathon' and 'Home' are both directed by him, and all of his episodes that I have seen are generally excellent, with 'Hooker' perhaps excelling even 'Marathon'; for here is another example of the series' range – a much more intimate piece, virtually a two-hander for Billie and (it seems to her) a very unconventional hooker, played by Dee Wallace. Billie meets her while investigating a series of murders of prostitutes, and becomes fascinated by her when she learns that she is going to real estate school and plans to become an estate agent. Her attitude to her life as a hooker is that it's just a job, she seems very level-headed and 'normal', and to Billie, as far removed from the conventional stereotype as could be imagined. They become friends, Billie hoping to help her 'save herself' while, as the murderer is still at large, she is also concerned lest she become the next victim. In the event, she is busted the night before taking her final exams and, with only fifteen minutes or so between getting out of jail and sitting the exam, she uses this as an excuse not to go; thus, by implication, it has all been 'a dream'. Billie is confused and disillusioned. The 'unconventional' hooker was actually a stereotype after all.

A central ambiguity of attitude is maintained all through the episode, teetering us first to one, then to another side of the argument, and what holds the whole narrative together and makes the totality so spellbinding, is Dee Wallace's performance – particularly a scene in a coffee shop where she finally talks about herself, her broken home-life, being raped by her stepfather and other painful memories, which Singer directs as if a near-improvisation, his concern that Linda Kelsey be truly at one with her showing in her wonderfully judged and felt reactions of pain and sorrow. Thus, it is as if *we* were hearing the story ourselves in a bar. Stereotype it may be, but here's the human being it happened to sitting right across that table, hence the pain and feeling seems all the more real. This is writing, acting, directing of a very high order indeed.

If 'Marathon', and to a lesser degree 'Hostage', indicate the series' desire to be radical with form, and 'Home' illustrates the 'double curve' method of thematic storytelling, 'Hooker' is also a good example of the series' attitude to its regular characters. The way in which Billie gets involved in the story operates on a far more personal level than in much TV programming, and she becomes, by implication at least, a slightly different person because of this (transient) relationship. All the main characters are seen going through various emotional dramas as the series progresses; Lou every now and then is emotionally attracted to someone, though nothing ever comes of it; his relationships with his daughters are explored (in 'Denial' one daughter and her husband are in relationship trouble because she refuses to face the fact that their small son is going deaf), which throws life on his past (*The Mary Tyler Moore Show*) life and the breakdown of his marriage. Donovan's mother dies (in 'Dying', another beautifully judged Singer-directed episode, which won awards for writer Michele Gallery and actress Geraldine Fitzgerald); Animal (who you'd have sworn had been on peace marches) is shown to be a veteran of the Vietnam war (in 'Vet', which compassionately puts all the moral confusions of the war into a 'delayed-stress' perspective). Charlie Hume's relationship with his son (who joins a Hare Krishna group in 'Sect') and his slowly eroding marriage, Mrs Pynchon's past life with her husband (who founded the Trib), the stroke she suffers at the end of the fourth season ('Stroke'), a recurring narrative thread in the fifth season, all these give a kind of depth and an extra human dimension to the series. We might assume that *Hill Street Blues*, with its much more overt and consistent use of these personal narrative themes, was in part inspired by the way *Lou Grant* had earlier tried to use them. In retrospect, only the Joe Rossi character was hard done by in this 'human dimension' respect (although he features in the storylines as much as Billie). Perhaps I merely missed those episodes where he is more personally involved (such as 'Skids', where we learn of his father's death through alcoholism) – or perhaps there simply aren't many, for his basic character is the one least amenable for change and progression. As Billy says, 'Rossi feels that all public servants are corrupt. That's idealism for you.' Which is not to say that Robert Walden's performance isn't a consistently excellent one – for in episodes such as 'Rape' and 'Hunger', where the Rossi character is central, he brings a multi-dimensional spirit to the role. In 'Rape', black reporter Lynne Moody is raped by a prowler in her apartment, and while the episode explores the emotional and legal parameters of the subject, it is left to Rossi (not, as would have been logical – and possible easier – Billie) to bring Moody out of the pit of shame, horror and pain into which the assault plunges her. The emotional level of the interplay between them, and the two fine performances, are also tribute to producer Seth Freeman, here writing/directing for the first time.

'Hunger' starts off with a joking tone, with Rossi betting Lou that he can find (or make) an interesting story out of any passer-by on the street. The person he elects to follow – Uta Hagen – who first appears to be a bag lady, turns out to be working for a poverty group on a hunger scheme and persuades Rossi to follow up on a story of government corruption/exploitation in the food production chain. This he is required to do on his own time (nobody at the Trib can see where the story is) and all Rossi's crusading liberalism is needed as he is constantly plagued night and day with new information from Hagen. Walden's performance, shading through all the necessary emotions, is again first class.

'I think the characters that we laid out in creating the series are pretty much what we have on the screen,' says Reynolds. 'But what we do is like what we did in *M*A*S*H* – we *turn* the characters, it's like getting the dimension you have with sculpture. We move *around* the characters, see different sides of them, so they become more rounded. But Rossi has remained as he was – very aggressive, the kind of guy that would climb over his mother to get a story, a guy with an axe to grind but a guy who's a born reporter, who'll live and die a reporter, doesn't want to do anything else. Though he might be a good editor . . .'

The only character that wasn't 'laid out' in creating the series is that of Billie Newman – which may be one reason why the episodes featuring her character seem the more memorable. For in the first three episodes, 'Carla Mardigian' (played by Rebecca Balding) is the Trib's young distaff reporter. As Reynolds recounts:

> She's a very talented actress, but younger [than Linda Kelsey] with more of an ingenue quality. Eventually Linda, as Billie, became the regular character because she's not only gifted as an actress but she's blessed with intelligence and you can somehow believe that whatever situation she's in, she understands the problems and is able to make sense of a great variety of situations. She's exceptional.

As with most of the regulars (Lou, of course, excepted) Linda Kelsey was not an overly-familiar face from previous series. She turned up in a *Barnaby Jones* episode from 1975 during the *Lou Grant* London run, however, and is very poor in it. Which is not to say that she is necessarily bad, but that, as an actress, she seems unable to cope with the blandness of what's required of her. I wondered – if such work was anything like a norm – how she came to be in *Lou Grant*. And naturally enough there had been a previous connection with Gene Reynolds:

> She's very well trained. She's from the theatre. She was at the Tyrone Guthrie Theatre in Minneapolis and she's toured a lot. I first became acquainted with her on *M*A*S*H*. We did a dynamite episode about nurses, directed by Joan Darling, which explored the problems of Hotlips, her martinet relationship with the nurses under her command and the conflict with her own emotional needs. Linda played a nurse whose husband had come off the line and the girls got the pair of them together and switched tents so that they could spend a night together. Linda was terrific.

And of all the *Lou Grant* regulars, it's the Billie Newman character which is seen to develop the most. Her first major episode is 'Nazi', where she investigates the American Nazi party and six episodes later, in 'Housewarming', she's investigating wife-beating. So far, she's an emerging member of 'the team', enjoying a love/hate rivalry with Rossi, with Lou as a sort of father figure (though we sense he'd like to be more) and Donovan making plays for her (with the impression that he's scored, but that she wants nothing permanent). So far, more or less par for the TV course. Then, in the 31st episode, 'Babies', there's the first reference to the fact that Billie was once married – a 'revelation' which arises naturally out of the storyline (she and Rossi are posing as a married couple to expose a black market baby racket), though perhaps more logically we'd have heard about this in the preceeding, 30th, episode, 'Singles',[2] where she and Rossi check out the various kinds of dating agency. (This, incidentally, is a wonderful episode, written and directed by 'newcomers' to the series, if not to the MTM stable, and is therefore the exception to the rule that the best episodes are done by the regular talent.) In episode 59, 'Brushfire', her father Paul appears on the scene (causing lots of jokes like 'Paul Newman – where have I heard of him before?' 'There's a minister in Rapid City with the same name.') As played by Marshall Thompson, he appears in a few subsequent episodes. In episode 77, 'Catch', she has her first 'meaningful relationship' (apart from her affair with Donovan) with ex-baseball catcher Ted McCovey (Cliff Potts). She really falls for him, but he leaves town to work as a scout now his career is over, though a hook's left in the water. In the 90th episode, and fifth season opener, 'Wedding', he turns up again – and at episode's end they get married. And in episode 108, 'Fireworks', Billie comes across her first husband again, now successfully established in politics (and involved in possible suspect activities ...).

Doubtless future episodes would have explored the tensions of the marriage (the relative incompatibility between the bright and brainy woman and the charming but not so clever man – which was seen to be a little strained in 'Beachhead'), and continued to watch Lou, Donovan and all the others grow, if not change. But there never was to be a sixth season.

It would be foolish – and quite wrong – to suggest that every one of *Lou Grant*'s 113 episodes is some kind of masterpiece. There are many duds, and there was a period when it seemed as if all the awards and acclaim that the show had by then received had gone to the team's collective head, making it self-satisfied and very smug. But then along came an 'Andrew' (a two-part story investigating the treatment of mental illness in America), a 'Hollywood' (one of those 'different' episodes, with the investigation of a 25-year old murder in the movie colony, with a delightful voice-over from Lou in homage to the style of the Marlowe-type private eye movie), a 'Lou' (where Lou gets the equivalent of battle fatigue and is forced to reappraise his life), and the smugness was shaken off as quickly as it had appeared.

And a strong, delightfully orchestrated episode like 'Witness' would turn up. A judge is beaten up, the Trib searches for a possible villain among his past cases and can't find a single friendly figure. Billie (inevitably) is contacted by one of the thugs in question and told that McQueen, a popular game show host, paid for the attack. This seems unlikely – especially as the game shows turn out to be Animal's favourite viewing along with the soaps – but the anonymous thug turns up dead, Billie's brakes are tampered with (while Rossi is driving the car – a splendidly 'natural' car-chase-type sequence with a terrified Rossi, in contrast to all the cop show action of other series) and she agrees to serve as a Grand Jury witness. She is sequestered in a hotel with Richard Jaeckel as bodyguard. The parallel story, incidentally, is of Lou and the door to door pool salesman who falls down Lou's step and twists his ankle. Helping him up, Lou cracks his bad back and spends the rest of the episode in pain and embroiled with attorneys, he having not yet taken out home-owners' insurance (after two plus years in Los Angeles, he has finally bought his own house in this episode's opening sequence).

Gary David Goldberg's script and Peter Levin's silky smooth direction, the narrative's concentration on Trib characters, give diversity and compulsion to the proceedings, which exist primarily on a sort of black comedy level which is quite unusual for the series (two men die in the course of the episode, there's the business with Rossi in the brake-less car, and a red-herring suspense sequence with Billie alone in the hotel room and we're led to feel that it's *not* room service, but hitmen, at the door; typically, it *is* room service). Yet though there's more conventional melodrama in the situation than normal, Levin and Goldberg defuse it (or make it, simply, less melodramatic) by their use of humour. For instance, Donovan's role consists largely of a series of cruel putdowns. 'Oh, oh – someone stayed too long at the disco,' he murmurs as we cut to a painful shot of Lou shambling to his desk. Lou delightedly discovers that his attorney is 'ex-ambassador to Paraguay under Eisenhower'. 'Sounds just the kind of guy to handle your case,' mutters Donovan with a sly smile – the irony lost on Lou, who beams in agreement, still impressed by the credentials. Rossi is his usual vain self ('I'm a reporter. Sometimes I have to creatively agitate people'). But the main strength of this episode is when it bends in a quite unexpected direction of detailing the love/hate relationship of Billie and Jaeckel holed up in the hotel. He's a splendidly right-wing cop with old-fashioned views on women, which initially bug Billie – until she realises he has equally old-fashioned views on everything else. This is all signalled very subtly – the way he 'naturally' makes assumptions about why she frequents a particular bar (looking for a husband). When she views a corpse without fainting he calls her a 'gutsy lady'; he figures 'your women's intuition' can't be far off when she guesses at a motive for the crimes. All this is merely 'irritating' to her – but then she learns he's to be her bodyguard (the female cop who was to be assigned to her 'called off sick. Probably one of those women's things') and it becomes all-out war. Through their incarceration together, they are found arguing about nuclear war, he orders steaks but of course she's a vegetarian ('You want to call room service or just go out and kill something to eat?' she taunts him – but he roars with appreciative laughter). Ultimately, both of them confirm the stereotype each has of the other, and the banter – always deeply felt – comes off like something in a Tracy/Hepburn *Pat And Mike*-type movie.

At the close, Lou has settled out of court for $500 damages and $700 attorney fees – and Billie walks from the courthouse after the trial with Jaeckel. The second thug has been found, and has told all. She has done well on the stand, he feels. 'You rambled a bit, but you were clear. You looked good too. Not too much make-up.' 'Us pacifist vegetarians don't usually have slit skirts in our wardrobes,' she jibes. And it looks like we're going to get some kind of sentimental end, when he says 'I've been with you for a week, got to know about you, got to like you. There's something I want to say.' Could it be 'I'd like to see you again'? Billie's reaction implies that she expects this (and, still in her unmarried state, might welcome it). But no. Looking very concerned, Jaeckel advises her 'Get a gun.' Billie seethes – and he laughs, 'just kidding', for he understands her far more than she is prepared to understand him. But they part amicably, the tantalising relationship over, and symbolically, and literally, take separate paths through the park outside the courthouse.

It would be foolish to suggest that there was universal acclaim for *Lou Grant*. Many radical observers for whom 'liberal' is a dirty word protested that *Lou Grant* was *always* soft and cosy and a pack of lies. 'Lou Grant is an archetype, a mythical character,' says Edwin Diamond in *American Film* July-August 1980. 'His values are genuine; they are the familiar shibboleths professed by the journalistic establishment, the American Society of Newspaper Editors and the American Newspaper Publishers Association. They make up what Herbert Gans, in his excellent study *Deciding What's News*, calls the hidden values of the news: moderation as opposed to "extremism", individualism as opposed to "collectivism", reform as opposed to "tearing down the system", independence, the dignity of work, enlightened democracy, responsible capitalism. On *Lou Grant*, the progressive moderation of the man and the progressive moderation of his newspaper are in step. But real life isn't like that . . .'

To which one can only say, *of course* it isn't. And, *of course* 'Lou Grant' is a mythical character. He is no more 'real' than the Henry Fonda character, or any of the other eleven, in *12 Angry Men*. Drama, in this regard, has never, ever, been 'real'. It is a vehicle to explore ideas, and the conflict of ideas. Gene Reynolds described his attitudes to drama like this: 'I love to have a conflict of ideas, and I like to deal with them even-handedly, to have both sides well represented because, who was it said, "Let all the opposing ideas be mounted and if Truth is in the field, Truth will prevail." I don't suppose it always does, but that's a damn good premise, both ideologically and in terms of drama.'

'Episodic television is a weekly thing,' says writer/producer/director Seth Freeman. 'So it can be a wonderful forum to deal with issues that you wouldn't necessarily put into a movie that you're going to spend millions of dollars on. For a writer it's a great thing. Always in television there have been some people who have tried to do things that have some meaning and significance and there always will be. Cynicism's frequently a cop-out. People will say, "we're just doing stuff about girls in bikinis because that's all they're buying." And it's not true that that's all they're buying. It's just that it's harder to make entertaining drama that is grounded in reality, where the human behaviour is recognisable and honest.'

There really is no answer to the charge that *Lou Grant*, beneath the 'illusion' and the 'myth' and the 'archetype', is merely serving up reactionary ideas because it doesn't advocate the destruction of capitalism by violent means. Perhaps it's true that the overall 'message' of the series is not, as Gene Reynolds hoped, 'truth will prevail', but the more establishment message '*reason* will prevail', meaning, by implication, that the status quo will be preserved. How ironic, nevertheless, that at the end of its fifth season, *Lou Grant* should have been cancelled by its network because of the outspokenness of Edward Asner in the political arena.

On Film, issue 11, Summer 1983 has a piece by Luli McCarroll detailing the rise of the 'New Right' in America and the consequent 'fall' of *Lou Grant*. The show's ratings had diminished to a 27 share, which is a borderline number; '... had it not been for Asner's conspicuous politics, the show's prestige would probably have compensated for the drop in ratings and it would likely have been renewed.' On the other hand, a five year run of a series is the 'magic' number for syndicators, who have sufficient episodes to 'strip' throughout the week, and it is through syndication that profits are made on TV series. Very likely we will never know the truth behind *Lou Grant*'s cancellation. Very likely too, we will soon cease to care.

Ironically, by the time *Lou Grant* left the screen, it had already been supplanted for experimentation, innovation, imagination and dramatic impact by another MTM series, *Hill Street Blues*, which, whether consciously or not, developed and expanded on many of the areas which *Lou Grant* had opened up.

In that final season, Billie had got married, Lou had been shot in a mugging, and there had been another outstanding 'different' episode, 'Obituary', paralleling the deaths of three reporters in a plane crash with the preservation vs. extinction of a rare species of butterfly. On paper this sounds like desperate (or wilful) plotting, but on screen it has logic and a fine sense of organic 'rightness', while there is an added poignancy because Billie, Lou and Charlie all have reasons for feeling 'guilty' about the loss of the reporters: Billie because she was due to be on the plane; Lou because he lied to get her on it; Charlie because he ordered it to be chartered. Subsequently Billie and Lou work on in-depth obits of the three reporters, and we are given a range of insights into the kind of people they were. Animal, meantime, is required to get pictures of the mating of the rare butterfly. But, a photographer not a reporter, the story to him, unlike them, is not paramount. An obsessive private collector (Simon Oakland) hopes Animal will lead him to the mating grounds. Perfect male specimens of the butterfly are worth $700 apiece and such collectors have no concern over the ecological balance which, Animal learns, will be threatened if collectors can have their way. Animal declines to get the story. The overall feeling of the episode is a little self-serving, but captures the solidarity of the profession (even though each of the dead reporters was screwed-up in some way, personal lives having been 'sacrificed' for the job) while, in the conclusion of the Animal story, there's a solidarity with the wider world in his gesture in not getting the pictures. There's also a greater-than-usual freedom of form, with Billie having brief flashbacks of the trio of reporters, while voice-overs of the obits which they have written cover some of the action. Thus, on several levels, though 'obituaries' are ostensibly the central theme, the show is really a celebration of life itself. Civilised entertainment indeed, for uncivilised times.

Notes

1. *Film Comment*, March-April 1984.
2. It should perhaps be noted here that in London the episodes were often screened in a different order from their American telecasting. It's possible, therefore, that this information had already been imparted. But it's certainly news to Rossi in 'Babies' and after all he *is* a reporter.

The following articles on *Lou Grant* may usefully be consulted:
Edwin Diamond, '*Lou Grant* – Too Good, Too True?', *American Film*, July-August 1980.
David Keller, 'Producing *Lou Grant*: The Prime Time Personality with the Documentary Look', *millimeter*, April 1979.
Luli McCarroll, 'Who Killed *Lou Grant*? The Implications of Liberal Politics in the Conservative 80s', *On Film*, Summer 1983.
Round table discussion on TV drama, including *Lou Grant*, in *Primetime* vol. 1, no. 1.
Christopher Wicking, 'Hello, City Desk ...', *Time Out* no. 524, 2–8 May 1980.

Hill Street Blues

Steve Jenkins

Anyone writing about *Hill Street Blues* has to confront the idea that this series is 'different'. This is not simply a matter of the supposed singular nature of this cop show against others – its intersection with soap opera, its realism, its mix of drama and comedy, its more complex narrative strategies – but of the ways in which it is talked and written about, and of the image of the series which emerges. And this image relates not only to *Hill Street* itself, but to the ways in which a wider image of television is constructed. Through the texts which accrue to it, the series becomes a point of definition for an institution and the limits of what can be accomplished within it. The point is made by Todd Gitlin in his book *Inside Prime Time*, which contains an excellent chapter on *Hill Street Blues*. Gitlin suggests that: 'In network television, even the exceptions [of which *Hill Street* is one] reveal the rules . . . the system that cranks out mind candy occasionally proves hospitable to something else, while at the same time betraying its limits.' It should be noted that in invoking the idea of the 'system', Gitlin is actually qualifying the sense of *Hill Street*'s uniqueness: he is embedding the series within the system. He argues that: 'for all its singularity, *Hill Street* in the end was also commercial television banging up against its limitations, revealing at the moment of its triumph just how powerful are the pressures and formulas that keep prime time close to dead center.' The series, in other words, rather than being a unique entity in itself, actually marks out an area of tension, and possibly contradiction, where certain forces intersect and come into conflict, while at the same time producing an object for consumption. These forces are often reduced to the crude and familiar opposition between creative personnel and industry/market pressures, and this terrain is thoroughly explored by Gitlin (who convincingly demolishes any such easy opposition en route).

If, however, one includes within the institution of television the ways in which programmes are discussed, then *Hill Street*, because it is seen as operating at the outer limits of mind candy, is clearly of particular interest. And the writings around the show which start to accumulate can be seen as part of the disparate forces which produce the consummable object. They intervene between the series and the spectator, shaping the show's image for the viewer, either before or after it is watched. Certain terms come into play in accounts of the series which, as mentioned, also refer to common-sense notions of how television in a wider sense is to be understood. And it may well be that these terms are more problematic than their users would have their readers believe, and also that the match between the writings, the series' image and the workings of individual episodes may be less than perfect. The latter point is important since, despite the fact that so much has been made of *Hill Street*'s 'texture' – its 'complexity and congestion, a sense of entanglement' (Gitlin) – very little, if any, close analysis of episodes has been undertaken. This is probably due to several factors: television's ephemerality; the desire to give a sense of the series rather than individual segments within it; and a desire to match the series' 'busyness', tensions and open-endedness with an appropriate kind of coverage. The purpose of this chapter is therefore merely to (re)construct the image of *Hill Street Blues* from various surrounding discourses, and then to compare the resulting picture with aspects of three episodes looked at in more detail, perhaps even read against the grain.

It should be stressed that this is not an attempt to provide a 'correct' reading in the face of previous misrepresentation. It is arguable, in fact, that the application of film studies-style textual analysis to individual episodes of a television series is inappropriate. Certainly, by plucking episodes out of the series' flow and treating them as discrete units, one is compounding the kind of attitude displayed by British programme schedulers, who show episodes out of series order and split longer 'specials' into two parts, as well as altering the series' slot and dropping it entirely for weeks at a time. Of the three episodes dealt with here, for example, (which were chosen at random) the first (A), entitled 'Shooter', was the second to last of the second series, part of a longer episode in the States, shown in two parts here. 'The Rites of Spring' (B) was a two-part episode (this was the second half), shown midway through the first season in the States, but at the end of that season here (resulting in a somewhat puzzling return of Larue's supposedly cured alcoholism). 'Moon Over Uranus' (C) was a three-parter in the third series (this was the first segment). Hopefully, however, the arbitrary selection process and the 'forced' analysis will precisely draw attention to aspects of the series which are concealed by its flow, and will produce meanings different to those explored elsewhere in this book.

Undoubtedly the most commonly-used term to encapsulate the series' interest is its supposed 'realism'. The term is invoked across a spectrum of writings and is used in different ways. The trade paper *Variety* (21 January 1981), reviewing the pilot episode, immediately identified a 'slice of life kind of approach', claiming that 'The pervading flavor of the series opener was reality (and thus believability).' The idea then crossed the Atlantic. *TV Times* (17–23 January 1981) talked about the producers being 'determined not to forsake reality'. They extended the point in two ways. First, realism as a kind of equivalent of reality: the programme featured characters who were 'Just the normal hotchpotch of cops you would find if you walked into a police station in any big American city.' Secondly, the realism was used to distinguish this cop show from others. The magazine quoted Steven Bochco: 'We're not doing a show about cops and robbers ... We're more concerned with the cops themselves.' He claimed that 'most policemen watching the show will recognise and identify with what they see.' Thus when *TV Times* (9–15 January 1982) previewed the second series, they described it as 'no *Starsky and Hutch* glamour show. This is police life complete with the warts.' The idea of 'believable realism' was constantly picked up and confirmed by newspaper reviewers. Thus, Mary Kenny (*Daily Mail*, 4 March 1982) found that 'Monday's episode was a little raw for my taste, but I did believe it. And believing is what counts.' The *Daily Express* (6 March 1982) mentioned 'the tangy taste of truth ... as a reflection of the rough and tough flood of life and debris that sweeps through an inner city police station.' In the same paper (15 March 1982), Ross Benson noted that 'The violence like real life is random and often fatal.' Martin Jackson (*Daily Mail*, 28 February 1981) found 'characters you can believe in', while Joe Steeples (*Daily Mail*, 21 May 1982) suggested 'an effort to achieve an even greater sense of jagged reality than cop shows like *Kojak*.'

These crude conceptions of a realism which merely, as Bochco put it, 'reflects what is going on in the street', as opposed to reflecting other cop shows, was made problematic by the fact that *Hill Street*'s 'realism' was so obviously carefully constructed and stylised. Thus *Variety* mentioned 'Robert Butler's direction [which] permitted an awful lot of activity to go on without the viewer losing track of the story line continuity' (a verdict not everyone was to agree with). This sense of orchestrated bustle was matched by a certain look (and sound) which was again carefully contrived: '*Hill Street* gives the impression of spontaneity and improvisation. To aid this, the soundtrack is deliberately muddied, the lighting is subdued and moments of tension and speed are made more effective by the use of hand-held cameras [which equals] a very distinctive style.' (Ray Connolly, *The Standard*, 26 May 1982) The difficulty, clearly, is how to account for this style in terms of 'window on the world' transparent realism. Avoiding the issue means ending up in a kind of paradox. Thus Michael Pollan in *Channels* magazine (March/April, 1983) linked the series' style to television news and documentary, and described how '*Hill Street*'s restless hand-held camera, its shadowy lighting and richly-layered soundtrack combine to give the show an authentic, nonfiction look.' But how to close the gap between 'authentic' and 'look' (as in appearance, probably deceptive)? An attractive answer, as provided by Gitlin, might simply be to collapse the stylisation into the world being represented, so that the style becomes an expression, rather than reflection, of that world: 'Quick cuts, a furious pace, a nervous camera made for complexity and congestion, a sense of entanglement and continuous crisis that matched the actual density and convolution of city life. . . . The show should look messy because the problems police deal with are messy. . . . The fragmentation and juxtaposition of shots and conversations would reproduce the fragmentation and simultaneity of society . . . The shaky hand-held frame reinforced the sense of irreverent, antic, raucous, sometimes hung-over cops at seven in the morning.' Q.E.D.

However, while this equation between style and the real might be convenient as regards the show's 'feel', it is not much help in accounting for the structural organisation of *Hill Street*'s narratives/episodes. Because these involve an unusually large number of regular characters and intercut stories, the generic term which has been invoked is soap opera. It is used by both Gitlin and Pollan to account for the show's narrative ordering. And it is around the idea that the series is actually a combination of genres – cop show and soap opera – rather than merely 'realist' that the most interesting divergences occur in terms of how it is discussed. The show's split identity becomes, for its champions, a sign of its progressive status within television drama (and television generally), while negative views of the same factor turn it into a sign of failure within their terms of definition. The latter viewpoint was most succinctly expressed by Joe Steeples in his *Daily Mail* article, which is very revealing about how mainstream TV criticism functions. The key question is exactly one of definition. He describes the 'format' as 'a gritty mix of comedy, police procedure and domestic melodrama.' This mix, however, according to the gulf between Emmy nominations and 'abysmal ratings', suggests that 'the format appeals more to critics than it does to viewers.' Because the programme is difficult to pin down, the critical function, as Steeples sees it, is threatened and he therefore abandons his professional role in order to join the ranks of the 'millions who fail to succumb [and who] can't all be wrong.' Instead of succumbing to the possible pleasures involved in the generic stew, Steeples decides that the series *is* a cop show and that because 'cops and robbers . . . is a childhood game that instills in us the need for dramatic certainties like beginnings, middles and endings, TV producers tamper with such conventions at their peril.' Because the episodes 'career wildly between scenes of brutal realism and comic relief, leaving more loose ends dangling than a colander full of spaghetti,' the ordinary-viewer Steeples is 'never quite certain what is going on.' Again, pleasure is ruled out because 'brilliant bits don't add up to a good programme.' Hand in hand with the implicit assumption that the business of television criticism is to spot 'good' programmes, goes a desire to fix the series' identity, which leads to the verdict that 'It's a bit like watching Roger Graef's fly-on-the-wall documentary on the Thames Valley Police. Real maybe, but it isn't drama.' The implications of all this, as regards a 'common-sense' view of how television should work, are both obvious and striking: programmes should function as discrete, conventionally ordered units within generically definable limits. The pleasure to be derived from these genres depends on certain interior rules not being broken and genre lines not being crossed; the point of the exercise is to fix the spectator in a place from where everything is identifiable, familiar and clear, from where she or he is 'certain what is going on'.

It is important to stress the 'common-sensical' status of this view. It emerged very clearly, for example, when *Hill Street Blues* was discussed on the talking-about-television programme *Did You See?* (BBC 2). The participants (actor John Thaw, former head of BBC Television Current Affairs John Gau, writer Jill Craigie and host Ludovic Kennedy) between them duplicated almost exactly Joe Steeples' position. The series could be characterised by the fact that 'right up to the punchline you seldom know which way it's going' (Kennedy). The latter found that 'It doesn't have a clear identity which you know and this is confusing, isn't it?' John Thaw agreed, while admitting that 'what I do find that I can't get at all is the humour allied with the seriousness' and stating that he thought it 'was just too diffuse having five stories running together.' Interestingly, in this context, John Gau tried to suggest that ' . . . it's not actually a police serial. It's a soap opera that takes place in a police station.' But this aspect was then dealt with moralistically, by setting it against the show's 'realist' surface. It becomes 'rather a meretricious soap opera because . . . they pretend this reality, this realism . . .. It's formula but it tries to pretend it's something else. And I find that a bit dodgy . . . in the end it's slightly distasteful.' Which is simply a moralising variation on Steeples' notion that the series' mimicking of fly-on-the-wall documentary meant that it failed as 'drama'. What was crucial in the discussion and, almost literally, rendered *Hill Street* 'unspeakable', was once again the problem of definition. The other programmes dealt with (a celebration of *Tonight*; the BBC adaptation of *Fame is the Spur*) presented no such difficulties, but with *Hill Street* every observation on, and criticism of, the series stumbled over the question of what it was exactly they were talking about. This meant, for Kennedy, that 'you don't really know where you are and I think you should.' To which Jill Craigie offered the only possible rejoinder (not taken up): 'Not knowing where you are makes you think and that's a change.'

This perhaps represents the bottom line for *Hill Street*'s champions and the series' progressive image. It becomes an achievement in itself that the programme not only demands attention and thought, but that this demand is inseparable from its generic and narrative weave. As Steven Bochco put it: 'Television audiences are creatures of comfort. They want something easy and recognisable. Maybe the biggest problem with *Hill Street*, in terms of popular success, is that it is a show that demands to be watched. And most people do not watch television. They are simply in its presence. They use television as a narcotic. And when television grabs you by the throat and says, "Wait a second, pay attention to what's going on here," you're gonna get a remarkable resistance. And I think we do.' The point of much of the negative criticism is exactly that the series is 'unrecognisable' (Kennedy: 'Well, it isn't quite a soap opera, you see'), it can't be easily labelled, 'realism' is not appropriate for a soap opera, and so on. But all this is simply viewed positively by the show's supporters. Michael Pollan, for example, claims that it 'demands a new way of watching television. An episode juggles so many characters (13 regulars) and so many plots (often half a dozen), that it frustrates our habit of watching television with one eye, while reading or talking. ... It's this illusion of improvisation that makes *Hill Street* new and earns our close attention.' In other words, Bochco and Pollan are suggesting, *Hill Street* is significant due to the very fact that it is watched, as opposed to simply unfolding in the presence of the ostensible viewer. It would thus seem to challenge, for example, the model for television viewing outlined by John Ellis in his book *Visible Fictions*, where he distinguishes between the look (directed at the cinema screen) and the glance (offered casually to the TV). And this challenge then manifests itself throughout the institution of television – in the kind of criticism outlined above, in the 'ratings war', in the Emmy awards, or in the pages of *City Limits* (27 April–3 May 1984), where Paul Kerr uses the programme to threaten the magazine's readers' supposed sense of 'quality' television: 'Of course, championing a cop show in *City Limits* is about as diplomatic as inviting Mike Belker to Buck House.'

But if the series thus becomes an 'issue' – perhaps the essence of its image – then the problem arises that the sides in the debate(s) seem too easily and obviously drawn up. On the one side are the supporters of a show which is a generic mutant, offering formal and structural delights hitherto unknown in a TV drama series, which wins awards, and which, as Paul Kerr suggests, is 'More imaginative then any British one-off drama in recent memory, and still better written, directed and acted than any long-running series from either side of the Atlantic.' And on the other – the programme schedulers, who repeatedly shift its slot and show episodes in the wrong order, and the establishment critics, pundits and TV professionals who simply bluster in confusion. Clearly there is no contest. The danger, however, is that the series' 'difference' becomes an almost mythical given, taken for granted in order to be celebrated or rejected. It can be qualified only on its own terms, which means that from the second series onwards, *Hill Street* is seen by its champions as slightly less anarchic, slightly more like other television. Thus, as Paul Kerr writes, 'There have certainly been changes ... NBC instructed MTM to settle at least one story line each week and, perhaps inevitably, some stylistic innovations have hardened into mannerisms, some character eccentricities have atrophied into new stereotypes. The series has suffered, if not in the ratings.' He asserts, however, that 'Nevertheless, it remains one of the best shows on the box.' Its difference, in other words, what makes it 'one of the best', endures. The only other crack which appears in this kind of position is around the series' politics; whether it can be accused of 'humanising the police', whether it 'offers an aestheticised or even anaesthetised image of the operation of law and order in Reagan's America' (Kerr). Or, alternatively, there is Gitlin's view that '*Hill Street Blues* was the first postliberal cop show' and that 'the energy swarming through in *Hill Street* was the energy of American liberal-middle-class ideology turned on itself, at a loss for direction.' These questions, however, tend to run alongside, or arise out of, the series' 'energy' which, again, is taken as read, subject to criticism only of the inane negative kind.

What is needed, unless the show's image is to become completely atrophied, is a shift of position on this 'energy'. This can be approached in two ways. First, an examination of specific episodes in terms of style and structure, rather than reference to the entire series' supposed free-form confusion which delights some and befuddles others. And secondly, though the points are related, a (re)consideration of how *Hill Street* and its image relate to soap opera. To take the latter point first, it is noticeable that soap opera is invoked with regard to questions of both 'form' and 'content'. It is a matter of structure (the number of sub-plots which are contained within any one episode) and of a certain kind of subject matter. The latter is characterised by Michael Pollan in terms of 'emotional complications' and 'adultery'. These elements are set against their cop-show generic counterparts: 'loads of action-adventure' and 'the jeopardy of police work'. However, Pollan also relates this distinction to the show's supposed audience, claiming that '*Hill Street* attracts the women who like soaps and the men who like cop-shows in roughly equal numbers.' Having introduced the idea of sexual difference in these generic terms, Pollan then attempts to erase it by describing how *Hill Street*'s combination of conventions works to strengthen the inherent weaknesses of both soap opera and cop show. The hybrid is a superior blend of both genres. It is interesting, however, to reinflect this question, to look at how sexual difference emerges and is dealt with both in the series and in how it is described.

Perhaps the strongest reason for so doing is that it is precisely a recurrent sexual encounter – between Captain Frank Furillo and Public Defender Joyce Davenport – which regularly anchors the 'busyness' which seems to epitomise the show's difference. For example, Pollan compares the unfolding of a *Hill Street* episode to a jazz performance, with the central intertwining of various subplots being equivalent to an improvisation. This is then replaced by 'the familiarly melodic: Furillo unwinding at day's end in the company of Joyce Davenport.' Richard T. Jameson (*Film Comment*, March/April 1981) makes a similar point, but in a way which underlines that this is not simply a matter of 'pure' structure: 'Not all the warmth that *Hill Street* gives off is communal: any episode that fails to wend its way to Veronica Hamel's bed or bath is going to leave habitual viewers feeling erotically deprived.' This link between sexuality (with here an assumed male heterosexual viewer) and a sense of satisfactory closure reverberates back on the function of the Joyce Davenport character. Jameson describes her as 'a tanned, leggy beauty from the Public Defender's Office', and this split/link between physical appearance and professional role crops up almost whenever the character is mentioned. From Clive James in *The Observer*, 14 March 1982, ('She has Clarence Darrow's sense of justice, the figure of Cyd Charisse and the face of an angel') through Jeffrey Robinson ('The sexy girlfriend ... who often gets into Furillo's way at work, but also into his bed at home.' – source unknown) to Todd Gitlin. The latter cannot avoid the trap, even though he is asserting Davenport as an example of how 'By television's standards, several of the characters were new departures. [She] was the first television regular at once professional, tough, elegant, intelligent, and sexy.' The point here is not at all to censure the writers for sexism, but to stress that these descriptions are absolutely appropriate as regards how the character was conceived and functions. According to Gitlin, the 'biggest fight' between the series' producers and NBC's casting people was over the Davenport character, with NBC (the villains) wanting a 'voluptuous bomb-shell type', an idea resisted by MTM, with everyone settling happily for 'a slender former cover girl.' (!)

The sense of sexuality balanced with professionalism around the Davenport figure becomes particularly significant given the series' other two main female characters: Patrolwoman Lucy Bates and Faye, Furillo's ex-wife and mother of 'his' son. The former's sexuality is effectively repressed: she is conceived as a professional, as one of the boys, the 'partner' of Joe Coffey. One of the threads of episode B (see below for episode synopses) is exactly the possibility of her becoming his sexual partner, a notion which she rejects, and for which both characters are punished (Joe with a bullet; Lucy, in a classic no-win bind, with feelings of guilt for having turned down his offer). That she must remain sexless (as Howard Hunter puts it, to him she is 'just a person'), was subsquently confirmed when Joe finally spent the night with her in a hospital bed after *she* had been injured: it was later revealed that they did not make love. Faye represents an opposite stereotypical extreme: constantly hovering on the edge of hysteria as, in various permutations, she tries to reconcile her female, non-'professional' role (divorced mother) with the problem of sexuality. Thus, in episode A, she is worried about Frank Jnr and a young female friend playing doctors; in B, she is being threatened by an angry wife with whose husband she is having an affair; and in C, Frank Jnr has discovered her in bed with another lover.

Around these opposing and limited constants, the episodes introduce other female characters, but it is noticeable that they are conceived almost entirely in terms of problems for the male running characters. The bottom line of this is the never-seen figure of Mike Belker's mother (actually another series regular) whose phone calls to the station are his main emotional burden in life (a verbal equivalent of Faye's intrusions into Frank's professional life). In episode A, the wife of Jack Halloran, the shot policeman, is posed as a problem for Furillo: he has to break the news of her husband's death to her and becomes the object of her hysterical aggression. In B, several variations are worked on the use of female characters to 'humanise' and 'flesh out' the male cops. Bobby Hill deals with an 'unfit' mother, who leaves him determined to change her life; his performance is watched admiringly by a female social worker whom he then asks out. She initially refuses, but relents when he says that 'these blues come off at night.' This possibility of a balanced, satisfactory relationship out of uniform is, however, offset by the ending of two other affairs within this episode. J. D. Larue's alcohol problem, which here comes to a head, is partly defined by his unsatisfactory relationship with air-hostess Jen, while Renko's treatment of Sandy helps colour him as possessive and emotionally unstable. The point of these, and other similar relationships introduced throughout the series, is exactly that they are transient: the female characters fade out; the males remain, *their* characters developed through the encounter with, and the subsequent loss of, the desired object. In C, this process is applied, unusually for the character, to Mike Belker, who is about to start a relationship with another officer, Tatalia. Again, however, the coupling will not be sustained, leaving Belker's loner image fuller and intact. The other women in this episode serve related functions. The violent rape of Lieutenant Jack Donleavy's daughter is used to explore emotional extremes in her father, culminating in his shooting of the wrong prisoner (which, in turn, ironically confirms the validity of the male survivalist's paranoid fantasies). Similarly, Mary Hicks presents herself as being under threat from her boyfriend; her subsequent murder proves her right, adding to Lieutenant Henry Goldblume's constant, recurrent feelings of guilt and inadequacy with regard to his job.

It is arguable, given this particular representation of male/female roles, that the eternal return to Frank and Joyce's bed is not therefore a matter of structure (calm after the storm) or of satisfying the male spectator, but rather of regularly correcting a very un-soap-opera-ish imbalance. Of the series' thirteen regular leading cast members (an unusually large number – a sign of the show's difference) only three are women. Of these three one is largely subsumed to professional maleness by her uniform, while another functions as an hysterical, non-professional intruder (Faye constantly *interrupts* Frank at moments of crisis); and there is a concomitant emphasis on male pairings (Hill/Renko; Larue/Washington) and male loners (Goldblume, Belker, Hunter). In terms of characters, in other words, the invocation of soap opera as a comparable model might seem somewhat arbitrary. Why not the 'all-male group' of classical Hollywood cinema? A series like *Cagney and Lacey*, for example, which centres on two women police officers, is much more conventional (i.e. un-soap-opera-like) in structure than *Hill Street*. But as a soap opera/cop show crossover (i.e. a series which plays on the personal/professional mix of its characters' lives), it exposes just how little *Hill Street* seems to offer its supposed female viewers. It is tempting here to think of the 87th Precinct novels of Ed McBain, to which *Hill Street* has been compared; there, the wife of Steve Carella, the rhyming equivalent of Frank Furillo, is beautiful, deaf and dumb, and graced with a man's name, Teddy. If *Hill Street* avoids this somewhat dubious, idealised vision of womanhood, it nevertheless, in the form of the Furillo/Davenport relationship, asserts a sense of heterosexual, male/female/, private/professional balance in the face of its own imbalance; it returns the spectator, after the supposed chaos, to a space where things are in their correct place, as they should be. Although this relationship is often interrupted (the bleeper call which summons Frank at the end of B) and occasionally threatened (the new job/other man which arises at the end of C), the important point, again, is that it endures.

There is a sense, however, in which it is misleading to isolate the Furillo/Davenport relationship in this way. In terms of structure, as opposed to characters and content, it fulfils an opposite role, duplicating and consolidating a previous tendency rather than being differentiated from it. It is arguable that Pollan's musical analogy (the improvisation followed by the 'familiarly melodic') is actually not a very useful model for describing the structure of *Hill Street* episodes. If one thinks of structure in terms of style, then there are actually three distinct modes which recur. The first, and most oft-noted in terms of the show's image, is the mock cinéma vérité which is used for the opening roll-call sequence. This epitomises the notion of 'busyness': hand-held camera, no fixed viewpoint, a large number of characters, and several narrative possibilities being raised through the various

Daniel J. Travanti as Frank Furillo and Veronica Hamel as Joyce Davenport in *Hill Street Blues*

'items' mentioned and by odd bits of business which are picked up in passing (in B, Larue's hung-over entrance, or the note passed from Joe to Lucy inviting her to dinner or a midnight swim). Although Sergeant Esterhaus provides an ostensible focal point, our attention is constantly distracted by alternative demands, by characters who block our view, and general background 'noise' (both aural and visual). The style works here to suggest the 'anything could happen' chaos which characterises the streets outside and which is in turn finally evoked by Esterhaus' repeated roll-call warning: 'Let's be careful out there.' However, it is equally apparent that the style in this sense is deceptive, that it is used to mask, or render less obvious, the specific ways in which our attention is being directed and fixed, the ways in which the upcoming contents of episodes are being laid out. There is very little in the roll-call sequences which is not later developed; they are tight rather than, as they are made to appear, loose. This is important, since it runs counter to Gitlin's argument that the series' rough and edgy style – here at its most pronounced – simply mirrors and expresses the world being represented. The point is that the 'world' outside the roll-call room is explored and represented through specific, and carefully structured, arrangements of characters, confrontations, encounters, incidents and situations, which constitute the body of each episode. The series, and each episode, in other words, constructs a narrative world, and it is to this, rather than to 'reality', that the style must be seen to relate. It was originally a possibility that the whole show should be shot with hand-held cameras, but due to producers' worries that this 'stretched the conventions too far' (Gitlin) the device was restricted to what director Robert Butler called 'certain heightened sequences'. But the fact that the style here tends to mask the actual construction is interesting not so much in terms of 'stretching conventions' and violating rules as in suggesting a direction that, in dramatic terms, it would be somewhat perverse to follow.

The point becomes clearer when one examines the second stylistic stage. This, which consists of the whole bulk section between roll-call and the Furillo/Davenport conclusion, is precisely a half-way house between these two extremes, shading into both. Thus between the end of roll-call and the credits are a number of exchanges between characters outside the roll-call room which often pick up on and develop elements introduced in the previous scene. In B, there is further business around the Lucy/Joe date, as Joe reluctantly agrees to take on Renko's night shift, followed by an elaboration of the Larue drinking problem (Renko jokes with him about the previous night's car-wrecking incident; Belker tells him he's been video-taped passing jewellery in a pawn-shop which is under surveillance). In C, Renko is summoned into Furillo's office and told his punishment for a 'public exposure' incident that had been mentioned during roll-call. While these exchanges are surrounded by a sense of bustle – inevitably in the constantly crowded Hill Street station – which carries forward the 'feel' of the roll-call, it is noticeable that the free-ranging focus is narrowed down to a concentration on characters dealt with predominantly in pairs. Thus, in A, Renko and Hill are followed by Belker plus prisoner, while in B, Renko and Larue give way to Larue and Belker. And in C, there is the Furillo/Renko confrontation. Stylistically, given this shift of focus, the vérité approach – which generally signifies an attempt to follow situations over which you have no structuring control – would be inappropriate (faked or not). As the group gives way to the pairs, and as the pairs move into the (narrative) world, a different formal strategy is required. And while a degree of roughness is retained – for example, picking up and following characters as they move into shot, then abandoning them to follow someone else – it is equally apparent that the 'settling down' around the characters is marked by a move towards a more conventional televisual grammar. This is based on a shot-reverse pattern which constructs a sense of space centred round two, sometimes three, characters, with the spectator positioned alternately with one then the other (while remaining outside both). This is important because it is exactly the kind of stylistic device which champions of *Hill Street* claim that the show rejects. Paul Kerr, for example, writes of an 'outright rejection of television's conventional visual grammar. It minimises, if not altogether eliminates, the tired rhetoric of the establishing shot, the two-shot, the close-up, the over-the-shoulder shot. The *HSB* team replaced it with an emphasis on character and camera mobility.' But certainly in the three episodes examined there is a very heavy reliance on exactly that kind of rhetoric – or at least an effective equivalent – in order to structure the narrative world. This is indeed centred on character, but camera mobility is reduced to a pleasurable (and sometimes, as it is deliberately used to conceal cuts, deceptive) icing on the stylistic cake, always anchored by a balanced view. Examples are really too numerous to list, but in B one might cite encounters between Larue and Jen, between Belker and a faker in a wheelchair, between Washington/Goldblume and the brother of the dead Curtis Gilford, between Furillo and Chief Daniels, between Hill and the female social worker, between Larue and a barmaid, between Faye and Furillo, between Renko and Sandy, and so on.

In other words, as we move, after the credit sequence, into the narrative(s) proper, we enter a world which is highly and significantly organised at a basic level. It may, on the surface, be crowded and noisy, it may veer suddenly between comedy and drama, it may consist of a large number of subplots, but it is ultimately explicable, resolvable and understandable through this interplay between combinations of individual characters. This is obviously manifest in different ways across the three episodes. In A, for example, firearms become an 'issue' which is examined through various narrative strands. Thus, at one point, we cut from the bodies of two shot policemen to guns on a table, as a weapons salesman performs for the benefit of Furillo and other cops. And, in the final scene, we discover, along with Furillo, that Joyce

Davenport now carries a gun to protect herself. Of these three threads, only the hunt for the killer of Halloran, the policeman who dies, is satisfactorily resolved. The search for the owner of the murder weapon breaks down into a series of confrontations with those through whose hands it passed, before the killer is shot dead as he is firing a rifle (the ultimate shot/reverse shot?). But because the other threads do not lend themselves to this kind of resolution, the issues involved are simply displaced until they disappear. Furillo moves from discussing the best use of police financial resources (guns or bullet-proof vests) to a sexually suggestive encounter with a female arms dealer, before they are interrupted by Esterhaus, who has news of the cop killing. Similarly, the question of the Davenport gun is evaded by 'Frank, come to bed ... We'll talk about it tomorrow.' This kind of evasion and irresolution is not to be found in B, where, for example, the problem of Sherette's unfitness as a mother can be dealt with in a face-off with Bobby Hill, where she simply has to acknowledge the correctness of his position (why she cannot keep her children) before determining to change her life. Similarly, the question of the (white) law protecting its own after a young black has been shot dead by Weeks, a cop, can be resolved in a confrontation between Chief Daniels and Furillo, where the issue becomes one of Daniels' political opportunism versus Furillo's sense of fair play. (Weeks was a bad cop but was acting correctly in this particular instance.) And in the case of Larue's alcoholism, although it threatens to become an irresolvable 'wider issue' (with his outburst directed at the rest of the Hill Street force) a one-to-one solution is found in the Alcoholics Anonymous meeting: there Furillo, by mirroring, in a cleansed state, Larue's problem, can turn it back on the sufferer, who will cure himself. It's worth noting here how in both scenes the camera moves across the group (the policemen, the anonymous alcoholics) before coming to rest on Furillo and his gaze. This duplication, in which the wider view/issue is reduced to the reciprocal relation, neatly encapsulates a significant tendency, the only possible solution.

Given this structuring method, the Furillo/Davenport finale – the third stylistic stage, with background interference reduced to the bleeper – can be read as a logical extension of the narrative, rather than as a kind of calming coda to it. In the case of A, which was intended as a rather different kind of episode (with its strong central thread around the murder weapon) this is particularly clear. The final scene takes the firearms issue firmly into the realms of the personal – the gun placed in front of a picture of Frank and Joyce, happy, laughing, out of uniform – but cannot resolve it or even talk about it. Resolution is provided instead by the very presence of the couple. The tomorrow referred to by Joyce never comes, of course. Similarly, in B, when Furillo leaves Joyce to go to the scene of Joe Coffey's shooting, he fails to understand or answer Lucy's feelings of guilt. Nevertheless he fulfils his structural role – the camera pulls back to show the two of them facing each other, surrounded by police and ambulance vehicles. Again, what's at stake for Lucy will not be taken up, is displaced; Joe simply recovers from the shooting. It is no accident that the only suspended resolution which *is* followed through is in C, where it is the Furillo/Davenport relationship itself which is under threat. That there is perhaps a paranoid edge to the reassurance sought in the Furillo/Davenport coupling is suggested by another tendency in the *mise en scène*. Towards the end of many episodes, particularly here in A, as night descends the darkness is often accompanied by high angle shots, rolling thunder on the soundtrack, wet, glistening streets, and occasional visual effects like the slow motion death of Halloran's killer. This expressive stylisation represents the opposite, but in a sense corresponding, tendency to the vérité 'chaos' of the roll-call. The body of each narrative, and the Furillo/Davenport resolution, can be read as ways of avoiding and repressing these different excesses.

What, hopefully, emerges from this is that a slightly closer look at *Hill Street*'s narrative strategies at least throws into question the show's received image, in both its positive and negative faces (which are effectively identical). In order for it to become a cause célèbre within the television system, a fantasy version had to be constructed, in which rules are gleefully and disturbingly broken, in which genres collapse into each other, style runs riot and anything goes. Terms such as realism and soap opera are thrown into the critical pot when their relation to the product in question is actually very tenuous. *Hill Street* may affect a surface realism, but what is 'realist' about a show which anchors every issue it attempts to deal with in characters with whom the spectator is intended to identify and empathise? And can soap opera be reduced to structure, given that, compared to *Coronation Street* or *Dallas, Hill Street*'s world is ultimately so male-oriented, with Furillo as its patriarchal centre? Certainly, it is likely to pull more surprises around character, incident and mood than any other drama series. But the importance of its image seems to go beyond the pleasures thus afforded, to the point where the text disappears; it becomes an abstraction of itself, distorted by the challengers and defenders of commercial television's 'limitations'. And as a result, the series seems to engage in self-criticism, dealing with those problems which have to be ignored, or quickly passed over, by its supporters. The fourth series seems, at time of writing, to be avoiding the Furillo/Davenport conclusions and is developing Faye's character beyond glib caricature. A burgeoning affair between Lucy Bates and a doctor seems to have been quickly dropped, but two out of three is progress. In any case, it remains, of course, the best show on the box.

A 'Shooter'

While arms salesmen are visiting the Hill Street station, two cops are shot in a stereo shop; one of them, Halloran, dies. Furillo has to break the news to his widow. The murder weapon is traced to the owner of a liquor store; it transpires, however, that the man was killed and the gun taken as police evidence. Wallins, of the police property department, admits passing the weapon on to his brother-in-law. The latter claims the gun was stolen. An arms dealer, forced to plea bargain, gives the name of a burglar, Billy Harris, who has a lot of 'hot' guns. Larue forces Sammy, an informant, to give Harris' address. The police, having found stereo equipment in Harris' apartment, shoot him dead when he returns and resists arrest. Furillo is disturbed to discover that Joyce is now carrying a handgun for protection. Sub-plots include: Howard trying to sell places in an underground condominium; Belker taking his driving test; Renko coping with his sick father.

B 'Rites of Spring'

Larue's alcohol problem is at an acute stage, and he has been recorded passing stolen jewellery in a pawn shop under surveillance by Belker. Howard Hunter supervises a weapons search at the Jefferson Avenue Playground. Larue tries to persuade Jen, from whom he took the jewellery, to tell Furillo that she loaned it to him; she ends their relationship. After Frank recommends that he transfer out, Larue directs an emotional tirade against the assembled cops in the station. Curtis Gilford, a young black, has been shot dead by Weeks, a corrupt cop, and Chief Daniels is determined, for political reasons, to 'hang Weeks out to dry' (despite Furillo's belief that, in this instance, Weeks acted correctly). Bobby Hill deals with a young black woman, Sherette, who is neglecting her child, and persuades an attractive social worker to see him 'out of uniform'. Washington and Goldblume obtain evidence which proves Weeks' innocence and he is freed after the inquest, much to Daniels' annoyance. Larue, after drinking in various bars, takes Frank's advice and attends an Alcoholics Anonymous meeting. There he finds . . . Frank. The latter is later summoned to where Joe Coffey has been shot while on patrol with Lucy Bates. She feels guilty, having taken the duty to stall Joe in his romantic advances towards her.

C 'Moon over Uranus'

Police Lieutenant Jack Donleavy's daughter Kathleen has been violently raped. While visiting the Hill's 'Black Hole' (as part of his election year clean-up-the-city campaign), Chief Daniels is bitten by a rat which he shoots and wounds. He instructs Larue and Washington to catch the creature. Renko, on scooter duty as punishment for a 'mooning' incident, has a run-in with vice-cop Sal Benedetto; Renko challenges him to fight later at Mulligan's bar. Leonard Smithers is found in possession of Kathleen's credit card; the man from whom he claims to have obtained it is then identified by Kathleen from a photo as her attacker. Mary Hicks asks Henry Goldblume to arrest her boyfriend Richard Brady, whom she claims has killed her cat and from whom she feels in danger. Lucy Bates and Joe Coffey bring in Petrakis, a crazed survivalist, and later aid in the arrest of the rapist. Henry talks to Brady, but gets nowhere. Larue and Washington have shot a rat, which they pretend is the beast which bit Daniels; the creature turns out to have hydrophobia, necessitating a painful injection for the Chief. Donleavy, mistaking Petrakis for the rape suspect, shoots him dead. At Mulligan's bar, Officer Tatalia asks about Belker, with whom she is working and to whom she is clearly attracted; he arrives. Benedetto and Renko go outside for their fight, but Benedetto attacks him from behind, leaving him unconscious in the snow. Joyce tells Frank she has to go to Washington for an interview for a job in the Justice Department. She mentions Clark Galloway, who taught her in Law school and whom she found attractive. Frank says he's jealous, and thinks she'll get the job.

MTM Productions: A Guide

MTM Series

The Mary Tyler Moore Show (CBS, 19/9/70 – 3/9/77)* Film. 30 mins.
Created by James L. Brooks and Allan Burns. *Producers*: Allan Burns, James L. Brooks, David Davis. *Director:* Jay Sandrich. *Associate producer/unit production manager*: Lionel A. Ephraim. *Music composed and conducted by* Pat Williams. *Theme song* 'Love Is All Around' *written and sung by* Sonny Curtis. *Director of photography*: Paul Uhl. *Film editor:* Douglas Hines. *Assistant director*: John C. Chulay. *Art director*: Lewis E. Hurst Jr. *Set decorator*: George R. Nelson. *Script supervisor*: Marjorie Mullen. *Title visualisation*: Reza S. Badiyi. *Assistant to producers*: Lorenzo Music. *Camera co-ordinator*: Gil Clasen. *Music editing*: Ed Norton, Music Inc. *Make-up*: Ben Nye II. *Hairstyling*: Mary Keats. *Men's costumes*: Don MacDonald. *Women's costumes*: Leslie Hall. *Wardrobe for Mary Tyler Moore furnished by* Evan-Picone. *Men's wardrobe furnished by* Palm Beach. *Designer*: John Weitz. *Filmed in Hollywood before a live audience. An MTM Enterprises Inc. Production.* [Credits taken from première episode only]
Producers (following seasons): Stan Daniels, Ed Weinberger. *Directors (following seasons)*: Jay Sandrich, Marjorie Mullen, James Burrows, Harry Mastrogeorge, Mel Ferber, Doug Rogers.
Cast (regular and various seasons): Mary Tyler Moore, Valerie Harper, Edward Asner, Ted Knight, Gavin MacLeod, Cloris Leachman, Lisa Gerritsen, John Amos, Nancy Walker, Harold Gould, Georgia Engel, Betty White, Nanette Fabray, Bill Quinn, Joyce Bulifant, Benjamin Chuley, Priscilla Morrill, John Gabriel, Sheree North, Robbie Rist, Peter Hobbs, Chuck Bergansky, Brad Trumbull, Nora Heflin.

1. 'Love Is All Around'
Première: Trying to get over a 4-year romance Mary moves to Minneapolis, becomes associate producer at WJM-TV newsroom.
2. 'Today I Am A Ma'am'
Concerned about their age, Rhoda and Mary look up old boyfriends.
3. 'Bess, You Is My Daughter Now'
Mary discovers she'd make a great mother after she babysits Phyllis's daughter.
4. 'Divorce Isn't Everything'
Mary and Rhoda join a club for the divorced in order to get a discount trip to Paris.
5. 'Keep Your Guard Up'
Mary finds herself attached to a former pro football player who's seeking a sportscaster's job.
6. 'Support Your Local Mother'
Rhoda refuses to see her mother when Mrs Morgenstern visits Minneapolis.
7. 'Toulouse-Lautrec Is One Of My Favourite Artists'
Mary becomes romantically involved with an author, a man shorter than her.
8. 'The Snow Must Go On'

*In accordance with British practice, all dates in this section are in the order: day, month, year.

Mary is forced to produce her first TV news show after a snowstorm prevents the others getting to the station.

9. 'Bob & Rhoda & Teddy & Mary'
Rhoda becomes angry when her boyfriend appears to like Mary more.

10. 'Assistant Wanted, Female'
Chaos rules when Mary hires Phyllis as her newsroom assistant.

11. '1040 Or Fight'
An Internal Revenue Service man (Paul Sand) comes to audit Mary's accounts.

12. 'Anchorman Overboard'
Ted Baxter freezes up when he's forced to confront an audience without a script.

13. 'He's All Yours'
Lou Grant's nephew chases Mary.

14. 'Christmas And The Hard Luck Kid II'
Mary is forced to work on both Christmas Eve and Christmas Day.

15. 'Howard's Girl'
The mother of Mary's date believes that she is engaged to her other son, and gets upset.

16. 'Party Is Such Sweet Sorrow'
Mary is almost lured to a job at a rival news station.

17. 'Just A Lunch'
Mary dates a professional heartbreaker.

18. 'Second-Storey Story'
Mary's apartment is twice burgled.

19. 'We Closed In Minneapolis'
A play that Murray Slaughter writes flops.

20. 'Hi!'
In hospital for a tonsillectomy Mary has to share a room with a cantankerous patient.

21. 'The Boss Isn't Coming To Dinner'
Lou and Edie (Mrs Grant) have marriage problems.

22. 'A Friend In Deed'
A visiting childhood friend of Mary's drives everyone crazy.

23. 'Smokey The Bear Wants You'
Rhoda falls for a man with ideas of becoming a forest ranger.

24. 'The 45-Year-Old Man'
Lou worries about his age and job possibilities when he nearly gets fired from the station.

25. 'The Birds ... And ... Um ... Bees'
Bess is given the facts of life by Mary.

26. 'I Am Curious Cooper'
Lou sets Mary up with a friend who's pleasant but no turn-on.

27. 'He's No Heavy, He's My Brother'
Mary and Rhoda plan a vacation.

28. 'Room 223'
Mary goes to night school and gets involved with the professor.

29. 'A Girl's Mother Is Not Her Best Friend'
Rhoda's mother tries to 'relate' to her daughter as an equal.

30. 'Cover Boy'
Ted's brother shows up and rivalry flares.

31. 'Didn't You Used To Be ...Wait ... Don't Tell Me'
Mary returns to her high school for a reunion.

32. 'Thoroughly Unmilitant Mary'
Lou has to do the news on the air during a strike at the station.

33. 'And Now, Sitting In For Ted Baxter'
Ted's vacation stand-in shows him up.

34. 'Don't Break The Chain'
Mary receives a chain letter.

35. 'The Six And A Half Year Itch'

Lou discovers his son-in-law having an affair.
36. ' . . . Is A Friend In Need'
Rhoda loses her window-dressing job.
37. 'The Square-Shaped Room'
Lou's living room is decorated by Rhoda.
38. 'Ted Over Heels'
Ted falls for the daughter of Chuckles the clown.
39. 'The Five-Minute Dress'
Mary dates a high-powered politician.
40. 'Feeb'
Feeling guilty about it, Mary hires an inept assistant.
41. 'The Slaughter Affair'
Murray's newsroom work suffers when he moonlights to get his wife a car.
42. 'Baby Sit-Com'
Lou babysits for Bess.
43. 'More Than Neighbors'
Ted nearly moves into Mary's apartment building.
44. 'The Care And Feeding Of Parents'
Mary is pressured by Phyllis to get Bess' composition published.
45. 'Where There's Smoke, There's Rhoda'
After a fire at Rhoda's apartment she moves in with Mary, putting their relationship on the edge.
46. 'You Certainly Are A Big Boy'
Mary is pursued by an amorous architect.
47. 'Some Of My Best Friends Are Rhoda'
A new girlfriend of Mary's turns out to be anti-semitic.
48. 'His Two Right Arms'
Mary meets what appears to be the world's most inept politician.
49. 'The Good-Time News'
Mary's assignment is to convert the news into 'happy talk'.
50. 'What Is Mary Richards Really Like?'
A newspaper columnist and fan of the Las Vegas Gold-diggers show comes on to Mary.
51. 'Who's In Charge Here?'
Lou gets promoted.
52. 'Enter Rhoda's Parents'
Mr and Mrs Morgenstern encounter marriage problems.
53. 'It's Whether You Win Or Lose'
Murray's long-repressed gambling compulsion surfaces.
54. 'Rhoda The Beautiful'
Even though she wins a beauty contest, Rhoda still feels fat and homely.
55. 'Just Around The Corner'
Mary's parents move a little too close for comfort.
56. 'Farmer Ted And The News'
Ted enters the world of TV commercials, and does a knockout dogfood spot.
57. 'But Seriously, Folks'
Mary goes out with an aspiring standup comic whose act is terrible.
58. 'Have I Found A Guy For You'
Mary goes on a date with a friend's ex-husband.
59. 'You've Got A Friend'
Mary invites her father to dinner – but not her mother.
60. 'It Was Fascination, I Know'
Bess' 12-year-old boyfriend, a precocious but likeable kid, goes nuts over Mary.
61. 'Operation: Lou'
Lou has to enter hospital.
62. 'Rhoda Morgenstern: Minneapolis To New York'

Rhoda nearly decides to move back to New York.
63. 'The Courtship Of Mary's Father's Daughter'
Mary encounters an old boyfriend who's now engaged.
64. 'Lou's Place'
Lou decides to buy a bar.
65. 'My Brother's Keeper'
Phyllis tries to set up her brother with Mary, unaware that he's gay.
66. 'The Georgette Story'
Ted uses Georgette to do some domestic work.
67. 'Romeo And Mary'
A man pesters Mary with proposals of marriage.
68. 'What Do You Say When The Boss Says, "I Love You"?'
The new station manager has a gleam in her eye when she spots Lou.
69. 'Murray Faces Life'
Depression hits Murray when he hears that an old classmate has won a Pulitzer Prize.
70. 'Remembrance Of Things Past'
An old flame returns, breaks Mary's heart again.
71. 'Put On A Happy Face'
Mary has a 'bad day', the day when everything goes wrong.
72. 'Mary Richards And The Incredible Plant Lady'
Rhoda discovers that she has a green thumb.
73. 'The Lars Affair'
Phyllis' husband goes on a fling with Sue Ann Nivens.
74. 'Angels In The Snow'
Mary goes on a date with a younger man.
75. 'Rhoda's Sister Gets Married'
While Rhoda's mother thinks she'll be depressed.
76. 'The Lou And Edie Story'
Mr and Mrs Grant visit a marriage counsellor.
77. 'Hi There, Sports Fans'
Mary hires a new sportcaster for the station.
78. 'Father's Day'
Ted receives a call from his wayward father.
79. 'Son Of "But Seriously Folks"'
Mary is courted by a comedy writer.
80. 'Lou's First Date'
Mary sets up Lou with a date following his marriage breakup.
81. 'Love Blooms At Hemples'
Rhoda's love is unrequited.
82. 'The Dinner Party'
Mary finds she doesn't have enough food when she gives a dinner party.
83. 'Just Friends'
Mary engineers to get Lou and Edie back together again.
84. 'We Want Baxter'
Phyllis pushes Ted to run for local office.
85. 'I Gave At The Office'
Murray's daughter gets a job in the newsroom.
86. 'Almost A Nun's Story'
Georgette catches Ted in a clinch with another woman.
87. 'Happy Birthday, Lou'
Mary lays on a surprise party for Lou – an idea he hates.
88. 'WJM Tries Harder'
Mary goes out with the anchorman of a rival TV news show.
89. 'Cottage For Sale'
Lou's house is sold by Phyllis.

90. 'The Co-producers'
Mary and Rhoda try to co-produce a new show – featuring Ted and Sue Ann.
91. 'Best Of Enemies'
Rhoda and Mary end up in a major battle.
92. 'Better Late . . . That's A Pun . . . Than Never'
Mary is nearly fired from her job.
93. 'Ted Baxter Meets Walter Cronkite'
CBS news star meets WJM's news man.
94. 'Lou's Second Date'
Office gossip almost spoils Lou's dates with Rhoda.
95. 'Two Wrongs Don't Make A Writer'
Ted and Mary enter a writing class, and Ted cribs an assignment from Mary.
96. 'I Was Single For WJM'
Researching a story, Mary hangs out in a singles bar.
97. 'Will Mary Richards Go To Jail?'
Mary is locked up for refusing to reveal a news source.
98. 'Not Just Another Pretty Face'
Mary dates an All-American-Male type.
99. 'You Sometimes Hurt The One You Hate'
Lou Grant softens, becomes almost docile.
100. 'Lou And That Woman'
Lou goes crazy over a girl-about-town.
101. 'The Outsider'
The style of WJM's newcasts is changed by a young consultant.
102. 'What Are Friends For?'
Mary and Sue Ann go on a business trip to Chicago and Sue Ann finds herself sexually rejected.
103. 'A New Sue Ann'
An ambitious young thing is after Sue Ann's 'Happy Homemaker' job.
104. 'Not A Christmas Story'
Sue Ann invites the staff to an early Christmas dinner.
105. 'I Love A Piano'
Murray teeters on the edge of an affair.
106. 'A Boy's Best Friend'
Ted discovers his mother has a boyfriend.
107. 'Menage-À-Phyllis'
Phyllis starts seeing another man, but on a non-sexual basis.
108. 'A Son For Murray'
Murray and his wife decide to adopt a boy.
109. 'Neighbors'
Lou moves into Rhoda's vacant apartment, just upstairs from Mary.
110. 'A Girl Like Mary'
Lou wants to recruit a female newscaster – and Sue Ann gives a classic audition.
111. 'An Affair To Forget'
Ted informs everyone he's having an affair with Mary.
112. 'Mary Richards: Producer'
Mary produces the show, but with a problem attached to each problem.
113. 'The System'
Ted creates an absurd betting system that miraculously works.
114. 'Phyllis Whips Inflation'
Lars orders Phyllis to cut down on her spending.
115. 'The Shame Of The Cities'
Lou's documentary exposé plans backfire.
116. 'Marriage Minneapolis Style'
Ted proposes to Georgette, then tries to back out.

117. 'You Try To Be A Nice Guy'
Lou becomes nervous of making a speech.
118. 'You Can't Lose 'Em All'
Mary helps a prostitute to go straight.
119. 'Ted Baxter's Famous Broadcaster's School'
Ted becomes the victim of a scam.
120. 'Anybody Who Hates Kids And Dogs'
Mary gets to hate the child of a man she's going out with.
121. 'Edie Gets Married'
Lou is crushed when his ex-wife gets married, but nevertheless attends the wedding.
122. 'Mary Moves Out'
Mary becomes bored with her life and Ted advises her on how to change it.
123. 'Mary's Father'
Mary thinks that a priest may leave the church in his love for her.
124. 'Murray In Love'
Murray wants somehow to tell Mary he's in love with her.
125. 'Ted's Moment Of Glory'
Ted is nearly a network TV quiz-master.
126. 'Mary's Aunt'
Mary's famous journalist Aunt Flo pays a visit and has a fling with Lou.
127. 'Chuckles Bites The Dust'
The bizarre circumstances of the death of Chuckles the clown are laced with comedy and tragedy.
128. 'Mary's Delinquent'
Mary and Sue Ann become 'big sisters'.
129. 'Ted's Wedding'
Mary's apartment is the setting for Ted and Georgette's wedding.
130. 'Lou Douses An Old Flame'
Lou dumps a former love who dumped him during the war.
131. 'Mary Richards Falls In Love'
Mary is head-over-heels for a macho type who's playing the field.
132. 'Ted's Tax Refund'
Ted gets audited by the IRS.
133. 'The Happy Homemaker Takes Lou Home'
Sue Ann tricks Lou into coming over for dinner.
134. 'One Boyfriend Too Many'
Two eligible men bid for Mary's attention.
135. 'What Do You Want To Do When You Produce'
Murray becomes Sue Ann's producer and nearly gets skinned alive.
136. 'Not With My Wife I Don't'
Ted is faced with impotence.
137. 'The Seminar'
Mary and Lou in Washington DC, with a guest appearance by First Lady Betty Ford.
138. 'Once I Had A Secret Love'
Lou is finally trapped between Sue Ann's sheets, and he desperately tries to keep it quiet.
139. 'Menage À Lou'
One of Lou's old girlfriends makes him jealous.
140. 'Murray Takes A Stand'
Murray almost quits his job.
141. 'Mary's Aunt Returns'
Aunt Flo throws a challenge to Lou's journalistic know-how.
142. 'A Reliable Source'
Mary nearly quits over a matter of principle.
143. 'Sue Ann Falls In Love'
An opportunist has Sue Ann on a string.

144. 'Ted And The Kid'
Ted and Georgette decide to adopt.
145. 'Mary Midwife'
Georgette gives birth in Mary's apartment.
146. 'Mary, The Writer'
Mary fails badly at creative writing.
147. 'Sue Ann's Sister'
Sibling rivalry breaks out between Sue Ann and her sister.
148. 'What's Wrong With Swimming?'
Mary hires a female sportscaster who's all wet.
149. 'Ted's Change Of Heart'
Ted's personality is temporarily transformed following a mild heart attack.
150. 'One Producer Too Many'
Indecision rules as Mary and Murray co-produce the news.
151. 'My Son, The Genius'
Ted's adopted son turns out to be a mini Einstein.
152. 'Mary Gets A Lawyer'
Mary finds her lawyer more interested in her than in her case.
153. 'Mary's Insomnia'
Mary's forced to use sleeping pills.
154. 'Lou Proposes'
Lou hears wedding bells when he's with Mary's Aunt Flo.
155. 'Murray Can't Lose'
Murray is all set to win a Teddy Award.
156. 'Ted's Temptation'
A hot-to-trot Los Angeles reporter tries to jump Ted's bones.
157. 'Look At Us, We're Walking'
Mary and Lou make a stand for a pay increase.
158. 'The Critic'
The ultimate snob becomes house critic at the station.
159. 'Lou's Army Reunion'
An ex-army buddy of Lou's tries to reconnoitre Mary.
160. 'The Ted And Georgette Show'
Ted and Georgette are given the chance of a TV show.
161. 'Sue Ann Gets The Ax'
The Happy Homemaker's show gets cancelled.
162. 'Hail The Conquering Gordy'
Ted becomes jealous of station weatherman Gordy Howard's good fortune.
163. 'Mary And The Sexagenarian'
Without her knowing, Mary dates Murray's father.
164. 'Murray Ghosts For Ted'
Ted's 'article' is picked up by *Reader's Digest*, but everyone suspects the truth.
165. 'Mary's Three Husbands'
Murray, Lou and Ted each have their fantasies about being married to Mary.
166. 'Mary's Big Party'
Mary's throwing a party and Johnny Carson comes by – during a blackout.
167. 'Lou Dates Mary'
Lou and Mary wonder if friends can become lovers.
168. 'The Last Show'
Everyone is fired, except Ted Baxter. Phyllis and Rhoda show up to cheer Mary – and the entire show gives a final bow.

The Bob Newhart Show (CBS, 16/9/72 –26/8/78) Film. 30 mins.
Executive producers: David Davis, Lorenzo Music. *Producers*: Tom Patchett, Jay Tarses. *Creators*: David Davis, Lorenzo Music. *Music*: Pat Williams.

Cast: Bob Newhart *(Robert Hartley)*, Suzanne Pleshette *(Emily Hartley)*, Bill Daily *(Howard Borden)*, Peter Bonerz *(Jerry Robinson)*, Marcia Wallace *(Carol Kester Bondurant)*, Patricia Smith *(Margaret Hoover)*, Larry Gelman *(Dr Bernie Tupperman)*, Pat Finley *(Ellen Hartley)*, Will Mackenzie *(Larry Bondurant)*, Jack Riley *(Elliot Carlin)*, Florida Friebus *(Mrs Bakerman)*, Penny Marshall *(Miss Larson)*, Renee Lippin *(Michelle Nardo)*, John Fiedler *(Mr Peterson)*, Noam Pitlik *(Mr Gianelli)*, Lucien Scott *(Mr Vickers)*, Oliver Clark *(Mr Herd)*.

Robert Hartley is a Chicago psychologist, married to Emily, who is a school teacher. The stories move between Dr Hartley's home life and his office life. The Hartleys' neighbour is Howard Borden, a divorced airline navigator with a clumsy ability to intrude at any time. At the office there's Carol, the receptionist who can't help interfering in her boss' work, and Jerry, Bob's orthodontist friend, a bachelor in search of the perfect woman. In addition to his neurotic friends and family, Bob also has to cope with the problems of his real patients, the types of neuroses covered ranging from parent trouble and insecurity to fear of geese.

Bob Newhart's first TV series, also entitled *The Bob Newhart Show*, had been shortlived. It ran from October 1961 to June 1962 on the NBC network. It had, however, been a variety hour rather than a thirty-minute comedy series and this format had failed to display the comedian's talents to their best effect. When that show was cancelled Newhart went on to work in other variety shows, including *The Entertainers* and *The Tonight Show* before turning to feature films like *Catch 22, Hot Millions* and *Cold Turkey*. In 1971 Newhart had a starring role in *Thursday's Game*, a feature made by ABC Circle Films, directed by Robert Moore and scripted by James Brooks. The Brooks connection seems significant – as does the presence alongside Newhart in the cast of Cloris Leachman, Nancy Walker and Valerie Harper, all *Mary Tyler Moore Show* regulars. The film, however, was never released commercially and was eventually screened as an ABC Saturday Night Movie on 14 April 1974.

Around this time the part of a tax accountant was written into *The Mary Tyler Moore Show* for Newhart, but he was unavailable and instead Paul Sand got the part. But Newhart, like Mary Tyler Moore, had Arthur Price as his manager, and in 1972 he was finally – and this time successfully – brought back to television by David Davis and Lorenzo Music.

Newhart's career as a comic raconteur, his very persona as a performer in nightclubs, on the radio and record albums as well as in television variety and talk shows, was based on his role as a reactor. In sketches like 'The Driving Instructor' and the 'Tobacco/Sir Walter Raleigh' sketch he perfected the style which he was later to define as 'listening to people and having to be nice to them no matter what they do. The recurring theme is that the person, through no fault of his own, is put in the middle of a situation and forced to sort it out. There's a put-upon quality to him. Those stories have always worked the best for me.' (*New York Times*. 26/12/82)

Davis and Music came up with the concept for a series in which Newhart would play a practising psychologist – a 'situation' whose comedy could capitalise on Newhart's characteristic image as a deadpan, 'buttoned-down' reactor. The pilot episode even included one of Newhart's now classic phone monologues; one particular sketch in his days as a comic had been a transatlantic phone call from Sir Walter Raleigh in America to England trying to describe the wonders of tobacco smoking.

Davis and Music had been comedy writers for Glen Campbell and The Smothers Brothers and they had even supplied Newhart himself with successful material before. Music, for instance, was the author of Newhart's classic 'Flight Control Operator' monologue (interestingly, the *Bob Newhart Show* pilot also incorporated a series of flying jokes). Both of them, furthermore, were well aware of Newhart's preferred persona and the series format they created was made to measure. Says Music:

> He's a reactor. He listens funny. We made him a psychologist because he can bring the work home . . . It also supplies us with our basic joke – the psychologist who is a whiz at dealing with other people's frailties, foibles, hangups, but not so hot at dealing with his own. (*TV Guide*, 20/1/73, pp. 22–23)

Like *The Mary Tyler Moore Show*, *The Bob Newhart Show* could be called character comedy rather than sitcom. The series constructed two 'familiar' worlds in which Newhart could operate – the professional sphere, populated by neurotic patients and long-suffering staff, and the domestic sphere occupied by Newhart and his wife (played by Suzanne Pleshette) and their zany neighbours. According to the producers: 'We resisted the temptation to surround Bob with eccentrics. We favour the identifiable face. We're not trying to do Archie Bunker. We're selling class and charm and wit.' (*TV Guide*, op. cit.)

Like MTM's première programme, *The Bob Newhart Show* started slowly and *Variety*'s review of the pilot episode is characteristic: 'At present, series has likeable leads and occasional amusing moments, but not yet jelled into a genuinely funny sitcom.' (*Variety*, 20/9/72) By the end of its first season the series had improved dramatically; the cast had acted their way inside the roles and the two spheres of comic action (home and surgery) were intertwining well. But ironically, for all its successful six-year run, *The Bob Newhart Show* came to a voluntary end, but not before a new brand of prime-time comedy had begun to make major inroads on its popularity. The demographic shift 1969–70 which had elevated the 18–49 year-old urban (and often female) audience had been supplanted by another shift toward a still younger audience. The *New York Times* has described how in the final season of *The Bob Newhart Show* the scriptwriters came up with the idea of Emily becoming pregnant as if to open up new avenues of 'kidvid' humour for the series. Newhart was unenthusiastic:

> I called up the producer and asked him who he was going to get to play my part. When I left ... one of the reasons was that I saw shows coming out that seemed aimed at pre-teenagers. Even if we said, 'OK, let's sell out and give them that kind of stuff, if that's what they want' I'm not sure our writers would have known how to write it. I left partly out of frustration and partly because of internecine wars. (*New York Times*, 26/12/82)

The combination of the imposition of Family Hour – and hence *Newhart*'s earlier scheduling – and hectic counterprogramming from NBC convinced those creatively involved in the series that it should come to an end before either CBS or the audience completely lost interest in it. According to Newhart:

> We hadn't slipped in any way. The show was still funny, which is the time to get off. But I felt like a club fighter, the way the other networks threw everything at us. I was very proud of our show but chagrined that the show and the people on it were never truly acknowledged by the TV industry – not one Emmy. We had so many good people – Suzanne Pleshette, Billy Daily, Marcia Wallace, Peter Bonerz and the rest, and they all made it look too easy. (*New York Times*, op. cit.)

MTM could no longer sell 'class and charm and wit' in sitcom formats – *The Mary Tyler Moore Show* had come to an end the previous year and by the end of the last *Bob Newhart Show* season a new MTM drama series, *Lou Grant*, with a great deal of class, charm and wit of its own, was already making its impact on the Emmys. Being 'the number two gun in the MTM arsenal' didn't mean that *The Bob Newhart Show* lacked the calibre to earn itself a place in the awards but that *The Mary Tyler Moore Show* had already won them for MTM.

Rhoda (CBS, 9/9/74 – 9/12/78) Film. 30 mins.
Executive producers: James L. Brooks, Allan Burns. *Producers*: Lorenzo Music, David Davis, Charlotte Brown. *Executive story consultants*: Geoff Neigher, Chick Mitchell. *Created by* Burns and Brooks, *developed by* Davis and Music. *Music*: Billy Goldenberg.
Cast: Valerie Harper *(Rhoda Morgenstern Gerard)*, Julie Kavner *(Brenda Morgenstern)*, David Groh *(Joe Gerard)*, Nancy Walker *(Ida Morgenstern)*, Harold J. Gould *(Martin Morgenstern)*, Lorenzo Music *(voice of Carlton the Doorman)*, Cara Williams *(Mae)*, Candy Azzara *(Alice Barth)*, Todd Turquand *(Donny Gerard)*, Barbara Sharma *(Myrna Morgenstern)*, Scoey Mitchell *(Justin Culp)*, Ron Silver *(Gary Levy)*, Anne Meara *(Sally Gallagher)*, Michael Delano *(Johnny Venture)*, Ray Buktenica *(Benny Goodwin)*, Ken McMillan *(Jack Doyle)*,

Rafael Campos *(Ramon Diaz Jr)*, Nancy Lane *(Tina)*.

Rhoda returns to her New York roots and family (sister Brenda, mother Ida), meets and falls in love with Joe Gerard, marries him, they quarrel, separate, divorce and, finally, Rhoda is left once again to try and 'make it on her own'.

Variety raved about the first episode, describing it as 'an instant hit, a well-conceived, well-written and well-executed sitcom that was off and running like clockwork from the opening minute.' (*Variety*, 11/9/74) *Hollywood Reporter*, however, was far from enthusiastic, noting that it 'comes across like a bad copy of *That Girl*' (*Hollywood Reporter*, 9/9/74) – an ironic reference point since *The Mary Tyler Moore Show* was initially conceived in contrast to *That Girl*'s kookiness.

The decision to spin-off a series starring Valerie Harper had been made long before the 1974 season. According to then CBS chief Fred Silverman, 'I looked at her very first piece of film in the first show, way back in 1970. And from that moment we knew we were going to star her in her own series.' (quoted in Rick Mitz, *The Great TV Sitcom Book*, p. 35) Apparently there was serious talk about a *Rhoda* series in 1973 and since MTM producers had had a number of pilots turned down by CBS they went to ABC with the idea of a Rhoda spin-off. CBS learnt of the idea and offered an on-air commitment to *Rhoda*, which went out in 1974.

In the première episode of the series Rhoda returned to Manhattan on a brief trip away from (*The Mary Tyler Moore Show*'s) Minneapolis. At the airport Mary waved Rhoda goodbye while a fellow traveller and a customs official (played by MTM's Patchett and Tarses) hindered her exit. By the end of this first episode Rhoda had moved in with her sister and fallen in love with Joe, owner of a building demolition company.

On 28 October, after four years as a husband-hungry single woman on *The Mary Tyler Moore Show*, Rhoda was married in an hour-long special which featured the whole cast of the original show as wedding guests. The episode was the top-rated special of the television season and *Rhoda* stayed in the top ten for the next two years.

The idea for marrying off Rhoda had emerged shortly after the idea for the spin-off series had been agreed. According to Sally Bedell, '[Fred] Silverman met with Brooks, Burns and Tinker for lunch one day to discuss its direction. Brooks brought up the question of Rhoda's love life with Joe. "Let's get them married!" exclaimed Silverman, hoping to succeed where he had failed with Mary Tyler Moore.' (Sally Bedell, *Up The Tube*, p. 85)

Silverman's idea was to hype the event in the same fashion that the *I Love Lucy* series had done with the 'televised' birth of Desi Jr to Lucille Ball and Desi Arnaz, and which had won an incredible 71.7 ratings share for the network. *Rhoda* was already one of the top prime-time shows before the wedding special, which was watched by some 40 million viewers. By the end of the first season it was placed 6th in the top ten.

Later Silverman was to admit that marrying Rhoda and Joe was '. . . the worst programming idea ever. What made *Rhoda* work was that she was a highly neurotic single girl. The moment she fell in love and got married the whole series lost its bite. The source of all the comedy conflict in the show was gone. That stunt hurt the show.' (Bedell, p. 85)

In 1976 MTM tried to revive *Rhoda* by having her get a divorce. After all, this had been Brooks' and Burns' ambition for the premise of *The Mary Tyler Moore Show* itself. (Lou Grant also got divorced on *The Mary Tyler Moore Show*, as if to spite CBS for their resistance to casting Mary as a divorcee.) Commenting on the idea before the show was scripted Brooks added that, 'If we were able to treat a separation in a marriage realistically and find the humor in that, then we have done something pretty spectacular.' (Horace Newcomb and Robert S. Alley, *The Producer's Medium*, p. 215) The ploy failed, however. According to Tinker, 'The audience let us know they hated it. They didn't like the divorce. We got a lot of negative mail and the ratings dropped.' (Bedell, p. 86)

Perhaps Burns' theory of the longitude of 'well-populated' shows helps to explain the fact that *Rhoda* never quite rose to the heights expected of it. Certainly, according to Gitlin, 'Burns thinks . . . that Rhoda did not have enough noteworthy company.' (Todd Gitlin, *Inside Prime Time*, p. 214)

The decision to separate Rhoda and Joe was taken because of creative unease rather than audience dissatisfaction – the series was still in the top twenty prime-time programmes. One of *Rhoda*'s producer-writers, Charlotte Brown, decribed what happened:

> It began in the middle of last season. We all suddenly realised we were getting bored with our show. Maybe the audience wasn't bored – yet – but we figured that at some time in the future it was inevitable the way we were going. Everything was so nice for our Rhoda in her happily married life. She had no vulnerability; she wasn't the underdog any more. We kept ending up with plots that featured the funny insecurities of poor sister Brenda. It got so that we'd say 'When in doubt, go to Brenda.' It was scary. Sometimes we'd sit around for days, to think up a single story with some conflict that could focus on Rhoda. (*TV Guide,* 11/12/76, p. 25)

Another writer-producer, David Davis, agreed:

> The ratings didn't lull us, because we all had the same nagging doubt, which none of us wanted to express openly at first. Instead we had meeting after meeting to come up with something to spice up Rhoda's placid existence. We thought of having Joe lose his business and just hang around the house while Rhoda supported him. We had Rhoda go back to work, as she had in Minneapolis on *The Mary Tyler Moore Show*. For a few minutes, we even considered someone's suggestion that Rhoda get pregnant and have a multiple birth. None of this worked and we finally had to face up to the problem that maybe what we always thought was our biggest triumph actually was our biggest mistake. (*TV Guide,* 11/12/76, p. 25)

Brooks agreed that the decision to marry Rhoda off had been a short term triumph and a long term disaster: 'I guess we had the conceit that we could do a show about marriage that was different. We couldn't. We just succeeded in making Rhoda dull.' (*TV Guide,* op. cit.) The answer, one they resisted for some time, was separation and, ultimately, divorce:

> We thought about all this for maybe six months, and the answer came out of the questions we had posed to ourselves. In essence, who was the original Rhoda Morgenstern on *The Mary Tyler Moore Show*? She was insecure, self-effacing, struggling to cope with problems of still being single at 34, the daughter of a destructive and pesky mother. Then, on our show, this bundle of doubts marries a man who has been unsuccessfully married before. In real life, would such a marriage succeed? Probably not. Would a separation not be typical of what is happening to thousands of such impetuously married couples today? Definitely. Could the separation be used to generate wry laughs, if not the old joke-type laughs? We weren't sure. (Allan Burns talking in *TV Guide*, op. cit.)

Once agreed on this new direction, Brooks, Burns, Davis and Brown talked to Grant Tinker about it. Tinker took some convincing of the concept, largely because of his past difficulties with CBS over the proposal to make the original Mary Richards character a divorcee. The response of the critics was to denounce the new move as soap-opera (for instance, see *TV Guide,* 27/11/76, p. 36), which is ironic since the decision to reshape the show was based on a desire to reflate the comedic elements. The *TV Guide* article seems to assess that the executive decision to separate Rhoda and Joe was based on a desperate desire to increase ratings – an assumption that is insubstantiated by the actual ratings the series was still receiving at that time. Whatever the executive explanation for the fictional separation, the article points out that no credible crisis in the relationship motivated such a separation: 'In an early episode, when Rhoda went to Joe's office to try to lure him back, all she said was "We still have these basic problems that haven't been solved." What problems?' (*TV Guide* review, 27/11/76, p. 36)

The Texas Wheelers (ABC 13/9/74 – 24/7/75) Film. 30 mins.
Executive producer: Dale McRaven. *Producer*: Chris Hayward. *Director* [pilot]: James Frawley.
Creator: Dale McRaven. *Theme music composed and sung by* John Prine.
Cast: Jack Elam *(Zack Wheeler)*, Mark Hamill *(Doobie Wheeler)*, Gary Busey *(Truckie Wheeler)*, Karen Oberdiser *(Boo Wheeler)*, Tony Becker *(T. J. Wheeler)*, Lisa Eilbacher *(Sally)*.

A comedy series about the four motherless children of the Wheeler family in rural Texas and their 'no good' father.

> By all rights, MTM Enterprises should have yet another hit on its hands with *The Texas Wheelers*, a marvelously constructed piece of family comedy-drama featuring the long underrated Jack Elam as clan head Zack Wheeler and the sensitive, intelligent acting of Gary Busey as his oldest son, Truckie.
>
> The series opener is concerned with Truckie's attempts to keep the family together in the wake of his mother's death and the absence of father Zack, who deserted the family several months before. The sudden return of Zack produces initial problems, but later resolves a conflict between Truckie and younger brother Doobie – Mark Hamill – who wants to leave school.
>
> However, the decision to use John Prine's 'Illegal Smile', a song about smoking marijuana, as the show's theme tune is a strange one. (*Hollywood Reporter*, 13/9/74)

In the autumn of 1974 Richard Wiley, the FCC chairman, arranged a meeting with executives from ABC, NBC and CBS, and urged a reduction in levels of sex and violence on the networks. Arguing that he himself was acting under pressure from Congress Wiley secured a promise from CBS president Arthur Taylor to refrain from scheduling anything which could be decreed 'inappropriate for general family viewing' (Sally Bedell, *Up the Tube* p. 101) before 9.00pm.

NBC and ABC followed suit and the National Association of Broadcasters ratified the proposal as 'Family Viewing Hour'. It was ABC, however, which took these new restrictions most to heart. According to Sally Bedell, while CBS had only really agreed to eliminate excessive, explicit violence from prime-time's first hour ABC were inclined to stretch the definition of 'Family Viewing' so as to be able to exclude the topical permissiveness of the sort of sitcom that was CBS' stock-in-trade:

> When CBS censor Thomas Swafford met in January 1975 with ABC's censor Alfred Schneider, to concoct the policy, Schneider said, 'What the hell is CBS going to do about *All In The Family*?' By including such shows as *All In The Family* and *M*A*S*H* in the Family Viewing definition, ABC sought to eliminate any ratings advantage CBS might derive from the policy. It was a canny ploy that many believe forced CBS to transfer *All In The Family* from its powerhouse position at the head of Saturday night to 9.00 on Mondays . . . The primary victims of the Family Viewing policy were the adult comedies still scheduled before 9.00 . . . (Bedell, p. 101)

At that time MTM was associated almost exclusively with CBS. But ABC's strategy was to create casualties on its own schedule too. One such was MTM's *The Texas Wheelers*. Indeed, it's ironic that *All In The Family* was one source of that series' conception. The *Los Angeles Herald-Examiner* described the series as 'having an aspect of *All In The Family* in the occasional sardonic touches', and the series' star Jack Elam was quoted as saying 'I've got a little bit of Bunker in me. But I'm not a bigot – I'm just a poor slob. I'd be a bigot if I was smart enough.' (*Los Angeles Herald-Examiner*, 13/8/74)

Both *Variety* and *Hollywood Reporter* reviewed the series very positively – in fact the former was positively effusive:

> MTM Enterprises looks as if it has another hit on its hands. The company responsible for *The Mary Tyler Moore Show* (CBS) of long-standing and the new and highly lauded *Rhoda* (CBS) has contributed *The Texas Wheelers* to ABC-TV and it may be the best of the lot – if not

the best sitcom ever to hit the homescreen. (*Variety*, 18/9/74)

Indeed, *Variety*'s enthusiasm for the series led it to suggest that it should have been scheduled earlier in the evening: 'ABC may have made a mistake in slotting this at 9.30pm on Friday. It would seem that they have as good a shot with this to beat *Sanford And Son* as they will ever have.' (*Variety*, op. cit.)

But *Sanford And Son*, another family comedy, went out at 8.00pm, while *Variety*'s own synopsis of *The Texas Wheelers* reveals why the series may have seemed inappropriate for general family viewing in the atmosphere of that season:

> Imagine, if you will, a hero who is a runaway father, a liar, a drunk and a loafer. And his son – for all the manly qualities displayed in keeping his three younger siblings together – is a convicted car thief, a reformed barroom brawler and a high-school dropout. The 16-year-old brother can hardly wait to become a regular drinker and leave school himself and even the two children showed signs in the first episode of having unplumbed streaks of rottenness to go along with their kid sweetness. This series, if it lives up to the first show, may be the closest TV sitcom has come to reality . . .

That very 'realism' was probably responsible for its exclusion from Family Viewing Hour and, consequently, from the family viewers that might have guaranteed it enough ratings to evade cancellation. The series was taken off the air in October and revamped for the following summer but ran only from June to July 1975, albeit in an earlier 8.30–9.00 slot.

Paul Sand In Friends And Lovers (CBS, 14/9/74 – 4/1/75) Film. 30 mins.
Executive producers: James L. Brooks, Allan Burns. *Producer*: Steve Pritzer. *Associate producer*: Michael Zinberg. *Photography*: Bill Cline. *Music*: Pat Williams. *Art director*: Lew Hurst. *Filmed at CBS Studio Center, Studio City, California.*
Cast: Paul Sand *(Robert Dreyfuss)*, Michael Pataki *(Charlie Dreyfuss)*, Penny Marshall *(Janice Dreyfuss)*, Dick Wesson *(Jack Riordan)*, Steve Landesberg *(Fred Meyerbach)*, Craig Richard Nelson *(Mason Woodruff)*, Jack Gilford *(Ben Dreyfuss)*.

Paul Sand stars as Robert Dreyfuss, a bass violinist with the Boston Symphony Orchestra. His life as a bachelor and his problems with an over-protective brother and sister-in-law provide the humour for the series. The character of Robert is a shy and sensitive fellow, and Sand makes the most of his funny, foot-in-mouth uncertainties.

This was to be the last sitcom Brooks and Burns were to create together, for MTM or indeed any other company. (Their next and last collaboration was for the sixty-minute drama series *Lou Grant*.) James Brooks has commented that 'Excellence is extraordinarily difficult to achieve and sometimes you achieve it only by accident.' *(TV Guide*, 23/9/78, p. 29) Danny Thomas, producer-writer of *Barney Miller*, a non-MTM series, has noted:

> You do a show like *M*A*S*H* or *The Mary Tyler Moore Show* or *Barney Miller* and you pour your energy into it. It doesn't necessarily follow that everything else you do will be good or will have that same inspiration. Just because Allan Burns and Jim Brooks did a great job on *The Mary Tyler Moore Show* doesn't mean they can do four other shows too. You spread yourself too thin. . . . But you can't tell a company with a huge success . . . 'No, that's all you can do. You can't mass produce. You can't make more money.' So they make more shows and they're just not as good as the original. *(TV Guide*, 23/9/78)

Paul Sand had played an IRS man in *The Mary Tyler Moore Show* and the company were keen to star him in a series of his own. Brooks himself, when asked why *Paul Sand* failed, provides an interesting explanation of how in the very process of producing something for American television the original concept and motivation can get lost but the momentum prevents recognition of that loss:

> I think what happened to that show was just about totally my fault. We had a good cast and we had a terrific pilot. We'd done brilliant post-production where we worked so intensely I had an experience I'd never had before. I was in the editing room, and an editor literally collapsed. They took him away, and a new editor replaced him, and I didn't notice until about a half hour later. But for some stupid reason which I'll never understand, I changed the thing about the show that I always wanted to do. It was built on the premise that 'lovers come and go but friends go on forever'. We had a man having a girlfriend, where it's a sexually viable relationship and every once in a while they fool with it, but basically they're each other's best friend. And then the girl who was supposed to be the best friend, we took out the part. We didn't think it was working, but instead of fixing it, we just walked away from it. Just stupid, just wrong. (Brooks interviewed by Kenneth Turan, *Film Comment*, April 1984, pp. 19–20)

The show was received very favourably at first. *Hollywood Reporter*, for instance, enthused that 'The best new show on CBS this fall by far is MTM Enterprises' *Paul Sand In Friends And Lovers*. Of all the new people in the CBS shows, Sand would seem to have the most potential of becoming a television staple.' *Hollywood Reporter*, 13/9/74) When it became clear that it wasn't working out producer Steve Pritzer and story editors Monica and Andrew Johnson were joined by Elias Davis, David Pollock and Bob Claver. *Hollywood Reporter* quoted an unnamed CBS executive:

> The first three shows shot were not what we had in mind. However, the last two they have done have come together and we are now happy with what they are doing, and I think they are finally on the right track. We won't air the first three episodes they shot until much later in the season. Paul Sand is a great talent but he's very special and it takes time to make a vehicle for him work. *(Hollywood Reporter*, 9/9/74)

Doc (CBS, 16/8/75 – 30/10/76) Tape. 30 mins.
Executive producers: Ed Weinberger, Stan Daniels. *Producers*: Norman Barasch, Carroll Moore. *Created by* Ed Weinberger, Stan Daniels, *developed by* David Lloyd. *Associate producer*: Bill Schwartz. *Story consultant*: Roy Kammerman.
Cast: Barnard Hughes *('Doc' Joe Bogert)*, Elizabeth Wilson *(Annie Bogert)*, Mary Wickes *(Miss Tully)*, Irwin Corey *('Happy' Miller)*, Judy Kahan *(Laurie Bogert Fenner)*, John Harkins *(Fred Fenner)*, Herbie Fay *(Ben Goldman)*, Audra Lindley *(Janet Scott)*, David Ogden Stiers *(Stanley Moss)*, Ray Vitte *(Woody Henderson)*, Lisa Mordente *(Teresa Ortega)*.

A comedy about 'Doc' Joe Bogert, a general family practitioner who treats symptoms with a larger dose of concern and understanding than pills. His practice, set in an old New York brown-stone, revolves around his relationships with his patients and his large Catholic family consisting of a multitude of grandchildren whose identities he can never keep straight.

Barnard Hughes had previously played a memorably crusty doctor in the medical black comedy *Hospital* and had been a familiar face on CBS' *All In The Family* (as a Polish priest) and *The Bob Newhart Show* (as Newhart's father). Indeed the original concept of *Doc* drew on this familiarity by combining elements of these personae and situations. Thus 'Doc' Joe Bogert was saddled with a son-in-law he disliked (like Archie Bunker's Mike 'Meathead' Stivic) and a waiting room full of weird and troublesome patients (like Bob Newhart's). Indeed, he was signed to do the pilot for the series before it was even written and, at the time, all that executive producer Weinberger had was the concept of a Manhattan GP, 'a decent man with decent instincts and a nice cut to his tongue'. *(TV Guide*, 16/10/76)

The plot established Doc as having a wife who is much tougher with his patients than he is and a son who is a pest. As a summer replacement series – replacing the cancelled *Paul Sand In Friends And Lovers* – *Doc* was no more successful than its predecessor. Before its second season the show was given a major overhaul, shedding the cosy format of the family and friends and relocating him out of Manhattan and into a private clinic. None of these changes, however, prevented the series being cancelled two months later.

Phyllis (CBS, 8/9/75 – 30/8/77) Film. 30 mins.
Executive producers: Ed Weinberger, Stan Daniels. *Producer*: Michael Leeson. *Created by* Ed Weinberger, Stan Daniels, *based on a character created by* James L. Brooks and Allan Burns. *Title song by* Stan Daniels.
Cast: Cloris Leachman *(Phyllis Lindstrom)*, Lisa Gerritsen *(Bess Lindstrom)*, Liz Torres *(Julie Erskine)*, Richard Schaal *(Leo Heatherton)*, Jane Rose *(Audrey Dexter)*, Henry Jones *(Judge Jonathan Dexter)*, Judith Lowery *(Mother Dexter)*, John Lawlor *(Leonard Marsh)*, Garn Stephens *(Harriet Hastings)*, Carmini Caridi *(Dan Valenti)*, Burt Mustin *(Arthur Lanson)*, Craig Wasson *(Mark Valenti)*; Barbara Colby, originally cast as Julie Erskine, died after completing the first three episodes and Liz Torres assumed the role from early October 1975.

Phyllis features Cloris Leachman as (the now) widowed Phyllis Lindstrom, the role she created on *The Mary Tyler Moore Show*, who moves to San Francisco with her daughter Bess, to her mother-in-law's home to make a new life for herself. In a short time, Phyllis is settled in her new home and after a series of discouraging attempts to get a job she becomes a 'gofer' at a photography studio.

If *Rhoda* was an almost ideal spin-off character, combining familiarity with amiability, *Phyllis* was far less successful. Starting off with optimistic observations from *Variety* ('If the CBS Monday schedule in general does as well as anticipated, *Phyllis* could be the top-rated new show and give MTM another big winner'; 10/9/75) and *Hollywood Reporter* ('Well, it looks like those people at Mary Tyler Moore Enterprises have hit upon another winner in their second new series of the season, *Phyllis*'; 8/9/75), after two seasons the series was cancelled. Sally Bedell describes why the series failed:

> Despite endless tinkering with her personality, Phyllis as a solo act failed to captivate the audience. She had been an effective supporting player on *The Mary Tyler Moore Show* because her producers had used her sparingly. Like a dash of Tabasco sauce. Once removed from the buffering characters surrounding her she seemed stark and shrill. The producers tried to soften her and to make her more sympathetic, but they only succeeded in blurring her image even more. *(Up The Tube*, p. 86)

But the blurring was also the result of increasing CBS censorship. On *The Mary Tyler Moore Show* Phyllis' outspokeness had been 'balanced' by Mary's 'common sense'. In her own show, and in the worsening network atmosphere of mid-70s censorship with the imposition of the Family Viewing Policy, that outspokenness suffered. As Bedell says, 'The primary victims of the Family Viewing Policy were the adult comedies still scheduled before 9.00 . . . Pressure from CBS censors . . . dulled the topicality of the MTM spin-off *Phyllis*.' (Bedell, p. 101–102)

Ed Weinberger goes further into how this new network censorship effected *Phyllis*:

> I'm used to dealing with the network programme practices people. They've been friends all these years. Reasonable. Honest. On questionable times in a script, it's been give-and-take. What's best for the show is best for CBS and vice versa. Now, suddenly, day into night. Phyllis has an important line, paying off a story she has told: 'Of course, they were gay.' That line has to come out, the network guy says. Offensive. 'But don't you agree the line's proper in its context?' Oh yes, he agreed . . .
>
> What would not be offensive, he had been authorised to say, would be a hand gesture that implied the word gay . . . The last three lines of the script also had to be cut. In the story, which is about mother-daughter communication, Phyllis insists that her 17-year-old, Bess, has spent the night in a ski lodge in the same room with a young man. Phyllis and Bess disappear into the girls' room for an old heart to heart. We go to commercial. Then, in the 'tag,' the final scene, Phyllis emerges, leans over and whispers to her mother-in-law: 'Nothing happened.' Freeze-frame. Then we are in freeze-frame and Phyllis adds: 'Unless she lied . . .' Those little words, a simple, wry comment about

mother-daughter communicating, were deemed a peril to the minds of young America. *(TV Guide, 2/8/75, pp. A1–A2)*

Three For The Road (CBS, 1975) Film. 60 mins.
Executive producer: Jerry McNeely. *Producer*: William F. Phillips. *Creator*: Jerry McNeely. *Photography*: Richard Rawlings. *Music*: David Shire, James Di Pasquale. *Editor*: Michael Brown.
Regular cast: Alex Rocco *(Pete Karras)*, Vincent Van Patten *(John Karras)*, Leif Garrett *(Endy Karras)*.

A drama series revolving around the assignments of photo-journalist Pete Karras as he travels around the United States in a custom motor home with his two sons, John and Endy.

'Fear'
Writers: Dick Bensfield, Perry Grant. *Director*: Barry Crane. *Guest cast*: Kathleen Cody, James Van Patten, Christopher Stone.
Despite his deep-rooted fear, John goes along with Pete and Endy in taking flight instructions from a hang-gliding pilot. Unexpectedly, John likes the beginner's lessons. However, he doesn't realise that the advanced stages of the sport entail flying off 200-foot cliffs.
'Match Point'
Writer: Jerry McNeely. *Director*: Bernard McEveety. *Guest cast*: Gary Lockwood, Jane Alice Brandon, Tim Matheson.
While his father is shooting a photo layout for a sports magazine, John almost defeats tennis star Tom Aberling (Matheson) in a pick-up match, but Tom's father feels the nonchalant game could ruin his son's reputation.
'The Ghost Story'
Writer: William Kelley. *Story by* Nina Laemmle and William Kelley. *Director*: Barry Crane. *Guest cast*: Stephanie Powers, Arlene Anderson, Alex Henteloff, Judy Lewis.
While covering an exhibit featuring the works of a deceased young artist, Pete receives a bizarre request from her twin sister, who wants a photograph of the artist's ghost, which is reportedly haunting the family estate.
'Ride On A Red Balloon'
Writer: Jerry McNeely. *Director*: Claudio Guzman. *Guest cast*: Larry Hagman, Anne Lockhart, James Gavin.
A drinking problem prevents Pete's long-time friend, a hot air balloon pilot, from assisting with an advertising photo layout Pete is doing for a soft drink company.
'The Fugitives'
Writers: Del Reisman, Perry Grant, Dick Bensfield. *Director*: Bernard McEveety. *Guest cast*: Bradford Dillman, Tracie Savage, Martin West, Med Flory, Phyllis Claire.
The father of a young girl is being stalked by a mysterious man with a gun.
'The Cave'
Writer: Jack Turley. *Director*: Barry Crane. *Guest cast*: Clu Gulager, Clint Ritchie, Hal Bokar, Wyatt Johnson.
Peter's wartime buddy Dan Marshall (Gulager) undertakes daring exploits in a huge, dark and treacherous cave, with an admiring John Karras following close behind him.
'The Ripoff'
Writers: Arnold and Lois Peyser. *Director*: Claudio Guzman. *Guest cast*: Kathleen Quinlan, Brendan Burns, Martin Kove, Noble Willingham, Kenneth E. Hansen, Lloyd A. Gash.
A young girl hitchhiker creates a nightmare for Pete Karras and his sons when she and her boyfriend execute a plot to steal the Karras' motor home.
'Prisoner In Sneakers'
Writer: Jack Miller. *Director*: Ralph Senensky. *Guest cast*: Michael Le Claire, James Antonio, Anne Convy, Nicholas Beauvy, Jack Stauffer, Tierre Turner.
A friendship develops between Endy Karras and a bitter, street-wise youth in a detention home.

'Trail Of Bigfoot'
Writer: Michael Kozoll. *Director*: Claudio Guzman. *Guest cast*: Dean Stockwell, Anne Schedeen, Woodrow Chambliss, Steven Liss, Parley Baer, James Ray, Eldon Quick.
One of man's most puzzling mysteries is the subject of Pete's photo assignment when he sets out to find the elusive Bigfoot.
'The Albatross'
Writer: not available. *Director*: not available. *Guest cast*: Meg Foster, Kristopher Marquis, Brian Cutler, Kathleen O'Mall, Pitt Herbert, Albert Reed, Don "Red" Bealle, Michael Link.
Pete Karras and his sons stop to help a young mother whose car has broken down, but find themselves giving Patti Hardy (Foster) and her son more than just a lift to the next city.
'Adventure In Los Angeles'
Writer: Dick Nelson. *Director*: Herschel Daugherty. *Guest cast*: Beth Brickell, Giorgio Tozzi, Elyssa Davalos, Charles Frank, Nate Esformes, John Medici, John Goff, Eleni Kiamos, Frank Leo.
Pete Karras has been assigned to photograph the daughter of an international shipping magnate while she is visiting Los Angeles, but he arrives to find that threats have been made on the young girl's life and that the job has been given to someone else.
'Odyssey In Jeans'
Writer: Michael Kozoll. *Director*: Lou Antonio. *Guest cast*: Jane Actman, Harry Gold, Tom Wheatley, Dean Smith, J. Jay Saunders, Charles Wagenheim, Paul Linke, Mel Gallagher, Robyn Lundin, Janis Carroll, Lew Palter, Cissy Wellman.
Peter Karras, working on a photo assignment at a guest ranch, falls from a horse and is rushed to the hospital, leaving John the difficult task of dealing with young Endy's fright and confusion.

Three For The Road was MTM's first sixty-minute drama series, as well as being their first ninety-minute pilot. Long-time TV scriptwriter Jerry McNeely *(Dr Kildare, Slattery's People, The Eleventh Hour*, etc.), the series' writer-producer, describes the show's genesis:

> Grant Tinker invited me to do the pilot for *Three For The Road* for MTM and for CBS. We talked to Fred Silverman at CBS – they were looking for a show for early Sunday evening (this was before *60 Minutes* was in place in the Sunday schedules). They wanted a family show – something that would give a canvas for some action/adventure but not about crime and I came up with the premise of a widowed photographer who in order to do his work has to go all over the world, to go where his subjects are. Boris Sagal directed the pilot which went out as the opening show of the series. The series never made it – we made 13 episodes but episode 13 was never aired. This was my introduction to MTM and I stayed there for about 6 years. (Interview with the authors, 1983)

Variety's review noted the series' accommodations to the recently imposed Family Hour and to the network's shortlived concern about crime-based series. Indeed, pointing to the surprising casting of Alex Rocco as the photographer/ father rather than in his more familiar role as hood/heavy, *Variety* added:

> When the series hits its regular spot [the pilot went out on a Thursday, 8.30 – 10.00, the series itself on Sundays, 7.00 – 8.00], Rocco's warmth figures to increase in line with the supposed audience. And the violence in this pilot, which played at 9.30pm, will be toned down. Theme of the series is not dissimilar to *The Fugitive, Run For Your Life* or *Then Came Bronson*, in that it provides the central character with an excuse (if not a reason) for wandering all over the country in search of stories that fit his needs as a freelance photographer. Only difference is those two kids, and Vincent Van Patten and Leif Garrett appear capable of taking the attention of youngsters in the weekly audience, while Rocco should satisfy as a strong father image for their elders. *(Variety*, 10/9/75)

Ironically, having been so clearly and perhaps even cynically prepared for Family Hour,

Three For The Road suffered from the shrinking of prime-time. *Variety* noted '"The MTM Road" hour leading off the CBS Sunday night schedule short-changed on clearances as affiliates stayed with news shows'. *(Variety*, 24/9/75) CBS, by trying to beat their competitors by starting prime-time earlier, simply failed to attract enough affiliated stations to gather audiences. The series was cancelled after only ten weeks.

The Bob Crane Show (aka **Second Start**) (NBC, 6/3/75–19/6/75) Film. 30 mins.
Writer-producers: Norman S. Powell, Martin Cohan.
Cast: Bob Crane *(Bob Wilcox)*, Trisha Hart *(Ellie Wilcox)*, Todd Susman *(Marvin)*, Jack Fletcher *(Dean Lyle Ingersoll)*, Ronny Graham *(the landlord, Mr Busso)*.

Second Start featured Bob Crane as an insurance man who decides to become a doctor in middle life. Crane had played a doctor before – as Dr Dave Kelsey in *The Donna Reed Show* – but was probably best remembered for his Col. Hogan role in the long-running *Hogan's Heroes*. He had worked with Mary Tyler Moore a number of times on *The Dick Van Dyke Show* and hopes were high for the new series. Furthermore, the series' format was adventurous since it implied that the protagonist would become financially dependent on his working wife. The series tried, in sitcom style, to dramatise the stresses this involved and, in one particular episode, when Bob's wife won a business award, he refused to attend the ceremony and moved out of the house and into a college dormitory.

The Lorenzo And Henrietta Music Show (Syndicated, 13/9/76 – 15/10/76) 60 mins.
Executive producers: Lorenzo Music, Lewis Arquette. *Producer*: Albert J. Simon. *Director*: Bob Lally. *Writers*: Lorenzo Music, John Gibbons, Sandy Helberg, Richard Philip Lewis, Ira Miller, Dennis Reagan, Lewis Arquette. *Orchestra*: Jack Eskew. *Hosts*: Lorenzo Music, Henrietta Music. *Regulars*: Samantha Harper, Dave Willock, Bob Gibson, Erick Darling, Bella Bruck, Sandy Helberg, Murphy Dunne.

This short-run series was spun off from the unsuccessful pilot *The New Lorenzo Music Show*. Rejected by the networks, MTM produced this series directly for syndicated local stations to which it was distributed by Metromedia Producers Corporation.

'The format is obviously aimed at establishing an "old shoe" low-key type of diversion,' reported *Variety* of the première episode, 'with the Musics not taking themselves too seriously as Lorenzo bumbles about as the well-intentioned klutz-in-charge (who is never quite on top of anything).' The review went on to consider that it was 'an amusing concept for a musical-variety skein', taking in the show's relaxed attitude. The final 30 minutes were taken up with an interview with Mary Tyler Moore, but what this actually contained or dealt with was not discussed by *Variety*:

> What is appealing about the concept is the easy familiarity with the viewer that the Musics generate by approach and manner, plus Lorenzo's droll wit – which is doubly effective because of his bumbler's stance. It's the kind of thing that could grow on an audience if it sticks with them on a regular basis. But there's enough promise to suggest that the series may make it in a moderate way, primarily due to the likeableness of the Musics' personalities and approach. *(Variety*, 15/9/76)

Whether any more durable relationship with Metromedia resulted from this series is unknown. Certainly it was Viacom which had the syndication rights to *The Mary Tyler Moore Show* and *The Bob Newhart Show* – both of which went into local station reruns in the next two years. But Metromedia did provide the studios for the videotaping of MTM's Project Peacock special *How To Eat Like A Child* in 1981.

The Tony Randall Show (ABC, 23/9/76 – March/77; CBS, September/77 – 25/3/78) Film. 30 mins.
Producer-writers: Tom Patchett and Jay Tarses.
Cast: Tony Randall *(Judge Walter Franklin)*, Barney Martin *(Jack Terwilliger)*, Allyn Ann

McLerie *(Miss Reubner)*, Rachel Roberts *(Mrs Bonnie McClellan)*, Devon Scott *(Bobby Franklin,* 1976–7*)*, Penny Payser *(Bobby Franklin* 1977–8*)*, Brad Savage *(Oliver Wendell Franklin)*, Diana Muldaur *(Judge Eleanor Hooper)*.

A comedy series about the lives of a widowed court-room judge and his children.

The Tony Randall Show was created by Patchett-Tarses, the fourth pair of writer-producers to graduate from *The Mary Tyler Moore Show* and create a series of their own.

> Thursday nights on network prime-time complete the Fred Silverman circle. It was Silverman who reduced CBS' heavy load of situation comedies by way of such family situation drama as *The Waltons* and *The Jeffersons*. Now, CBS has thrown its high-rated *The Waltons* against ABC's high-rated early evening sitcoms – *Welcome Back, Kotter* and *Barney Miller*. Silverman has responded by adding more sitcoms – *Tony Randall* and *Nancy Walker* – and if he has any revenge in his heart he may well have the satisfaction of seeing *The Waltons* go down the tubes with the rest of the CBS schedule on Thursdays. The pop-sociology opinion that the country is back in the couldn't-care-less mood of the '50s looks truer all the time.
>
> The show is populated with wise-acres who converse in wisecracks, and nobody is better at it than Randall. At home, the judge talks to his housekeeper (the capable Rachel Roberts) and his children (Devon Scott, Brad Savage) in a series of one-liners. He is dominated by the housekeeper at home and by his secretary (Allyn Ann McLerie) in his chambers. Between the distantly maternal housekeeper and the shrewish secretary, women are not well-considered on the show. The programme is likely to carry its time period and could be an important factor in throwing the entire evening ABC's way. (*Variety*, 29/9/76)

There are divergent explanations for the series' failure to find an audience. Co-producer Hugh Wilson attributes it to poor scheduling: 'Tony was an upper-middle-class white judge and they put it on after a black show like *The Jeffersons*. That's borderline insanity.' *(TV Guide* 30/9/78, p. 36) Grant Tinker, on the other hand, is less willing to lay all the blame on the network: 'If people wanted to see *Tony Randall* bad enough, they'd watch it no matter when it was on. We just made some mistakes. We probably should've stayed in the court room more and not gone home with him so much. That deflated the show, slowed it down.' *(TV Guide,* op. cit.)

But as *TV Guide* pointed out, MTM's success had been based on the successful formula of combining work-based and home-based ensemble comedy and Patchett and Tarses were reluctant to risk flouting that receipe for success – it seemed almost an obligatory component of MTM's house style. Eventually, as ratings began to fall, the networks began to apply pressure. Jay Tarses recalls:

> They wanted us to get Tony Randall involved with a ten-year-old girl and a couple of sweathogs. We did what we thought was workable: we had Tony teach a night-school class to get him out of the house and the court-room and involved with young people. We shouldn't have done it. We shouldn't have compromised. You lose whatever integrity you have when you start doing that and it didn't help the show anyway. *(TV Guide,* 20/9/78, p. 36)

Like his predecessor protagonists in MTM's series, Randall's Judge Walter Franklin is acted upon rather than being an activator. Indeed the role of judge – like that of Newhart's psychiatrist – ensures the reactive persona. He is a put-upon character, constantly beleaguered by defendants, by his children, his secretary, his housekeeper. In a combination of ABC's Family Hour format, MTM's demographic targetting and the company's traditional 'topicality' the series focuses on four members of the Franklins – Walter himself, his eccentric father, his liberal 18-year-old daughter Bobby and his precocious 11-year-old son Oliver. But the network's uncertainty over its target audience resulted in its being shifted in the schedule, from Thursday 9.00 – 9.30 on its launch in

September to Thursday 9.30 – 10.00 from December to March. Then, at the end of the 1976–7 season, it was cancelled by ABC and taken up by CBS, MTM's traditional network.

CBS ran the series on Saturdays, first at 9.30 – 10.00 and then, in January of 1978, at 8.30 – 9.00. MTM's relationship with ABC had never been a good or fruitful one (witness *The Texas Wheelers'* failure in 1974). According to Robert Sklar, ABC had options on three MTM series for the 1977–8 season but rejected all of them. *The Tony Randall Show* was snapped up by CBS, but two MTM pilots – *Bumpers* and *The Chopped Liver Brothers* – were not considered worth developing into series. And since pilots are produced under contract to a particular network they could not be put up for consideration to CBS or NBC.

The Betty White Show (CBS, 12/9/77 – 9/1/78) Tape. 30 mins.
Executive producer: Bob Ellison. *Co-producers*: Dale McRaven, Charles Raymond. [Première episode credits read: *Executive producers*: Ed Weinberger, Stan Daniels. *Producer*: Bob Ellison.] *Executive story consultant*: David Lloyd. *Story editor*: Sheldon Bull. *Music*: Dick De Benedictis.
Cast: Betty White *(Joyce Whitman)*, John Hillerman *(John Elliot)*, Georgia Engel *(Mitzi Maloney)*, Charles Cyphers *(Hugo)*, Alex Henteloff *(Doug Porterfield)*, Caren Kaye *(Tracy Garrett)*, Barney Phillips *(Fletcher Huff)*.

Betty White stars as a witty and outspoken veteran movie actress who finds a new career in television starring in a CBS series called 'Undercover Woman'. She also finds the renewal of a love-hate relationship with her former husband, John Elliot, who is hired to direct her series. Joyce's friend and room-mate, Mitzi, is flighty but has the talent to calm Joyce in her more turbulent moments; also on the scene are an assortment of off-beat characters who work on 'Undercover Woman'.

MTM assigned its elder statesmen, writer-producers Ed Weinberger and Stan Daniels, who had been responsible for *Doc* and *Phyllis*. Ed Weinberger takes up the story:

> The first thing we considered, of course, was to transfer Sue Ann, the Happy Homemaker, to some suitable environment and simply let her career along her woman-hating, man-hungry, acerbic course. But we had tried something like that with Cloris Leachman in *Phyllis* and it was becoming more and more apparent in the ratings that it hadn't been our most brilliant decision. Besides, as Betty astutely added, 'The only reason the character of Sue Ann worked at all was that sweet Mary tolerated her and so the audience also tolerated her. Without Mary she would quickly get swamped in her own vinegar and become thoroughly unpleasant.' *(TV Guide*, 24/9/77, pp. 23–4)

The Sue Ann Nivens/Happy Homemaker role didn't seem suitable. (Indeed it may only have come about in *The Mary Tyler Moore Show* itself because Moore's first TV role herself had been as an advertising model for the Happy Hotpoint commercial, a role that had clearly concealed a good deal of frustration and resentment. Brooks and Burns may have fashioned a role for Betty White out of Mary's memories of that role/actress distinction.) And so, having rejected the idea of the continuation of the Sue Ann role, Weinberger and Daniels themselves tried the same 'biographical' approach:

> Then, digging for something in Betty's own background, we hit on the idea of a woman working in the chaos of a summer stock company. We liked the play-within-a-play idea – a bunch of wild people trying to put on a new stage production every week – but it would require too big a cast and would become unwieldly. (*TV Guide*, op. cit.)

From there Weinberger and Daniels came up with the idea of a show about a sitcom star but quickly realised that, 'We'd end up having to write two funny shows for every episode – one about Betty and the people backstage and the other about what they're doing on the air.' So they dropped the show-within-a-show idea and the next concept involved Betty and the ex-*Mary Tyler Moore Show* actress Georgia Engel as nuns teaching in a Catholic school run by a priest played by John Hillerman who, along with Engel, had been signed

The Betty White Show (l. to r.): John Hillerman, Betty White, Georgia Engel

up by MTM to co-star in whatever format emerged for Betty White's show. The nuns idea didn't work out, however, and eventually Weinberger and Daniels returned to the idea of a show-within-a-TV-show. Betty White herself suggested the idea of behind-the-scenes of a science fiction series but that, in Daniels' words, was 'too expensive, too many special effects.' (*TV Guide*, op. cit.) From that point, however, it didn't take long before the idea for a crime show format was agreed. After all, while the 1975–6 season ratings had boosted two MTM series, *Rhoda* and *Phyllis*, in the top ten by the end of the 1976–7 season, they had been squeezed out by two new ABC entries, *Charlie's Angels* and *Baretta*. In the 1977–8 lineup *Rhoda* was running opposite *Six Million Dollar Man, The Tony Randall Show* was scheduled against *Starsky and Hutch*, and the new *Lou Grant* competed with NBC's *Police Woman*. In Weinberger's words:

> Someone said *Charlie's Angels*; someone said *Police Woman*; someone said *Baretta*; someone said *Starsky And Hutch* – and then we all said, 'How about a melange of the worst aspects of all of them?' It just so happened that the worst aspects of *Police Woman* seemed to match best with the meager talents of the actress character we had in mind for Betty. (*TV Guide*, op. cit.)

But for all its appeal *The Betty White Show* was an early casualty of increased network competition. *TV Guide* quotes an unnamed MTM producer as criticising CBS' decision to cancel the series, suggesting that it would have found a very large audience given time:

> Everyone at the network forgets that it took us half a season to get our act together on *Mary* back in 1970. The ratings were low for a while. Some shows just take time to find themselves and their audience. They're uneven at first, weak, but they develop. *Mary* did. *Lou Grant* did. *Betty* would have too. (*TV Guide*, 30/9/78, p. 38)

But CBS were no longer the top network and while they had given both *Mary* and *Lou Grant* on-air commitments to make half a season of episodes (and then invested considerable amounts in them) no such deal had been done for *The Betty White Show*.

Lou Grant (CBS, 1977–82) Film. 60 mins.
Executive producers: James L. Brooks, Allan Burns, Gene Reynolds. *Associate producer*: Roger Young. *Creators*: Allan Burns, James L. Brooks, Gene Reynolds. *Developed by* Leon Tokatyan. *Photography*: William K. Jurgensen. *Music*: Patrick Williams, Michael Melvoin. *Editors*: Doug Hines, Ken Koch.
Regular cast: Edward Asner *(Lou Grant)*, Mason Adams *(Charlie Hume)*, Robert Walden *(Joe Rossi)*, Linda Kelsey *(Billie Newman*; replacing Rebecca Balding [*Carla Mardigian*] after three episodes), Nancy Marchand *(Margaret Pynchon)*, Jack Bannon *(Art Donovan)*, Darryl Anderson *(Animal)*.

A drama series with comedic overtones, revolving around the lives and activities of the city editor's office of the fictitious *Los Angeles Tribune*, a struggling newspaper under the autocratic rule of its owner-publisher, Margaret Pynchon.

'Cophouse'
Writer: Leon Tokatyan. *Director*: Gene Reynolds. *Guest cast*: Peter Hobbs, Danil Torppe, Norman Bartold, George Cooper, Paul Larson, Wallace Rooney, Laurence Haddon, Rachel Bard, Michael Bond.
Lou Grant has scarcely settled in to his new job as city editor of the *Los Angeles Tribune* when his leadership is tested by zealous reporter Joe Rossi, who claims that a police veteran is holding down details of a departmental scandal.
'Hostage'
Writer: Seth Freeman. *Director*: Charles Dubin. *Guest cast*: John Rubinstein, Patrick Tovatt, Joyce Jillson, Robert Phalen, Rachel Bard, Austin Stoker, Pepe Hern, Richard Saunders, Fred Stuthman, Donnegan Smith, Michael Irving, Wallace Rooney.
The brother of a dead robber holds Rossi at gunpoint until his version of the holdup sees print.
'Hoax'
Writer: Gordon Dawson. *Director*: Jay Sandrich. *Guest cast*: Eugene Roche, Booth Colman, Diana Douglas, Rod McCary, Fred Stuthman, John Alvin, Ivan Bonar, Michael Irving, Wallace Rooney.
Lou must assess the credibility of a former colleague known for passing bad tips when the old man comes in with a hot lead on the location of a missing tycoon.
'Hen-House'
Writer: Leonora Thuna. *Director*: Richard Crenna. *Guest cast*: Claudette Nevins, Geoffrey Lewis, Parry Mattick.
A squabble develops between Lou and the arts-and-leisure editor over which department should cover the murder of a famous writer.
'Nazi'
Writer: Robert Schlitt. *Director*: Alexander Singer. *Guest cast*: Peter Weller, Brian Dennehy, Janet Brandt, Jack A. Lukes, Lee Wallace, Davis Roberts, Than Wyenn, Daniel Chodos.
During her investigation of a Nazi group, Billie Newman discovers that their leader was raised as an Orthodox Jew.
'After-Shock'
Writer: Del Reisman. *Director*: Jud Taylor. *Guest cast*: Joyce Van Patten, Clyde Kusatsu, Betty Ann Rees.
Lou's first experience of a California earthquake only underscores his emotional upheaval when a reporter's widow accepts his comfort but then grows overly dependent on him.
'Barrio'
Writer: Seth Freeman. *Director*: Mel Damski. *Guest cast*: Margarita Cordova, Felipe Turich, Guillermo San Juan, Phillip Antora, Joe Santos, Kiki Quiralta, Edward Gallardo, Janice Karman, Rosa Turich, Bert Rosario.

Billie and Lou, following up on the shooting of a barrio woman, learn that the victim's son blames gang rivalries for the incident and is out for revenge.
'Scoop'
Writer: Gene Kearney. *Director*: Harry Falk. *Guest cast*: Billy Beck, George Murdock, Reni Santoni, Ted Gehring, Paul Kent, Rod Colbin.
Rossi scores two page-one scoops, both of which turn out to be inaccurate.
'Judge'
Writer: Leon Tokatyan. *Director*: Irving J. Moore. *Guest cast*: Barnard Hughes, Phillip E. Pine, Joe Mantell, Timothy Jerome, Guy Raymond, Paul Tulley.
Acting on a lead that an ageing Superior Court judge may be growing senile, Lou goes along as court observer, and gets thrown in jail by the cantankerous magistrate while trying to exit quietly.
'Psych-Out'
Writer: Seth Freeman. *Director*: Alexander Singer. *Guest cast*: Michael Zaslow, Phillip R. Allen, Lisle Wilson, Tom Tarpey.
Pushed by Lou to 'get into' stories, Rossi commits himself to a mental hospital he is investigating.
'House-Warming'
Writer: Leonora Thuna. *Director*: Mel Damski. *Guest cast*: Julie Kavner, Fredi Olster, Janice Kent, Edward Winter, Robert Rothwell.
For her article on wife-beating Billie meets a battered wife who fears to serve as even an anonymous source for the story.
'Take-Over'
Writer: Leon Tokatyan. *Director*: Gene Reynolds. *Guest cast*: John Anderson, Jerry Fogel, Paul Kent, Allen Williams, William Bogert, Gail Bowman, Michael Prince, James Cahill, Wallace Rooney.
Mrs Pynchon strikes up a friendship with a man known for buying out respectable newspapers and turning them into sensational tabloids.
'Christmas'
Writer: David Lloyd. *Director*: Jim Burrows. *Guest cast*: Verna Bloom, Tim O'Connor, Ben Hayes, Carol O'Leary.
One week before Christmas, Billie's story of a homeless family brings in thousands of sympathy dollars. Meanwhile, Lou gives Rossi a seemingly dull assignment as punishment for unethically quoting a source.
'Airliner'
Writer: Charles Einstein. *Director*: Mel Damski. *Guest cast*: Jack Grapes, Allan Miller, Lou Cutell, Penny Stanton, Laurette Spang.
Coverage of an LA-bound airliner with faulty landing gear takes on a new dimension when the Trib staff learn that Charlie Hume's daughter in on board.
'Sports'
Writer: Bud Freeman. *Director*: Harvey Laidman. *Guest cast*: Vaughn Armstrong, Michael D. Henry, David Ackroyd, Elizabeth Herbert, Michael Morgan, Keene Curtis, Sandy Kenyon, John A. Randolph, Michael Riving.
Lou locks horns with a famous Trib sportwriter and sparks an outcry from angry readers when he attempts to disclose football-recruiting violations by a much-admired college coach.
'Hero'
Writer: Seth Freeman. *Director*: Mel Damski. *Guest cast*: Marlene Warfield, Hazel Medina, Lola Mason, Jim McMullan, Kerry Sherman, Marilyn Coleman, William Bryant.
To Lou, a story about an ex-convict who saves a judge's life seems like good human-interest material, until the hero blames the news of his past for the loss of business and fiancée.
'Renewal'
Writer: Ken Trevey. *Director*: Gene Reynolds. *Guest cast*: Robert Earl Jones, James Karen, Phillip R. Allen.

The Trib staff hope to block the demolition of a newspaper vendor's condemned apartment to save the murals he painted in honour of his late wife. [Murals by Rozzel Sykes.]
'Sect'
Writer: Michele Gallery. *Director*: Alexander Singer. *Guest cast*: James Beach, Peggy McCay, William Boyett, Richard Erdman, Melissa Newman, David Hunt Stafford, Jean Gillespie, Bucklind Berry, John Carter.
Charlie Hume and his wife are distraught over their son's conversion to Krishna.
'Scandal'
Writer: Seth Freeman. *Director*: Mel Damski. *Guest cast*: Gail Strickland, James Olson, Brian Farrell, Paul Jenkins, Virginia Bingham, Betty McGuire, Bob Watson.
Rossi is taken off a county supervisor's re-election campaign and replaced by a woman he suspects is romantically involved with the candidate.
'Spies'
Writer: Leon Tokatyan. *Director*: Charles Dubin. *Guest cast*: Peter Hobbs, Laurette Spang, Michael Strong, Jean Allison, Robert Casper.
The arrest of a businessman's son draws CIA involvement, and arouses suspicion among the Trib staff that they're harbouring an informant.
'Poison'
Writer: Michele Gallery. *Director*: Gene Reynolds. *Guest cast*: Guy Boyd, Belinda J. Montgomery, Jennifer Rhodes, Robert Rothwell, Arthur Batanides.
A grieving Rossi strives to continue the investigation into radioactive contamination begun by a good friend who met an 'accidental' death.

Lou Grant (Second Season: 1978–9)
Executive producer: Gene Reynolds. *Associate producer*: Roger Young. *Photography*: Robert Caramico, Hugh R. Gagnier. *Music*: Hod David. *Art director*: Ken Reid.
Regular cast: Edward Asner *(Lou Grant)*, Mason Adams *(Charlie Hume)*, Robert Walden *(Joe Rossi)*, Linda Kelsey *(Billie Newman)*, Jack Bannon *(Art Donovan)*, Darryl Anderson *(Animal)*, Nancy Marchand *(Margaret Pynchon)*, and Allen Williams in the recurring role of *Adam Wilson*.
'Pills'
Writer: Michele Gallery. *Director*: Jay Sandrich. *Guest cast*: Steve Nevil, Richard Bull, Jean Rasey, Dean Santoro, Joey Aresco, Michael Mullins.
Just after finishing a story about the flow of illegal pills, Rossi witnesses a teenage girl collapse from a combination of alcohol and drugs that, tragically, proves to be lethal.
'Prisoner'
Writer: Seth Freeman. *Director*: Gene Reynolds. *Guest cast*: Silvana Gallardo, Peggy McCay, Frank Ramirez, Jorge Cervera Jr., Enrique Novi, Tony Perez, Tonyo Melendez.
While Mrs Pynchon plays hostess to the wife of a Latin ruler, Rossi and Billie investigate charges of repression in her country; and Charlie Hume is oddly reluctant to print their findings.
'Hooker'
Writer: Seth Freeman. *Director*: Alexander Singer. *Guest cast*: Dee Wallace, Paul Lambert, Gail Edwards, Michael Alldredge, Mary Robin Redd, Earl Boen, Jeffrey Chandler, Barbara O. Jones, Michael Bond, Hugh Gillin, Gerry Black, J. Kenneth Campbell, Allen Williams, Rod Masterson.
Billie, while investigating a prostitute's murder, befriends a massage-parlour hustler who wants a better life.
'Mob'
Writer: Leon Tokatyan. *Director*: Corey Allen. *Guest cast*: Nicholas Colasanto, Mary Ann Chinn, Carmen Argenziano, Phillip Pine, Dennis Robertson, Dennis Holahan, Gary Pagett, Barry Cahill, Merrie Lynn Ross, Nick Angiotti.
While organising the Trib's annual tennis tournament at a California resort, Lou and Rossi become suspicious over the presence of 'holidaying' underworld bosses.
'Murder'

Writer: Gary David Goldberg. *Director*: Mel Damski. *Guest cast*: Alan Fudge, Jane Rose, Ketty Lester, Thalmus Rasulala, Ralph Wilcox, Saundra Sharp, Veronica Reed, Ray Oliver.
Rossi's piece on a dowager who fought off four thieves with a golf club gets front-page coverage, while Billie's story about the murder of a young mother is 'buried' on a back page.
'Dying'
Writer: Michele Gallery. *Director*: Alexander Singer. *Guest cast*: Geraldine Fitzgerald, Larry Gates, Joan Hotchkiss, Stephen Johnson, Raleigh Bond, Lois Foraker, Allen Williams.
Donovan, despite Lou and Billie's help, is unable to cope with the fact that his mother is dying.
'Schools'
Writer: Gary David Goldberg. *Director*: Burt Brinckerhoff. *Guest cast*: Lee Chamberlain, Kevin Hooks, Lloyd Hollar, Justin Lord, Lorry Goldman, Mary Carver, Sidney Clute, Veronica Reed, Michael Irving.
While Rossi and Billie investigate violence at a local high school, Lou forms a friendship with an optimistic guidance counsellor who shares his interest in a reformed student now vying for a Tribune college scholarship. [This story includes an award-ceremony speech delivered by the Rev. Jesse Jackson.]
'Slaughter'
Writer: Bud Freeman. *Director*: Roger Young. *Guest cast*: Stephen Elliott, Sandy McPeak, Sally Kirkland, Danny Goldman, Sybil Scotford, John Petlock, Tony Becker, Allen Williams, Stephen Keep.
Lou and his former boss, the editor of a small-town newspaper, investigate a mysterious cattle disease that may affect humans.
'Singles'
Writers: Gina Frederica Goldman, Sally Robinson. *Director*: Michael Zinberg. *Guest cast*: Peter Donat, Frances Lee McCain, Sam Freed, Philip Charles MacKenzie, Karen Landry, Michael Alaimo, Melodie Johnson, Paul W. Davidson.
Billie and Rossi investigate the LA singles scene at the urging of a media consultant bent on giving the Trib a youthful look.
'Babies'
Writer: David Lloyd. *Director*: Alexander Singer. *Guest cast*: Joseph Mascolo, John Carter, Russell Johnson, Judyann Elder, Robert Broyles, Anny Mathias, David Brandon, Virginia Bingham.
Rossi and Billie pose as a child-seeking couple to investigate a baby-selling racket.
'Conflict'
Writer: Michele Gallery. *Director*: Mel Damski. *Guest cast:* Norman Burton, Peggy McCay, Fred Holliday, Helen Kleeb, Eve Roberts, Alan Haufrect, Michael Irving, Laurence Haddon, Allen Williams, Michael Alnimo, John Gilgreen, Rod Gist, Charles Bracy, Barbara Edelman.
Mrs Pynchon is infuriated by the Trib's derogatory piece on the director of a charity with which she is affiliated; and Rossi ruffles more feathers when, as the paper's new media critic, he accuses city-room staff of having conflicts of interest.
'Denial'
Writer: Leonora Thuna. *Director*: Charles Dubin. *Guest cast*: Ann Sweeny, Robert Pine, Fred Beir, Dennis Redfield, Meeno Peluce, Alba Francesca, Ric Mancini, Art Batanides.
Lou's daughter refuses to accept her son's advancing deafness, a situation which threatens to destroy her marriage.
'Fire'
Writer: Seth Freeman. *Director*: Roger Young. *Guest cast*: Tom Atkins, Tom Bower, Ann Ryerson, William Joyce, Ellen Blake, Richard Balin, G. W. Bailey, Janet Brandt, Hal Bokar, Clarke Gordon, Thomas W. Babson.
Following a string of apartment-house fires, the city-room staff suspect an insurance scam.
'Vet'

Writer: Leon Tokatyan. *Director*: Alexander Singer. *Guest cast*: Lionel Smith, George Pentecost, Charlie Robinson, John Wyler, B. J. Bartlett, Eddie Hailey, Hank Ross, Maurice Sneed.
Vietnam War still affects news at the Trib – with Animal getting accusing calls from the widow of a soldier he served with, and Lou trying to find a job for a down-and-out veteran.
'Scam'
Writer: Gary David Goldberg. *Director*: Gerald Mayer. *Guest cast*: John Considine, J. Pat O'Malley, Peggy McCay, Barney Phillips, Booth Colman, Hal England, Ross Elliott, William Beckley, William Lally.
Whilst toying with how to spend a $15,000 gift, Lou stumbles onto what may be an investment scam involving Charlie Hume's financial counsellor.
'Sweep'
Writer: Steve Kline. *Director*: Charles Dubin. *Guest cast*: Maureen McCormick, Rafael Campos, Jonathan Banks, Cynthoa Avila, Maria Elena Cordero, Arthur Rosenberg, Eric Server, James Gallery, Felipe Turich, Rene Enriquez, Allen Williams, Ron Godines, Charles Bracy, Eric Greene, George De Lao, Jose Flores.
Rossi, Billie and Animal probe the influx of illegal aliens to Southern California, while Lou breaks in a new copy 'boy' – Mrs Pynchon's niece.
'The Samaritan'
Writer: Eliot West. *Director*: Paul Leaf. *Guest cast*: Richard B. Schull, Ben Piazza, Marcia Rodd, John Larch, Bill Watson.
The Trib receives an ominous letter signed 'Samaritan', the name of a psychopathic killer who once stalked the city and threatens to do so again.
'Hit'
Writer: Michele Gallery. *Director*: Peter Levin. *Guest cast*: Allyn Ann McLerie, Ed Harris, Ivan Bonar, Michael Champion, Paul Sorensen, Allen Williams, Edwin Owens, Lou Felder, Bart Burns, Janice Carroll.
Rossi is intrigued by a woman's two-year search for her son's hit-and-run killer.
'Home'
Writer: Gary David Goldberg. *Director*: Alexander Singer. *Guest cast*: Jack Gilford, Ed Grover, Patricia Smith, Lee Kessler, Jessamine Milner, Nina Wilcox, Mari Gorman, Meshach Taylor, Eve McVeagh, John Devlin, Ann Nelson, Allen Williams, Lisle Wilson, Jed Mills.
Billie takes a job in a nursing home to investigate mistreatment of patients, while Lou befriends a retiree who yearns to be productive again.
'Convention'
Writer: David Lloyd. *Director*: Charles Dubin. *Guest cast*: Kenneth McMillan, Ivor Francis, Amanda McBroom, Laurie Heinman, Robert Rothwell, James Mitchell, Robert Snively, Paul Tuerpe, Joe Bratcher.
Lou accompanies Charlie Hume and Mrs Pynchon to a newspaper convention, where there's a rumour that terrorists plan to kidnap a prominent publisher.
'Marathon'
Writer: Gene Reynolds. *Director*: Alexander Singer. *Guest cast*: Peter Hobbs, Michael Warren, John Petlock, Emilio Delgado, Rebecca Stanley, Ken Letner, Lee Delano, Scott Ellsworth, J. P. Finnegan.
A day inside the city room. A tunnel collapses at a construction site burying workers; Lou calls for a TV set to monitor the rescue, but the city room is visited by a group of junketing Swedish businessmen, none of whom speak English; Donovan, tired of Lou's editorial judgments, contemplates leaving the Trib for a job offer as the Governor's press secretary.
'Bomb'
Writer: Seth Freeman. *Director*: Gene Reynolds. *Guest cast*: Dinah Manoff, Joe Spano, Frank Marth, Norbert Weisser, Paul Kent, Terry Wills, Richard Doyle, Allen Williams, John Finnegan, Gail Bowman.
Terrorists send Rossi their blueprint for an atomic bomb, which they threaten to detonate in Los Angeles unless their demands are met.

'Skids' [aka 'Skid Row']
Writer: Steve Kline. *Director*: Burt Brinckerhoff. *Guest cast*: Andrew Duggan, Al Ruscio, Virginia Gregg, Scoey Mitchell, James Hong, Tom Spratley, James O'Connell, Don Hanmer, Allen Williams, Jed Mills, Eric Helland.
Coverage of a string of skid-row stranglings disturbs Rossi, whose father died of alcoholism; and Lou, who meets an old friend who's now a bum.
'Romance'
Writer: Michele Gallery. *Director*: Roger Young. *Guest cast*: Frances Lee McCain, Terri Nunn, Devon Ericson, Craig Wasson, Robert Costanzo, Lark Geib, Shannon Terhune, Allen Williams, James Dale Ryan, Virginia Bingham, Christian Juttner, Deanna Martin.
Lou gets an unexpected offer from Susan (McCain) and Billie meets teenagers who have babies in order to escape from home.

Lou Grant (Third Season: 1979–80)
Executive producer: Gene Reynolds. *Photography*: Robert F. Liu. *Music*: Patrick Williams. *Art director*: Elizabeth Bousman. *Editor*: A. David Marshall.
Regular cast: Edward Asner *(Lou Grant)*, Mason Adams *(Charlie Hume)*, Robert Walden *(Joe Rossi)*, Linda Kelsey *(Billie Newman)*, Jack Bannon *(Art Donovan)*, Darryl Anderson *(Animal)*, Nancy Marchand *(Margaret Pynchon)*, and Allen Williams in the recurring role of *Adam Wilson*.
'Cop'
Writer: Seth Freeman. *Director*: Roger Young. *Guest cast*: Ron Max, Don Draper, Bob Hackman, Joe Medalis, Gene Sua, Allen Williams, James Oliver, Joe Penny, Ed Winter.
When Lou is the only witness to a neighbourhood murder, he is mystified at the way police handle the case, and discovers a touchy area of crime.
'Exposé'
Writer: David Lloyd. *Director*: Gene Reynolds. *Guest cast*: William Schallert, Lousie Troy, Richard Brestoff, Julie Cobb, Michael Irving, Allen Williams, Steve Tannen, Don Diamond, Barbara Jean Edelman.
The hard-drinking husband (Schallert) of a popular woman politician makes headlines, while a gossip magazine does a well-researched piece on what goes on behind the scenes at The Trib.
'Slammer'
Writer: Johnny Dawkins. *Director*: Alexander Singer. *Guest cast*: Kene Holliday, Alan Fudge, J. Jay Saunders, Robert Davi, Danny Glover, Rosana Soto, Eric Holland, Lance Rosen, Garty Pagett, Ken Letner, Art Le Fleur, Heshimu Cumbuka, Allen Williams, Phil Montgomery.
After agreeing to be guest speaker at Rossi's journalism class, Lou learns his students are tough state prison inmates angered by the shut-down of their newspaper.
'Charlatan'
Writer: Michael Vittes. *Director*: Roger Young. *Guest cast*: Mesach Taylor, Ruth Silveira, Kenneth Tigar, John Carter, Carmen Argenziano, Ellen Travolta, William Cort, Michael Fairman, Charles Cyphers, William H. Bassett, Ric Carrott, Ken Hill, Allen Williams.
Freedom of religion and freedom of the press pose sticky problems for Lou and The Trib as a naked man on a church steeple and the editor of a sleazy porno magazine test the two rules.
'Frame-Up'
Writer: Steve Kline. *Director*: Burt Brinckerhoff. *Guest cast*: Stephen McHattie, Wendy Phillips, Paul Kent, Edward Marshall, Bill Smillie, M. G. Kelly, Nigel Bullard.
The Trib is taken to court and Billie is taken to task after her exposé on a manufacturing firm turns out to be based on a forged document.
'Hype'
Writer: Michele Gallery. *Director*: Peter Levin. *Guest cast*: Harold Gould, David Huffman, Craig Wasson, Silvana Gallardo, Paul Sparer, Clarke Gordon, James Saito, Robert Rothwell.

Lou's participation in a cancer-research study leads the Trib into a story on industry funding of university programmes.

'Gambling'

Writer: Bud Freeman. *Director*: Alexander Singer. *Guest cast*: Charles Lane, Michael Shannon, Sandy Kenyon, Alan Mason, John Karlem, Donald Bishop, Lorry Goldman, John Aquino, Alma Beltran, Allen Williams, Buck Young, Judy Sardo, Dorothy Meyer, Grace Simmons.

Gambling fever strikes the Trib as Lou is touted on a longshot, Animal learns the meaning of vigorish and Billie makes a risky loan to a gambler.

'Witness'

Writer: Gary David Goldberg. *Director*: Peter Levin. *Guest cast*: Richard Jaeckel, Peter Marshall, Charles Hallahan, Bartlett Robinson, William Bryant, Raleigh Bond, Jack Lukes, Allen Williams, Timothy C. Burns, Jack Lindine.

Billie is given police protection after the death of her source for a story about a beating.

'Kidnap'

Writer: Bud Freeman. *Director*: Alan Cooke. *Guest cast*: Parley Baer, Jonathan Banks, Jordan Rhodes, Stanley Kamel, Curt Wilson, Virginia Bingham, Raleigh Bond, Read Morgan, Michael Currie, Emilio Delgado, Allen Williams, Gerry Black, Susan McClung, Dominique Dunne.

While the city-room staff cover the story of a missing plane, Mrs Pynchon ponders an offer from a large newspaper chain.

'Andrew' (Part I: 'Premonition')

Writer: Seth Freeman. *Director*: Roger Young. *Guest cast*: Bruce Davison, Barbara Barrie, Joan Hotchkis, Nita Talbot, Ellen Regan, Robert Hirschfeld, Nick Angotti, Nocona Aranda, Allen Williams, Eddy C. Dyer, Gail Bowman

Donovan's cousin Andrew (Davison) is on the verge of a potentially violent psychological breakdown.

'Andrew' (Part II: 'Trial')

Writer: Seth Freeman. *Director*: Peter Levin *Guest cast*: Bruce Davison, Barbara Barrie, Charles Aidman, Joan Hotchkis, Mary Gregory, Michael McGuire, Russ Martin, Ken Sansom, Sarah Miller, Jon Terry, Pat Corley, Allen Williams, Nick Angotti, Nocona Aranda.

Donovan's cousin is charged with the murder of a young woman.

'Hollywood'

Writer: Michele Gallery. *Director*: Burt Brinckerhoff. *Guest cast*: George Chandler, Laraine Day, Howard Duff, Nina Foch, Margaret Hamilton, John Larch, Paul Stewart, Dave Wilcox, Marie Windsor, Allen Williams.

Lou's fascination with an abandoned Hollywood nightspot puts the Trib staff onto the case of an unsolved murder committed there some 30 years earlier.

'Kids'

Writers: Michael Vittes, Shep Greene. *Director*: Alexander Singer. *Guest cast*: Matthew Laborteaux, Nicholas Pryor, Melinda Cordell, Jenny Sullivan, Elizabeth Bliss, Peggy Ann Garner, Michael J. Fox, Barbara Jane Edelman, Gail Bowman, Allen Williams, Gene Bua.

Problem children and children's problems are examined in encounters with a young boy in need of attention, a shy child star reluctant to tell her story and a lawyer specialising in youngsters' rights.

'Brushfire'

Writers: Allan Burns, Gene Reynolds. *Director*: Donald A. Baer. *Guest cast*: Peggy McCay, Marshall Thompson, Jeff Corey, Brian Farrell, Tony Perez, William Joyce, Allen Williams, Michelle Downey, Matthew Faison, Kurtwood Smith, Charles Bracy, John Christy Ewing.

A brush fire disrupts the lives of many Trib employees, and consequently affects the paper's coverage of it.

'Indians'

Writer: April Smith. *Director*: Ralph Senensky. *Guest cast*: David Yanez, Ned Romero, Julie Carmen, Ray Tracey, Tom Rosqui, Alex Kubic, Henry Bal, Ivan Naranjo, James Dale Ryan, Paul Bryar, Allen Williams.
The Trib's research on urbanised American Indians gains insight when Animal befriends a youngster running away from a boarding school.
'Cover-Up'
Writer: Paul Ehrmann. *Director*: Gerry Mayer. *Guest cast*: Andrew Rubin, David Hollander, Edward Power, Ross Bickell, William Jordan, Ann Sweeny, Booth Colman, Viola Harris, Augusta Dabney, Allen Williams, Ron Gilbert, Ken Hill, Robert Rothwell, David Cooper, Arthur Hanson, Billy Jacoby, Seven Anne McDonald.
Rossi is taken off a probe of movie-industry kickbacks when a producer interested in one of his stories is implicated.
'Inheritance'
Writer: April Smith. *Director*: Roger Young. *Guest cast*: Allyn Ann McLerie, Marshall Thompson, Sands Hall, Carol Bagdasarian, Buck Kartalian, Keene Curtis, Magda Harout, Gregory Rozakis, Arthur Space, Jean Howell, Allen Williams, Michael Irvingin, Emilio Delgado, John Alvin, James R. Winker, Bill Baldwin, Ed Vasgersian, Ted Lehmann, Jerry Anello.
Billie's story on the potential effects of synthetic estrogen on unborn children leads her to suspect that her mother may have taken the hormone.
'Censored'
Writer: Joanne Pagliaro. *Director*: Alexander Singer. *Guest cast*: Richard Dysart, Laurie Heineman, Paul Lambert, Dan Spector, James Gallery, Karen Ingenthron, Brent Davis, Vernon Weddle, Pat Finley, Lindsay Workman, Allen Williams, Emilio Delgado, Jon Terry, Clete Keith, Marte Post, Susan McClurg, Michael Irving, Flora Plumb.
The issue is censorship as the Trib considers dropping a controversial comic strip, while Rossi is sent to a small town to cover a series of book burnings.
'Lou'
Writer: Michele Gallery. *Director*: Roger Young. *Guest cast*: Richard B. Shull, Elta Blake, Michael Bond, Ray Oliver, Billy Beck, Don Janmner, Allen Williams, Barbara Jane Edelman, Rae Dawn Chong, Charles Bracy, Daniel Chodos.
Lou's single-minded devotion to his job begins to wear on his stamina, causing concern among his co-workers.
'Blackout'
Writer: Steve Kline. *Director*: Allen Williams. *Guest cast*: Richard Evans, Margie Impert, Stanley Grover, Paul Jenkins, Walter Brooke, Ray Oliver, Lynn Seibel, Lawrence Cook, Ivan Bonar, Drew Katzman, Charles Bracy.
The Trib has never missed a press deadline, a record it may lose after power is knocked out by a combination of lightning and earth tremors.
'Dogs'
Writer: Seth Freeman. *Director*: Burt Brinckerhoff. *Guest cast*: Geoffrey Lewis, Alan Vint, Michael Jeter, Eric Server, Pat Corley, John Blyth Barrymore, Read Morgan, Sam Edwards, Grant Owens, Mickey Knox, Allen Williams, Eric Holland.
Rossi infiltrates a dog-fighting ring when the disappearance of Mrs Pynchon's Yorkshire terrier is linked to trainers suspected by the Humane Society.
'Influence'
Writer: April Smith. *Director*: Gene Reynolds. *Guest cast*: James Whitmore Jr., Sheila Larken, Allen Williams, Bartlett Robinson, Al Ruscio, Fred Beir, John Alvin, John Holland, Arthur Batanides, Barry Cahill, Michael Irving, Ivan Bonar, Bernadette Pelletier.
While Mrs Pynchon listens to influence-peddlers seeking her support for an airport project, Lou becomes increasingly aware that Adam (Williams) has a drinking problem.
'Guns'
Writer: Seth Freeman. *Director*: Bob Sweeney. *Guest cast*: Rue McClanahan, Redmond Gleeson, Michael Alldredge, Jack Dodson, Deirdre Lenihan, John Considine, Kenneth

O'Brien, Kate Zentall, Bob Hastings, Nigel Bullard, Naomi Caryl, Kurtwood Smith.
St Patrick's Day is the occasion for an episode examining 'the troubles' in Northern Ireland and Irish-American support for the IRA.
'Hazard'
Writer: Michele Gallery. *Director*: Burt Brinckerhoff. *Guest cast*: Tom Rosqui, Phillip R. Allen, Ed Harris, Clete Keith, Edward Bell, Carl Lumbly, Elizabeth Berger, Barbara Jane Edelman, Allen Williams, Michael Irving, Laurence Haddon.
Cheque-book journalism is at issue when Rossi can't get the facts about dangerous motorbikes unless he pays his informant.

Lou Grant (Fourth Season: 1980–1)
Executive producer: Gene Reynolds. *Photography*: Robert F. Liu. *Music*: Patrick Williams. *Art director*: Richard Berger.
Regular cast: Edward Asner *(Lou Grant)*, Mason Adams *(Charlie Hume)*, Robert Walden *(Joe Rossi)*, Linda Kelsey *(Billie Newman)*, Jack Bannon *(Art Donovan)*, Darryl Anderson *(Animal)*, Nancy Marchand *(Margaret Pynchon)*, and Allen Williams in the recurring role of *Adam Wilson*.

'Nightside'
Writer: Michele Gallery. *Director*: Gene Reynolds. *Guest cast*: Richard Erdman, David Paymer, Millie Slavin, Alexandra Johnson, Charles Bloom, Robert Rockwell, John Furey, Allen Williams, Ross Elliott.
Lou has to work a double shift and gets an eye-opening encounter with the Trib's eccentric nightside staff.
'Harassment'
Writer: April Smith. *Director*: Roger Young. *Guest cast*: David Spielberg, Lynn Carlin, Marilyn Jones, Michael Talbot, Candy Ann Brown, Brenda Hillhouse, Joe Medalis.
Billie jolts the Trib when she uses what goes on at the newspaper for her angle on a story about sexual harassment on the job.
'Pack'
Writer: Steve Kline. *Director*: Burt Brinckerhoff. *Guest cast*: Eileen Heckart, Ed Nelson, John Hillerman, James Callahan, Ivor Francis, Joe Regalbuto, Jorge Cevera Jr, Buck Young, Allen Williams, Emilio Delgado, Michael Irving, Jay Tarses, Michael Kagan.
Billie is given an inside view of politics as well as a rough initiation from the press bus when she goes on the road to cover a hotshot politican.
'Sting'
Writers: Patt Shea and Harriet Weiss. *Director*: Peter Levin. *Guest cast*: Larry Linville, John Considine, Peggy McCay, Michael Alldredge, Cliff Norton, Mo Malone, Jacquelyn Hyde.
After renting his house to a strangely-acting couple, Charlie Hume gets suspicious when neighbours report mysterious goings-on.
'Goop'
Writer: Seth Freeman. *Director*: Alexander Singer. *Guest cast*: Parley Baer, Dominique Dunne, Alex Henteloff, Jordan Rhodes, Med Flory, Curt Wilson, Terry McGovern, Vernon Weddle, Allen Williams.
Just how far to go to get an important story becomes a problem when the Trib cannot nail down what's causing a mysterious bulge near a small-town dump site.
'Libel'
Writer: William Hopkins. *Director*: Burt Brinckerhoff. *Guest cast*: Robin Gammell, Alan Oppenheimer, Marie Windsor, Bernard Fox, Dean Santoro, Logan Ramsey, James Van Patten, Irena Ferris, Allen Williams.
The Trib's exposé of a scandal sheet results in a whopping libel suit from the publisher.
'Streets'
Writer: Bud Freeman. *Director*: Donald A. Baer. *Guest cast*: Carl Franklin, Mark Bell-James, Larry B. Scott, Beverley Todd, Lawrence Cook, Veronica Redd, Esther Sutherland.
Rossi's overbearing manner angers a black Trib reporter working with him on a difficult story about the surprising community response to a ghetto killing.

'Catch'
Writer: Michele Gallery. *Director*: Roger Young. *Guest cast*: Cliff Potts, Jordan Charney, Robert Hirschfeld, Allen Williams, Eve McVeagh, Erin Donovan, David Wiley, Helen Siff.
Billie goes out on a story and falls in love with her news source, a professional baseball player who's having a bad season.
'Rape'
Writer: Seth Freeman. *Director*: Seth Freeman. *Guest cast*: Lynne Moody, Linda Carlson, Jonathan Banks, Julia Duffy, Allen Williams, Macon McCalman, Maggie Gwinn, Kurtwood Smith, Ellen Blake, Carrie Freeman.
The horror of 'everyday' crime is brought home to the city room in a shocking way when one of the Trib's own reporters is raped.
'Boomerang'
Writer: Steve Kline. *Director*: Alexander Singer. *Guest cast*: Michael Constantine, Roger Newman, Drew Snyder, Charles Parks, Emilio Delgado, Laurence Haddon, Allen Williams, Barbara Beckley, Timothy Stack.
Lou's authority and ego are undermined by an old pal, a high-paid writer working on a story about dumping – the practice of sending dangerous or defective goods overseas.
'Generations'
Writer: Johnny Dawkins. *Director*: Harvey Laidman. *Guest cast*: Arthur Space, Charles Lane, Whitman Mayor, Peggy McCay, Shirley Jo Finney, Ken Sansom, Brad Savage, Tony Perez, Matthew Broderick, David Baron.
The problems of the older generation touch the Trib when an elderly neighbour of Lou's is hassled by mischievous kids and Charlie Hume's father escapes the boredom of retirement by shoplifting.
'Search'
Writers: Everett Greenbaum and Elliott Reid. *Director*: Allen Williams. *Guest cast*: Alley Mills, Millie Slavin, Carolyn Coates, Juliana McCarthy, Antony Ponzini, Robert Casper, Jane Atkins.
The skill it takes to track down a news story get a tough test when Rossi tries to help a Trib staffer searching for her real mother.
'Strike'
Writer: April Smith. *Director*: Gene Reynolds. *Guest cast*: Nancy Malone, Tom Atkins, Bruce Kirby, Ray Wise, Phillip Pine, John Petlock, Allen Williams, Sidney Clute, Ivan Bonar, Ray Oliver, Arthur Batanides.
A bitter strike over automation, led by an aggressive reporter, splits the city room and forces Lou to take management's side against his staff.
'Survival'
Writer: April Smith. *Director*: Burt Brinckerhoff. *Guest cast*: Keene Curtis, Ed Harris, Doreen Lang, Ray Oliver, Marc Bentley, Barbara Jane Edelman, Buck Young, Eric Server, Lance Guest, Allen Williams.
A Trib story about a doomsday group – people preparing at all costs to survive in a disaster – comes to life for Lou and Rossi when they are caught in a killer storm.
'Venice'
Writers: Harriett and Patt Shea. *Director*: Paul Stanley. *Guest cast*: James Callahan, Frank Aletter, Claire Malis, Colby Chester, Elizabeth Halliday, Trinidad Silva, Terry McGovern.
While Animal is drawn into a strange quest to find out more about a pretty girl's tragic death, Trib management is shaken by a threat to make public a list of staff salaries.
'Campesinos'
Writer: Michael Vittes. *Director*: Peter Levin. *Guest cast*: James Victor, Bill Lucking, Jeff Corey, Pepe Serna, Emilio Delgado, Ted Gehring, Buck Kartalian, Chuy Franco, Allen Williams, Abel Fernandez.
Rossi gets a real insider's report on an explosive labour dispute when he's asked to publicise the plight of striking farm workers and winds up behind bars himself.

'Business'
Writer: Steve Kline. *Director*: Alan Cooke. *Guest cast*: Ed Winter, David Spielberg, Richard Erdman, Philip Abbot, Paul Kent, Kenneth Tigar, Allen Williams.
Lou has to go on the defensive when the Trib is accused of being anti-business in its coverage of a factory fire while ignoring labour problems of its own.
'Violence'
Writer: Johnny Dawkins. *Director*: Georg Stanford Brown. *Guest cast*: Fred Williamson, Tyne Daly, Fred Dryer, Chick Hearn, Faye Hauser, Michael Fairman, Allen Williams.
When a hard-hitting pro football star is sued for injuring an opponent it raises questions at the Trib over how well it covers the touchy subject of violence in sports.
'Depression'
Writer: Gene Reynolds. *Director*: Peter Levin. *Guest cast*: Peter Hobbs, James Sloyan, Priscilla Pointer, Sands Hall, Allen Williams, Ivan Bonar, Bart Burns.
Be it depression, midlife crisis, job burnout, it catches up with the Trib's hard-drinking police reporter, who tries a drastic way out.
'Stroke'
Writer: April Smith. *Director*: Roger Young. *Guest cast*: Alan Fudge, Philip R. Allen, Jim Antonio, Paul Sparer, Harris Kal, Victoria Lynn Johnson, Susan McClung, Pat Finley, Allen Williams, Emilio Delgado.
Mrs Pynchon suffers a massive stroke and as she lies near death the Trib editors get into a fight with her money-hungry nephew over control of the paper.

Lou Grant (Fifth Season: 1981–2)
Executive producer: Gene Reynolds. *Photography*: Robert F. Liu. *Music*: Patrick Williams. *Art director*: Richard Berger. *Editor*: James Galloway.
Regular cast: Edward Asner *(Lou Grant)* Mason Adams *(Charlie Hume)*, Robert Walden *(Joe Rossi)*, Linda Kelsey *(Billie Newman)*, Jack Bannon *(Art Donovan)*, Darryl Anderson *(Animal)*, Nancy Marchand *(Margaret Pynchon)*, Lance Guest (irregular role as *Lance Rienarky)*, and Allen Williams in the recurring role of *Adam Wilson*.

'Wedding'
Writer: Seth Freeman. *Director*: Alexander Singer. *Guest cast*: Cliff Potts, Parley Baer, Barbara Dirickson, Arthur Rosenberg, Michael Griswold, Joe Rassulo, Fran Bennett, Art Kimbro, Allen Williams, Charles Bracy, Beth Le Grant, Ann Sweeny, Jeff Severson.
Billie gets a marriage proposal from baseball scout Ted McCovey but is so busy on a story there's a big question as to whether she can take time to accept.
'Execution'
Writer: April Smith. *Director*: Burt Brinckerhoff. *Guest cast*: Terri Nunn, Christopher Cazenove, George Wyner, Mariclare Costello, Sharon Spelman, Bill Baldwin, Kres Mersky, William Edward Phipps, Matthew Faison, Allen Williams.
Rossi covers the sensational case of a young woman who won't appeal her death sentence for murder and is attracted in spite of himself when he talks to her about why she wants to die.
'Reckless'
Writer: Steve Kline. *Director*: Alexander Singer. *Guest cast*: Michael McGuire, William Shilling, Michael Tucci, Chip Lucia, Milt Kogan, Allen Williams.
While Charlie sets up a controversial news tip hotline for the Trib, Lou has one drink too many and lands in trouble with the law for drunk driving.
'Hometown'
Writer: Michele Gallery. *Director*: Gene Reynolds. *Guest cast*: Robert Prosky, Georgann Johnson, Kenneth Kimmins, Anthony Costello, Sandy Ward, Stacy Keach Sr, Thom Bray, Jonathan Woodward, Michael Irving.
A bittersweet visit for Lou when he goes back to his hometown and runs into an unexpected and troubling news story, as well as an old flame.
'Risk'

Writer: Seth Freeman. *Director*: Allen Williams. *Guest cast*: Lynne Moody, J. Jay Saunders, Michael Alldredge, Kario Salem, Sandy Martin, Kate Zentall, Ken Smolka, Wendy Lynne, Lance Guest.
A little girl who performs in porno movies and the exploits of a search-and-rescue team raise a disturbing question for two reporters – how much should they risk to get their stories?
'Double-Cross'
Writer: Michele Gallery. *Director*: Roger Young. *Guest cast*: Lin McCarthy, Barbara Cason, Peter Fox, Roger Kern, Jeff Lester, Lynn Thigpen, Lou Fant, Jane Edleman, Jon Lormer, Allen Williams.
A bitter feud, family secrets and a gem-studded golden cross emerge when a time capsule from a demolished building is opened, but Billie suspects all is not as it seems.
'Drifters'
Writer: Bud Freeman. *Director*: Peter Levin. *Guest cast*: W. K. Stratton, Tom Atkins, Conchata Ferrell, James Callahan, Peggy McCay, Bruce Gray, Charlie Stavola, Emilio Delgado, Allen Willliams.
Charlie Hume's nervous young nephew shows up looking for a job and turns out to be a mental case shakily balanced by drugs he doesn't want to take.
'Friends'
Writer: Seth Freeman. *Director*: Seth Freeman. *Guest cast*: Larry Breeding, Dick Anthony Williams, Logan Ramsey, Paul Kent, Murphy Dunne, Jennifer Holmes, Jean Howell, Allen Williams, Carmen Argenziano.
Rossi learns about dirty politics the hard way when an old friend runs for office, while the city room is abuzz over whether Donovan really slugged someone.
'Jazz'
Writer: Rogers Turrentine. *Director*: Burt Brinckerhoff. *Guest cast*: Todd Susman, Richard Erdman, Med Flory, Joe Williams, Louis Bellson, Ray Brown, Paula Shaw, Danny Wells, Allen Williams, Paul Hampton, Marte Boyle Slout. [Appearing in both dramatic and musical roles are jazz singer Joe Williams, Med Flory, of the Grammy-winning Super Sax group, drummer Louis Bellson, and bass player Ray Brown.]
While Lou wrestles with the unexpected break-up of a top team of reporters, everyone else is excited by Rossi's 'Where are they now?' story on a famous jazz group.
'Ghosts'
Writer: April Smith. *Director*: Roger Young. *Guest cast*: Jacqueline Brooke, Milton Selzer, Penelope Windust, Lionel Smith, Peter Maloney, Pat Finley, Ellen Blake, Allen Williams.
The sceptical Billie is on hand after a haunted house is the scene of a murder and the man accused of the crime pleads that ghosts are to blame.
'Cameras'
Writer: David Lloyd. *Director*: Peter Levin. *Guest cast*: Marcia Rodd, Jack Collins, Robin Rose, Kenneth Tigar, Corinne Michaels, Vincent Caristi, Lisa Blake Edwards, Read Morgan, Kevin Breslin, Danny Borshell, Neil Flanagan, Allen Williams.
When an angry mother claims her son was damaged in a sensational hostage case it sets off a controversy over how news can be slanted by press and television coverage.
'Review'
Writer: Jeffrey B. Lane. *Director*: Nell Cox. *Guest cast*: Margaret Hamilton, Karen Carlson, Diana Douglas, Don Plumley, Yolanda Marquez, Mary Ann Gibson, Allen Williams.
Lou knows he'll get unofficial criticism from outspoken Thea Taft, retired city editor, but hits the roof when an official complaint against the Trib comes before a watchdog committee on the press headed by an unfriendly chairwoman.
'Immigrants'
Writer: Steve Kline. *Director*: Alexander Singer. *Guest cast*: Raleigh Bond, John Carter, Kieu Chinh, Doan Chau Mau, J. D. Hall, Le Tuan, Antony Ponzini, Gregory Sierra, Nguyen Cu, William Bronder, Allen Williams, Drew Katzman.
The Trib discovers the plight of frightened and exploited refugees after it hires a Vietnamese photographer whose talent almost makes up for his breaking the city room rules.

'Hunger'
Writer: Gene Reynolds. *Director*: Peter Levin. *Guest cast*: Uta Hagen, Tonyo Melendez, Ivan Bonar, Alan Haufrect, Stanley Grover, Allen Williams, Georgina Schmidt.
On a bet with Lou that he can get a good story no matter what, Rossi follows a passerby who gives him such a challenging assignment he risks his job to work on it.
'Recovery'
Writer: Michele Gallery. *Director*: Roger Young. *Guest cast*: Clyde Kusatsu, Clint Howard, Pat Morita, Allen Williams, Lee McDonald, Arthur Taxier, Eunice Christopher.
Charlie tries to protect an ailing Mrs Pynchon when Rossi's dogged probe of war-time profiteers takes an embarrassing turn.
'Obituary'
Writer: April Smith. *Director*: Paul Stanley. *Guest cast*: Michael Bond, Simon Oakland, Barney Phillips, Rae Allen, Peter Michael Goetz, William Jordan, Lance Guest, Ward Costello, John Dukakis, Susan Barnes, Allen Williams.
A dash to make a breaking story brings tragedy to the city room and turns the routine job of writing newspaper obituaries into an extraordinary assignment for Lou and Billie.
'Blacklist'
Writer: Seth Freeman. *Director*: Burt Brinckerhoff. *Guest cast*: Freddye Chapman, William Schallert, Graham Brown, Jeff Corey, Rick Lenz, Helen Stenborg, Lance Guest, Sam Weisman, Allen Williams, Camila Ashlend.
The old days of the blacklist are revived in a personal way for Rossi and his reporting partner, Abby McCann, while the Trib comes under fire from parents angered by a straight-talking sex column.
'Law'
Writer: Steve Kline. *Director*: Burt Brinckerhoff. *Guest cast*: Charles Cioffi, Harold J. Stone, Charles Hallahan, Mary Louise Wilson, Bartlett Robinson, Sally Kirkland, James Canning, Fredd Wayne, Joel Lawrence, Allen Williams.
Legal waters become a whirlpool when Lou runs into home repair problems and a wily city councilman uses one of Animal's photos in a revenge law suit.
'Fireworks'
Writer: Michele Gallery. *Director*: Jeff Bleckner. *Guest cast*: Vincent Baggetta, Parley Baer, Sandy McPeak, Ken Letner, Lance Guest, Emilio Delgado.
Billie's Washington DC assignment is complicated by her ex-husband (Baggetta), a shrewd lobbyist who does his best to undermine her work.
'Unthinkable'
Writer: April Smith. *Director*: Allen Williams. *Guest cast*: Lane Smith, Bonnie Bartlett, Warren Kemmerling, Dean Santoro, Peggy McCay, Michael Fairman, David Wiley, Matthew Faison, Lily Mariye, Emilio Delgado.
What couldn't happen does: the unthinkable prospect of nuclear war, sparked by a crisis in the Middle East, sends Lou and his staff gearing for the biggest disaster story of all.
'Suspect'
Writer: Seth Freeman. *Director*: Alan Cooke. *Guest cast*: Lance Guest, Dixie Carter, Ron Woods, Christina Pickles, Roxanne Reese, Ron Vernan, Ron Recasner, Allen Williams.
A hit-and-run death turns into a bizarre story for eager cub reporter Lance, who keeps digging up more – and dangerous – details about the victim.
'Beachhead'
Writer: Gene Reynolds. *Director*: Roy Campanella. *Guest cast*: Cliff Potts, Michael Constantine, Robert Peirce, Bill Ostrander, William Traylor, K. Callan, Marc Vahanian, Lillian Garrett, David Graf, Al Fann, Emilio Delgado, Allen Williams.
While rival surfing gangs give the Trib headlines that land Lou in trouble, Billie and Ted move into their own home and wind up on opposite sides of a neighbourhood feud.
'Victims'
Writer: Steve Kline. *Director*: Peter Bogart. *Guest cast*: Steve Marachuk, Bruce Kirby, Barry Primus, James Gallery, Lincoln Kilpatrick, Wyn Saunders, Kate Zentall, Ann Sweeny, Bob Larkin, Michael Mitz, Bill McLaughlin, Allen Williams, Amy Kirkpatrick.

An armed hold-up in the Trib parking lot leaves Lou the victim and a policeman tormented with a guilty conscience.
'Twenty-Two'
Writer: Michele Gallery. *Director*: Seth Freeman. *Guest cast*: Lance Guest, Macon McCalman, Freddye Chapman, Joanna Cassidy, Betty Kennedy, Richard Lineback.
It may be routine for Charlie when he has to fire two incompetents, lend a sympathetic ear to Donovan and consider assignments for Billie and Rossi, but for a cub reporter the story he's working on is anything but routine.

We've Got Each Other (CBS, 1/10/77–14/1/78) Tape. 30 mins.
Executive producers: Tom Patchett, Jay Tarses. *Created by* Patchett and Tarses. *Producer*: Jack Burns. *Executive script consultant*: Sy Rosen. *Associate producer*: Ted Kaye. *Theme*: 'We've Got Each Other Theme' composed and sung by Nino Candido.
Cast: Oliver Clark *(Stuart Hibbard)*, Beverly Archer *(Judy Hibbard)*, Tom Poston *(Damon Jerome)*, Joan Van Ark *(Dee Dee Baldwin)*, Ren Woods *(Donna)*, Martin Kove *(Ken Redford)*.

Stuart and Judy Hibbard, a young married couple, have found their roles reversed, but face life's frustrations secure in the knowledge that 'they've got each other'. Stuart works at home as a copywriter for a mail order catalogue, while Judy goes to the office as manager of the studio of an eccentric but talented photographer, Damon Jerome. The bane of Judy's existence is Dee Dee, a strikingly attractive but terribly vain model whose petty demands are unceasing.

The plot premise of this sitcom was that of role-reversal; the female protagonist goes out to work in an office, while her husband stays at home to do the cooking and cleaning – as well as his home-based employment as a catalogue copywriter. This basic premise points to the demographic area of the series and its relation to the 'relevance' wave that had launched MTM itself seven years earlier. But as *Variety* noted in an otherwise very positive review, *We've Got Each Other* was launched into a 'changing sitcom acceptance pattern, which sees a diminished appeal to such adult-targeted product.' *(Variety*, 5/10/77)

Jay Tarses, co-creator of the series, is honest about its failure:

> I thought it was a good show but it was about two plain, lonely people, and you just didn't care about them. If I were a network executive, I wouldn't have bought the show in the first place. I'm not even sure I would have watched it myself if I wasn't involved with it. I have better things to do with my time. (*TV Guide*, 30/9/78, p. 36)

The professional photographer idea was also an MTM patent – having been career-subplotted already with *Three For The Road* and *Phyllis*, while the role reversal premise had been tested on *The Bob Crane Show/Second Start*. Created, like *The Tony Randall Show*, by Patchett and Tarses it joined that show and *The Bob Newhart Show* on CBS' Saturday night schedule, but was cancelled in January.

TV Guide's Robert MacKenzie has the last word: 'The show is one of a type, and the type has lost a good deal of its original steam.' (*TV Guide*, 17/12/77)

WKRP In Cincinnati (CBS, 18/9/78–20/9/82) Tape. 30 mins.
Producer: Hugh Wilson. *Associate producer*: Ted Kaye. *Story editors*: Tom Chehak, Bill Dial, Blake Hunter. *Art director*: Ken Johnson. *Lighting director*: Harold Guy. *Set decorator*: Jacque Webber. *Wardrobe*: Warden Neil. *Make-up*: Raye Steele. *Hairstyling*: Janis Clark. *Casting*: Sharon Himes. *Music*: Tom Wells. *Post-production consultant*: Rod Daniel. *Video-tape editor*: Chip Brooks. *Technical director*: Ray Conners. *Audio*: Jerry Pattison.
Cast: Gary Sandy *(Andy Travis)*, Gordon Jump *(Arthur Carlson)*, Howard Hesseman *(Dr Johnny Fever)*, Loni Anderson *(Jennifer Marlowe)*, Richard Sanders *(Les Nessman)*, Tim Reid *(Venus Flytrap)*, Frank Bonner *(Herb Tarlek)*, Jan Smithers *(Baily Quarters)*, Sylvia Sidney *(Lillian Carlson)*.

Radio station WKRP in the American midwest is losing money and listeners by playing the hit tunes of twenty years ago. To put the business back on its feet young Andy Travis is hired as the new Programme Director – and he meets the challenge by revamping the station's format to one of hard-driving rock music, aided and abetted by Dr Johnny Fever, a balding, washed-up disc jockey, and Venus Flytrap, a suave and debonair black DJ known as 'The Sultan of Sound'.

WKRP In Cincinnati, like *The Mary Tyler Moore Show*, is an ensemble sitcom about a broadcasting station in the midwest. But its surrogate working family regulars and show-within-a-show format aside, what separated the series from *The Mary Tyler Moore Show* in particular and past MTM product in general was far more striking than its similarities. For WKRP Cincinnati is not a TV news station like WJM Minneapolis – it is a rock radio station. And the series was symptomatic of MTM's decision to go for a different demographic slice and, in consequence, a different kind of comedy. *TV Guide* observed:

> *WKRP* is going after a broader, somewhat different audience. The rock sitcom provides instant identification for young viewers, of course. It helps, too, that the male lead is a handsome young man – and that there's a black character, a jive-talking disc jockey named Venus Flytrap. But the most egregious accommodation is the casting of a stunningly sexy blonde, clad in tight sweater and skirt, who manages, in the course of the pilot show, to thrust her very noticeable breasts under the noses of the two different characters at particularly appropriate parts in the dialogue. (*TV Guide*, 30/9/78, p. 38)

Nor was this 'accommodation' only visible within the series. 'Jiggle' television – which NBC executive Paul Klein defined as 'when you have a young, attractive television personality running at top speed wearing a limited amount of underwear' (Sarah Bedell, *Up The Tube*, p. 204) – had come to MTM. CBS trailers for *WKRP* had Loni Anderson, the actress playing the blonde receptionist, 'wearing a low-cut dress and purring "You can see more of me on Monday night."' Ironically, this bid for ratings via an accommodation to conventions was one of the few elements of the series that met with audience resistance. According to Sally Bedell, 'When *WKRP In Cincinnati* featured a witless blonde receptionist in its initial run . . . viewers rejected the show, CBS pulled it so the producers could make some changes. The series returned and presto: the blonde had been transformed into a shrewd mother figure . . .' (Bedell, p. xvii)

Although this meant little more than replacing one female stereotype with another it helped the series to steer away from the 'jiggle' shows that were already prevalent in prime-time and back toward MTM's perennial preferred arena – quality television. The series remained a compromise but, in a sense, an uncompromised one. Grant Tinker, for instance, was emphatic that while the show was 'our attempt to have it both ways – to do our kind of comedy but still get an audience in this new comedy cycle' (*TV Guide*, 30/9/78, p. 38) it would retain 'character development in the MTM vein'.

WKRP In Cincinnati was scheduled on CBS at 8.00 on Monday nights. It was MTM's solution to the problem Tinker posed in conversation with Robert Sklar: 'The biggest and crying need is for material for the early evening. If it isn't Fred Silverman's frothy things, it's very hard to programme early evening. We're sort of typecast. Our label is comedy.' (Robert Sklar, *Prime Time America*, p. 86) *WKRP* was a combination of Silverman froth (rock 'n' roll, 'jiggle', jive) and MTM style and format.

One of the ways in which *WKRP* evaded accusations of accommodation was by making it the theme of its own show. Thus the first episode of the series concerned the appointment of a new programme director, Andy Travis, to a radio station that had previously specialised in sedate, romantic music. Brought in to boost the station's ratings/advertising, Travis made no bones about transferring WKRP into a rock station, and was unconcerned about alienating the station's predominantly elderly audience and its few sponsors (Barry's Fashions for the Short and Portly, Shady Hill Rest Home, etc.). If this parodied MTM's own shift toward the changing audience it also replayed CBS' 'new wave' of relevance in 1969–70 on the crest of which MTM and *The Mary Tyler Moore Show* had come into being.

The series did badly in the ratings at first and CBS withdrew it from their schedules for some fine-tuning before returning it to the air in January. This time it was slotted later in the evening – between *M*A*S*H* and *Lou Grant* at 9.00, and it captured a much larger, and more adult, audience.

After four successful seasons *WKRP* was cancelled (in the same week as *Lou Grant*, another casualty of CBS timidity with its advertisers). That autumn it was in syndication, as an example of Victory Television's *Variety* advertisement demonstrates:

Dramatic debut!

'WKRP in Cincinnati' is New York's Number One 6:30 strip and the hottest new sitcom in syndication, according to trade press reports after the November 'sweeps.'
Sold in 90 markets, mostly for future starts, 'WKRP' premiered on 28 stations in Fall '82 with dramatic time-period increases . . .

'WKRP' Average Increase Over Year-Ago Program in Time Period.

84% more men 18-34 in 26 markets!
71% more men 18-49 in 24 markets!
44% more women 18-34 in 22 markets!
51% more women 18-49 in 22 markets!
21% more total homes in 19 markets!
35% higher share in 16 markets!
36% higher DMA rating in 15 markets!

(from *Variety*, 16/2/83)

Mary (CBS, 24/9/78–8/10/78) 60 mins.
Producers: Tom Patchett, Jay Tarses.
With: Mary Tyler Moore, Dick Shawn, James Hampton, Swoosie Kurtz, David Letterman, Judy Kahan, Michael Keaton.

Running for only three weeks, this hour-long variety show was a brave attempt to diversify Miss Moore's roles and, in *Variety*'s words, 'to reverse the evaporation of variety shows'. (*Variety*, 27/9/78) *Variety* confidently predicted that 'CBS no doubt will allow *Mary* plenty of time to establish itself', but it was unable to challenge ABC's *Battlestar Galactica* and was whipped off the schedules with almost indecent haste. With traces of *Saturday Night Live* and *The Carol Burnett Show* in its format, it offered no guest stars, concentrating instead on its own intrinsic interest and the talents of its little-known stars; it did include, however, traditional MTM in-jokes, like a dance troupe of bald, pot-bellied, middle-aged men named the Ed Asner Dancers, and frequent references to Mary's husband Grant Tinker – who was off-screen (like Phyllis' husband Lars in *The Mary Tyler Moore Show*). Amongst the co-stars was Judy Kahan, who had been in the MTM pilot *Love, Natalie* and the series *Doc*.

The show was produced by Patchett and Tarses, following a long period of sitcom scripting chores, which meant it was an attractive assignment for them. In 1977 James Brooks, Stan Daniels, Ed Weinberger and Dave Davis had all left the MTM fold (and CBS) for Paramount (and ABC), and Patchett and Tarses were much in demand. Said Patchett, 'It's the first time I've been excited in two years. If this show hadn't come up I would have left MTM too.' (*TV Guide*, 23/9/78, p. 27)

The creation of *Mary* was multi-determined. There was, of course, the desire to find a new show for MTM's brightest star. There was also the feeling that MTM-type comedies were no longer what the network wanted. Grant Tinker suggests, via the same *TV Guide* article, that MTM's comedies were being replaced by 'witless comedy for the mindless . . . tight leotards and short skirts.' ABC, under Fred Silverman, had shot to the top of the ratings ladder with what the trade described as 'jiggle' programming – bouncing breasts under tight T-shirts. Tom Patchett commented on this at the start of the season: 'The most popular comedies on television today don't have any story. They're just jokes . . . This year will be the worst ever. You're going to see stuff so putrid you won't believe it. It's all going to be carbon copies of the hit shows.' (*TV Guide*, op. cit.)

But MTM itself, at least until the 1977–8 season, could also have been accused of copying its own hit shows. Only when the television ecology changed and prime-time itself shifted its preferences did MTM begin to change. The move into variety (prefigured by *The Lorenzo And Henrietta Music Show* in 1976) epitomised this shift. But the company also moved into made-for-TV movies, mini-series and sixty-minute drama series.

Robert Sklar observed the demise of *Mary*. Having opted for a variety format for her return to prime-time television MTM produced an hour-long show and CBS scheduled it at 8.00 in the presumably secure Sunday night slot following *60 Minutes*. At first the series got 'respectable ratings and respectful reviews' (Robert Sklar, *Prime Time America* p. 192) but critics and audience were soon disenchanted. *Mary* plumetted to near the bottom of the weekly prime-time ratings list. In early October, the show was pulled by 'mutual agreement' between CBS and her production company, with the added news that she would soon be back on the air in a new format – with big-name guest stars of the kind *Mary* had so obviously lacked.

Jay Tarses was less enthusiastic afterwards. Interviewed in *Emmy* magazine he reacted, 'We told Grant we didn't want to do it. But he can sell you anything. He was always straight with you. He made us think we could carry this thing off. And of course there was a lot of money in it for us. But it was terrible – there was no way the show would work. I didn't think Mary should have been in a variety show because, for one thing, America wasn't ready for it. Also, she's a terrific talent, but she's not a great singer or dancer.' (*Emmy*, Spring 1981, p. 25)

The White Shadow (CBS, 1978–81) Film. 60 mins.
Executive producer: Bruce Paltrow. *Creator*: Bruce Paltrow. *Music*: Mike Post, Pete Carpenter.
Regular cast: Ken Howard *(Ken Reeves)*, Jason Bernard *(Jim Willis)*, Joan Pringle *(Sybil Buchanan)*, Kevin Hooks *(Morris Thorpe)*, Eric Kilpatrick *(Curtis Jackson)*, Nathan Cook *(Milton Reese)*, Timothy Van Patten *(Mario Salami)*, Ken Michelman *(Abner Goldstein)*, Ira Angustain *(Ricky Gomez)*, Robin Rose *(Katie Donahue)*, Jerry Fogel *(Bill Donahue)*.

A drama series based in and around the fictitious Carver High School in Los Angeles, California, where Ken Reeves, a former pro basketball player now retired due to a knee injury, coaches a rough and third-rate ghetto school basketball team; the series' title refers to Reeves' comment that he'll stick behind the team like a white shadow.

Pilot Episode
Writer: Bruce Paltrow. *Director*: Jackie Cooper. *Guest cast*: Bethel Leslie, Thomas Carter, Marilyn Coleman.
Coach Reeves hopes to persuade a promising athlete to stay on in school.
'Here's Mud In Your Eye'
Writer: Bruce Paltrow. *Director*: Jackie Cooper. *Guest cast*: Thomas Carter, Christine Belford, Lincoln Kilpatrick.
Reeves helps a young athlete with a severe drinking problem seek psychiatric care.
'The Offer'
Writer: Marc Rubin. *Director*: Bruce Paltrow. *Guest cast*: Fawne Harriman, Ed Grover, Lupe Ontiveros, Lew Brown, Rosana Soto.
While Reeves weighs a tempting offer to become a network sportscaster, he tries to aid a player troubled with failing school grades and a shoplifting arrest.
'Bonus Baby'
Writer: Robert DeLaurentis. *Director*: Jackie Cooper. *Guest cast*: Art Metrano, Annazette Chase, Charlie Robinson, Hilda Haynes, Tony Monaco, Robert Phalen.
A fast-talking agent tries to entice Coolidge into quitting school and turning pro.

'Pregnant Pause'
Writer: Steven Bochco. *Director*: Jackie Cooper. *Guest cast*: Ren Woods, Gail Cameron, Naomi Caryl, Phillip Robinson.
Reese, Carver High's star player, is pressured to finish school by his girl friend, who says she's pregnant and desperate to get married.
'Wanna Bet'
Writer: Michael Kane. *Director*: Jackie Cooper. *Guest cast*: Michael Warren, Booth Colman, Justin Derosa, Richard Reicheg, Leone James, Richard Marcus, Simmy Bow, David Himes, Lionel Decker.
Reeves encourages a troubled youth with a penchant for basketball, then discovers the boy is wanted by gangsters.
'That Old Gang Of Mine'
Writers: Marc Rubin, Gary Knott. *Director*: Bruce Paltrow. *Guest cast*: James Victor, Richard Cansino, Jesse Dixon, Robert Huerta, Manuel Padilla Jr, Alma Beltran.
A Chicano player seeks self-esteem by leaving school to join a violent street gang.
'Air Ball'
Writer: Marc Rubin. *Director*: Jackie Cooper. *Guest cast*: Penelope Willis, Nick Latour, Georgie Paul, Jenny Sullivan, Jonelle Allen.
The jet airliner that the team is taking to an invitational tournament develops a malfunction.
'Just One Of The Boys'
Writer: John Falsey. *Director*: Bruce Paltrow. *Guest cast*: Robin Rose, Peter Horton, Paul Marin, Bruce Weitz, Karole Selmon.
A transfer student is mercilessly taunted by his schoolmates when rumours circulate that he is homosexual.
'We're In The Money' (aka 'The Tournament')
Writer/director: Mark Tinker. *Guest cast*: Ric Mancini, Regina Brown-Hooks, Michael T. Williamson.
The team heads for Las Vegas to compete in a basketball game, but ends up competing, and losing, at the gaming tables instead.
'Spare The Rod'
Writer: Marc Rubin. *Director*: Victor Lobl. *Guest cast*: Brian Mitchell, Philip Sterling, Royce Wallace, Fred Pinkard, Renny Temple.
Reeves' opposition to corporal punishment is sorely tested when a student takes a swing at him.
'The Great White Dope'
Writer: John Falsey. *Director*: Michael Zinberg. *Guest cast*: Robin Rose, Jay Varela, Robert Costanzo, Cynthia Sziegeti, Carlos Palomino.
Salami shows promise as an amateur boxer, but his biggest opponent is his father, who is bitter about failing at the sport himself.
'Mainstream'
Writer: George Geiger. *Director*: Victor Lobl. *Guest cast*: Deborah White, Barbara Babcock, James Cromwell, Jason Green, Ketty Lester, Luisa Leschin.
Reeves is disturbed by his own reaction to an autistic student placed on the basketball team without the coach's approval.
'Little Orphan Abner'
Writer: John Falsey. *Director*: Ernest Pintoff. *Guest cast*: Eda Reiss Merin, Michael Pataki, John Bleifer, Ralph Bryers.
Depressed by his grandfather's illness, Goldstein is a passive target for his teammates' barbs.
'Le Grande Finale'
Writer: Marc Rubin. *Director*: Mark Tinker. *Guest cast*: Alexandra Johnson, Milt Kogan, Sarah Miller, Harry B. Danner, Fil Formicola.
Thorpe is attracted to a white girl whose bad reputation and prejudiced parents make the relationship difficult to pursue.

The White Shadow (Second Season: 1979–80)
Executive producer: Bruce Paltrow. *Associate producer*: Scott Brazil. *Photography*: Hugh K. Gagnier. *Music*: Mike Post, Peter Carpenter. *Art director*: William McAllister.
Regular cast: Ken Howard *(Coach Ken Reeves)*, Ed Bernard *(Jim Willis)*, Joan Pringle *(Sybil Buchanan)*, Thomas Carter *(Hayward)*, Kevin Hooks *(Thorpe)*, Nathan Cook *(Reese)*, Eric Kilpatrick *(Jackson)*, Byron Stewart *(Coolidge)*, Ken Michelman *(Goldstein)*, Timothy Van Patten *(Salami)*, Ira Angustain *(Gomez)*.

'On The Line'
Writers: Gary Knott, Dusty Kay, Joshua Kott. *Director*: Mark Tinker. *Guest cast*: David Hubbard, Ralph Wilcox, Russell Phillip Robinson, Deborah Lacey.
A reporter for the school paper believes that Jackson's interest in the numbers game may extend to point shaving.
'Albert Hodges'
Writer: Bruce Paltrow. *Director*: Marc Rubin. *Guest cast*: Richard Cummings Jr, Saundra Sharp, Ella Rains Edwards, Russell Phillip Robinson, Richard Derr, R. William Parker, Mary Moon, Eric Douglas, Jesse D. Goins.
After spending 18 months imprisoned for a crime he didn't commit, an embittered black student directs his resentment of 'white man's justice' toward Reeves, labelling the coach a racist.
'The Cross Town Hustle'
Writer: Steve Kline. *Director*: Mark Tinker. *Guest cast*: Wayne Heffley, Dennis Howard, Isabel Cooley, Hari Rhodes, Keny Long, Ronald McQueen, Dori Keller, Jeff Bannister, Peter Reynolds.
Reese is impressed with the promises of a smooth-talking rival coach, impressed enough to consider leaving Carver High.
'Sudden Death'
Writer: Joshua Brand. *Story by* Tom Chehak. *Director*: Victor Lobl. *Guest cast*: Haywood Nelson, Madge Sinclair, Hall Williams, David Ankrum, Jennifer Marmon, Rason Ross, Phil Rubenstein, John Mengatti, Jeff Bannister, Joe Eiland.
Feeling responsible, Reeves wrestles with his conscience after a promising freshman lapses into a coma during a rigorous practice.
'A Silent Cheer'
Writer: Steve Kline. *Director*: Victor Lobl. *Guest cast*: Robert Doqui, Taylor Lacher, Kim Hamilton, Glenn-Michael Jones, Larry Farmer, Steven M. Obradovich.
A pro scout tries to talk Reeves out of retirement; and a deaf transfer student tries out for the team.
'No Place Like Home'
Writer: Marshall Herskovitz. *Director*: Betty Goldberg. *Guest cast*: Hilda Haynes, Mary Moon, Erin Blunt, Dana Richardson.
After a fire destroys his family's appartment, Collidge accepts Reeves' offer to put him up until alternate housing can be found.
'Globetrotters'
Writer: John Masius. *Director*: Bruce Paltrow. *Guest cast*: Hubert 'Geese' Ausbie, Fred 'Curley' Neal, Nate Branch, Robert 'Baby Face' Paige, James Blacklock, James 'Twiggy' Sanders, Louis 'Sweet Lou' Dunbar, John Mengatti, Russell Phillip Robinson, Bob Delegall, Stanley Brock, James E. de Friest, Renee Jones, Barbara Jane Edelman, Joseph Burns, Mark James, Richard J. Baker.
The team have inflated egos from a 10-game winning streak, so Reeves challenges them to play some 'old men off the street' – the Harlem Globetrotters.
'Me?'
Writer: Sam Hefter. *Director*: Thomas Carter. *Guest cast*: Rosanne Katon, Judyann Elder, Mary Moon, Becky Gonzalez, Judy Sardo, Lisle Wilson, Teri Taylor, Erica Lyon.
Reeves' sex-education class has special meaning for Thorpe.
'Needle'

Writer: John Falsey. *Director*: Victor Lobl. *Guest cast*: Thomas Carter, Marc Jefferson, Leopoldo, Hope Clark, Eric Laneuville, Bryan O'Dell, Hal Hawkins, David Harris.
Hayward (Carter) seeks revenge on the dealer reponsible for his cousin's overdose death.
'Sliding By'
Writer: Charles Johnson. *Director*: Victor Lobl. *Guest cast*: Brian Frishman, Jerry Hardin, Lisle Wilson, S. John Launer, Phillip L. Allan, Mary Moon, Georgie Paul.
The 'perfect' student transfers to Carver High: a highly recruited basketball star with a very high grade-point average.
'Delores, Of Course'
Writer: Sam Hefter. *Director*: Leon Carrere. *Guest cast*: Deborah Morgan-Weldon, Taurean Blacque, Susan Davis, Jan Hill, DeCarla Kilpatrick, Michael O'Dwyer, Jay Fletcher, Deanne Mencher, Joseph Sicari.
Jackson is reunited with his long-lost love, unaware that she's now a prostitute.
'A Christmas Present'
Writers: John Falsey, Joshua Brand. *Director*: Betty Goldberg. *Guest cast*: Theodore Wilson, Rod Browning, Trinidad Silva, Deborah Lacey, Nancy Pearlberg, Mary-Gail Hobbs, J. Rob Jordan, Don Diamond.
It's Christmas, and Reeves has no place to go; his sister and brother-in-law are spending the holidays out of town; Buchanan is getting back together with her ex-husband (Wilson); Willis is going snorkelling; and the team is planning a party, without the coach.
'Feeling No Pain'
Writers: Marc Rubin, John Falsey. *Story by* Michael Halperin. *Director*: Victor Lobl. *Guest cast*: Andy Romano, Todd Susman, Maurice Snead, Jerry Lacy, Patricia Conklin, Lloyd McLinn, Julius J. Carry III, Dick Baker, Jessica Nelson, Merv Hawkins.
Looking for something to dull the pain of a knee injury, Salami goes shopping for drugs – on campus.
'Artist'
Writer: Marc Rubin. *Story by* Leroy Robinson, Marc Rubin. *Director*: Leroy McDonald. *Guest cast*: Gloria Foster, Herbert Jefferson Jr, Hazel Medina, Crystal Mukes, Art Washington, Gary D. Martin, Michael Montalvo, Charles Currie, Billy Crawford, Dick Baker.
A teacher tries to steer Thorpe away from his dream of NBA stardom and toward a career in art.
'Salami's Affair'
Writers: David Assael, Joshua Brand. *Director*: Tom Chehak. *Guest cast*: Darleen Carr, Fran Myers, Verria Whitehead, Theresa Hayes, Michael Karm, Rosanne Katon, Darnell Williams, Theodore Wilson.
While Carver's girls hunt dates for the annual Sadie Hawkins Dance, a wanton history teacher (Carr) seeks a tryst with Salami.
'Links'
Writers: Mark Tinker, John Masius. *Director*: Mark Tinker. *Guest cast*: Robert Alda, Simone Griffeth, Stacey Kuhne, Ed Call, Felix D. Scott, Jeff Bannister.
Reeves takes Salami, Thorpe and Coolidge on a golf outing at an exclusive country club, unaware of an unwritten course rule – no blacks allowed.
'The Stripper'
Writer: John Falsey. *Story by* Steve Kline, Marc Rubin. *Director*: Victor Lobl. *Guest cast*: Randee Heller, Robert Costanzo, Gloria LeRoy, Eric Server, Montana Smoyer, Jon St Elwood, Abbie Scott, Shaun Raphiel Harrie, Dean Miller, Juliette Marshall.
Reeves discovers that the dance teacher he's romancing is moonlighting as a stripper.
'Gonna Fly Now'
Writer: Steve Kline. *Director*: Mark Tinker. *Guest cast*: Kathleen Lloyd, Carl Crudup, Veronica Redd, Rudy Lowe, Lark A. Hackshaw, Joseph X. Flaherty, Nicholas Mele, Terry Cammack, Eleanor McCoy, Russell Phillip Robinson.
Team manager Phil Jeffers (Robinson) becomes the innocent victim of 'angel dust' when his drink is spiked at a party.

'Out At Home'
Writer: Barry Gold. *Story by* Marc Rubin. *Director*: Victor Lobl. *Guest cast*: James McEachin, Beverley Hope Atkinson, Meshach Taylor, Arnold Johnson, Nicholas Mele, Dorothy Butts, Jeff Gallagher, Brenda Elder, Mary Margaret Lewis.
Reeves is appointed athletic director, a move resented by a fellow coach with more experience.
'The Russians Are Coming'
Writers: Joshua Brand, David Assael. *Story by* Robert Di Pietro. *Director*: Victor Lobl. *Guest cast*: Chris Mulkey, Kenneth Kimmins, Zitto Kazann, Brad Maule, Jonathan Gries, Gregory Fisher, Gene Scherer, McKee Anderson, Jaison Walker, Penelope Krompier.
Carver High plays host to a touring Russian high-school basketball team.
'The Hitter'
Writer: Tom Di Martini. *Director*: Marc Norman. *Guest cast*: Hector Elias, Lupe Ontiveros, Carmen Zapata, Jan Stratton, Bubba Smith, Garcia, Gerald Castillo, Natalie Devis, Ira Angustain.
Reeves discovers that Gomez (Angustain) is the victim of parental abuse.
'The Death Of Me Yet'
Writer: Marc Rubin. *Director*: Victor Lobl. *Guest cast*: Fran Myers, James Cromwell, Beany Williams, Leland Smith, Norman Alexander Gibbs, Will Gill Jr, Craig Thomas, Theresa Hayes, Grant Wilson, Dick Baker.
Carver High wins a shot at the championship, but one of the starters isn't going to make tap-off.
'Coolidge Goes Hollywood'
Writers: Marc Rubin, John Falsey. *Director*: Marc Norman. *Guest cast*: George Wyner, Peter Jurasik, Harry Danner, Marty Ferrero, Paul Willson, Susan Krebs, Teddi Siddall, David Assael, Colby Chester, John Cewey-Carter.
Coolidge's latent acting talent is discovered by a television producer.
'A Few Good Men'
Writers: John Falsey, Joshua Brand. *Director*: Thomas Carter. *Guest cast*: Glynn Turman, Fran Myers, Carl Franklin, Dee Timberlake, Eleanor McCoy, Karole Selmin, Mike Finneran, Ron Pinkard, Darnell Williams, Teri Taylor, Morgan Kester, Jerry Bell.
As graduation approaches, the seniors consider life after high school.
'Reunion' (Part I)
Writer: John Falsey. *Director*: Bruce Paltrow. *Guest cast*: James Whitmore, Robert Hooks, Jobeth Williams, Thomas Carter, John Laughlin, Peter Hobbs, Mickey Mantle.
In Part I Ken Reeves flies home for a 20-year high-school reunion and a visit with his father (Whitmore), a hard-headed Irishman who's hiding the fact that he's dying of a brain tumour.
'Reunion' (Part II)
Writer: Joshua Brand. *Director*: Bruce Paltrow. *Guest cast*: as above.
Part II sees Reeves extending his New York visit to make one last attempt at becoming friends with his dying father; and the basketball tryouts turn out the new series regulars: Stone (Larry Flash Jenkins), Rutherford (Wolfe Perry), Falahey (John Laughlin), Mitchell (Stoney Jackson), and Franklin (Art Holliday).
'Georgia On My Mind'
Writer: Marc Rubin. *Director*: Victor Lobl. *Guest cast*: Rosey Grier, Melinda Cordell, Ken Sansom, with the Harlem Globetrotters as themselves.
Coolidge is in serious academic trouble and believes that a tryout with the Harlem Globetrotters is the way out.

The White Shadow (Third Season: 1980–1)
Executive producer: Bruce Paltrow. *Photography*: William Mendenhall. *Music*: Mike Post, Pete Carpenter. *Art director*: Carl Braunger.
Regular cast: Ken Howard *(Ken Reeves)*, Joan Pringle *(Sybil Buchanan)*, Kevin Hooks *(Thorpe)*, Byron Stewart *(Coolidge)*, Timothy Van Patten *(Salami)*, Larry Flash Jenkins

(Stone), John Mengatti *(Vitaglia)*, Wolfe Perry *(Rutherford)*, Stoncy Jackson *(Mitchell)*, John Laughlin *(Falahey)*, Art Holliday *(Franklin)*.

'If Your Number's Up ... Get It Down'
Writer: Joshua Brand. *Director*: Mark Tinker. *Guest cast*: Rosey Grier, Elgin Baylor, Sparky Anderson, Red Auerbach, Willie Tyler & Lester, Chet Walker, Jimmie Walker, the LA Rams Cheerleaders.
When Reeves reluctantly takes charge of a fund-raising drive to fight high blood pressure, his ball players resort to an imaginative pitch to collect money when all else fails.
'Christmas Story'
Writers: Joshua Brand, John Falsey. *Director*: Victor Lobl. *Guest cast*: Penny Peyser, Craig T. Nelson, Shavar Ross, Dain Turner, Adrian Ricard, Holly Irving, Eron Jackson.
As the holidays approach, a priest persuades Reeves to conduct a boys' clinic, while his team's idea of holiday spirit is to sell Christmas trees, for their own gain.
'No Blood, No Foul'
Writer: Joshua Brand. *Director*: Thomas Carter. *Guest cast*: Lee Chamberlain, Randy Brooks, Robert Costanzo, Lawrence Cook, Paul Larson, Gamy L. Taylor, Dana Gladstone, Eric Laneuville, Robert Phalen.
Pugnacious Salami throws a jaw-breaking punch on the basketball court, and is charged with assault.
'Vanity Fare'
Writers: Mark Tinker, John Masius. *Director*: Mark Tinker. *Guest cast*: John Laughlin, Ray Girardin, Frazer Smith, Sandra Will, James Staley.
Reeves is offered a television commercial and his ball players win a recording contract.
'Mr Hero'
Writer: Marshall Herskovitz. *Director*: Marc Norman. *Guest cast*: Sandra Sharpe, Eleanor McCoy, Bryan O'Dell, Karl Bruck, Charles Alvin Bell, Walter Janowitz, Hugo L. Stanger, J. Flash Riley, Gene Bua, Susan Keller, Fred Holliday.
Perpetual looney Stone becomes a hero in spite of himself when he carries an old woman from her car seconds before it explodes.
'B.M.O.C.'
Writer: Steve Kline. *Director*: LeRoy McDonald. *Guest cast*: Bill Russell, Michael Edwards, Eugenia Wright, Liz Sheridan, John Wyler, Maidie Norman, Jere Lea Rae, Corkey Ford, Violette Winge, Marsha Ragwell, Deena Freeman.
Embarrassed by his towering height, Coolidge exhibits a short fuse when it comes to wisecracks from his teammates and rejection by girls.
'Trial And Error'
Writer: Marc Rubin. *Director*: Victor Lobl. *Guest cast*: Rosey Grier, Jennifer Perito, Ron Pinkard, Jessica Potter, Jan Crawford, Marc Ross, Dick Baker, Al Fann.
Falahey tells a few lies to avoid basketball practice, and even Reeves is tempted to stretch the truth to avoid jury duty.
'Car Repo'
Writer: Joshua Brand. *Director*: Mark Tinker. *Guest cast*: Robert Constanza, John Steadman, Mark Brown, Helen Martin, Francis E. Williams, Marlena Giovi, Tom Patchett, J. Rob Gordon, Tony Perez, Dana Halsted, James G. Tinker.
Salami and Vitaglia get involved in the dangerous profession of automobile repossession when Salami's father (Constanza) forces them to find work.
'Psyched-Out'
Writer: Joanne Pagliaro. *Director*: Victor Lobl. *Guest cast*: Christina Pickles, Michael Winslow, Nicholas Mele, Leslie Speights, Renee Jones, Barbara-O, Dwayne McGee, Mel Waters.
A new teacher is cruelly harassed when word gets around that she's recovering from a nervous breakdown.
'Cops'
Writers: Erwin Washington, David Assael. *Director*: Lawrence Levy. *Guest cast*: Bob

Delegall, A. Martinez, Louis Giambalvo, Stephanie Faulkner, Stack Pierce, Wyatt Johnson, Becky Gonzalez, Ken Rector, Steve Jones.
The school community becomes a time bomb of violence when Thorpe is mistaken for an armed-robbery suspect and shot by police.
'Burnout'
Writers: Dennis Danziger, Eric Stunzi. *Director*: Mark Tinker. *Guest cast*: Richard Lawson, Lynne Moody, Ella Raino Edwards, Brandyn Artise, Nicholas Mele, Mykel T. Williamson, Merv Hawkins, Juney Smith, Don Cervantes, Bill Lodge.
Twelve years at Carver leaves a teacher (Lawson) burned out and he starts to give up on his students and his career.
'A Day In The Life'
Writer: Joshua Brand. *Director*: Victor Lobl. *Guest cast*: Nathan Cook, Thomas Carter, Ken Michelman, Ira Angustain, Ella Fitzgerald, Dennis Holahan, Jonathan Ian, Marilyn Coleman, Gerald Castillo, Christopher St John, Jusy Sardo, Martin Garner, Eda Reiss Merin, Luisa Leschin, Arthur Adams.
An alumi game returns four former regulars – *Reese* (Cook), *Hayward* (Carter), *Goldstein* (Michelman) and *Gomez* (Angustain) – to Carver High; Ella Fitzgerald appears as a former jazz great.

MTM's move towards drama series with sixty-minute episodes and away from thirty-minute comedies necessitated attracting new creative personnel from outside the company whose on-staff writer-producers were specialists in sitcom but inexperienced at drama. The next MTM drama series, *The White Shadow*, epitomises this uneasy shift, since it premièred as a mid-season replacement for the temporarily dropped *WKRP In Cincinnati*. Like *Room 222*, *The White Shadow* concerned the relationships between black and whites in a multiracial high school, but where the former had been a sitcom with a black history teacher protagonist, the latter was a drama about a white basketball coach.

Since MTM did not have a profusion of drama writer-producers on contract, *The White Shadow* originated as a package brought to the company by a talent agency, International Creative Management. Where in the early days Arthur Price, as the manager of Miss Moore and Bob Newhart, and MTM Enterprises as the preferred stable of a number of creative comedians, had been able to create new series 'in-house', *The White Shadow* was actually a package put together with the star Ken Howard, writer-producer Bruce Paltrow and director Jackie Cooper. Other 1978 series which ICM, as a 'packaging agency', had created for the prime-time schedule included *Taxi, Charlie's Angels* and *The Waltons*. (Back in 1970 they had also been responsible for acquiring the American rights to *Till Death Us Do Part* and, since they already had Norman Lear on their books as well as Carroll O'Connor, Rob Reiner and Sally Struthers, the formation of *All In The Family* was almost inevitable.) ICM had also been responsible in 1977 for the creation of the John Charles Walters Company, composing four of MTM's writer-directors – Jim Brooks, Stan Daniels, Ed Weinberger and David Davis – so the presentation to MTM of *The White Shadow* package may have seemed some sort of reparation.

Whereas CBS sitcoms were under fire from heavy pre-teen fare network competition, their drama had a somewhat stronger place in the schedules. Thus Sally Bedell, for instance, could comment that: 'CBS . . . continued to convince the world that its first initial stood for Class, thanks to the survival of *60 Minutes, Lou Grant, The White Shadow, M*A*S*H* and *Archie Bunker's Place*.' (Sally Bedell, *Up The Tube*, p. 283)

Grant Tinker, however, was aware that *The White Shadow* might be a ratings failure, as well as causing concern among CBS brass because it 'is about real and frequently unresolveable problems and situations.' (Quoted in Horace Newcomb and Robert S. Alley, *The Producer's Medium*, p. 225) Indeed the series was 'softened' in an abortive attempt to bolster its ratings and Tinker admitted that:

> We did try to make them [the stories] lighter. We and CBS decided inner city problems that didn't have solutions and therefore couldn't be wrapped up neatly and happily at

the end were depressing people, and/or they weren't watching to begin with. (Quoted in *Emmy*, Spring 1981)

Mark Tinker, son of Grant Tinker, began working with Lorimar Productions as production assistant on *The Waltons, Apple's Way*, and numerous television movies and pilots. He joined MTM in 1975, where he worked as associate producer on *Three For The Road, The Bob Newhart Show* and *The Chopped Liver Brothers* pilot. He also served as producer on the *Operating Room* pilot, *The White Shadow* and the *Thornwell* TV movie. Mark has directed *The Bob Newhart Show*, written and directed multiple episodes of *The White Shadow* and also directed a CBS comedy series, *Making The Grade*. He also serves as producer on MTM's *St Elsewhere* series. Here he discusses his involvement with *The White Shadow* series:

> Well, in the beginning, Bruce [Paltrow] and I just basically talked the script over with Jackie Cooper. Jack has quite a reputation in town. He's been in the business for ever and I think he may have been a waiter at the Last Supper, I'm not sure. But, Jack is invaluable in getting a project off the ground. Bruce's script was fabulous. Jack knew in what areas we needed to bolster understanding for the audience – and he's had quite a success with the pilots he's made for TV – so we were delighted to have him with us. And he was quite helpful in just getting the script into something that would really mean a lot to the audience. There would be no holes for them at all – in logic, story or otherwise. Plus, Jackie is one of the best shooters around and so he really brought a lot to it, despite the fact that he knew nothing about basketball. Bruce and I filled in those holes for him and it was a delightful experience.
>
> Basically, *The White Shadow* was about a white coach, basketball coach, in a black ghetto neighbourhood. This white coach had been a professional basketball player, had injured his knee and his old college roommate, a black gentleman who was now the principal of that high school, convinced him to coach basketball at his high school. Of course, there were quite a few misfits and tough guys and poor kids and uneducated kids, as well as a number of bright kids in the school – and they related to this guy, this big white basketball player, who they thought initially was going to be a big problem and not be able to relate to them. Quite the opposite; he was quite helpful to them when they would allow him to be. They [CBS] probably thought the show was a little too heavy from time to time and wanted it to be lighter in tone. We agreed to do that in the last season and I think the last season suffered for that very reason. The shows got fluffy and light and often silly, and I think we sort of lost sight of the gritty reality that we had in the early episodes that the network thought may have been too heavy. They may be right. Maybe we could have walked a finer line and established a better balance. However, we weren't able to do it in year three and in the first two years – I think we did pretty well at that, but by and large we did not have problems with the strong themes if they were timely and handled properly. They just didn't want them to be too much of a downer. They wanted them to be realistic, as we did of course. We fought with them over certain themes that they thought were too depressing but, for the most part, they let us do what we wanted. They really didn't come to see the dailies after the first few shows and we only bumped heads with them a few times and they gave us our rein. (Interview with the authors, 1983)

The Last Resort (CBS 19/9/79–17/3/80) Film. 30 mins.
Producer-writer: Gary David Goldberg.
Cast: Larry Breeding *(Michael Lerner)*, Stephanie Faracy *(Gail Collins)*, Zane Lasky *(Duane Kaminsky)*, Walter Olkewicz *(Zach Comstock)*, Ray Underwood *(Jeffrey Barron)*.

The Last Resort flopped in the ratings on its first outing and was removed from the schedules by CBS after only three episodes. In December it returned to the air but failed once again to accumulate an audience and was cancelled in March. *Variety* described it as 'one of the poorer examples to come out of the MTM production foundry.' (*Variety*, 26/9/79)

The series concerned a group of students working through their summer vacation in a mountain restaurant, The Last Resort. Writer Gary David Goldberg, who was later responsible for MTM's *Bureau* pilot dealing with American war correspondents in Vietnam, had started with MTM writing scripts for *The Bob Newhart Show, The Tony Randall Show*, and had eventually become a staff writer for *Lou Grant. The Last Resort*, though, was much more conventional, much lighter and (maybe as a result) much less successful. It was based on Goldberg's experiences as a waiter.

The show was one of three series on the networks that season obviously indebted to the cinematically successful depiction of student antics in *National Lampoon's Animal House*. The 26 September 1979 issue of *Variety* noted under the headline 'Last Resort Ploy': 'In an effort to boost what the web considers its best new sitcom prospect, CBS-TV has set a one-shot special airing of *The Last Resort* for Monday ... Prem show ratings were terrible for *Resort* ... and, to compound the fracture, reviews tended to dismiss the *Resort* premise as another *Animal House* ripoff project, which is not how MTM envisioned the skein nor plotted its development.'

Paris (CBS, 1979–80) Film. 60 mins.
Executive producer: Steven Bochco. *Associate producer*: David Anspaugh. *Producer*: Greg Hoblit, Edward De Blasio. *Creator*: Steven Bochco. *Photography*: Chuck Arnold. *Music*: Fred Karlin. *Art directors*: Jim Hulsey, Richard Berger. *Editor*: Lee Burch.
Regular cast: James Earl Jones *(Woodrow Paris)*, Lee Chamberlain *(Barbara)*, Hank Garrett *(Deputy-Chief Bench)*, Cecilia Hart *(Stacy Erickson)*, Jake Mitchell *(Charlie Bogart)*, Frank Ramirez *(Ernie Villas)*, Michael Warren *(Willie Miller)*.

A drama series centering on the activities of LAPD Captain Woodrow Paris who heads a special squad of detectives assigned to intricate investigations; stories move between Paris' police work, his criminology classes at UCLA, and his home life with wife Barbara, a nurse.

Pilot Episode
Writer: Steven Bochco. *Director*: Jackie Cooper. *Guest cast*: Vic Morrow, Barbara Babcock, Candy Brown, Kiel Martin, Frank Marth.
Captain Woodrow Paris is brought in to solve the murder of a prominent councilman's wife.
'Dear John'
Writer: Steven Bochco. *Director*: Arnold Laven. *Guest cast*: Lawrence-Hilton Jacobs, Harold J. Stone, Clinton Derricks-Carroll, Danny Glover, Royce Wallace, Taurean Blacque.
After his mother is crippled by muggers a rookie cop under the command of Captain Paris tries to take the law into his hands.
'Pawn'
Writer: Edward De Blasio. *Director*: Georg Stanford Brown. *Guest cast*: Wendy Phillips, David-James Carroll, Stephen Pearlman, Irene Tedrow, Joan Darling.
Paris finds that identifying a killer-rapist is a lot easier than coming up with evidence to convict him.
'Friends And Enemies'
Writer: Edward De Blasio. *Story by* Michael Kozoll. *Director*: Alex March. *Guest cast*: Mark Slade, Rudy Ramos, Alice Hirson, Barrie Youngfellow.
Paris investigates the slaying of an unarmed restaurant owner by a policeman.
'Once More For Free'
Writer: Burton Armus. *Director*: Alexander Singer. *Guest cast*: Michael Conrad, Dan Hedaya, Victor Brandt, Lee Paul.
Two quite different police philosophies cause conflict between Paris and his old mentor in a case of an elusive drug dealer.
'Dead Men Don't Kill'
Writer: Steven Bochco. *Director*: Jerry McNeely. *Guest cast*: Georg Stanford Brown, Stephen Pearlman, Marya Small, Jordan Clarke.
In a desperate effort to save a possibly innocent man on death row Paris searches for

evidence linking a suave robber to a six-year-old cop killing.
'Burnout'
Writer: Del Reisman. *Director*: Alf Kjellin. *Guest cast*: James B. Sikking, Bruce Weitz, Ellen Geer, Herb Braha, David Himes, Vahan Moosekian, Abel Franco.
Paris' delicate investigation of a gun-running gang is jeopardised by the insatiable ambition of a fellow officer.
'Decisions'
Writer: Irv Pearlberg. *Director*: Jack Starrett. *Guest cast*: John Quade, Sandy McPeak, James Oliver.
Paris' conscience is deeply troubled when an innocent man is killed by hijackers in the course of an undercover investigation.
'Fitz's Boys'
Writers: Larry Alexander and Burton Armus. *Director*: Alf Kjellin. *Guest cast*: Joe Penny, Tom Clancy, Laurence Lau, John P. Ryan, W. T. Zacha, Carolyn Conwell, Richard X. Slattery.
Paris becomes an honorary Irishman when he and his squad investigate thefts from the docks and the suspicious death of an old stevedore.
'The Price Is Right'
Writer: Jack Gillis. *Director*: Georg Stanford Brown. *Guest cast*: Don Gordon, Ron Feinberg, Frank Ronzio, Granville Van Dusen.
With a juicy political appointment on the line, Paris persists in his investigation of crooks who are driving elderly people from their beach-front homes.
'The Ghost Maker'
Writer: Burton Armus. *Director*: Bruce Paltrow. *Guest cast*: Nicholas Coster, Ben Piazza, James Gallery.
Paris locks horns with federal agents when he tries to prosecute a killer who, as star witness in a gangland trial, is being protected by the government.
'Pay The Two Bucks'
Writer: David Solomon. *Director*: Alan Rachins. *Guest cast*: Joe Santos, Ken Swofford, Jonathan Frakes, Anne Sward, Karlene Crocket.
When a good friend is framed for murder due to an extortionist's plot, Paris works to exonerate the innocent man.
'America The Beautiful'
Writer: Burton Armus. *Director*: Victor Lobl. *Guest cast*: Paul Koslo, Dolph Sweet, Ed Harris, Betsy Slade.
Paris finds himself caught in the middle when violence erupts between a neighbourhood association and American Nazis on the eve of a 4th of July rally.

For *Variety*, *Paris* was always a vehicle for its star, James Earl Jones: 'What gave the opener its distinction was black actor James Earl Jones' performance in the title role, which invested a wide scope of personality into the part – including a large dollop of the unique brand of big-friendly-bear warmth that has become a Jones trademark.' (*Variety*, 29/9/79, p. 46) However, according to Bochco:

> I used to get into really big arguments with James Earl [Jones] . . . He had a very different sense of heroism. He very much wanted to be a much more traditional hero in, no pun intended, a black-and-white sense. He wanted to be a symbol of law and order. You go after those bad guys and you nail them. And I always found that what interested me about doing *Paris* was exploring the limits of the power and realities of compromise, and how can you be effective under that constriction. (Quoted in Todd Gitlin, *Inside Prime Time*, p. 313)

And, for Bochco, the experience of *Paris* was ultimately disappointing. 'I was personally so dismayed with the work. I wasn't happy with what I did at all. And so I sure wasn't looking to do another cop show.' (Gitlin, p. 280)

MTM had been interested in drama about blacks for some time. They had produced a TV movie, *Just An Old Sweet Song*, a pilot called *Kinfolks*, a series idea for PBS entitled *Going Home Again*, and the racially mixed arena of *The White Shadow* series.

Variety noted that *Paris* recalled *Columbo* in plot structure. It also looked forward to *Hill Street Blues*. It brought Bochco together with co-writer Michael Kozoll and producer Bruce Paltrow. It also linked actors Michael Warren, Kiel Martin, Joe Spano, all of whom were to be reunited in *Hill Street Blues*. Kozoll's comments on the series reflect a rather 'routine chore' view: 'As far as the *Paris* series goes all I ever did was help Steve out on a couple of stories. It seemed like a strange combination of *Columbo* and *Delvecchio* with a black cop lead. It was a pretty average television series. The demise of *Paris*, I think, we can credit to the fact that it wasn't very good.' (Interview with Tise Vahimagi and Paul Kerr, 1984)

Kozoll's latter statement is, one imagines, a natural opinion on a series that 'failed' in commercial terms, failed to run into acceptable syndication figures at least. However, on a more aesthetic note one of the more remarkable episodes (one that managed to stun the viewing audience with a deep sense of helplessness, of despair and emotional reaction) was the Steven Bochco-scripted 'Dead Men Don't Kill' episode. Better than any trade review, J. Fred MacDonald describes the episode from his point of study in *Blacks and White TV* (Nelson-Hall, 1983, p. 227):

> One of the most powerful indictments of capital punishment in TV history occurred in an episode entitled 'Dead Men Don't Kill'. The episode was aired on 4 December 1979, and was written by Steven Bochco. The story featured Georg Stanford Brown as a wrongly convicted prison inmate awaiting execution. Although Woody Paris discovered the prisoner's innocence, the state governor refused to halt the execution. Brown graphically enacted the last moments in the prisoner's life as he sat strapped to a chair, eyes bulging, muscles tensed, agonizingly holding his breath and sweating profusely, then screaming his final exhalation as a cyanide capsule released its toxic justice into the gas chamber.

Paris was cancelled because the network failed to schedule or promote the series to any effect. It was shown five times on Saturday nights then six times on Tuesday nights – but with a ridiculous break of four weeks between the time-slot changes. It folded with a Nielsen rating of 12.7, ranking the series at 92.

Christopher Wicking writes:

To most viewers the name of Steven Bochco first made an impact with *Hill Street Blues* – yet he had been working in TV as a writer/producer for many years, most often in the cop genre. It was of curious retrospective interest, therefore, that *Paris* should start circulating on the British stations after *Hill Street Blues*'s arrival – for many a familiar *Hill Street Blues* name was already present in the *Paris* lineup: Bochco himself as creator/executive producer and occasional writer; co-*HSB* creator Michael Kozoll; directors Alexander Singer, Arnold Laven, Georg Stanford Brown and Jack Starrett, all of whom contributed to *Hill Street Blues*; and, of most iconographic interest, Michael Warren in the regular cast, plus Barbara Babcock, Kiel Martin, Joe Spano (all in the pilot), Taurean Blacque, James B. Sikking and Michael Conrad (six of the regular *HSB* team plus one irregular-regular, Babcock) guesting in various episodes.

However, *Paris* ran for 13 episodes, then was cancelled. Yet, perhaps with *Hill Street Blues*-related hindsight, it has many more virtues than Bochco and Kozoll remember. James Earl Jones in the leading role for a start. He is one of America's finest contemporary actors, and brings a Shakespearian weight to the blandest of lines, making every emotion one of nuance and shade, and bringing a genuine anguish to the many moral questions which the series poses.

The pilot (which runs a normal hour length) makes no attempt to set the series' concept out in the way a pilot usually does, but after a few episodes it generally becomes clear that Captain Woodrow Paris has been put in charge of a special squad of young detectives (though what their 'gimmick' is remains, for the most part, a mystery) and, as he also teaches night classes in criminology at UCLA, presumably he is designed to articulate the moral and legal parameters of police work. Certainly, at its best, the series tackles such conundrums – though never with the open-endedness of *Lou Grant* or the feeling for life's quick tragedies that *Hill Street Blues* exudes.

'Dead Men Don't Kill' comes near to the *Hill Street Blues* flavour. Used to last minute rescues and/or cop-outs, we're relatively sure that an eleventh hour reprieve will come. Amazingly, in the 70s prime-time TV context, it doesn't come and Paris is compelled to watch the execution. (This, incidentally, sounds reminiscent of the famous 'Prime of Life' episode of *Naked City* in 1963.) Certainly this *Paris* episode has an inexorable power, while we – and Paris – feel utter impotence and rage, all the more so because Holmes had previously been resigned to his fate and implored Paris not to raise his hopes merely to solve a current problem. Paris is wholly genuine when he makes his promise – and is thus all the more appalled when it proves to be a hollow one. The tears that he cries at the end are, so to speak, lovingly engendered by fine writing and direction.

Less 'important' in terms of subject matter, but an even better episode overall – perhaps the series' best – is 'Once More For Free', written by cop expert (and ex-cop?) Burton Armus, a veteran of *Kojak* where he was technical advisor as well as a contributing writer (he was also co-producer of this particular episode).

There's nothing too 'original' about the episode – unless 'style' is original, which it is of course in the cop show leagues. Essentially it is an examination of the 'hard man', the 'killer with a badge', the old-fashioned anachronism that Michael Conrad represents, and is engrossing and hypnotic, given Armus' script and Alexander Singer's seemingly effortless authority as director. Conrad plays Sam Beecher, Paris' ex-partner/mentor, who we learn got him through the streets safely as one of 'the first black detectives'. Beecher is back from Arizona and a divorce, working in LA as a security man. In an early sequence, he is provoked by two roughnecks in a bar, and clearly relishes the prospect. He puts the two men into hospital and although he's got to have twelve stitches in a knife wound 'that's the only thing that makes it look fair', says Paris. Then we learn that, just as Beecher helped Paris through the early years of training, so Paris got Beecher through his last years on the force when all he did was kick down doors and pull out his gun. Eventually the department was glad to get rid of him. Paris is now working on a case, trying to bust a leading narcotics dealer, who is an old nemesis of Beecher's. Learning this, and resentful of the fact that they could never bust him in the 'old days' ('Shoulda broke his legs and let him sell his drugs on his knees', he snarls), he makes nailing him a priority – once more for free – on a personal level. There's a great scene where he pounces on one of the dealer's henchmen, pinning him up against a wall, choking him, looming over like a predatory beast: 'Tell your boss – I marked him years ago and I'm coming for his skin. He belongs to me!' The henchman duly reports back, and has an apt description of Conrad the actor and his usual (pre-*HSB*) roles: 'He's got eyes like a machine. He ain't like real people.'

Yet Paris' wife Barbara modifies our view of the beast, this machine, who so far has been presented in appropriately unsavoury tones. For, at one time Paris had been shot in the stomach, and Beecher had come to comfort her. This was the first time she had actually met him, though she already hated him because Paris himself was becoming colder, harder-edged because of Beecher's influence. But she remembers how 'he sat with me, touched me, cried with me' in her distress. 'I've always loved him for that.'

So while the department works within the law with its stake-outs and procedural niceties, Beecher works in parallel, an insane private citizen, breaking any laws he likes in order to achieve a successful resolution. At one point, trying to provoke a gunfight so he can 'legally' kill the dealer, he flushes $150,000 of drugs down the sink – but thereby unwittingly destroying carefully 'planted' evidence, and wrecking the department's plan. He also tries to provoke Paris into a confrontation ('you're nothing but the city's house nigger!'), but he won't let himself be drawn. 'We were friends,' he says at one point, but Paris rejoins: 'You don't have friends. You just have people you remember because they respected you.'

Finally, having lost all his henchmen, the leader is getting the last of his stash. Beecher bursts in, 'Take that out and eat it.' 'You crazy?' the other responds, 'I'll O.D.' 'It's the painless way,' says Beecher, advancing with a wicked grin in a low-angle set-up. Guns bark, Beecher kills him – as he has the legal 'right' to do. The Grand Jury lets him off (Paris testifying to the legalities – but, quite specifically, *not* as a friend, for he strongly disapproves of Beecher's activities). Beecher decides to return to Arizona, where 'there's less people to interfere with you.' The last image is a freeze-frame as he walks away, back to camera – but with a 'second' Beecher reflected in the shiny wall of the courthouse.

Thus another of America's beloved gunslinger-types is seen as a dinosaur – but not without Paris laying some of the blame on the department for, in earlier times, Beecher's methods made the department look good and nobody ever told him different. If we're more interested in his 'style' than in the 'morality' that's an interesting angle in itself. If too much respect is paid Beecher, that's partly due to Conrad's wonderful performance, and after all the character is a kind of American heritage.

Mainly, therefore, this episode is a marvellous character study, but touches on many interesting points in the manner of a *Lou Grant* 'debate', while also incidentally 'revealing' previously 'unknown' facts and information about Paris himself, again in the 'sculptural' style of *Lou Grant*. But, perhaps because its subject matter is less 'important', it is always bound to be overlooked, certainly in comparison with 'Dead Men Don't Kill', for example. Yet the episode's *attitude* to its subject matter, and the brilliant way that director Singer works with his actors and Armus' screenplay, creates a little episodic gem, for essentially it is 'reworking' a theme, which is one of the essences of genre – which in turn brings us back to the concept of 'style'.

Few other *Paris* episodes have any standout qualities to remain in the memory, although the series was rarely unintelligent; which in turn suggests that its creators never quite got the mix to work, or indeed clarified for themselves their ambitions. But it does continually raise moral questions and encourage its audience to think as well as react, and in Earl Jones has an actor of the highest stature who alone is a reason to watch the programme. Also, in the relationship between Mr and Mrs Paris there's a clear precursor of the Furillo/Davenport relationship of *Hill Street Blues*, for Paris is also married to a professional (she is a nurse) and uses 'home' as contrast to cop-house, a place for peace and reflection, the relationship itself (warm, 'equal') allowing for doubts, fears, worries to be expressed. So, if *Paris* doesn't work overall (and it certainly doesn't), its value is quite clear if only because it was Bochco's last stop before the masterly series *Hill Street Blues*.

The Mary Tyler Moore Hour

(CBS, 4/3/79–6/5/79 [one extra episode tx 6/6/79]) Tape. 60 mins.
Producer: Perry Lafferty. *Director*: Robert Scheerer. *Executive production consultant*: Jim Hirschfeld. *Head writer*: Arnie Kogen. *Art director*: Rene Lagler. *Choreographer*: Tony Stevens. *Costume designer*: Bill Hargate. *Musical director*: Alf Clausen. *Special musical material*: Stan Freeman. *Technical director*: Harry Tatarian. *Audio*: Neil Weinstein.
Cast: Mary Tyler Moore *(Mary McKinnon)*, Michael Keaton *(Kenneth Christy)*, Michael Lombard *(Harry Sinclair)*, Ron Rifkin *(Artie Miller)*, Joyce Van Patten *(Iris Chapman)*, Dody Goodman *(Ruby Bell)*.

A one-hour situation comedy/variety series; Mary Tyler Moore portrays a television variety star coping with life at a TV studio and at home. The series uses a show-within-a-show format with Ms Moore starring as the host of a weekly television variety show.

When *Mary* was pulled from the schedules in October 1978 MTM worked fast to come up with a more successful format for their founder, their first and still most popular star. By December *The Mary Tyler Moore Hour* was already being recorded. But when the first episode was transmitted in March of 1979 the ratings and reviews were even more negative than *Mary* received. Robert Sklar's verdict is quite interesting. Noting that CBS was no longer leading the other networks, and thus that less time was given to their shows to find their audience, Sklar suggests that:

The hasty reconstruction of the [*Mary*] show into *The Mary Tyler Moore Hour* was based on the flimsy assumption that the public would accept a compromise version of the real Mary Tyler Moore – the Laura Petrie/Mary Richards fictional personality in the guise of a television variety-show star. The format was a mistake from the beginning. It showed her behind-the-scenes preparation for 'The Mary McKinnon Show', centering on the difficulties of finding a weekly guest star. It did give Moore a chance to dance at least one number a show and to sing and trade quips with her guests. But the inside show-business plot was tired from the start, and often grotesquely gauche, as when someone said to Dick Van Dyke (a guest on one programme), 'Don't you think Mary looks a lot like the gal that played Laura Petrie on your show?' and Van Dyke, shaking his head, said, 'No'. That line (and others like it on the same programme) may have been planted in a desperate effort to distance Mary Tyler Moore from her prior fictional characters. As the difficulties of the past season have shown, this is no easy task. (Robert Sklar, *Prime Time America*, pp. 195–6)

Hill Street Blues (NBC, 1980–) Film. 60 mins.
Executive producer: Steven Bochco. *Associate producers*: Scott Brazil, David Anspaugh. *Creators*: Michael Kozoll, Steven Bochco. *Photography*: William H. Cronjager, ASC. *Music*: Mike Post. *Art director*: Jeffrey L. Goldstein. *Editors*: A. David Marshall, Ray Daniels.
Regular cast: Daniel J. Travanti *(Capt. Frank Furillo)*, Michael Conrad *(Sgt. Phil Esterhaus)*, Michael Warren *(Officer Bobby Hill)*, Bruce Weitz *(Det. Mike Belker)*, James B. Sikking *(Lt. Howard Hunter)*, Joe Spano *(Sgt. Henry Goldblume)*, Barbara Bosson *(Fay Furillo)*, Taurean Blacque *(Det. Neal Washington)*, Kiel Martin *(Det. Johnny 'J. D.' LaRue)*, Rene Enriquez *(Lt. Ray Calletano)*, Betty Thomas *(Officer Lucy Bates)*, Charles Haid *(Officer Andy Renko)*, Veronica Hamel *(Joyce Davenport)*.

A humorous police drama series centering on a beleaguered group of cops assigned the bewildering, unenviable and dangerous task of maintaining law and order in the blighted Hill Street precinct of an Eastern metropolis.

'Hill Street Station'
Writers: Steven Bochco, Michael Kozoll. *Director*: Robert Butler. *Guest cast*: Trinidad Silva, Panchito Gomez, Jonathan Dasteel, Gary Grubbs.
Furillo juggles the conflicting advice of a SWAT-team commander, a police psychologist and a gang leader in his attempt to free hostages taken during a liquor-store holdup.
'Presidential Fever'
Writers: Steven Bochco, Michael Kozoll. *Director*: Robert Butler. *Guest cast*: Barbara Babcock, Rocky Echevarria, Trinidad Silva, David Caruso.
Hill and Renko meet for the first time after being shot; Esterhaus contends with Grace Gardner (Babcock), who's assigned as the station's interior decorator; and Furillo learns that the President plans to visit the precinct.
'Politics As Usual'
Writers: Steven Bochco, Michael Kozoll. *Director*: Robert Butler. *Guest cast*: Dan Hedaya, John Brandon, Lou Joffred, Jonathan Dasteel, Nick Savage.
Hill and Renko want their partnership dissolved; Johnny LaRue is offered a payoff; and, amid chaotic preparations for the President's visit, Furillo is hounded by Fay over child-support payments.
'Can World War III Be An Attitude?'
Writers: Steven Bochco, Michael Kozoll. *Director*: Robert Butler. *Guest cast*: Charles Fleischer, Barbara Babcock, Dan Hedaya, Charles Seaverns, Louis Giambalvo.
A rapist continues to elude police as he claims his 12th victim; Hill and Renko arrest a car thief who turns out to be a real handy-man around the station; and LaRue, charged with accepting a bribe, faces an Internal Affairs hearing.
'Dressed To Kill'
Writers: Steven Bochco, Michael Kozoll. *Director*: Robert Butler. *Guest cast*: Dan Hedaya,

Barbara Babcock, Louis Giambalvo, A. C. Weary, Jonathan Dasteel.
The DA has to let LaRue go in the bribery case; psychologist Goldblume fails to talk a jumper down from a building, and a squad of Hill Street's finest dress in pantyhose and halter tops in the grim manhunt for the rapist, who has just claimed his 13th victim.
'Film At Eleven'
Writer: Anthony Yerkovich. *Director*: Georg Stanford Brown. *Guest cast*: Andrea Marcovicci, Mark Metcalf, Robert Bryan Berger, Tony Plana, Joe Sicari.
Furillo probes the 6-month-old shooting of Hill and Renko; a TV news reporter arrives to film the activities at the station.
'Choice Cut'
Writer: Lee David Zlotoff. *Director*: Arnold Laven. *Guest cast*: Andrea Marcovicci, Panchito Gomez, Jay Moreno, Kent Williams, Dana Gladstone.
Furillo contends with yet another hostage-taking perpetrated by Hector Ruiz (Gomez); and Esterhaus is distraught over a memorandum from headquarters cancelling funds for Grace's redecorating project.
'Up In Arms' [aka 'Clap Trap']
Writers: Geoffrey Fischer, Anthony Yerkovich, Michael Kozoll, Steven Bochco. *Director*: Georg Stanford Brown. *Guest cast*: Robert Bryan Berger, Andrea Marcovicci, Jeff Seymour, Gela Jacobson, Mark Metcalf.
Dogged by the TV news reporter, Furillo tries to calm vigilante merchants; meanwhile, Esterhaus prepares for a confrontation with an ex-con he helped put away; and Renko senses increasing aloofness in Hill.
'Your Kind, My Kind, Human Kind'
Writers: Bill Taub, Anthony Yerkovich, Michael Kozoll, Steven Bochco. *Director*: Arnold Laven. *Guest cast*: Andrea Marcovicci, Robert Bryan Berger, Jeff Seymour, Panchito Gomez, Kent Williams.
LaRue invites Cynthia, the TV reporter, to a stakeout; Santini (Seymour) has serious doubts about his police vocation; and the Dekker Avenue Protective Association sets up headquarters in the station.
'Gatorbait'
Writer: E. Jack Kaplan. *Director*: Georg Stanford Brown. *Guest cast*: Carl Weintraub, Dolph Sweet, Jordan Charney, Don Cervantes, George Dickerson.
Furillo gets word that he's up for promotion; and LaRue and Washington play a practical joke on Hunter, who's patrolling the city sewers for alligators.
'Life, Death, Eternity, Etcetera'
Writers: Gregory Hoblit, Lee David Zlotoff. *Director*: Jack Starrett. *Guest cast*: Dolph Sweet, George McDaniel, Dwight Schultz.
Despite his imminent promotion, Furillo pushes an investigation linking a city councilman to a prostitute's murder; Belker is antagonised by a fellow cop; and LaRue recruits investors for his latest business venture – a combination bar and laundromat.
'I Never Promised You A Rose, Marvin'
Writer: Anthony Yerkovich. *Director*: Robert C. Thompson. *Guest cast*: Phil Schultz, Dennis Holahan, Don Cervantes.
Furillo frustrates his superiors by refusing to ignore murder evidence that incriminates a city councilman; LaRue continues to push his idea for 'saloondromats'; and Howard Hunter is itching to test a new armoured tank in 'sniper alley'.
'Fecund Hand Rose'
Writer: Alan Rachins. *Director*: Gregory Hoblit. *Guest cast*: Lisa Lindgren, Dan Hedaya, Michael Tucker, Barbara Babcock, George Dickerson.
Esterhaus nervously prepares to marry his teen-aged fiancee; and Furillo must provide police protection for Macafee (Hedaya), the cashiered detective who turned state's evidence for immunity from prosecution.
'The Rites Of Spring'
Writers: Michael Kozoll, Steven Bochco, Anthony Yerkovich. *Director*: Gregory Hoblit. *Associate producer*: David Anspaugh. *Photography*: William Cronjager. *Music*: Mike Post. *Art*

director: Jeffrey L. Goldstein. *Editor*: Tom Stevens. *Guest cast*: Charles Hallahan, Ed Marinaro, James Remar, Van Nessa Clarke, Mimi Rogers, Freddye Chapman, Starletta Du Pois, Tony Perez, Myrna White, Marc Cassella, Robert Hirschfeld, Vincent Lucchesi, Rony Clanton, Terry Alexander, Jack Andreossi, Sam Scarber, Frantz Turner, Jim Tartan, Neil Brooks Cunningham, Jan Stratton [US tx 19 May 1981; 100 mins].
Narcotics cop Weeks (Hallahan) faces manslaughter charges after he guns down a black youth; Hill takes a protective interest in a prostitute (Clarke) and her two children; LaRue hits the bottle on the job; and Henry is distraught over his young son's hospitalisation for an undiagnosed ailment.
'Jungle Madness'
Writers: Steven Bochco, Michael Kozoll, Anthony Yerkovich. *Director*: Corey Allen. *Associate producer*: David Anspaugh. *Photography*: William Cronjager. *Music*: Mike Post. *Art director*: Jeffrey L. Goldstein. *Editor*: Clay Bartels. *Guest cast*: Ed Marinaro, Van Nessa Clarke, Robert Hirschfeld, Charles Hallahan, Mimi Rogers, Freddye Chapman, Terry Alexander, Jeanetta Arnette [US tx 26 May 1981; '2 hours'].
Problems with liquor and money plague LaRue, further straining his relationship with Washington; Furillo presses an investigation that might clear a narcotics officer of manslaughter; Fay finds romance with her orthopedist.

Hill Street Blues (Second Season: 1981–2)
Executive producer: Steven Bochco. *Associate producer*: Scott Brazil. *Photography*: John C. Flinn III, Jack Cooperman, William H. Cronjager. *Music*: Mike Post. *Art director*: Jeffrey Goldstein. *Editors*: David Rosenbloom, Andrew Chulack, Ray Daniels.
Regular cast: Daniel J. Travanti *(Frank Furillo)*, Veronica Hamel *(Joyce Davenport)*, Michael Conrad *(Sgt. Phil Esterhaus)*, Michael Warren *(Officer Bobby Hill)*, Charles Haid *(Officer Andy Renko)*, Rene Enriquez *(Lt. Ray Calletano)*, Bruce Weitz *(Det. Mike Belker)*, Kiel Martin *(Det. Johnny LaRue)*, Taurean Blacque *(Det. Neal Washington)*, Barbara Bosson *(Fay Furillo)*, James B. Sikking *(Lt. Howard Hunter)*, Joe Spano *(Det. Henry Goldblume)*, Betty Thomas *(Officer Lucy Bates)*, Ed Marinaro *(Officer Joe Coffey)*, Robert Hirschfeld *(Leo)*.

'Hearts And Minds'
Writers: Steven Bochco, Anthony Yerkovich. *Director*: Gregory Hoblit. *Guest cast*: Teddi Siddall, Danny Glover, Sandy McPeak, Nathan Cook.
It is Furillo's 40th birthday, but before anyone can console him a prisoner grabs an officer's gun and opens fire on the precinct house; meanwhile, there's a search for a missing child; a paroled gang leader (Glover) is back on the Hill and out to regain control of his troops; Belker collars a purse snatcher, which turns out to be an orangutan; an officer is accused of arresting a young woman because she refused his sexual advances; Furillo wants more out of his sporadic relationship with Joyce; and Esterhaus just wants out of his torrid, and strenuous, affair with Grace. (Part 1 of 4)
'Blood Money'
Writers: Steven Bochco, Anthony Yerkovich. *Story by* Bochco, Yerkovich, Michael Kozoll. *Director*: Gregory Hoblit. *Guest cast*: John Dennis Johnston, Danny Glover, Karen Austin, Sandy McPeak, Nathan Cook, Sandra McCabe.
LaRue and Washington investigate the fatal stabbing of a prostitute; Belker and Henry pose as cabbies to get a mugger who's a disguise artist; a local gang is suspected of having a large cache of stolen weapons. (Part 2 of 4)
'The Last White Man On East Ferry Avenue'
Writers: Steven Bochco, Anthony Yerkovich, Robert Crais. *Story by* Michael Kozoll, Bochco, Yerkovich. *Director*: David Anspaugh. *Guest cast*: Danny Glover, Jose Flores, Nathan Cook, Reuven Bar-Yotam.
An elderly man, resenting the influx of minorities into his neighbourhood, shoots a Hispanic boy and barricades himself in his home; Belker loses contact with the officer who infiltrated the Black Arrow gang; Esterhaus starts dating his ex-wife. (Part 3 of 4)
'The Second Oldest Profession'

Writers: Steven Bochco, Anthony Yerkovich, Robert Crais. *Story by* Bochco, Yerkovich, Michael Kozoll. *Director*: Arnold Laven. *Guest cast*: Danny Glover, Sandy McPeak, Jon Cypher, Rosanna Huffman, M. E. Loree.
Lucy allows a prostitute to shoot up before going to jail; Jesse John Hudson (Glover) is arrested; and Esterhaus goes to lunch for the first time in 24 years. (Part 4 of 4)
'Fruits Of The Poisonous Tree'
Writer: Jeffrey Lewis. *Director*: Rod Holcomb. *Guest cast*: Jeffrey Tambor, Allan Rich, Mickey Morton, Ralph Manza, Essex Smith.
LaRue and Washington may have entrapped a welfare-cheque thief; a ten-year-old girl is accidentally killed by a gang out to get her brother; and Grace informs Esterhaus that he may soon be a father.
'Cranky Streets'
Writer: Robert Crais. *Story by* Michael Kozoll, Steven Bochco. *Director*: Randa Haines. *Guest cast*: Livia Genise, Robert Sampson, Stephen McHattie, Eddie Zammit, Tony Perez.
Hill covers for an officer who used excessive force during an arrest; Coffey arrests a family acquaintance for dealing in stolen goods; a breakdown in contract negotiations presages an epidemic of 'blue flu'.
'Chipped Beef'
Writer: Jeffrey Lewis. *Story by* Michael Kozoll, Steven Bochco. *Director*: Georg Stanford Brown. *Guest cast*: Robert Sampson, Lynn Whitfield, Art Evans, Daphne Maxwell, Stephen McHattie, Dori Brenner, Nick Savage.
Belker stalks a gang that mugs customers at automatic tellers; Fay's fiancé cuts short a fund-raising luncheon; and nobody wants to arrest a citizen who aids Renko but is wanted on an old felony charge.
'The World According To Freedom'
Writer: Michael Wagner. *Director*: Jeff Bleckner. *Guest cast*: Dennis Dugan, Victor Campos, Trinidad Silva, Andy Winner, Richard Foronjy, Julia Calderon, Fritz Turner.
First call of the day takes the officers to a neighbourhood bar, where three men wearing gang colours used the patrons for target practice the night before; appalled by the carnage, Furillo issues a swift ultimatum to the Hill's gang chieftains, to bring in those responsible or else; meanwhile, Belker's attempt to collar a robber is scuttled by the inept assistance of Captain Freedom (Dugan), a would-be superhero who believes that his mother lives in a bottle on the moon. (Part 1 of 4)
'Pestolozzi's Revenge'
Writers: Anthony Yerkovich, Jeffrey Lewis, Michael Wagner. *Story by* Michael Kozoll, Steven Bochco. *Director*: Randa Haines. *Guest cast*: Dennis Dugan, Jon Cypher, James O'Sullivan, Marcelino Sanchez, Charlie Robinson, Luke Andrews, Bob Basso.
Captain Freedom interferes with the capture of a purse snatcher; Furillo, Howard and Ray are subpoenaed by a grand jury; and Renko's gun is stolen. (Part 2 of 4)
'The Spy Who Came From Delgado'
Writers: Steven Bochco, Anthony Yerkovich, Jeffrey Lewis, Michael Wagner. *Story by* Michael Kozoll, Bochco. *Director*: Georg Stanford Brown. *Guest cast*: Dennis Dugan, Jon Cypher, Robin Gammell, John Karlen, Wayne Heffley, Janet DeMay, Jerome Thor, Harry Moses.
Furillo considers retaining a high-priced lawyer (Gammell) when it looks like the Sullivan Commission is out for blood; Belker tends bar to catch city officials on the take; and Howard attempts to track a wild-dog pack with a pair of basset hounds. (Part 3 of 4)
'Freedom's Last Stand'
Writers: Steven Bochco, Anthony Yerkovich, Jeffrey Lewis, Michael Wagner. *Story by* Michael Kozoll, Bochco. *Director*: Gregory Hoblit. *Guest cast*: Dennis Dugan, Jon Cypher, James O'Sullivan, Vincent Lucchesi, Scott Paulin, Jerome Thor, Harry Moses, Pamela Hayden, Richard Marcus.
Captain Freedom (Dugan) makes his last stand against crime, and is killed; Furillo forces a showdown with the Sullivan Grand Jury; and Lucy competes in the interdepartmental poker finals. (Part 4 of 4)

'Of Mouse And Man'
Writers: Steven Bochco, Anthony Yerkovich, Jeffrey Lewis, Michael Wagner. *Story by* Michael Kozoll, Bochco. *Director*: Thomas Carter. *Guest cast*: Jeffrey Tambor, Edward James Olmos, Al Ruscio, Kene Holliday, Howard Witt, Jonathan Frakes, Gary Miller, Karen Ragland.
A public defender is gunned down outside a restaurant; Hill's election as vice-president of the Black Police Officers' Coalition strains his relationship with Renko; Washington and LaRue put the 'sting' on a cocaine dealer.
'Zen And The Art Of Law Enforcement'
Writers: Anthony Yerkovich, Jeffrey Lewis, Michael Wagner. *Story by* Thom Thomas, Michael Kozoll, Steven Bochco. *Director*: Arnold Laven. *Guest cast*: Edward James Olmos, Alley Mills, Morgan Woodward, Al Ruscio, Kene Holliday, George Wyner, William Schilling.
The murderer of Joyce's friend may go free on a technicality; Henry and Belker step outside the law to put pressure on a slum landlord; LaRue comes off the wagon; Renko works without Hill; and Grace asks Esterhaus to quiet a barking dog.
'The Young, The Beautiful And The Degraded'
Writers: Anthony Yerkovich, Jeffrey Lewis, Michael Wagner. *Story by* Wagner, Michael Kozoll, Steven Bochco. *Director*: Lawrence Levy. *Guest cast*: Dennis Lipscomb, Eric Laneuville, Kene Holliday, J. A. Preston, George Wyner, Ricco Ross, Howard Witt, Peter Iacangelo, Barbara Brownell, Richard Marsion, John Brandon.
A witness to a murder seems too good to be true; LaRue may lose his job; Belker fears he's getting old; and Esterhaus confronts Grace about their physically satisfying, but emotionally sterile, relationship.
'Some Like It Hot-Wired'
Writers: Steven Bochco, Anthony Yerkovich, Jeffrey Lewis, Michael Wagner. *Story by* Michael Kozoll, Bochco. *Director*: Thomas Carter. *Guest cast*: Jon Cypher, Morgan Woodward, Rosanna Huffman, Debi Richter, Meg Tilly, Allan Rich, Bill Ratzenberger, Eric Server.
Henry loses a promotion; Esterhaus loses his car; Ray loses his pay; Joyce loses her cool in court – and all are thinking about quitting.
'Personal Foul'
Writers: Steven Bochco, Anthony Yerkovich, Jeffrey Lewis, Michael Wagner. *Director*: David Anspaugh. *Guest cast*: Trinidad Silva, Morgan Woodward, Alley Mills, Hope Clarke, Felton Perry.
Washington and Belker stake out a porno theatre to catch a mugger; Hill and Renko try to stop a family dispute before it becomes violent; and the precinct plays basketball against the gang's all-stars.
'Shooter'
Writers: Steven Bochco, Anthony Yerkovich, Jeffrey Lewis, Michael Wagner. *Director*: Thomas Carter. *Guest cast*: Morgan Woodward, Tracey Walter, Alan North, Karen Kondazian, Chip Fields.
Two police officers are ambushed with a handgun that had been evidence in another crime.
'Invasion Of The Third World Mutant Body Snatchers'
Writers: Steven Bochco, Anthony Yerkovich, Jeffrey Lewis, Michael Wagner. *Director*: Gregory Hoblit. *Guest cast*: Alley Mills, Morgan Woodward, Thomas Carter, Gail Strickland, Michael C. Gwynne.
Belker poses as a wino to catch a man who's knifing drunks; and Joyce defends a rape suspect whose alibi won't admit she was with him at the time of the crime.

Hill Street Blues (Third Season: 1982–3)
Executive producers: Steven Bochco, Gregory Hoblit. *Associate producer*: David Latt. *Photography*: John C. Flinn III. *Music*: Mike Post. *Art director*: Jeffrey L. Goldstein. *Editors*: David Rosenbloom, David Marshall, Ray Daniels.
Regular cast: Daniel J. Travanti *(Frank Furillo)*, Veronica Hamel *(Joyce Davenport)*, Michael

Conrad *(Sgt. Phil Esterhaus)*, Michael Warren *(Officer Bobby Hill)*, Charles Haid *(Officer Andy Renko)*, Rene Enriquez *(Lt. Ray Calletano)*, Bruce Weitz *(Det. Mike Belker)*, Kiel Martin *(Det. Johnny LaRue)*, Taurean Blacque *(Det. Neal Washington)*, Barbara Bosson *(Fay Furillo)*, James B. Sikking *(Lt. Howard Hunter)*, Joe Spano *(Det. Sgt. Henry Goldblume)*, Betty Thomas *(Officer Lucy Bates)*, Ed Marinaro *(Officer Joe Coffey)*, Robert Hirschfeld *(Leo)*.

'Trial By Fury'
Writer: David Milch. *Director*: Gregory Hoblit. *Guest cast*: Gerry Black, Gloria LeRoy, Ruth Silveira, George Wyner.
The precinct house is besieged by irate citizens demanding the blood of two suspects in custody for the savage beating of a nun.
'Domestic Beef'
Writers: Anthony Yerkovich, Jeffrey Lewis, Michael Wagner. *Director*: Jeff Bleckner. *Guest cast*: Robert Hogan, Jon Cypher, Vincent Lucchesi, Arnold Johnson.
With atmospheric temperature rising on the hill, Furillo becomes embroiled in a departmental trial over a fellow captain's alleged negligence; Hill and Renko try to settle a domestic squabble; LaRue is looking for a job in the Bahamas; and Belker forgets his mother's birthday and she's steaming.
'Heat Rash'
Writers: Anthony Yerkovich, Jeffrey Lewis, Michael Wagner. *Director*: David Anspaugh. *Guest cast*: Jon Cypher, Leo Rossi, Trinidad Silva, Robert Gray.
Bates and Coffey collar a 'space case' who claims he's an E.T. and needs the phone that the phone company wants to confiscate; Washington and LaRue quarrel over job offers in the Bahamas; but Belker is sizzling because he's got to chaperone a movie star.
'Rain Of Terror'
Writers: Anthony Yerkovich, Jeffrey Lewis, Michael Wagner. *Director*: Thomas Carter. *Guest cast*: Jon Cypher, Leo Rossi, Robin Coleman, Phil Peters, Michael Fairman, Francine Lembi.
The celebrations are few on Renko's birthday as LaRue and Washington set up a trap for bad cops; Belker takes Gennaro (Rossi) on a narcotics buy; Furillo tries to clear Henry of misconduct charges; and Howard finds an angel of mercy.
'Officer Of The Year'
Writer: Karen Hall. *Director*: David Anspaugh. *Guest cast*: Helen Shaver, Jon Cypher, Jesse John Bochco.
Ray Calletano, at the dinner honouring him Hispanic Officer of the Year, loses his cool; Lucy is upset with Joyce for humiliating her on the witness stand; Renko's mad at an assault victim for refusing to press charges; and Frank Furillo Junior goes missing.
'Stan The Man'
Writer: David Milch. *Director*: Thomas Carter. *Guest cast*: Robert Davi, Kathleen Lloyd, Jeffrey Tambor, Peter Jurasik, Frances E. Williams.
LaRue's law suit against a man who bumped his car is nothing compared with the head-on collision he has with a narc (Davi) over who's going to bust a dealer; meanwhile, Belker needs a bank loan so he can hire a private nurse for his father; Joyce is attacked at the station; and a condemned building has most of the Hill serving eviction notices and trying to keep one unhappy tenant from jumping off the roof.
'Little Boil Blue'
Writer: Robert Earll. *Director*: David Anspaugh. *Guest cast*: Jon Cypher, Vincent Lucchesi, Jeffrey Tambor, Michael Fairman, Larry Riley, C. C. H. Pounder, George Wyner.
Belker goes undercover to expose a personal-injury insurance scam involving skid-row inhabitants; Coffey has a Mexican standoff with a troubled Vietnam vet; Renko is caught trying to make a doctor change his report on a shooting victim.
'Requiem For A Hairbag'
Writer: Mark Frost. *Director*: Robert Kelljan. *Guest cast*: Jeffrey Tambor, Gerry Black, Jon Cypher, Vincent Lucchesi, Michael Fairman, Lynne Moody, Sumant, Kathleen Lloyd, Dominique Dunne.

Mizell's safe-deposit box contains evidence proving he was crooked, and Chief Daniels (Cypher) seeks Furillo's help to keep it from smearing the department; Belker, LaRue and Washington raid a doctor's office; Wachtel (Tambor) gets a different view of law enforcement. ('This episode is dedicated to the memory of Dominique Dunne')

'A Hair Of The Dog'

Writers: Steven Bochco, Anthony Yerkovich, Jeffrey Lewis. *Director*: Gregory Hoblit. *Guest cast*: Jon Cypher, Pat Corley, Michael Fairman, Helen Shaver, Donald Carter, Lynne Moody, Franklyn Seales, Trinidad Silva, Betty McGuire, Donnelly Rhodes, Charles Levin.

One of the six new recruits on the Hill may be a coward; a delay with the autopsy report on a murder victim may allow his killer to go free; Belker gets a new snitch; Fay is thrown into jail; a departmental party at a local bar shakes up a happy couple; and, while the governor is on a hand-shaking tour of the district, his dog is stolen.

'The Phantom Of The Hill'

Writers: Michael Wagner, David Milch. *Story by* Steven Bochco, Anthony Yerkovich, Jeffrey Lewis. *Director*: David Anspaugh. *Guest cast*: Helen Shaver, Pat Corley, Lynne Moody, Trinidad Silva, Donnelly Rhodes, Franklyn Seales, George Wyner, Charles Levin.

The hunt for the governor's dog continues; Eddie (Levin) brings in information on his lover that involves a multiple murder; Furillo is running out of time to book a murder suspect whose victim seems to have disappeared; Teresa (Shaver) dumps Renko and sets her sights on Coffey; Esterhaus sends Belker to fetch a ring for Grace; and the 'Phantom' strikes.

'No Body's Perfect'

Writers: Michael Wagner, David Milch. *Story by* Steven Bochco, Anthony Yerkovich. *Director*: Randa Haines. *Guest cast*: Pat Corley, Helen Shaver, Charles Levin, Franklyn Seales, George Wyner, Trinidad Silva, Lynne Moody, Irene de Bari.

Furillo wants Nydorf (Corley) to fake a case of flu to avoid testifying at a preliminary hearing; a drug dealer pegs Eddie (Levin) as a snitch; Renko fights it out with Coffey for Teresa; Crawford (Seales) is teamed with Hill; and the precinct's furnace, and Grace, have Esterhaus's temperature rising.

'Santaclaustrophobia'

Writers: Steven Bochco, Anthony Yerkovich, Jeffrey Lewis. *Director*: Jeff Bleckner. *Guest cast*: James McEachin, Khalif Bobatoon, Earl Billings, Gina Gallego, Micole Mercurio, Royce Wallace, Jan Stratton.

It's Christmas Eve on the Hill and festive cheer is hard to come by as Washington's guilt over his shooting of an innocent bystander surfaces; Hill's vagabond, cash-poor father comes to visit; Belker has his Santa Claus cover blown by a street kid; and a gang terrorises the neighbourhood with a string of fatal attacks.

'Gung Ho!'

Writers: David Milch, Jeffrey Lewis, Michael Wagner. *Director*: David Anspaugh. *Guest cast*: Peter Donat, Jeannetta Arquette, Elayne Heilveil, Peter Lownds, Ed Grover, Myrna White, Lisa Sutton.

The station is invaded by reporters when an armoured-car robbery leads to the arrest of a fugitive radical who's been sought for twelve years.

'Moon Over Uranus'

Writers: Anthony Yerkovich, Jeffrey Lewis, Michael Wagner, David Milch. *Story by* Joseph Gunn, Steven Bochco, Lewis. *Director*: Christian Nyby II. *Guest cast*: Bruce Kirby, Dennis Franz, Karen Carlson, Lisa Sutton, Alexandra Johnson, Jon Cypher, Sandra J. Bertrelle, Jack Starrett, Patrick Collins.

A policeman's daughter is raped and stabbed, the third victim of the same criminal; a woman asks Henry for help when her ex-boyfriend threatens to kill her; Lucy and Coffey confront a survivalist who's been stockpiling dynamite in his apartment; the search proceeds for a rat that bit Chief Daniels (Cypher); Renko is busted down to a moped and traffic patrol after he's arrested for 'public exposure'.

'Moon Over Uranus – The Sequel'
Writer: Mark Frost. *Story by* Frost, Steven Bochco, Jeffrey Lewis. *Director*: Oz Scott. *Guest cast*: Dennis Franz, Alexandra Johnson, Karen Carlson, David Downing, Bill Forsythe, Lisa Sutton, Jon Cypher.
Furillo halts the sweep of a crime-infested block, ordered by Chief Daniels (Cypher), when the arrests get out of hand; a battered, moped-mounted Renko risks his life to rescue people trapped in a burning building; Hill looks to avenge his partner's beating by Benedetto (Franz); and Joyce jets to Washington DC for an interview with the Justice Department.
'Moon Over Uranus – The Final Legacy'
Writers: Anthony Yerkovich, Michael Wagner, David Milch, Jeffrey Lewis. *Story by* Philip Combat, Steven Bochco, Lewis. *Director*: David Anspaugh. *Guest cast*: Jon Cypher, Lincoln Kilpatrick, Donnelly Rhodes, Gregory Sierra, Steven Williams, Richard Beauchamps, Mykel T. Williamson.
The courts move to stop Chief Daniels' (Cypher) 'Operation Big Broom'; La Rue continues to intimidate the criminal element with psychology, and a piece of army-surplus equipment; Henry tries some intimidation of his own on hostile gang members; Furillo confronts Joyce about her sleeping arrangements during her stay in Washington.
'The Belles Of St Mary's'
Writers: Anthony Yerkovich, Jeffrey Lewis, Michael Wagner, David Milch. *Director*: David Rosenbloom. *Guest cast*: Terry Kiser, Pat Corley, Harry Caesar, Whitman Mayo, Gregory Sierra, Dennis Burkley, Trinidad Silva, John O'Connell, Lisa Sutton.
Belker's over-protectiveness causes a rift between him and Tataglia (Sutton); Henry and Ray argue over who is ranking officer; Esterhaus conducts a tour for Catholic high-school girls.
'Life In The Minors'
Writers: Michael Wagner, David Milch, Karen Hall. *Story by* Steven Bochco, Anthony Yerkovich, Jeffrey Lewis. *Director*: Jeff Bleckner. *Guest cast*: Terry Kiser, Gregory Sierra, Ketty Lester, Stack Pierce, Ron Silver, Robin Gammell, Alley Sheedy, Pat Corley, Peggy Blow, Lionel Smith, Lisa Sutton, Arthur Taxier.
Coffey becomes the prime suspect in a prisoner's death; LaRue is losing his heart to a high-school student and his money to an inept comedian's career; Joyce reaches a decision about her future; and Fay tries to get the father of her unborn baby to admit paternity.
'Eugene's Comedy Empire Strikes Back'
Writers: Anthony Yerkovich, David Milch, Karen Hall. *Story by* Steven Bochco, Yerkovich, Jeffrey Lewis. *Director*: David Anspaugh. *Guest cast*: Ron Silver, Terry Kiser, Ally Sheedy, Lisa Sutton, Dennis Burkley, Gregory Sierra, Arthur Taxier, Ketty Lester, Ted Markland, George O. Petrie, Vahan Moosekian, Jane Alden, Joseph Reisman.
Lucy poses as a bus driver to catch a gang terrorising riders; the citizenry is becoming hostile over the jail death of an inmate, and City Hall may offer Coffey as a sacrifice; and the relationship of Furillo and Joyce takes an unexpected turn.
'Spotlight On Rico'
Writers: Jeffrey Lewis, Michael Wagner, David Milch, Karen Hall. *Story by* Steven Bochco, Lewis, Wagner. *Director*: Rick Wallace. *Guest cast*: Michael Lerner, Marion Yue, Dennis Burkley, Leonard Stone, Kathleen Lloyd, George Innes, Marco Rodriguez, Dennis Franz.
A brutal narcotic cop (Franz) has a special assignment on the Hill; Furillo and Henry interrogate a suspect with multiple personalities, one of which may be a killer; cash flow problems arise when vouchers are issued instead of pay-cheques.
'Buddy, Can You Spare A Heart?'
Writers: Michael Wagner, David Milch, Karen Hall. *Story by* Steven Bochco, Anthony Yerkovich, Jeffrey Lewis. *Director*: Thomas Carter. *Guest cast*: Dennis Franz, Jonathan Banks, Marco Rodriguez, Michael Lerner, Marion Kodama Yue, George Innes, Zerondrick Hubbard, David Fresco, Richard Roat, Sheldon Feldner.
Washington goes undercover in Benedetto's (Franz) scheme to nail a loan shark; an unclaimed bag of money plays on the consciences of an opportunistic Renko and a nervous

Hill; LaRue stacks the deck to clean up in the police betting pool.
'A Hill Of Beans'
Writers: Anthony Yerkovich, David Milch, Mark Frost. *Story by* Steven Bochco, Jeffrey Lewis, Milch. *Director*: Rick Wallace. *Guest cast*: Trinidad Silva, Dennis Franz, Marco Rodriguez, Michael Lerner, Jon Cypher, George Innes, David Fresco, Tom Ryan, Arnie Moore, Allan Rich, Stanley Kamel, Kale Williamson.
LaRue and Belker discover that Washington's blown undercover operation was a set-up by someone in the department; everyone is searching for the thief who heisted the precinct's overdue payroll; and Joyce is victimised by a sincere purse snatcher.

Hill Street Blues (Fourth Season: 1983–4)
Executive producers: Steven Bochco, Gregory Hoblit. *Associate producers*: David Latt, Ellen Pressman Sarid. *Photography*: John C. Flinn III, Terry K. Meade. *Music*: Mike Post. *Art director*: Ned Parsons. *Editors*: David Saxon, Ray Daniels, Joe Ann Fogle.
Regular cast: Daniel J. Travanti *(Capt. Frank Furillo)*, Veronica Hamel *(Joyce Davenport)*, Michael Conrad *(Sgt. Phil Esterhaus)*, Bruce Weitz *(Mike Belker)*, Michael Warren *(Officer Bobby Hill)*, Charles Haid *(Officer Andy Renko)*, Rene Enriquez *(Lt. Ray Calletano)*, Kiel Martin *(Det. Johnny LaRue)*, Taurean Blacque *(Det. Neal Washington)*, Joe Spano *(Lt. Henry Goldblume)*, Betty Thomas *(Officer Lucy Bates)*, James B. Sikking *(Lt. Howard Hunter)*, Barbara Bosson *(Fay Furillo)*, Ed Marinaro *(Officer Joe Coffey)*.

'Here's Adventure, Here's Romance'
Writers: Michael Wagner, David Milch, Karen Hall, Mark Frost. *Story by* Steven Bochco, Jeffrey Lewis, Milch. *Director*: Chris Nyby II. *Guest cast*: Lawrence Pressman, Martin Ferrero, Eugene Butler, George Wyner, Tracey Walter, George D. Wallace, Don Diamond, Bill Watson, Nick Savage, Rudy Ramos.
It's hot, it's humid and there's a power failure on the Hill; there's also looting, traffic jams, hair-trigger tempers and a crazy who thinks he's the Cisco Kid; a maniac has been shooting up gay bars and a lone witness, who happens to be one of Furillo's detectives, refuses to come forward; meanwhile, Fay searches for a childbirth 'coach'.
'Ba-Bing, Ba-Bing'
Writer: Karen Hall. *Director*: David Anspaugh. *Guest cast*: Jon Cypher, Ron Parady, George Coe, Kale Browne, Panchito Gomez, Harrison Page, Dian Gallup, Denise Gallup, Trinidad Silva, John Medici, William Schilling.
The Hill is caught in a political vice when Chief Daniels' opponent (George Coe) in the mayoral race takes up residence in the projects during a gang war; Belker is suspended for roughing up the deputy police chief; Hill wins $100,000 in a lottery; and Coffey scores big with a pair of female mud wrestlers.
'The Long Law Of The Arm'
Writer: Michael Wagner. *Director*: Alexander Singer. *Guest cast*: George Coe, Clinton Derricks-Carroll, Jon Cypher, Panchito Gomez, William Schilling, Harrison Page, Kale Browne, Larry D. Mann, Ron Parady.
Mayoral candidate Fisk (Coe) is taken hostage by Hector (Gomez), who demands that Martinez be returned to prison; Hill has problems dealing with his instant wealth and popularity; Joyce defends an immigrant accused of murder; and Assistant Police Chief Mahoney (Parady) continues his witch hunt on the Hill.
'Death By Kiki'
Writers: David Milch, Mark Frost. *Director*: Bill Duke. *Guest cast*: George Coe, Clinton Derricks-Carroll, William Schilling, Kale Brown, Trinidad Silva, Jon Cypher, Larry D. Mann, Ron Parady.
Chief Daniels (Cypher) becomes the clear front-runner when his opponent (Coe) 'drops out' of the mayoral race; Furillo makes a deal with Chief Daniels to call off the dogs, namely Assistant Police Chief Mahoney (Parady); Hill's fortune has created a monster out of him; and the Nigerian immigrant (Derricks-Carroll) accused of murder refuses to plea-bargain.
'Doris In Wonderland'

Writer: Peter Silverman. *Story by* Steven Bochco, Jeffrey Lewis, David Milch. *Director*: Arthur Seidelman. *Guest cast*: Jon Cypher, Ron Parady, Alfre Woodard, J. A. Preston, George Wyner, Larry D. Mann, Tony Perez, Sam Groom.
A black precinct captain (Preston) declares his candidacy for mayor, dividing political loyalties on the Hill; Officer Perez (Perez) shoots a child holding a toy gun; Furillo plants four detectives in a porn palace in another precinct; Bates is injured by a man on PCP.
'Praise Dilaudid'
Writer: Michael Wagner. *Story by* Steven Bochco, Jeffrey Lewis, David Milch. *Director*: Gabrielle Beaumont. *Guest cast*: Michael Horton, Sam Groom, Alfre Woodard, Larry D. Mann, Jeffrey Tambor, Kale Browne, Jon Cypher, Milton Selzer, George Wyner, J. A. Preston.
Ozzie Cleveland (Preston), the black precinct captain, and Chief Daniels (Cypher) square off in a televised debate; a drug bust at Murray's Wonderland results in a shoot-out; Mrs Robson (Woodard) appears in court on child-endangering charges; Henry negotiates with a desperate drug addict (Horton).
'Goodbye, Mr Scripps'
Writer: Mark Frost. *Story by* Steven Bochco, Jeffrey Lewis, David Milch. *Director*: Corey Allen. *Guest cast*: Jon Cypher, Kenneth Tigar, Jeffrey Tambor, Ron Parady, George Wyner, Tony Perez, Alfre Woodard, J. A. Preston.
On election day, Chief Daniels (Cypher) suggests that his election could benefit Furillo's career; feeling he's been made a scapegoat, Mahoney (Parady) vows to ruin the Chief; Henry contends with a slightly unhinged mayoral candidate (Tigar); Wachtel (Tambor) wants police protection for Murray's Wonderland.
'Midway To What?'
Writers: Jeffrey Lewis, Michael Wagner, Karen Hall, Mark Frost. *Story by* Lewis, David Milch, based in part on an unpublished story by Darrell Ray and Alan Toy. *Director*: Thomas Carter. *Guest cast*: Gary Frank, Guy Boyd, Michael Durrell, Robert Phalen, George Wyner, Barney Martin, Al Ruscio.
Suspecting that cops are on the take, Furillo orders a raid on a bookie joint; Bernstein (Wyner) is less than pleased that his manslaughter case rests on the eyewitness testimony of vagrants and perverts; Belker befriends a bitter man (Frank) confined to a wheelchair; Hill has second thoughts about representing the precinct in a boxing match.
'Honk If You're A Goose'
Writers: Michael Wagner, David Milch, Karen Hall, Mark Frost. *Story by* Jeffrey Lewis, Milch, based in part on an unpublished story by Darrell Ray and Alan Toy. *Director:* Arthur Seidelman. *Guest cast*: Gary Frank, Jon Cypher, Guy Boyd, Michael Durrell, George Wyner, Lisa Sutton, Barney Martin.
The bookie Seltzer (Martin) wants a deal, claiming he has proof of widespread corruption; Belker hits the streets in a wheelchair; Hill isn't so sure he'll win the precinct-championship fight; Bates and Coffey take on a mean-spirited guard goose.
'The Russians Are Coming'
Writer: Dennis Cooper. *Story by* Jeffrey Lewis and Cooper, based in part on an unpublished story by Stanley N. Wellborn. *Director*: Randa Haines. *Guest cast*: Allan Kolman, Natasha Shneider, Lynne Moody, Louis Giambalvo, Larry D. Mann, Bruno Kirby, Richard Brooks.
Howard gives three Russians a tour of the precinct; Belker poses as an ambulance attendant; Joyce gets a mentally disturbed youth (Brooks) released on his own recognizance; LaRue's brother-in-law (Giambalvo) is busted for soliciting; Henry and Fay discuss telling Furillo about their relationship.
'Ratman And Bobbin'
Writers: Jeffrey Lewis, Michael Wagner, Karen Hall, Mark Frost. *Story by* Steven Bochco, Lewis, David Milch. *Director*: Richard Compton. *Guest cast*: Vincent Baggetta, Lynne Moody, George Wyner, Jon Cypher, Ron Rifkin, Harrison Page, Dana Gladstone, Fred McCarren, Debi Richter, Ted Gehring.
The Chief (Cypher) approves Furillo's plan to investigate corruption in the new mayor's

former precinct; Henry, who's temporarily assigned roll-call duty, feels he's being treated 'differently' because of his relationship with Fay; a cop killer is on the loose; the Pied Piper of rat exterminators is hired to rid the precinct of its rodent problem.

'Nichols From Heaven'

Writer: Dennis Cooper. *Story by* Steven Bochco, Jeffrey Lewis, David Milch. *Director*: Thomas Carter. *Guest cast*: George Wyner, Fred McCarren, Vincent Baggetta, Lisa Sutton, Joe Pantoliano, Richard Stahl, Dana Gladstone, Larry D. Mann, Harrison Page.

Henry, filling in at roll-call for Esterhaus while he undergoes some hospital tests, instructs the troops to guard themselves against the maniacal cop killer; Furillo is ready to snap from the strain of the job and personal problems.

'Fuchs Me? Fuchs You?'

Writers: David Milch, Michael Wagner, Karen Hall, Mark Frost. *Story by* Milch, Steven Bochco, Jeffrey Lewis. *Director*: Arthur Seidelman. *Guest cast*: Linda Hamilton, Caroline McWilliams, Barry Tubb, George Wyner, Jon Cypher, J. A. Preston, Vincent Baggetta, Fred McCarren, Vincent Lucchesi, Dennis Lipscomb.

Furillo does some house cleaning when he orders the arrest of fellow cops for running a ring of corruption; two male cops draw guns over the love of a female officer who has fallen for the younger of the pair; Coffey becomes the latest target for the cop killer when he tries to aid an injured child.

'Grace Under Pressure'

Writers: Jeffrey Lewis, Michael Wagner, Karen Hall, Mark Frost. *Story by* Lewis, Steven Bochco, David Milch. *Director*: Rick Wallace. *Guest cast*: Barbara Babcock, Linda Hamilton, Jane Kaczmarek, Barry Tubb, Trinidad Silva, Lisa Sutton, John Hancock, Jon Cypher, George Wyner.

Sergeant Esterhaus dies suddenly in the arms of Grace Gardner (Babcock) and the entire station is grief stricken, with each officer trying to cope with the death by remembering good times; Furillo is named executor at Esterhaus' death and the Sergeant's legend grows as rumours abound about who will take his position; Lucy is put up as a reluctant candidate for roll-call officer; Fay is arrested for soliciting.

'The Other Side Of Oneness'

Writers: Michael Wagner, David Milch, Mark Frost, Roger Director. *Story by* Steven Bochco, Jeffrey Lewis, Milch. *Director*: Alexander Singer. *Guest cast*: Kay Lenz, Gail Strickland, Barry Tubb, Trinidad Silva, Jane Kaczmarek, Larry D. Mann, Jon Cypher, George Wyner, Vincent Lucchesi.

A prostitute held on murder charges intrigues Henry after porno videotapes emerge featuring her with government big shots, and Chief Daniels temporarily confiscates the tapes; Lucy finally takes the offer of roll-call sergeant.

'Parting Is Such Sweep Sorrow'

Writers: Jeffrey Lewis, Michael Wagner, David Milch, Mark Frost. *Story by* Steven Bochco, Lewis, Milch. *Director*: Gregory Hoblit. *Guest cast*: Linda Hamilton, Edward James Olmos, Clarence Williams III, Jane Kaczmarek, George Wyner, Jon Cypher, Barry Tubb.

A tense Sergeant Lucy Bates has a rocky start in her first roll call and finds that she must earn new respect among her fellow cops; Furillo must find the best way to follow Esterhaus' instructions to have his ashes scattered at the Hill's epicentre, the murder of the videotaped prostitute leads to another professional slaying.

'The End Of Logan's Run'

Writers: Jeffrey Lewis, David Milch, Karen Hall, Mark Frost. *Story by* Steven Bochco, Lewis, Milch. *Director*: Christian Nyby II. *Guest cast*: Scatman Crothers, Jane Kaczmarek, Jeffrey Tambor, Lisa Sutton, Tracy Reed, Jesse D. Goins, Andy Romano, Fritz Turner.

When Joyce is assigned to defend William Mullins (Goins) for murder, she notices the effect that his threatening brother Timothy (Turner) has on the prosecution's witness; Belker and others begin undercover surveillance of the Stop 'N' Cop drug emporium; Goldblume and Fay agree to remain friends.

'The Count Of Monty Tasco'

Writers: Jeffrey Lewis, Michael Wagner, Mark Frost, Roger Director. *Story by* Steven

Bochco, Lewis, David Milch. *Director*: Rick Wallace. *Guest cast*: Barry Corbin, Jonelle Allen, Jon Cypher, Jesse D. Goins, Jane Kaczmarek, George Wyner, Alan North, Larry D. Mann, Ken Olin, Alex Hyde-White, Debi Richter.
A horrendous day has Furillo slowly caving in to pressure when the mayor relieves him of his command; in addition, Furillo's personal life is rocked when one of the dangerous Mullins brothers promises him that Joyce will die; Renko is asked by a pregnant Daryl Ann (Richter) to marry her; Hunter stalks Fay.
'Nutcracker Suite'
Writers: Michael Wagner, David Milch, Karen Hall, Mark Frost. *Story by* Steven Bochco, Jeffrey Lewis, Milch. *Director*: Arthur Seidelman. *Guest cast*: Jon Cypher, Trinidad Silva, Jesse D. Goins, Andy Romano, Jane Kaczmarek, Ken Olin, J. A. Preston, Jeffrey Tambor, George Wyner, Debi Richter.
The disgruntled Blues try to sort things out in the wake of Furillo's departure while the harried captain is tempted to take his first drink in seven years; Goldblume quietly improvises a team of detectives to dog William Mullins (Goins); upset over his girlfriend's pregnancy and the possibility of unheralded matrimony, Renko makes an unlikely ally of gang leader Jesus Martinez.
'Hair Apparent'
Writers: Jeffrey Lewis, Michael Wagner, Karen Hall, Roger Director. *Story by* Steven Bochco, Lewis, David Milch, Mark Frost. *Director*: Corey Allen. *Guest cast*: Ken Olin, George Wyner, Randy Brooks, Trinidad Silva, Robert Costanzo, Joanna Kerns, Joe Santos, Beau Starr, Harold Sylvester, Michael Alldredge, J. A. Preston.
Belker's undercover operation is nearly blown by investigators from another agency; Garibaldi (Olin) does some unofficial police work for a citizen who has threatened to sue him for rear-ending his car; the mayor's personal appointee (Brooks) to the Youth Corps comes under fire from the gangs for giving jobs only to friends; Furillo pushes for a gang-treaty renewal before the violence escalates.
'Lucky Ducks'
Writers: Michael Wagner, David Milch, Karen Hall, Mark Frost. *Story by* Steven Bochco, Jeffrey Lewis, Milch, Hall. *Director*: Rick Wallace. *Guest cast*: Randy Brooks, Robert Costanzo, Joe Santos, Trinidad Silva, Beau Starr, Ken Olin, Jeffrey Tambor, Harold Sylvester, Debi Richter, Hunt Block, John McCook.
The gang violence erupts into a bloody war; Peabody (Brooks) goes to the loan shark Franco (Costanzo) to finance a drug deal; an assault suspect (Block) wants the wheels of justice to turn swiftly; Joyce tells Frank she needs some time alone; Ray prepares to be on a game show; Renko prods his best-men to get their tuxedos.
'Eva's Brawn'
Writers: Jeffrey Lewis, David Milch, Mark Frost, Roger Director. *Story by* Steven Bochco, Lewis, Milch. *Director*: Gregory Hoblit. *Guest cast*: Trinidad Silva, George Wyner, Susan Kellermann, Robert Costanza, Joe Santos, Beau Starr, Don Calfa, Andy Romano, Debi Richter, Jeffrey Tambor, Harold Sylvester, Ken Olin.
The loan sharks Belker busted commandeer a jail bus and want to exchange their hostages for Belker; Furillo asks Jesus Martinez (Silva) to mediate the gang summit; Renko is having second thoughts about his impending nuptials; Joyce wants to go to Paris by herself; Henry reluctantly tries a video-dating service; Coffey bets Renko's wedding-gift money on a horse race.

St Elsewhere (NBC, 1982–) Film. 60 mins.
Executive producer: Bruce Paltrow. *Associate producer*: Beth Hillshafer. *Creators*: Joshua Brand, John Falsey. *Photography*: John McPherson. *Music*: Dave Grusin. *Art directors*: James Hulsey, Jacqueline Webber. *Editor*: John Heath.
Regular cast: David Birney *(Dr Ben Samuels)*, Ed Flanders *(Dr Donald Westphall)*, David Morse *(Dr Jack Morrison)*, William Daniels *(Dr Mark Craig)*, Cynthia Sikes *(Dr Annie Cavanero)*, Howie Mandel *(Dr Wayne Fiscus)*, Terence Knox *(Dr Peter White)*, G. W. Bailey *(Dr Hugh Beale)*, Christina Pickles *(Nurse Helen Rosenthal)*, Denzel Washington *(Dr Phillip*

Chandler). Kavi Raz *(Dr V. J. Kochar)*, Norman Lloyd *(Dr Daniel Auschlander)*, Ed Begley Jr *(Dr Ehrlich)*, Ellen Bry *(Nurse Daniels)*, Kim Miyori *(Dr Armstrong)*.

A drama with comedy elements centering on the lives and careers of the doctors, residents and nurses of a teaching hospital in a deteriorating section of Boston; the hospital is called St Eligius but because of its 'skid row' status is generally referred to as 'St Elsewhere'.

Première Episode
Writers: Joshua Brand, John Falsey. *Director*: Thomas Carter. *Guest cast:* Barbara Whinnery, Dominique Dunne, Eric G. Laneuville, Rafael Campos, Lance Guest.
The notorious, and fictitious, St Eligius Hospital in Boston provides the setting for the operations of a staff that reluctantly considers chaos to be routine. In this première episode, a mental patient is missing; a surgeon with a social disease tries to recall with whom he did what; paramedics bring in the victims of a terrorist's bomb; and a smitten intern chases a new pathologist.
'Bypass'
Writers: John Falsey, Joshua Brand. *Director*: Thomas Carter. *Guest cast*: Heather McAdam, Barbara Whinnery, Robert Constanzo, Vivian Bonnell, Deborah White, Tara Buckman, Tim Robbins, Sandy McPeak, Frances Lee McCain, Peter Maloney.
Despite his personal feelings, Morrison treats the antagonistic bomber, whose victim remains in a coma as her husband arrives; Ehrlich has his first OR encounter with the demanding Craig, who intimidates a patient to consent to triple bypass surgery; Fiscus cures Martin (Whinnery) of guilt over their first encounter; Samuels gives Beale a swimming lesson.
'Down's Syndrome'
Writer: Tom Fontana. *Story by* Joshua Brand, John Falsey, Fontana. *Director*: Mark Tinker. *Guest cast*: Barbara Whinnery, Tony Bill, Mureen Anderman, Jack Bannon, Lance Guest.
Westphall plays host to visiting hospital board members: a couple learn their unborn child has Down's Syndrome; Fiscus and Martin have a date at a rifle range.
'Cora And Arnie'
Writer: Neil Cuthbert. *Story by* Joshua Brand, John Falsey, Cuthbert. *Director*: Mark Tinker. *Guest cast*: Doris Roberts, James Coco, Jack Bannon, Tim Robbins, Bernard Behrens, Anne Gerety, Lionel Smith.
A simple-minded soul and his wife (Coco and Roberts), a bag lady whose sore feet tip Morrison to a condition that threatens her life; meanwhile, residents run a battery of expensive tests to try to determine why a woman collapsed; and a parolee (Smith) enters the emergency room complaining of back pain and learns he's been shot.
'Samuels And The Kid'
Writer: John Masius. *Story by* Masius, Joshua Brand, John Falsey. *Director*: Thomas Carter. *Guest cast*: Jeremy Licht, Vivian Bonnell, Bonnie Bartlett, Eric G. Laneuville, Robert Davi, Ally Sheedy, Panchito Gomez, Domingo Ambriz, Paul Lieber.
Samuels develops more than a passing interest in an 11-year-old (Licht) with a football injury; Chandler accuses a veteran nurse (Bonnell) of incompetence; a teenager (Gomez) tries to deliver his neighbour's baby with telephone guidance from Cavanero.
'Legionnaires' (Part I)
Writer: Joel Surnow. *Story by* Surnow, Joshua Brand, John Falsey. *Director*: Thomas Carter. *Guest cast*: Barbara Whinnery, Karen Landry, Eric G. Laneuville, Christopher Guest, Rafael Campos, Albert Salmi, James Keane, Rita Taggart, Matthew Faison.
Westphall considers closing down an entire ward after three patients die with symptoms of Legionnaires' disease; a nurse (Taggart) shows inexplicable contempt for Cavanero; the expense of replacing his lost beeper puts added strain on White's home life.
'Legionnaires' (Part II)
Writer: as above. *Director*: as above. *Guest cast*: as above plus Laraine Newman, Ann Bronston, Richard Marcus, Carl Byrd.
Rumour has it that Westphall's job is on the line over his decision to close the ward; Fiscus is mugged in the emergency room after treating a street-gang member; Beale learns that his

mental patient was impregnated during her hospital stay.
'Tweety And Ralph'
Writer: Elizabeth Diggs. *Story by* Diggs, Joshua Brand, John Falsey. *Director*: Mark Tinker. *Guest cast*: Laraine Newman, Molly Cheek, Bonnie Bartlett, Eric G. Laneuville, Richard Marcus, Nan Martin, Charlie Robinson, Roxanne Reese, Lisa Rafel.
A nervous patient throws a party to celebrate her impending hysterectomy; Ralph, another mental patient, who believes he's a bird, builds a nest in the storeroom; Luther's pigeon is suffering from depression; the source of the Legionnaires' disease is discovered.
'Rain'
Writer: Tom Fontana. *Story by* Fontana, John Falsey, Joshua Brand. *Director*: Victor Hsu. *Guest cast*: Eric G. Laneuville, Karen Landry, Richard Marcus, George Morfogen, Deborah White, Sagan Lewis, Ray Liotta, Billy Ray Sharkey.
Morrison soon regrets acceding to a request for a house call; Fiscus, now carrying a gun, pulls it on a patient belonging to the same gang that mugged him; White's daughter swallows mothballs; Craig lectures Ehrlich on hand care for surgeons.
'Hearts'
Writer: John Masius. *Story by* Masius, Joshua Brand, John Falsey. *Director*: Mark Tinker. *Guest cast*: Dorothy Fielding, Conchata Ferrell, Richard Marcus, Jennifer Savidge, Rafael Campos, Eric G. Laneuville, Madelyn Cates, Peter Hobbs, Lance Guest.
Ralph poses as a member of staff; an obese woman learns her stomach discomfort is labour pains; Ehrlich faces another moment of truth assisting Craig in surgery; White accepts an offer from Morrison to move in.
'Graveyard'
Writers: Joshua Brand, John Falsey, John Masius, Tom Fontana. *Story by* Brand, Falsey. *Director*: Victor Lobl. *Guest cast*: Eric G. Laneuville, Dorothy Fielding, Jane Kaczmarek, Rummel Mor, Thomas Hulce, Richard Marcus, Drew Katszman, James Hong, Julius Harris, Marc Hayashi, Robert Pastorelli.
Rebuffed by Dr Paxton (Fielding), Samuels throws himself into a night-long struggle to save a critically wounded shooting victim; a Chinese boy's parents ask to perform an ancient ritual when they're told their son won't live through the night; and Ralph finally decides to leave the nest.
'Release'
Writers: Tom Fontana, David Assael. *Story by* Joshua Brand, John Falsey. *Director*: Victor Lobl. *Guest cast*: Dorothy Fielding, Thomas Hulce, Jane Kaczmarek, Andy Romano, Alice Hirson, Pat Corley, Sandy Ignon, Jonathan Luria.
Samuels and Paxton (Fielding) let a professional disagreement degenerate into attacks on each other's personalities; Craig's college room-mate enters the hospital for a sex change; White struggles to obtain his first autopsy consent form; Chandler tries to help a shooting victim regain his memory.
'Family History'
Writer: Andrew Laskos. *Story by* John Falsey, Joshua Brand. *Director*: Kevin Hooks. *Guest cast*: Dorothy Fielding, Keenan Wynn, Jane Kaczmarek, Thomas Hulce, Alan Feinstein, Karen Landry, Andy Romano, Joe Lambie, Claire Malis, Frank Campanella.
Hoping for reconciliation, White visits his wife (Landry); 'John Doe' meets his parents; Craig meets his college friend's therapist; Armstrong (Kim Miyori) works to correct an embarrassing oversight.
'Remission'
Writer: Lee Curran. *Story by* Joshua Brand, John Falsey. *Director*: Mark Tinker. *Guest cast*: Janis Paige, Michael Madsen, Dick O'Neill, Melody Anderson, Fred Dennis, Stacy Keach Sr, David Elliott, Robert Beecher, Sagan Lewis, Jennifer Savidge, Ben Stack.
Chemotherapy becomes essential for Auschlander; a teenager vows vengeance on the black youths who beat up his brother; Cavanero weighs her desire for a family life against a career opportunity; a 50-year-old female flasher walks the halls; an evicted Fiscus persuades Ehrlich to let him move in 'for a couple of days'.
'Monday, Tuesday, Sven's Day'

Writers: John Masius, Tom Fontana. *Story by* Joshua Brand, John Falsey. *Director*: Bruce Paltrow. *Guest cast*: Dick O'Neill, David Elliott, Lane Brinkley, Eric G. Laneuville, Karen Landry, Bonnie Bartlett, Erik Holland.
Mismatched with Daniels for a party at Craig's house, Ehrlich tries to cope by drinking; Morrison learns that the beating was not a case of black against white; Luther (Laneuville) has a special birthday party when a prostitute, who's in for an appendectomy, brings a horde of well-wishing co-workers.
'The Count'
Writers: Joshua Brand, John Falsey. *Director*: Kevin Hooks. *Guest cast*: Peter Michael Goetz, Michael Halsey, William Shilling, Liz Sheridan, Bonnie Bartlett, Jennifer Savidge, Roxanne Reese, Peter Van Norden.
Cavanero and Samuels help hide a porn star from a summons server; Armstrong confronts Craig with her suspicions that a doctor is unnecessarily inserting pacemakers in his heart patients.
'Brothers'
Writers: Mark Tinker, John Tinker. *Story by* Joshua Brand, John Falsey. *Director*: Mark Tinker. *Guest cast*: Karen Landry, Pat Hingle, Richard Hamilton, Alan Oppenheimer, Melody Anderson, Eda Reiss Merin, Christopher Thomas, Richard Chaves, Katie McClain, Frank White.
A man wants his terminally ill brother to die without prolonged suffering; Ehrlich asks for a second chance with Daniels; White celebrates his birthday with another attempt to reconcile with his wife (Landry); Rosenthal faces a mastectomy.
'Dog Day Hospital'
Writer: John Ford Noonan. *Story by* Joshua Brand, John Falsey. *Director*: Victor Lobl. *Guest cast*: Judith Light, Tom Atkins, Alan Oppenheimer, Sam Anderson, Elizabeth Kerr, Mary Margaret Lewis, Richard Kuss, Jennifer Savidge, Eric G. Laneuville, Howard McGillin, Sagan Lewis, Paco Vela, Henry G. Sanders, Beaumont Bruestle.
Ehrlich's first solo operation is interrupted by a gun-wielding pregnant woman demanding to see the doctor who gave her husband a vasectomy; Rosenthal deals with overkindness following her mastectomy; Fiscus and Daniel take Fiscus's feisty aunt on a hospital tour.
'Working'
Writer: Dennis Cooper. *Story by* Joshua Brand, John Falsey. *Director*: Bruce Paltrow. *Guest cast*: Ed Lauter, Rita Zohar, Melody Anderson, Laurie O'Brien, James Sutorius, Alan Haufrecht, Bella Chronis, Luise Heath, Don Blakely, Viola Kates Stimpson.
A patient dies on the elevator and his family hits Chandler with a lawsuit; an attractive surgeon (Zohar) draws another side out of Craig; a patient is doing his sober best to drink himself to death, for insurance purposes.
'Craig In Love'
Writer: Steve Lawson. *Story by* Joshua Brand, John Falsey. *Director*: Victor Lobl. *Guest cast*: Rita Zohar, Bonnie Bartlett, James Sutorius, Sagan Lewis, Tom Tully, Alice Cadogan, James Hardie, Harsh Nayyar.
Chandler is increasingly sensitive about the malpractice charge; White responds, violently, to Morrison's concern for his self-destructive behaviour; Craig, whose wife is away, continues to bask in the warmth exuded by Dr Anya (Zohar).
'Baron Von Munchausen'
Writers: David Assael, Paul Schiffer. *Story by* Joshua Brand, John Falsey. *Director*: Victor Hsu. *Guest cast*: Barbara Whinnery, Eric G. Laneuville, Louis Giambalvo, Micole Mercurio, Jennifer Savidge, James R. Winker, Frank Dent, Sagan Lewis, Paco Vela.
Fiscus may get pressed into a double date with a former girl-friend (Whinnery); Morrison and Ehrlich disagree on whether to operate on a man whose test results contradict his condition; Daniels is attacked in the ER by a crazed street woman.
'Addiction'
Writers: John Masius, Tom Fontana. *Director*: Mark Tinker. *Guest cast*: Barbara Whinnery, Eric G. Laneuville, Howard Duff, Deborah White, Ralph Seymour, Scott Paulin, Melody Anderson, Tom McFadden, Jean Allison, Karen Landry, Jack Heller, Howard George,

Alice Cadogan, Laurie Kennedy, Sagan Lewis.
White is suspected of a drug theft; Auschlander gets into a fist fight; Craig's med-student son gets a different high from medicine than his father; Morrison's wife goes into labour.

St Elsewhere (Second Season: 1983–4)
Executive producer: Bruce Paltrow. *Associate producer*: Beth Hillshafer. *Photography*: Marvin L. Gunter. *Music*: J. A. C. Redford, Dave Grusin. *Art director*: Jacqueline Webber. *Editors*: John Wm. Heath, Elodie Keene.
Regular cast: Ed Flanders *(Dr Donald Westphall)*, William Daniels *(Dr Mark Craig)*, Mark Harmon *(Dr Robert Caldwell)*, Nancy Stafford *(Joan Halloran)*, Christina Pickles *(Nurse Helen Rosenthal)*, Cynthia Sikes *(Dr Annie Cavanero)*, David Morse *(Dr Jack Morrison)*, Denzel Washington *(Dr Peter White)*, Howie Mandel *(Dr Wayne Fiscus)*, Ed Begley Jr *(Dr Victor Ehrlich)*, Kim Miyori *(Dr Wendy Armstrong)*, Norman Lloyd *(Dr Auschlander)*, Ellen Bry *(Nurse Shirley Daniels)*, Eric G. Laneuville *(Luther Hawkins)*.

'Ties That Bind'
Writers: John Masius, Tom Fontana. *Director*: Bruce Paltrow. *Guest cast*: Alan Arkin, Piper Laurie, Marian Mercer, Jean Bruce Scott, Barbara Whinnery, Jennifer Savidge, Sagan Lewis, Frank Koppala.
Jerry Singelton (Arkin), a gruff and outspoken man, creates problems for the hospital staff with his demands for instant and constant attention when his wife suffers a stroke.
'Lust Et Veritas'
Writer: Dennis Cooper. *Story by* John Masius, Tom Fontana, Cooper. *Director*: Mark Tinker. *Guest cast*: Alan Arkin, Piper Laurie, Marian Mercer, Peter Horton, Peggy McCay, Jennifer Savidge, Sagan Lewis, Frank Dent.
A new plastic surgeon, Dr Robert Caldwell, turns the head of every woman in the hospital but is revealed to have a very special relationship with administrative officer Joan Halloran.
'Newheart'
Writers: John Masius, Tom Fontana, Garn Stephens, Emily Small. *Director*: Mark Tinker. *Guest cast*: Alan Arkin, Piper Laurie, Marian Mercer, Bonnie Bartlett, Deborah White, Barbara Whinnery, Paul Linke.
Dr Craig tries to keep a beloved patient alive while awaiting a donor for heart transplant surgery; Dr White tries to overcome his irrational fear of radiation treatment; Dr Westphall clashes with Joan Halloran over proposed plans to use the hospital as a major centre in the event of nuclear war; Dr Cathy Martin (Whinnery) decides on drastic action when she learns that Dr Kochar, who is a virgin, will soon take a bride.
'Qui Transtulit Sustinet'
Writers: John Tinker, Mark Tinker. *Director*: Victor Lobl. *Guest cast*: Marian Mercer, Jeannetta Arnette, Peggy McCay, Michael Bond, Sagan Lewis, Milt Oberman, Vahan Moosekian.
Dr Morrison sinks into depression, blaming himself for his wife's accidental death; Dr Craig finally gets to perform St Eligius Hospital's first heart transplant; Luther and Dr Fiscus overhear a conversation between two wealthy doctors and decide to pool their money for a stock market killing.
'A Wing And A Prayer'
Writers: Raymond and Robert DeLaurentis. *Director*: Bruce Paltrow. *Guest cast*: Jane Wyatt, Marian Mercer, 'Bumper' Yothers, Gretchen Wyler, Barbara Whinnery, Sagan Lewis, Jennifer Savidge.
Dr Auschlander, weary from his battle against cancer, begins to contemplate suicide when he learns that a bright, trusting and loveable eleven-year-old patient is an apparent leukemia victim.
'Under Pressure'
Writers: Steve Bello, Tom Fontana, John Masius. *Director*: David Anspaugh. *Guest cast*: Austin Pendleton, Paul Sand, Marian Mercer, Eric Stoltz, Robert Hogan, Sydney Penny, Redmond Gleeson, Thomas De Weir.

Two young men, Eddie Carson (Stoltz) and Patrick Brennan (De Weir), are rushed to the hospital, near death, after a fight. They are discovered to be opposing Irish terrorists who bring 'The Troubles' to Boston.
'Entrapment'
Writers: Steve Bello, Tom Fontana, John Masius. *Director*: Mark Tinker. *Guest cast*: Eric Stoltz, Paul Sand, Marian Mercer, Bonnie Bartlett, Barbara Whinnery, Karen Landry, Sagan Lewis, Thomas De Weir.
Dr Peter White, trying to be kind to an indigent patient, finds himself facing a drug charge when she turns out to be a policewoman.
'All About Eve'
Writers: John Masius, Tom Fontana. *Director*: David Anspaugh. *Guest cast*: Eric Stoltz, Paul Sand, Marian Mercer, Joan Hotchkis, Barbara Whinnery, Jean Bruce Scott.
Dr Caldwell learns a very painful lesson about becoming involved with Irish terrorists; and Dr Ehrlich is shocked to find that his free-loving girlfriend, Roberta (Scott), has changed her life style after consulting a psychiatrist.
'Aids And Comfort'
Writers: John Masius, Tom Fontana, Steve Lawson. *Director*: Victor Lobl. *Guest cast*: Michael Brandon, Paul Sand, Marian Mercer, Caroline Smith, Karen Landry, Peggy McCay.
Anthony Gifford (Brandon), a happily married and highly successful young politician, finds his future shattered when it is learned that he is suffering of AIDS and he must admit his homosexuality. Dr White's wife is so fearful of the disease that she forces him to ask to be removed from the case; and St Eligius' blood drive collapses when it is learned that the hospital is treating an AIDS victim.
'A Pig Too Far'
Writers: John Tinker, Jay Kahn. *Director*: Linda Day. *Guest cast*: Linda Carlson, Paul Sand, Michael Goodwin, Philip Charles MacKenzie, Jean Bruce Scott, David Knell.
Dr Westphall is annoyed by a patient, young computer freak Matthew Brody (Knell), who uses his personal computer to diagnose other patients' ailments and break into hospital records and secret files.
'Blizzard'
Writers: Steve Lawson, Jamie Horton. *Director*: Kevin Hooks. *Guest cast*: James McEachin, Paul Sand, Bonnie Bartlett, Barbara Whinnery, Jean Bruce Scott.
A raging snow storm creates multiple problems for the patients and staff of St Eligius: the randy Dr Cathy Martin (Whinnery) decides to seduce psychiatrist Ridley (Sand); Dr Cavanero winds up as a patient when snow causes the hospital's ceiling to collapse on her; staff members become concerned after learning that Dr Craig is missing in deep snow; and Dr Ehrlich is overjoyed when his girlfriend accepts his proposal of marriage.
'Hearing'
Writers: Steve Bell, Robert Daniels. *Director*: Chuck Braverman. *Guest cast*: Joe Regalbuto, Conrad Janis, Jean Bruce Scott, Robert Daniels, Richard Roat.
Dr Auschlander has some very surprising results when he experiments with marijuana to control the nausea caused by his chemotherapy treatment; Dr White fights for his medical future when he faces a board accusing him of improper handling of drugs; and Dr Ehrlich prepares to meet his future in-laws.
'In Sickness And In Health'
Writers: John Masius, Tom Fontana. *Director*: Mark Tinker. *Guest cast*: William Windom, Paul Sand, Louise Lasser, Priscilla Pointer, Jean Bruce Scott, Lurene Tuttle.
Everything goes haywire when Dr Ehrlich finally weds Roberta (Scott). The day becomes crazy with the arrival of Ehrlich's hard-drinking Aunt Charice (Lasser) and Dr Craig's salty mother-in-law.
'Drama Center'
Writer: John Tinker. *Story by* John Masius, Tom Fontana. *Director*: David Anspaugh. *Guest cast*: Allyn Ann McLerie, Paul Sand, Jenny O'Hara, Michael Richards, Bonnie Bartlett, Michael Goodwin.

A beaming Dr Craig is the willing subject of an intrusive television documentary crew that has the run of the hospital but he begins to have second thoughts when they insist on staging scenes and poking into private matters.

'Attack'

Writers: Cynthia Darnell, Douglas Brooks West. *Director*: Kevin Hooks. *Guest cast*: Geraldine Fitzgerald, Paul Sand, Jean Bruce Scott, Dan Hedaya, Michael Goodwin, Barbara Whinnery.

When a ski-masked rapist continues to terrorise St Eligius, the female staff members grow increasingly restless with hospital security and paranoia reigns as the rapist boldly assaults women of all ages in and near the hospital.

'After Dark'

Writer: Steve Lawson. *Story by* Lawson, John Masius, Tom Fontana. *Director*: Eric Laneuville. *Guest cast*: Dan Hedaya, Peter Evans, Jean Bruce Scott, Bonnie Bartlett, Gretchen Wyler, Karen Landry.

Dr Ehrlich's 16-day-old marriage and his hopes for wedded bliss seem to be on the rocks; an expectant Dr Craig preens himself and prepares in case he should be named Doctor of the Year; Dr White is becoming increasingly obnoxious in his attitude toward the women of St Eligius.

'Vanity'

Writers: John Tinker, Ray DeLaurentis, Jorge Zamacona. *Story by* John Masius, Tom Fontana. *Director*: Mark Tinker. *Guest cast*: Austin Pendleton, Paul Sand, Bonnie Bartlett, Al Ruscio, Dan Hedaya, Michael Richards, Barbara Whinnery.

Dr Craig is livid when a television documentary casts him in an unflattering light and rails against the 'slanderous' treatment he received; Nurse Rosenthal undergoes a breast implant operation under Dr Caldwell's scalpel.

'Equinox'

Writers: Channing Gibson, Charles H. Eglee. *Story by* John Masius, Tom Fontana. *Director*: David Anspaugh. *Guest cast*: Thomas Byrd, Paul Sand, Barbara Whinnery, Reid Shelton, Charles Tyner, Gretchen Wyler.

Westphall is furious when Dr White is released from jail on a rape charge and allowed to resume his residency programme; Nurse Rosenthal, following her breast implant, ignores orders and returns to work too soon; Cathy Martin (Whinnery) gets professional help as she tries to cope with the effects of having been sexually assaulted some weeks earlier.

'The Women'

Writer: John Ford Noonan. *Story by* John Masius, Tom Fontana. *Director*: Bruce Paltrow. *Guest cast*: Eva LeGallienne, Brenda Vaccaro, Blythe Danner, Joseph Maher, Patricia Elliott, Tracy Nelson, Nicholas Mele.

Three patients with different maladies and distinctive personalities share a room at St Eligius: Evelyn (LeGallienne), a feisty octogenarian with a broken hip and a heart problem; Page (Danner) cannot resist inventing whopping stories to colour her otherwise pale existence; and Rose's (Vaccaro) eccentric behaviour makes it hard for her family to believe that, though she's around forty, she is suffering from Alzheimer's disease.

'Cramming'

Writers: Steve Lawson, Steve Bello. *Director*: Tim Matheson. *Guest cast*: Louise Lasser, Paul Sand, Conrad Janis, Barbara Whinnery, Patrick McNamara.

Pressure mounts on the young residents when the dreaded National Board exams approach. As everyone pores over books, Ehrlich is upset by the arrival of his eccentric Aunt Charice (Lasser) and her romantic designs on Westphall; while Dr White takes a big risk by agreeing to a polygraph examination with regard to his sexual-assault trial.

'Rough Cut'

Writers: Mitchell Fink, Susan Lindner. *Story by* Steve Lawson, Steve Bello. *Director*: Linda Day. *Guest cast*: Barbara Whinnery, Joey Arresco, Sagan Lewis, Starletta DuPois, Rebecca Robertson.

The scores of the recent National Board exams and the personal evaluation of the residents have Ehrlich, like the others, on the verge of paranoia as they await the decision that will

determine their medical future – knowing that some of them will be cut from the programme.
'Hello And Goodbye'
Writers: John Masius, Tom Fontana. *Director*: Mark Tinker. *Guest cast*: Scott Paulin, Helen Hunt, Tannis Valley, Bonnie Bartlett.
The ER is shut down for structural repairs; Morrison has his first date since his wife's death; Craig's son (Paulin) comes home after beating his drug problem; Auschlander collapses in a stuck elevator; and Luther goes on a wild-goose chase to fill an ailing child's request for a Cheshire cat.

Michael Leahy wrote about St Elsewhere *in* TV Guide (12/11/83):

... Despite all its talk about innovative quality, television remains a medium largely committed to numbers. So, in the early spring of 1983, when Brandon Tartikoff [of NBC] and his associates received reports that the numbers for their new medical drama, *St Elsewhere*, had not climbed, their reaction was swift: the show had to be canceled. ... The producers had accepted the decision calmly. It was as if they had been expecting the termination for some time, and later, when they spoke to each other of vacations and prospects for new shows, no one shed tears; no one mourned bitterly about the network's failure to promote the show. The cast reacted amicably as well. Ed Begley Jr, who had been nominated for an Emmy for his portrayal of Dr Victor Ehrlich, said *c'est la vie* about the cancellation, though something told him the issue was not yet closed. 'Just a feeling', he said. 'Nothing justifies it. The show wasn't doing very good. We were dead. ...'

They had been given their chance, and by the standards of commericial television, they had failed – miserably. Twice that season, *St Elsewhere* had been the lowest-rated show in prime-time, and though the numbers had improved somewhat, the show rarely found itself any higher than 30th among the opposition. No one had panicked immediately. *Hill Street Blues*, another MTM production, had zoomed after early ratings problems, and everyone agreed that *St Elsewhere*, like *Hill Street*, had strong characters and a compelling storyline. The bizarre happenings inside the battered Boston teaching hospital called St Eligius had an appropriate mix of the real and surreal; paternalistic administrators, dashing doctors and a pathologist who liked conducting her love affairs in the morgue.

Everyone waited awhile for the ratings to climb, and when they didn't suddenly everyone said there were problems; the show had no identifiable star, it needed a stronger leading man; it needed a stronger leading woman; whatever else, it *absolutely required* an injection of heavy romantic entanglements. NBC officials blamed the show's scripts, insisting that the writers had bogged down the show with too many subplots and peripheral characters. So changes were made; subplots reduced, more identifiable characters given longer scenes so that viewers could learn their faces. Even after favorable reviews from critics, the show's numbers went nowhere.

No questions remained now. The show had to be jettisoned, and so it was, informally, NBC telling the *St Elsewhere* staff not to expect a renewal of the program. Then in the middle of May, a call came to Mark Tinker, now *St Elsewhere*'s supervising producer, from a network executive. NBC had decided to renew, said the executive. A meeting was hurriedly arranged. The next day, everyone gathered in a Los Angleles conference room to hear NBC chairman Grant Tinker, Mark's father, say that yes indeed, the show would be coming back, noting that two of the last episodes had made an impressive jump in the ratings. The logic of the network's decision, even if it was benefiting them, struck the makers of *St Elsewhere* as dubious. 'Yeah, but why are you renewing us?' executive producer Bruce Paltrow kept asking, dumbfounded.

'If someone finds the answer,' said producer Masius, 'he'll have unraveled this studio's biggest mystery.' Conflicting rumors ran rampant: Grant Tinker had decided to renew because he wanted son Mark to have a show; MTM Productions had refused to sell NBC its promising new series, *Bay City Blues*, unless the network renewed *St Elsewhere*; Grant Tinker had forced the decision down Brandon Tartikoff's throat; no, Grant Tinker had not even been consulted; Tinker and Tartikoff did not speak; Tinker and Tartikoff were great friends. Some people questioned Tartikoff's decision to schedule the show againsty ABC's *Hotel*, which industry insiders had already tabbed as the new season's next blockbuster. 'We think we can compete,' said Tartikoff. 'It's presumptuous to say that we can't compete against a show that has never been on TV.' Was Tartikoff simply being devious? some wondered. . . .

Only Brandon Tartikoff in New York knew the answer to that mystery. 'Temporary insanity,' he sometimes said. He would laugh then and launch into a speech that had become something of the official NBC spiel for the show: *St Elsewhere* had shown slow but steady progress in the ratings; the show had been nominated for an Emmy; the show's numbers mirrored those of *Hill Street Blues* at a comparable period. He mentioned everything before casually saying the one world that mattered most. *Comp.* The show had good comp. Which meant that *St Elsewhere* had good audience composition; it attracted a large number of viewers from TV's prime advertising audience, those between the ages of 18 and 49 with sizable incomes and an instinct for buying. 'You know, the kinds of people who buy cleansers and all that crap,' said Begley. The show had a much higher comp than other programs with significantly higher ratings, and that, in the end, had saved it; that, and the realization of NBC executives that they had no pilot that could do better than their struggling medical drama. 'Thank God for people who like cleansers,' concluded Begley.

'The surveys keep getting more sophisticated,' Brandon Tartikoff said proudly from his Rockefeller Center office. An interesting thing, this *comp.* Tartikoff and other television executives had long waited for a device like it, something that could sift out the viewers with spending money from the multitudes without any. The implications were interesting, maybe ominous. Smaller audiences could shape programming, yet only if the smaller audiences had big money. An anemic rating could suffice, yet only if a show's viewers could afford the cleansers and cars. Perhaps in the end that will be *St Elsewhere*'s legacy: that a show with no major stars, bedeviled by script problems and wracked by mediocre ratings managed to survive because of the shape of its audience. It is programming by a new kind of numbers. '*St Elsewhere* has a promising look to it,' Brandon Tartikoff says these days.

Newhart (CBS, 8/11/82–) Tape. 30 mins.
Executive producer: Barry Kemp. *Producer*: Sheldon Bull. *Co-ordinating producer*: Stephen Grossman. *Associate producer*: Jay Klechner. *Executive story consultant*: Emily Marshall. *Executive script consultant*: Barbara Hall. *Music*: Henry Mancini.
Cast: Bob Newhart *(Dick Loudon)*, Mary Frann *(Joanna Loudon)*, Steven Kampmann *(Kirk Devane)*, Tom Poston *(George Utley)*, Jennifer Holmes *(Leslei Vanderkellen, the maid* 1982–3 season), Julia Duffy *(Stephanie Vanderkellen, the maid* 1983–4 season).

Newhart's ambitions for a new series were such that 'At one time I thought of simply picking up the old show four years later. I think it might have worked.' The idea was dropped though and instead, *TV Guide* suggests, the idea for the new series was Newhart's: 'We were staying at a little inn and I had some time to kill and I couldn't help noticing how many characters come and go in a place like that.' (*TV Guide*, 1/1/83, p. 19) If this sounds like an American *Fawlty Towers*, the comedy in *Newhart* rarely concerns the workings of the hotel or the relationship between staff and guests.

The script consultant on Paramount's series *Taxi* (a series, incidentally, created by ex-MTM alumni Brooks, Weinberger, Daniels), Barry Kemp, was called in to be executive producer and write the pilot script. Newhart has a contract with CBS so the series ran on that network, as had *The Bob Newhart Show*. But it also ran on CBS because Arthur Price, who is Newhart's manager (and Mary Tyler Moore's), is president of MTM and MTM still has a close relationship with CBS, the company which commissioned its first and founding series.

Once again, Newhart's role is, in his own words, 'listening to people and having to be nice to them no matter what they do. The recurring theme is that the person, through no fault of his own, is put in the middle of a situation and forced to sort it out. There's a put-upon quality to him.' (*New York Times*, 26/12/82)

The *New York Times* comments that Newhart's comedy is clearly aimed at a slightly older, more sophisticated audience than most contemporary television comedy and this places it alongside MTM's tradition of demographically specific targeting. In Newhart's own only half-jocular words: 'They're 35 to 40, college graduates, second marriage, a Mercedes and a station wagon, one kid from the first marriage, two from the second.' (*New York Times*, op. cit.)

Newhart plays Dick Loudon, the author of such dubious do-it-yourself guides as 'How To Panel In Hard-To-Reach Places', rather reminiscent of the husband's work in *We've Got Each Other*. The hotel setting enables the show to accommodate the MTM sitcom's traditional work and home fictions in the same site. If this is an effect of economy so too is the decision to shoot on tape.

Richard Hack's 'TeleVisions' column comment in *Hollywood Reporter* sums up the feeling perfectly: 'The welcome mat is out for Newhart the man and *Newhart* the show; and the only sound being heard is applause.' (*Hollywood Reporter*, 10/11/82, p. 4)

Remington Steele (NBC, 1982–) Film. 60 mins.
Executive producer: Michael Gleason. *Associate producer*: Carl Vitale. *Creators*: Michael Gleason, Robert Butler. *Photography*: Edward R. Brown. *Music*: Henry Mancini, Richard Lewis Warren. *Art director*: Richard Berger. *Editor*: James Galloway.
Regular cast: Stephanie Zimbalist *(Laura Holt)*, Pierce Brosnan *(Remington Steele)*, James Read *(Murphy Michaels)*, Janet DeMay *(Bernice Foxe)*.

A comedy drama about a female private investigator, Laura Holt, who creates a fictitious character to run her agency only to have him appear in person – and then take his job seriously; Murphy Michaels is her assistant and Bernice Foxe her secretary.

'Licence To Steele'
Writer: Michael Gleason. *Director*: Robert Butler. *Guest cast*: Joseph Hacker, Phil Casnoff, Robert Darnell, John Francis.
Private eye Laura Holt invents a male boss to lure clients reluctant to hire a woman. The ruse works until a mysterious character interferes with her job of protecting a $2 million jewel shipment. Enter Remington Steele.
'Tempered Steele'
Writer: Michael Gleason. *Director*: Robert Butler. *Guest cast*: Arlen Snyder, David Hayward, Diana Douglas, Brenda King, Curt Lowens, Charles Stavola.
Laura and Remington become involved with industrial espionage in an electronics firm, where an alarm-system failure results in the disappearance of trade secrets – and in murder.
'Steele Waters Run Deep'
Writer: Lee Zlotoff. *Director*: Jeff Bleckner. *Guest cast*: Peter Scolari, George D. Wallace, Betty Kennedy, Rozanne Hart, Rae Allen, Randy Rocca.
Laura and Remington have 24 hours to find a video-game genius who vanished on the eve of a successful merger, along with $5 million of his company's latest video-game plans.
'Signed, Steeled And Delivered'
Writer: Glenn Caron. *Director*: Robert Butler. *Guest cast*: Thom Bray, Philip Sterling, Alexandra Johnson, Marta Kristen, Christopher Lofton.
A CIA researcher, terrified by attempts on his life, is convinced that his own agency is trying to kill him.
'Thou Shalt Not Steele'
Writer: Lee Zlotoff. *Director*: Leo Penn. *Guest cast*: Beverly Garland, Cassandra Harris, James Blendick, Peter MacLean, Kurt Christian, Ben Slack, Ben Mittleman.
Laura dragoons Steele into protecting a museum painting that carries a curse, and a woman from his shadowy past wants him to help her steal it.
'Steele Belted'
Writer: Michael Gleason. *Director*: Robert Butler. *Guest cast*: Andrew Bloch, Barry Van Dyke, Raymond Singer, Ilene Graff, Lora Staley.

The agency takes a client charged with murder who simply can't win: the man's alibi – the only witness – is found murdered in Remington's apartment.
'Etched In Steele'
Writer: Glenn Caron. *Director*: Stan Lathan. *Guest cast*: Shannon Wilcox, George Morfogen, Richard Cox, Joel Colodner, Lyman Ward.
Laura thinks a best-selling sexy-book author murdered her own husband, until she discovers it was the woman's insipid spouse who really wrote the books.
'Your Steele The One For Me'
Writer: Lee Zlotoff. *Director*: Thomas Carter. *Guest cast*: Keye Luke, Marc Hayashi, Sab Shimono, Reid Shelton.
Laura ponders two suspicious deaths, a run-in with Army Intelligence and cryptic clues about a 'Palace of Heaven', and concludes that Remington was right in the first place – the death of a visiting Japanese was not caused by jaywalking.
'In The Steele Of The Night'
Writer: Joel Steiger. *Director*: Burt Brinckerhoff. *Guest cast*: Carlene Watkins, Philip Charles Mackenzie, Arthur Rosenberg, Jeff Pomerantz.
As the only outsider at a house party, Remington is asked to identify the killer in a group of Laura's former colleagues after one of them is found dead.
'Steele Trap'
Writer: Michael Gleason. *Director*: Sidney Hayers. *Guest cast*: Lynne Randall, Paul Hecht, Bruce Kirby, Brandis Kemp, Diane Stilwell, Robert Phalen, Erica Yohn.
Laura and Remington crash a party on a privately owned island after their client declines an invitation by committing suicide.
'Steeling The Show'
Writer: Peter Lefcourt. *Director*: Seymour Robbie. *Guest cast*: Bibi Osterwald, Frances Lee McCain, Duncan Ross, Richard Backus, Than Wyenn, Peter Jurasik, Michael Cornelison.
A Hollywood has-been thinks someone's trying to kill her, and Laura and Steele come to think she may have a point.
'Steele Flying High'
Writer: Richard Collins. *Director*: Nick Havinga. *Guest cast*: Francine Lembi, Michael Goodwin, Michael McGuire, Martine Bartlett, Blake Clark, Walter Beery, Paul Brennan.
Steele wonders why he's been asked to join a committee to save a bald eagle. Then he learns about the murder of a member who supposedly sent him a controversial report on land proposed as a sanctuary.
'A Good Night's Steele'
Writers: Lee Zlotoff and R. J. Stewart. *Director*: Seymour Robbie. *Guest cast*: Paul Reiser, Nancy Parsons, William Larsen, David Haskell, John Mansfield, Marley Sims, Nancy Linari, Gene Ramsel.
Laura and Steele go undercover as a doctor and patient at a sleep-disorder clinic that's missing morphine, and a physician.
'Hearts of Steele'
Writer: Glenn Caron. *Story by* Charles Rosin. *Director*: Robert Butler. *Guest cast*: Mark Hutter, Susan Kellermann, Linda Carlson, Caren Kaye, Alexandra Borrie, Mary-Joan Negro, Guy Boyd, Blake Clark.
Laura and Steele have an intoxicating romp posing as a man and wife whose marriage is on the rocks while they try to determine which of four angry and tippling ex-spouses is trying to knock off their husbands' divorce lawyer.
'To Stop A Steele'
Writer: Glenn Caron. *Director*: Sidney Hayers. *Guest cast*: Cliff Norton, Michael C. Gwynne, Donald Bishop, Frank Lanyer, Arnold Turner, J. J. Johnson, Douglas Warhit.
Laura and Steele don't know it, but they're working the same case – Laura and Murphy for the jeweller robbed of a $2 million diamond, and Steele for a frightened thief who has to explain to the syndicate that someone beat him to it.
'Steele Crazy After All These Years'

Writers: R. J. Stewart and Andrew Laskos. *Story by* Stewart, Laskos, Peggy Goldman. *Director*: Don Weis. *Guest cast*: Annie Potts, Todd Susman, Allyce Beasley, Tony Plana, John C. Becher, Mark King, Xander Berkely, Sharon Stone, Roger Hampton.
Murphy's college homecoming is interrupted by a class radical's murder, which recalls a decade-old bombing incident.
'Steele Among The Living'
Writer: Andrew Laskos. *Director*: Nick Havinga. *Guest cast*: Phil Rubenstein, Marilyn Jones, Reid Smith, Hansford Rowe, Peter Vogt, Judith Anna Roberts, Israel Juarbe, Blake Clark, David Byrd.
The paintings of a missing artist soar in value as Laura and Steele search for the *corpus delicti* amid evidence that the painter's demise will profit her estranged husband, as well as the gallery about to open her one-woman show.
'Steele In The News'
Writers: Michael Gleason, Fred Lyle and Duncan Smith. *Story by* Lyle, Smith. *Director*: Burt Brinckerhoff. *Guest cast*: J. D. Cannon, Maggie Roswell, John Reilly, Ron Frazier, Jenny O'Hara, Tracy Scoggins, Macon McCalman, Richard Moll, Alan Blumenfeld.
A saboteur in a TV studio makes the news team look like bumbling fools on the air. But no one's laughing when the weatherman tumbles from the rafters, dead.
'Vintage Steele'
Writer: Susan Baskin. *Director*: Larry Elikann. *Guest cast*: Wilson Jeffries, Beverlee McKinsey, James Widdoes, Michael Currie, Erik Holland, Michael O'Guinne, William Hootkins, Dorothy Buhrman.
A vintage caper involves Laura and Steele with a corpse that bobbed to the surface of a wine vat and keeps resurfacing in apparently unrelated places.
'Steele's Gold'
Writers: R. J. Stewart, Andrew Laskos, Michael Gleason. *Director*: Burt Brinckerhoff. *Guest cast*: James Callahan, Lois de Banzie, Barbara Stock, William Russ, Ellis Ren, Ernestine McClendon.
At an 'Old California' party where the agency is working security, a legendary prospector's journal is stolen and a guest is stabbed to death.
'Sting Of Steele'
Writers: Gary Kott and Michael Gleason. *Director*: Seymour Robbie. *Guest cast*: Efrem Zimbalist Jr, Beverly Garland, John Orchard, Peter Bromilow, Robert Denison, Gerry Gibson, Derek Partridge.
Laura is astonished to find con man extraordinaire Daniel Chalmers working a stylish sting with Steele, his one-time protégé – all the while making an equally polished play for her mother.
'You're Steele In Circulation'
Writer: Lee Zlotoff. *Director*: Don Weis. *Guest cast*: John Doolittle, Gina Gallego, Richard Kuss, Patsy Pease, Amanda McBroom, Martin Azarow, John Edwards, Thomas Newman, Adele Rosse, Ken Gibbel.
Laura and Steele try to thwart repeated attempts by a bank employee to end it all because he 'borrowed' $50,000 for a few days to help a damsel in distress, only to have both the money and the damsel disappear.

Remington Steele (Second Season: 1983–4)
Executive producer: Michael Gleason. *Associate producer*: Kevin Inch. *Music*: Henry Mancini, Richard Lewis Warren.
Regular cast: Stephanie Zimbalist *(Laura Holt)*, Pierce Brosnan *(Remington Steele)*, Doris Roberts *(Mildred Krebs)*.

The Laura Holt and Remington Steele characters continue as the investigators, with the addition of a new regular Mildred Krebs, an IRS auditor who assists the team; the Murphy Michaels and Bernice Foxe characters have been dropped.

Pierce Brosnan and Stephanie Zimbalist in *Remington Steele*

'Steele Away With Me' ('2-hour' season première episode)
Writer: Michael Gleason. *Director*: Seymour Robbie. *Guest cast*: Vincent Baggetta, Ray Girardin, Jack Blessing, David Warner, Pedro Armendariz Jr, Fausto Bara, Chloe Webb, Perla Walter, Richard Cansino.
Laura and Steele are in Mexico, after a tuna stuffed with diamonds and wrapped in an Acapulco newspaper is dropped on her doorstep by a dying man. As a smuggling conspiracy emerges, they're assisted by Mildred Krebs, an IRS auditor who's been tracking Steele.
'Red Holt Steele'
Writer: Lee Zlotoff. *Director*: Kevin Connor. *Guest cast*: Barbara Cason, Joel Polis, Lewis Arquette, Audrie J. Neenan, Thomas Randall Oglesby, Richard Brestoff, James Horan, Dee Dee Rescher, Blake Clark.
Laura moves in with Steele when her apartment is blown up and her life is endangered after the two investigate corporate sabotage.
'Altered Steele'
Writer: Jeff Melvoin. *Director*: Alex Singer. *Guest cast*: Fred McCarren, Monique Van De Ven, Delta Burke, Jane Kaczmarek, Carole Ita White, Clara Perryman.
A terrified client doesn't know his own name, or why someone is trying to kill him, but a fake funeral arranged by Laura and Steele produces five suspects, each claiming to be the man's widow.
'Steele Framed'
Writer: Brian Alan Lane. *Director*: Sheldon Larry. *Guest cast*: Guy Boyd, Gary Frank, Archie Hahn, Rod Corbin, Lynne Stewart, Gamy L. Taylor, Bill McLaughlin.
Speeding to a rendezvous, Steele hits a man and the question is – was it an accident? Certain evidence tells Laura that Steele was being blackmailed by the victim.
'A Steele At Any Price'
Writers: Mitch Paradise, Richard DeRoy, Michael Gleason. *Director*: Don Weis. *Guest cast*: Michael Cornelison, Jeffrey Jones, Susan Bey, Stefan Gierasch, Gillian Eaton, Ernest Harada.
Laura and Steele set up a competing syndicate in hopes of locating an investigative reporter who has disappeared inside a ring of international art thieves.
'Love Among The Steele'
Writer: Lee Zlotoff. *Director*: Seymour Robbie. *Guest cast*: Clive Revill, Susan French, Peter Hobbs, Al Ruscio, Kate Zentall, Robert Thaler, Ed Penney.
Laura and Steele set out to unravel the romantic and sinister mystery involving a driverless, runaway vintage car which almost runs them down.
'Scene Steelers'
Writers: Michael Gleason, Richard DeRoy, Joyce Armor, Judie Neer. *Director*: Peter Medak. *Guest cast*: Barrie Ingham, Bib Besch, Gwen Humble, Paul Kreppel, Faith Prince, Frances Bay.
When a parrot dies during the production of a food commercial, Steele and Laura go into action to find out who is trying to kill the stars and sabotage the operation.
'Steele Knuckles And Glass Jaws'
Writer: Jeff Melvoin. *Director*: Don Weis. *Guest cast*: Bert Remsen, Paul Stewart, Ken Foree, Julie Carmen, George McDaniel, Len Lesser, John Davey.
Laura and Steele become instant parents when they are left with an abandoned baby with dangerous ties to the underworld.
'My Fair Steele'
Writer: Brian Alan Lane. *Director*: Seymour Robbie. *Guest cast*: Stephen Elliott, Ann Dusenberry, Joanna Barnes, Thomas Hill, Judith Chapman, Ian Wolfe.
Laura and Steele are hired by a dying business tycoon to locate the twin sister of his jet-setting daughter but, following his death, one twin appears and the other disappears, presumably kidnapped.
'Steele Threads'
Writer: George Lee Marshall. *Director*: Karen Arthur. *Guest cast*: Joshua Shelley, Lara

Parker, Dean Santoro, John van Dreelen, Carl Weintraub, Michael Bond, Estelle Omens.
Laura goes undercover as a high fashion model and Steele plays a slightly vulgar wholesale buyer as they try to find out who's stealing their client's design secrets, and they find themselves involved in foreign espionage.

'Steele Eligible'

Writer: Michael Gleason. *Director*: Sheldon Larry. *Guest cast*: Roy Dotrice, Mimi Kuzyk, D. D. Howard, Frank Luz, Richard Backus, Michael Lemon.
A prominent magazine lists Steele among its five 'most eligible' batchelors but the honour soon turns into a nightmare when two of the bachelors are murdered.

'High Flying Steele'

Writer: George Lee Marshall. *Director*: Karen Arthur. *Guest cast*: Lisa Pelikan, Michael McGuire, A. Martinez, Joy Garrett, Jessie Lawrence Ferguson.
Laura and Steele join the circus, performing on the trapeze and eating fire as they investigate a homicide which occurred some years before.

'Blood Is Thicker Than Steele'

Writer: Richard DeRoy. *Director*: Barbara Peters. *Guest cast*: Eric Brown, Carolyn Seymour, Bridgette Andersen, Jack Betts, Ann Gee Byrd, Patricia Wittig, Ed Crick, Bruce Wright.
Walter Gallen (Betts), a Robert Vesco-like expatriate, is brought back from his tropical exile to testify on the government's behalf against his former employer. He hires Laura and Steele to protect his children against retaliatory harm.

'Steele Sweet On You'

Writer: Susan Baskin. *Director*: Don Weis. *Guest cast*: Maryedith Burrell, Michael Durrell, Patrick Collins, James O'Sullivan, Boyd Bodwell.
The business partner of Laura's brother-in-law, a dentist, is killed during a convention in Los Angeles. When Laura and Steele investigate the case becomes further complicated by the arrival of Frances (Burrell), Laura's sister.

'Elegy In Steele'

Writer: Brian Alan Lane. *Director*: Kevin Connor. *Guest cast*: Guy Boyd, Quinn Cummings, Michael Fairman, Peter Jason, Ric Mancini, Ruth Kilbart, Ed Hooks.
Magician Major Descoine (Boyd) gives Laura and Steele one hour to live when he pays a visit to their office and, after the threat, vanishes in a puff of smoke.

'Small Town Steele'

Writer: Jeff Melvoin. *Director*: Seymour Robbie. *Guest cast*: Paul Gleason, Ben Slack, Jacques Aubuchon, Carolyn Coates, Ford Rainey, Jennifer Parsons.
A missing persons case brings Laura and Steele to a small town where the entire populace is in on a secret involving hidden money and murder.

'Molten Steele'

Writer: Richard Collins. *Director*: Chris Hibler. *Guest cast*: Pippa Scott, Bill Morey, John Bedford-Lloyd, John Furey, Ellen Regan, Ellen Tobie, Andrea Moar.
Society matron Emily Dumont (Scott) hires Laura and Steele to track down the culprit who placed an ad in a sex magazine using her name and telephone number.

'Dreams Of Steele'

Writer: Brian Alan Lane. *Director*: Don Weis. *Guest cast*: Judith Light, Woodrow Parfrey, Jack Gwillim, Robert Harper, Lomax Study, Jineane Ford Passolt.
Laura and Steele are hired to transport the famous Royal Lavulite jewels from Santa Barbara to LA but somehow the gems are replaced by fakes en route, leading into a murder case.

'Woman Of Steele'

Writers: Susan Baskin, Richard DeRoy, Michael Gleason. *Director*: Chris Hibler. *Guest cast*: Cassandra Harris, James Laurenson, Christopher Stone, Eve Roberts, John Del Regno.
A gorgeous female operative re-enters Steele's life and Laura finds herself defending not only a priceless art collection, but her partner as well.

'Hounded Steele'

Writer: Jeff Melvoin. *Director*: Don Weis. *Guest cast*: Tom Baker, J. D Cannon, Sarah Marshall, Anita Talbot, Doris Belack.

Mildred's moonlighting as a detective turns up a dead Interpol agent and puts Laura and Steele on the trail of an international master thief.
'Elementary Steele'
Writer: Michael Gleason. *Director*: Seymour Robbie. *Guest cast*: Lynne Randall, Pearl Shear, Keone Young, William Griffis, Bob Elmore, Peter Evans.
Mystery buffs have signed up for a make-believe case that's actually a scheme to locate a murderous embezzler.

In 1982, just when the series was starting production, Stephen Dark interviewed the series' co-creator-director Robert Butler in California:

> I had the basic idea for the series and the title a long time ago and I knew at that time that if there was a woman posing as a detective, chauvinism being what it is, she would get more done that way. That's not a true idea, but that's a true show idea. As I worked on the idea I realised it would be more fun if there was our equivalent of the Orchid man and I had invented something and Michael invented something and so ultimately he wrote the pilot script and developed the material so that the sum total of it was that we created the situation together.
>
> But we didn't go in trying to combine Cary Grant and Jimmy Stewart out of two Hitchcock movies. We just realised that it would be fun if there was a very attractive man with a dangerous past opposite this lady he is thrown in there with. So you got this unbreakable bond and yet it must remain sexist because as she says if we crossed that bridge think of what the hell could happen ...
>
> Incidentally, when I had the original idea I couldn't tell whether it was chauvinistic or feministic. I just can't tell yet, whether the person who figured this all out is a feminist or an anti-feminist. I just can't tell. Because I can see it go both ways. He's arrogant and masculine and taciturn at times – which is to say chauvinistic and at times she is infuriated and bossy. It's both there. I guess it's going to come in the eye of the beholder.
>
> My evaluation is that the Remington character [in the pilot episode] was a little harsh, a little potentially less sympathetic than he should be; harsh, sharp, selfish, expedient. So NBC said alter the premise slightly. It's very complicated to follow and it sets our hero up as an extortionist, if you will, as opposed to an ex-cop or whatever. And also they wanted a thing that often they do not want and that is to show the original story, how the characters got to be in each other's lives, and that's the script we're doing now. So that instead of her 'inventing' a character that really came out of her memory from a guy she saw in a line-up once, we're intentionally taking a device from the movie *North By Northwest* – because the whole series is about an affectionate nod to the old movies – whereby Cary Grant raised his hand at an inopportune moment to call a pageboy to send his mother a telegram message and the two villains saw him answer a page. We're lifting that and bending it to suit our purposes, so that's how the two of them get together. So what they do in between scenes, as it were, is make an arrangement. It's in the agency's advantage to have a figurehead in the flesh rather than to have to fake him all the time, so they decide to make an arrangement, which is what this series becomes.
>
> [Regarding the cost of production, in comparison to *Hill Street Blues*] I wouldn't really say that the sets cost more on this show than on *Hill Street* – that's a balance, but *Hill Street*'s a slightly better buy in terms of production because you can go down into the bowels of Los Angeles and on a little street corner you can get five locations: you can get a parking lot, an alley, whatever. It's a good buy because everything is of similar character. It happens to work well. Now with *Remington Steele* you have to keep changing the arena. One week it will be an Italian race driver who lives in an hotel. Another it'll be a blue blood polo player who lives on an estate. The next week it'll be Howard Hughes who is trying to present a new car to the public in a ballroom. You have to keep changing the – well, it's an opulent show so it's not cheap – but more than that you have to keep changing your number.

[The writers] have a terrible task because what they have to do is figure out a case which is complicated with twists at the end and entertaining and surprises and revelations and all that. It's really hard to figure out and it takes a lot of time to put finger-prints on keys and broken glass in pockets and all that. And once having found that then they don't play on it much; they play on the people and what the people are doing in relationship to that. It takes those guys a long time to figure out those fearful lines of geometry that come out even in the end. So they've got to do Hitchcock every week which is hard. They can't do it. Nobody can. There are holes in *North By Northwest*; we started talking about them afterwards. And doing this show occasionally we talk about behaviour as opposed to plot. Well, occasionally people are doing things that behaviourally doesn't make sense, but you just have to go ahead and do them. You know, we keep telling each other – don't think just do it. Which is to say, the stories are very tough with the guys and they are doing a great job with it.

I do have an instinct though, not unlike *Hill Street*, that this show will have an audience, a very specific, a very worthwhile and product-buying but slightly limited audience.

Despite the 'arrangement' built between the show's central characters, the *Variety* verdict on the première episode was that 'NBC is obviously nervous about portraying a truly independent woman in a primetime series. Lone rogue males abound on every video mean street, but a woman handling tough situations often ultimately finds herself dependent upon the tender mercies of the other gender. Zimbalist does so in this show, and that's after running through a pattern of stereo-typical female behaviour that includes going instantly ga-ga over guest star Pierce Brosnan. . . .The [Steele] characterisation is particularly regressive because its premise provides the opportunity for a dynamic female lead role, rare enough in prime.' (*Variety*, 6/10/82, p. 46)

TV Guide reflects this view, but from another angle, as Robert MacKenzie reported: 'I think the producers, full of admirable liberal impulses, are trying to tell us about the unfairness of it all. It's the prejudice of her clients, after all, that forces Laura to use a man as a front. And Laura, I guess, represents the modern, all-but-liberated woman – competent, resourceful and ever so frank about [sexual] itches. As for Remington, he may signal a coming fashion in males – useless but decorative, a nice accessory for a woman who can afford him.' (*TV Guide*, 8/1/83, p. 31) But Tom Carson in *Village Voice* (3/5/83) called *Remington Steele* 'the merriest piece of fluff on TV – airy as cotton candy and nowhere near as sticky'.

Bay City Blues (NBC, 1983–) Film. 60 mins.
Executive producer: Steven Bochco. *Associate producer*: Jim Hart. *Creators*: Steven Bochco and Jeffrey Lewis. *Music*: Mike Post.
Regular cast: Michael Nouri *(Joe Rohner)*, Kelly Harmon *(Sunny Hayward)*, Pat Corley *(Ray Holtz)*, Bernie Casey *(Ozzie Peoples)*, Perry Lang *(Frenchy Nuckles)*, Patrick Cassidy *(Terry St Marie)*, Dennis Franz *(Angelo Carbone)*, Larry Flash Jenkins *(Lynwood Scott)*, Michele Greene *(Judy Nuckles)*, Ken Olin *(Rocky Padillo)*, Tony Spiridakis *(Lee Jacoby)*, Mykel T. Williamson *(Deejay Cunningham)*, Jeff McCracken *(Vic Kresky)*, Peter Jurasik *(Mitch Klein)*, Sharon Stone *(Cathy St Marie)*, Marco Rodriguez *(Bird)*. *Occasional cast*: Sheree North, Kevin McCarthy, Julius J. Carry III, Eddie Velez, Denise Galik.

A drama about the men and women associated with a minor league baseball team in a small California town.

Première episode
Writers: Steven Bochco, Jeffrey Lewis. *Director*: Gregory Hoblit. *Guest cast*: Kevin McCarthy, Barry Tubb, E. Erich Anderson, John Karlen, Art LaFleur, Lisa Kingston.
Manager Joe Rohner, like his players on the minor-league Bay City (California) Bluebirds, dreams of baseball's big leagues; team owner Ray Holtz dreams of profits; and the lonely banker's wife Sunny dreams of Rohner. In this debut episode, two players and their wives

find that pressures on the field spill over into the domestic life they share under the same roof.
'Beautiful Peoples'
Writers: Thad Mumford, Dan Wilcox. *Director*: Michael Rhodes. *Guest cast*: Robert Davi, Jeanetta Arnette, Beah Richards, Diane Franklin, Woodrow Parfrey, Elizabeth Daily, Leonard Stone.
On Ozzie Peoples Appreciation Day, the slugger strikes out and later is 'caught stealing'. Meanwhile, Rohner and Jacoby rebound after losing in love.
'Zircons Are Forever'
Writers: Jeffrey Lewis, David Milch. *Story by* Steven Bochco, Jeffrey Lewis. *Director*: Alan Reisner. *Guest cast*: Barry Tubb, Denise Galik, Diane Franklin, John Furey, Sunny Johnson, Robert Costanzo, Shane McCabe, David Sage, Rob Kim.
Potential superstar St Marie signs with a high-powered agent (Furey), spawning resentment in Frenchy; Rohner balks at going into business with Hayward (McCarthy); Jacoby wants to be not only Holtz's catcher but his son-in-law as well; pitcher Mickey Wagner (Tubb) returns to the Bluebirds after a cup of coffee in the majors.
'I Never Swung For My Father'
Writer: Joel Surnow. *Director*: Arthur Seidelman. *Guest cast*: E. Erich Anderson, William Lucking, Sunny Johnson, Barry Tubb, John Furey, John Karlen, Rob Kim, Ellen Blake.
The father-son reunion is anything but joyous for Vic and Moe Kresky (McCracken and Lucking); Hayward (McCarthy) becomes even more insistent about his business proposal and more perplexed by Rohner's resistance; Padillo, Scott and Jacoby pay a solemn final tribute to a fallen colleague.

Bay City Blues was hailed on its opening by an article in *Time* (31/10/83) written by Richard Stengel:

. . . '*Bay City Blues* follows the successful formula of its predecessor, but the show does more than replace nightsticks with Louisville Sluggers. The series features a repertory company brimming with quirky and distinctive characters, simultaneously strong and vulnerable. Each episode has multiple, intersecting plot lines, tight camera shots, overlapping dialogue à la Robert Altman movies (or locker rooms), private lives spilling over into public, and a concern with such human-size issues as embarrassment, anxiety, loyalty and how to hit a hanging curve. Knowledge of baseball lore is useful, not essential.

'The idea for the show popped into Bochco's head last July while he was watching an oldtimers game at Dodger Stadium. Eventually a meeting was arranged with Grant Tinker, the chairman of NBC, and other executives at the office of MTM Enterprises, the production company where Bochco works and that Tinker created. Bochco brought along a shopping bag full of major-league baseballs. The executives played with the idea and the baseballs. One hour later, Bochco left the room with a commitment for 13 shows. First on their agenda: the construction of a full scale $500,000 stadium in Sun Valley, Calif., with just the right rinky-dink look. . . .

'According to the producer, the current advertising-agency wisdom about a sports series is that women will never watch it. Bochco, who had boyish dreams of being a ball-player, admits that "baseball is essentially a man's fantasy, not a woman's." Accordingly, he has been careful to treat the unfulfilled longings of some of the players' wives as much as those of their husbands. Sharon Stone and Michele Greene play high-spirited but long-suffering companions who must put up with lingering slumps and Baseball Annies. The only weak character is a wealthy banker's wife, played by the luminous Kelly Harmon. Her role needs more reason for being around than simply to give the audience someone to stare at.

'Despite an occasional lapse, the Bay City Bluebirds are minor-leaguers in name only; this backwater is a microscosm of major-league concerns and emotions. When the skipper of the team strolls over to the local college and eavesdrops on a lecture, the teacher is reading aloud from Melville. "Passion," she says, "and passion at its profoundest, is not a thing demanding a palatial stage whereon to play its part . . ." Judging from the early episode of *Bay City Blues*, all it needs is a locker room.'

Following the show's première episode, *Variety* felt that 'Steven Bochco's *Bay City Blues* debuted with all the stylistic tricks of Bochco's much-honoured *Hill Street Blues* intact, but with a different content. That difference in content could make all the difference in *Bay City*'s chances for success.' (*Variety*, 2/11/83, p. 80) If this, like the initial comments regarding *St Elsewhere*, had an element of hope within the view then it also contained a certain reviewer's insight to the life-span possibilities: 'Granted that the slice-of-life reality style of *Hill Street* has a certain attraction of its own, but stylistically *Bay City Blues* reminded this viewer more of Abby Mann's *SKAG* [Karl Malden's working-class steel town family] series of the recent past, a skein that depressed viewers with its harsh dramatic reality unrelieved by balancing humour. *Bay City* could find it tough to win.' So tough, in fact, that NBC cancelled the series after only four episodes had been aired (25/10/83–15/11/83.)

The Duck Factory (NBC, 12/4/84–4/7/84) Tape. 30 mins.
Executive producer: Allan Burns. *Producers*: Rod Daniel, Dan Wilcox, Thad Mumford. *Creators*: Allan Burns, Herbert Klynn. *Animation producers*: Ted and Gerry Woolery Playhouse Pictures. *Executive script consultant*: Jordan Moffet. *Creative animation consultant*: Herbert Klynn. *Photography*: Robert F. Liu. *Art director*: Jacqueline Webber.
Cast: Jim Carrey *(Skip Tarkenton)*, Jack Gilford *(Brooke Carmichael)*, Don Messick *(Wally Wooster)*, Teresa Ganzel, Nancy Lane, Julie Payne, Clarence Gilyard Jr.

The title refers to the struggling animation studio which produces a cartoon character called Dippy Duck. The basic theme is that the offbeat employees are under constant fear that their cartoon will be cancelled by the network. The 'factory' workers consist of the young, unwilling producer, the aging artist who drinks too much, and the legendary voice-over man who can't remember which of his 600 voices is actually his own.

Tom Carson reviewed the first episode in the *Village Voice* (1/5/84):

. . . 'The comedy-drama mix, not to mention the comedy-action mix, obviously aren't completely new to TV. But they've become particularly important because the sitcom formulas have gotten even more worn out than those of the action shows, and aren't nearly as suspectible to revivifying outside influences. Hollywood just doesn't offer as much to steal that would fit the mechanical, laugh-jerking, ubiquitous breed of sitcom we all know, deplore, and probably still watch when there's nothing else on – even though we may feel like even the lowest common denominator just isn't the family it used to be. The shows just aren't doing their crass job properly: a show as bad as *We Got It Made* ought to be either a cultural monstrosity, or nothing. *The Duck Factory* is much, you know, worthier – in a line with all those determinedly grown-up and humane, MTM-derived '70s sitcoms which stayed enshrined as the form's definitive class act even after they started losing the battle for popular appeal with Fred Silverman's teeny shows. But in a way, the new series also has the effect of making the MTM style of sitcom seem, if not as threadbare as the standard crap, at least something of an anachronism. . . .

'Much of this was fairly funny – and being filmed on location rather than in front of a studio audience gave the show a visual mobility that turned its most throwaway lines into snappy asides. But what most MTM shows are about above all is personal relations – celebrated, rather statically, through whatever sentiments link people in common, despite the superficial differences occasioned by character. Here, however, the creators have had to invent a mouthpiece protagonist who can verbalize the emotional linkages. Skip brushes up against all sorts of events which ought to make his innocence appear fatuous, and sweeps them away by verbalizing even more. His adulation restores a sense of craftsmanly pride to an aging artist overcome by weary resignation (Jack Gilford); in half an hour, he makes three separate fervent speeches about how much the studio and keeping the studio family together means, all of the you-don't-know-how-*great*-you-are variety. When characters start making speeches like this, it's usually out of fear that the situation involved won't get the meanings across on its own. *The Duck Factory* seems to constantly overcompensate for a connection with the audience that's somehow lacking: for instance, while the aspirations of earlier MTM characters were immediately recognizable to us in their small scale (not to mention their failure), Skip's not only got a big-time mission – to make the world laugh again – but is presented as if he's going to succeed at it.

'The sentiments, once made explicit, only register as sentimentality – a sentimentality that's quite out of synch with the tone of the purely comic stuff, making for all sorts of contradictory effects. MTM has always hired the best comic writers around, and the prevailing style in comedy writing now is acerbic – merely mean-spirited at worst, rudely knowing at its best and most likable. *Duck Factory*'s writers catch the style all right, but its sardonic riffs and one-upping details don't belong in the same series with the emotional affirmations which are the MTM sitcom's reason for being.

'Now that *Duck Factory*'s predecessor in the Thursday time slot has gone off the air, *Cheers* is the only sitcom that feels as attuned to the audience as, say the old *Mary Tyler Moore Show* itself once did – and I think it's mostly because the good people on *Cheers* are seldom any better than they have to be. If one of them has a moment of vulnerability or idealism or self-knowledge, it's a response to a situation, not the opened page of their soul; the moment itself might be shown up by later events as fatuous, or lampooned even at the time. That kind of emotional fluidity is what puts the show squarely into the present tense, and it couldn't be more alien to most MTM shows' standard moment of epiphany: the discovery that nothing ever changes, and people always stay reassuringly the same. All in all, it seems quite fitting that, in this decade, the MTM sensibility has worked best not on sitcoms but on rather florid dramatic shows – where it isn't intended to be the comic relief.'

On 16 May 1984 *Variety* reported that NBC had decided to cancel *The Duck Factory*. For a while there were suggestions that it might be brushed up – as *WKRP* had been – and returned to the schedules later in the year, or alternatively, acquired by another network. But neither NBC's Tinker or MTM's traditional network CBS resurrected the series.

MTM Pilots

Bachelor At Law (CBS, 5/6/73) 30 mins.
Producer: Ed Weinberger. *Writer*: Ed Weinberger. *Director*: Jay Sandrich.
Cast: John Ritter, Sarah Kennedy, Harold Gould, Betsy von Furstenburg, Bill Zuckert, Kathleen O'Malley, Craig Nelson, David Frank, Richard Schaal, Curt Conway, Richard Gittings, Wayne Heffley, Ron Rifkin.

This was MTM's first pilot proper, which didn't get a screening until 1973, and which failed to pick up a series contract. Director Jay Sandrich comments: 'Very early on at MTM Ed Weinberger created a show about a young lawyer who goes to work for an older lawyer, who is a conman. It was a very funny show but it did not get on the schedules.'

Curiously enough, several years later, when Brooks, Weinberger and Daniels had left MTM, they created a short-lived series called *The Associates*, with a very similar theme and setting.

Of the cast members, John Ritter would go on to feature in ABC's *Three's Company* in 1977, and Harold Gould would reappear under the MTM aegis more prominently as Martin Morgenstern, Rhoda's father, in *Rhoda* (a part he originally played in *The Mary Tyler Moore Show*); Richard Schaal also went on to play Cloris Leachman's photographer co-worker in *Phyllis*.

This early pilot sets up a typical MTM family, this time in a Los Angeles law office. Ben Sykes is a naive, idealistic attorney whom we see applying for his first job with the cynical Matthew Brandon's law firm. Brandon takes Sykes on a 'trial' basis, giving him a case in which the client is obviously guilty. After interviewing the wrong client, Sykes eventually goes to court, only to discover (long after we do) that the case has been dismissed because somebody else confessed to the crime. At the end, Brandon tells him, 'I've decided to hire you – for another week.' A supporting comedy role involves Lester, an inept private investigator. The 'bachelor' part of the series is developed through Ben's relationship with a 'happily divorced' sexy neighbour, thus setting up the MTM home/office balance.

Much of the humour comes from the comic character, Lester, who keeps trying to demonstrate his savvy as a private eye (in much the same way Remington Steele would later). But all of his conclusions are either wrong or painfully obvious. In the tag, Lester enters, convinced the client was guilty. 'The Judge found Woodward innocent,' Sykes tells him. 'Close enough,' Lester replies as the pilot's final joke.

Bachelors 4: Friends & Lovers (CBS, 16/5/74) 30 mins.
Writers: Allan Burns, James L. Brooks. *Director*: Jay Sandrich.
Cast: Paul Sand, Lynn Lipton, Mike Pataki, Penny Marshall, Kathleen Miller, Dick Wesson.

Bachelors 4 was the umbrella title used by CBS to transmit four pilot films about single men in one 120-minute slot. Only the MTM pilot went on to a series, as *Paul Sand In Friends And Lovers* (1974–5).

> The successful half-hour, *Friends & Lovers*, is probably best described as a warm comedy. It has the advantage of an interesting setting, Boston, and an interesting profession for the young protagonist, bass player in the Boston symphony. Especially effective in the pilot was the scene in which Sand and other aspirants are at the audition for the orchestra. Uncredited support here was standout and the network would be smart to use them again if the casting director can find their names. (*Variety*)

Variety also noted that Penny Marshall, as the Paul Sand character's sister, exhibited 'comic flair'. The series that resulted from this pilot was shortlived, however, being cancelled after only thirteen weeks. One of the more successful series of the 1974 season on the other hand was *Happy Days*, which flagrantly flouted the 'contemporary' feel of the Lear and MTM comedies, opting instead for a teenage milieu set in the 1950s. By the 1976–7 season, *Happy Days* was the highest-rated series in prime-time and, in January 1976, Penny Marshall reappeared in a series spun-off from *Happy Days* entitled *Laverne And Shirley*. In 1978 Henry Winkler (the Fonz in *Happy Days*) and Penny Marshall also appeared in the pilot of another semi spin-off series, *Mork And Mindy*. All three of these series were produced by Garry Marshall who was to replace Lear and MTM as *the* sitcom producer of the second half of the seventies. All three were on ABC under its new (ex-CBS) president, Fred Silverman.

Friends & Lovers was the first of MTM's pilots to include 'an audition' as one of its narrative devices. Most new series start with the beginnings of things – new relationships, new jobs, new homes and so on – but MTM put its own stamp on this convention by regularly focusing on showbiz auditions in its pilots (e.g. in *The New Lorenzo Music Show, The Chopped Liver Brothers, Stephanie, Don't Call Us,* and *One Night Band*, not to mention *The Betty White Show*). Thus, while *Bachelor At Law* included an interview for a new job (as did the first episode of *The Mary Tyler Moore Show* itself) *Friends & Lovers* both 'naturalises' and at the same time foregrounds the actual function of pilots – as auditions for the networks.

Three For The Road (CBS, 4/9/75) 90 mins.
Writer: Jerry McNeely. *Director*: Boris Sagal.
Cast: Alex Rocco, Vincent Van Patten, Leif Garrett, Julie Sommars, John Beck, John McLiam, Katie Sagal, Larry McCormick, Alan McRae, Lucille Benson.

See section on MTM series for details.

Royce (CBS, 21/5/76) 60 mins.
Executive producer: Jim Byrnes. *Producer*: William T. Phillips. *Writer*: Jim Byrnes. *Director*: Andrew V. McLaglen.

Cast: Robert Forster, Marybeth Hurt, Moosie Drier, Terri Lynn Wood, Michael Parks, Eddie Little Sky, Dave Cass.

A Western drama set in the 1870s concerning an ex-gunfighter dealing with the harsh realities of frontier life.

> In the title role, Forster played a loner, as per the age-old formula for westerns, but he was not beyond lending a helping hand to women and children in trouble.
> Dependents in this case were a mother and two small children, alone on the prairie as they headed for California.
> Luckily for her, he stays close for a full quota of narrow escapes. But – and this may make it viable family hour fare – at one point, Royce told her ('what I've never told anyone else') that he'd never shot anyone – and she seemed to begin to recognise his real worth as a man. (*Variety*, 25/5/76)

Filmed on location in Arizona – an unusual expense for a pilot, if par for the course for MTM – this was a Western drama set in the 1870s about the exploits of an ex-gunfighter settling down to a more peaceful life on the frontier. Although this was MTM's first sixty-minute dramatic pilot, the mood was very visibly inflected – and infected – by the impact of 'Family Hour'. In 1975 *The Waltons* was the only family Western – indeed the only Western of any description – on network prime-time and *Royce*, in spite of the presence of an oater auteur director like McLaglen, was not to be the first of a new wave. MTM's only previous venture into the sixty minute slot, *Three For The Road*, had also involved the travels and travails of a single parent family, but this too had proved equally unsuccessful.

The New Lorenzo Music Show (ABC, 10/8/76) 30 mins.
Producer: Carl Gottlieb. *Writers*: Lorenzo Music, Carl Gottlieb, James L. Brooks, Jerry Davis, Allan Burns. *Director*: Tony Mordente.
Cast: Lorenzo & Henrietta Music, David Ogden Stiers, Jack Eagle, Steve Anderson, Roz Kelly, Lewis Arquette, Bandini Bros.

> MTM Enterprises' *New Lorenzo Music Show*, a busted pilot that was the genesis of syndicated *Lorenzo & Henrietta Music Show* that is readying for a September start, was an amusing half-hour that augurs well for the Musics' fling at the musical-variety brass ring.
> The droll pilot was in the form of an audition by Lorenzo Music for a talk-variety show of his own, after having been a TV writer for a long time [actually, Music is also a producer, having created the *Bob Newhart Show* and produced it, along with *Rhoda* in which he provides the voice of Carlton the doorman].
> The most pleasing aspect of the pilot was that the script showed an excellent awareness of what was funny in the overall concept and capitalised nicely on that awareness. The Musics have been pro performers before he turned to comedy writing, and they handle themselves quite well on camera. Script was by the cream of the MTM writing-producing stable. (*Variety*, 18/8/76)

This was MTM's first pilot for ABC, now headed by Fred Silverman who had previously presided over MTM's relationship with CBS. *The New Lorenzo Music Show* was an early example of MTM's decision to diversify its output (*Royce* was another symptom of this strategy) and it proved to be only the first of several attempts by the company to carve out a niche for itself in the field of television variety. Where MTM had simply turned to new projects when previous pilots were turned down by the networks, on this occasion the company approached a syndicate of local stations and persuaded them to take a first run option of a spin-off series, *The Lorenzo And Henrietta Music Show*. Once again, the pilot took its narrative cue from an audition.

Don't Call Us (CBS, 13/8/76) 30 mins.

Producers: Ed Weinberger, Stan Daniels. *Writer*: David Lloyd. *Creators*: Ed Weinberger, Stan Daniels, David Lloyd, *Director*: Robert Moore.
Cast: Jack Gilford, Allan Miller, Leland Palmer, Barry Miller, Richard Narita, Patty Maloney, Billy Barty, Tina Louise, James Luisi, Don Davis.

Another audition format pilot, *Don't Call Us* concerned the activities of Marty and Larry King and their theatrical agency, Talent Unlimited. Once again – another MTM speciality – the setting was regional, Philadelphia, but for the first time the focus was on two brothers – a concept reprised in two later MTM pilots, *Brothers* and *The Chopped Liver Brothers.*

Martinelli: Outside Man (CBS, 8/4/77) 60 mins.
Executive producer: Paul Magistretti. *Producer*: William T. Phillips. *Writer*: Paul Magistretti, *Director*: Russ Mayberry.
Cast: Ron Liebman, Woody Strode, Janet Margolin, Nicholas Colasanto, Al Ruscio, Pepper Martin, Robert Donner, Pat Corley, Fred Stuthman, Nicholas Pryor, William Wintersole, Michael Frost.

Crime drama featuring the exploits of a street-wise federal agent who goes undercover to apprehend criminals.

> Given the opportunity, it is obvious that Liebman could develop a regular following. Executive producer Paul Magistretti's script displayed a good understanding of Italian ethnic values that added considerably to the pilot's impact, but the fly in the ointment is the fact that cop dramas of any sort are currently in disfavor in plans for the 1977–8 season at all three webs – so *Martinelli* looms as an also-ran, despite its promising aspects. *(Variety,* 13/4/77)

Martinelli: *Outside Man* took the 'undercover cop' premise of the show-within-a-show fiction of *The Betty White Show* and simply ironed out the comedy. Another of the company's attempts to come up with a workable sixty-minute drama series, its apparent similarity to other non-MTM product meant that it was indistinguishable from contemporary cop shows; MTM's successful sixty-minute series, like *Lou Grant* and *Hill Street Blues*, were to extend the MTM 'house-style' into the drama field rather than simply dropping their differences. Four years later, the same undercover cop format was refashioned for *Nichols & Dymes* but without success. MTM have, however, been more fortunate with their uniformed cop shows, *Paris* and *Hill Street Blues*, and the private eye series *Remington Steele*.

Bumpers (ABC, 16/5/77) 30 mins.
Producers: David Davis, Charlotte Brown. *Writers*: David Davis, Charlotte Brown. *Director*: James Burrows.
Cast: Richard Masur, Stephanie Faracy, Michael L. McManus, Jack Riley, Tim Reid, Zane Buzby, Ray Buktenica, Brian Dennehy.

David Davis and Charlotte Brown who wrote and produced this pilot had both been at MTM for some time – Davis since its inception – but neither of them ever came up with a series. Once again, though, the 'failure' of *Bumpers* may be as much a consequence of cynical network strategy as of the programme's 'quality'. Robert Sklar has described *Bumpers* as 'a blue-collar comedy about a worker in an automobile factory' and he adds:

> ABC gave it a sneak preview in the half hour before the Ali-Evangelista heavyweight prizefight. Sneak preview indeed: *TV Guide* listed that time slot as: 'To Be Announced'. Predictably *Bumpers* scored an unimpressive rating. *(Prime Time America,* p. 85)

What this anecdote reveals is that by the time pilots are scheduled their respective networks have already decided on their fates. In the case of *Bumpers,* ABC were unwilling to commission a series on the basis of the pilot but were equally unwilling to allow MTM to take the project elsewhere. Since it is the networks who commission scripts and then pilots, it is the networks who hold copyright on those pilots and independent production companies like MTM are prohibited from offering them elsewhere, even after they have been rejected by the commissioning network. The same fate overtook another MTM pilot commissioned by ABC that same season, *The Chopped Liver Brothers* and Sklar describes Grant Tinker's frustration at ABC's attitude. On the admittedly second-hand evidence of the *Variety* synopsis and Sklar's own account, *Bumpers* sounds as if MTM were still persevering with their 'social realist' sitcom model in spite of ABC's success with such teenage programming (in terms both of audiences and protagonists) as *Happy Days*. It also provided Stephanie Faracy with her first starring role for MTM; the company was later to create a vehicle, *Stephanie*, for her – but without success.

The Chopped Liver Brothers (ABC, 20/6/77) 30 mins.
Executive producers: Tom Patchett and Jay Tarses. *Producer*: Michael Zinberg. *Writers*: Tom Patchett, Jay Tarses, Hugh Wilson. *Director*: Hugh Wilson.
Cast: Tom Patchett, Jay Tarses, Gwynne Gilford, Philip Bruns, Robert Emhardt, Michael Pataki, Phil Roth, Madeleine Fisher, Rick Podell.

Tom Patchett and Jay Tarses had begun their careers in show business as a pair of rather unsuccessful stand-up comedians. Spotted by Tom Smothers they worked for a while as scriptwriters for *The Smothers Brothers Comedy Hour* which (like *Lou Grant* more than a decade later) was eventually cancelled because of network nervousness about its politics. MTM, which was in a sense the beneficiary of CBS's decision to de-ruralise its audience, also benefited from the cancellation of the *Smothers Brothers* show because the network needed 'topical' comedy, if not quite as controversial as the latter series had proved. *The Mary Tyler Moore Show* had been the result and among the first writer-producer teams hired to back up Brooks and Burns and Weinberger and Daniels was Patchett and Tarses. The latter pair eventually moved on from producing *The Mary Tyler Moore Show* and *The Bob Newhart Show* and created a series of their own, *The Tony Randall Show* – also for ABC. This pilot, though unsuccessful, sounds closer than the *Randall* show to their, and MTM's own, territory. It was scripted by and starred Patchett and Tarses and re-created in fictional form their experiences on the nightclub circuit prior to their move into prime-time. ABC proved uninterested in the pilot; perhaps ethnic comedy (always more closely associated with Norman Lear than with MTM, in spite of Rhoda Morgenstern) was no longer acceptable in prime-time. Credited as co-writer and director was Hugh Wilson, who went on to create *WKRP In Cincinnati* (and later to write and direct the non-MTM feature film *Police Academy*). Co-star Rick Podell later turned up as co-writer of another MTM pilot, *Brothers*.

The Natural Look (NBC, 6/7/77) 30 mins.
Executive producer: Lillian Gallo. *Producers*: Leonora Thuna, Pamela Chais. *Writer*: Leonora Thuna. *Director*: Robert Moore.
Cast: Barbara Feldon, Bill Bixby, Brenda Forbes, Sandy Sprung, Caren Kaye, Michael MacRae.

MTM's longstanding relationship with CBS was finally being broadened out to include not only occasional flirtations with ABC but also, briefly, with NBC. *The Natural Look* concerned a newlywed couple, Edie, a cosmetics executive and Bud, a pediatrician. While thus retaining the MTM split between domestic and professional situations therefore, this pilot seems to have stretched the company's previously already noteworthy commitment to women (both in the industry and on the screen and, via vicarious identification, in the audience). The pilot was written, produced and executive produced by women and of the main cast of six, four were women. (Edie's 'cosmetics' work neatly reflected the main advertisers of women's products on TV.) But in 1977 female protagonists were rapidly becoming par for the prime-time course – in *Laverne And Shirley* and *Charlie's Angels* on ABC. NBC, meanwhile, already had *Bionic Woman* and *Police Woman* on its roster and perhaps they had heard rumours that MTM were already preparing to spoof the latter in that season's *The Betty White Show*. Certainly on this occasion NBC decided against the MTM show on offer.

Kinfolks (CBS, not tx'd, 1977–8 season) 60 mins.

The pilot episode was produced for the 1977–8 season, and after waiting in vain to see if CBS would give it a try as a replacement series, MTM released the cast . . . *Kinfolks* had a white producer, Philip Barry, and a white director, Fielder Cook, but a black writer, Melvin Van Peebles.

[Van Peebles is regarded as something of an urban black rebel, reflecting very much the lead character of his controversial 1971 film, *Sweet Sweetback's Baadasss Song*.] 'I got a letter inviting me to a cookout down South,' Van Peebles says. The cookout was for a reunion of a Van Peebles family, and Van Peebles suspected the family was white and had made a mistake, though he never went down to find out. He did, however, develop a story idea from the incident and took it to an agent. Eventually the incident made its way into the *Kinfolks* pilot, where a group of white Simmonses shows up at the black Simmonses home for a 'family reunion'. The white adults are befuddled or indignant, but a little white girl hugs the elderly black great-aunt, and a point about racism is made.

The agent soon reported back that a producer was interested in Van Peebles, but for a different idea. The producer was Philip Barry of MTM Enterprises, and the result was *Just An Old Sweet Song*, an award-winning television drama written by Van Peebles and directed by Robert Ellis Miller. . . .

The idea for *Kinfolks* grew out of the success of *Just An Old Sweet Song*. In the pilot show for *Kinfolks*, Robert Hooks continues [from the TV movies] as the husband, Madge Sinclair replaces Cicely Tyson as his wife, and Beah Richards, formerly the dying grandmother of *Just An Old Sweet Song*, is reincarnated as the great-aunt. Van Peebles got a chance to include his original television idea, the episode of the family reunion. But the story line turns on the murder of Nate Simmons' white business partner by a demented red-neck and the threat by the murderer's brother to do further harm to blacks – stereotyped bigots and conventionalized violence, as I viewed it. . . .

[Van Peebles] expresses good feelings about his work on *Kinfolks*. 'Many of the hassles are not indigenous to blacks,' he says, 'they're indigenous to television per se.' (Extracts quoted from Robert Sklar, *Prime Time America*, pp. 104–106)

The Many Loves Of Arthur (NBC, 23/5/78) 60 mins.
Producer: Philip Barry. *Writer*: Gerald DiPego. *Director*: Bill Bixby.
Cast: Richard Masur, Caroline McWilliams, Constance McCashin, David Dukes, Silvana Gallardo, Paddy Edwards, Linda Lukens, Harv Selsby, Lee Bryant, Robert Ridgely.

Shot in film-style with no laugh track, *Arthur* was a rather experimental comedy-drama about a veterinarian (Richard Masur) who, as a lead figure, was something of a 'loser'. Arthur feels like crying over the death of a lion, but tells his female colleague, 'what if I never love another human being as long as I live?' He lectures on the subject of extinction at a university, describing what it means from the animals' point of view. Arthur flies to a Seattle zoo to try to save a dying pregnant hippo's offspring from extinction. On the plane, he meets a stewardess and takes her to the zoo, where they talk about adopting the baby hippo. Eventually his involvement with the woman becomes too threatening and he breaks up with her by leaving a note on the back of a photo of them with the hippo. The mama hippo lives long enough to go into labour. Arthur delivers the baby, meanwhile phoning the woman and asking her to move back with him. The implication is that the birth of the baby hippo renews his faith in the possibility of human relationships.

Bill Bixby, who had starred in an earlier MTM pilot, *The Natural Look*, directed this one but with no more success with NBC. It was produced by Philip Barry, who also produced MTM's TV Movie *Just An Old Sweet Song* and its offshoot pilot *Kinfolks*. Originally entitled *Arthur Among The Animals* the pilot was renamed in an apparent attempt to attract a more 'adult' audience than the one composed entirely of pet-lovers which the network may have expected. As a sixty minute comedy, it occupied an uneasy place in terms of programming – and consequently scheduling – conventions and no series was commissioned.

Your Place Or Mine? (CBS, 27/5/78) 30 mins.
Producers: David Lloyd, Dale McRaven. *Writers*: Bob Ellison, David Lloyd. *Director*: Jim Burrows.
Cast: Jane Actman, Stuart Gillard, Peter Hobbs, Alice Hirson, Elizabeth Kerr, George Pentecost, Judy Graubart, Elizabeth Halliday, Martin Garner.

Written and produced by Bob Ellison and David Lloyd, *Your Place Or Mine?* nicely thematises the rural/urban polarity out of which MTM itself had emerged. It concerned the relationship between a male freelance writer living in Manhattan but longing for the countryside and a female editorial assistant living in a quiet part of Queens but working – and wanting to live – in Manhattan. The pilot's premise is that these two meet, fall in love and decide to exchange apartments to better suit their lifestyles.

The Busters (CBS, 28/5/78) 60 mins.
Executive producer: Stu Erwin. *Producer*: Jim Byrnes. *Writer*: Jim Byrnes. *Director*: Vincent McEveety.
Cast: Bo Hopkins, Brian Kerwin, Slim Pickens, Devon Ericson, Buck Taylor, Chris Robinson, Lance LeGault, Susan Howard.

Action drama about a couple of cowboys working the professional rodeo circuit.

> The rodeo environment could be a reasonably productive area for exciting action footage, but *The Busters* portion of same was thinly doled out – with the plot resorting to a night club brawl over Howard as its key action sequence. Hopkins is a persuasive performer with his own unique style, while Kerwin deftly limned the eager-to-rise neophyte. The rest of the cast was acceptable in generally stereotyped parts and the series idea could make a moderate series entry – if only networks were looking for moderate bread-and-butter skeins these days. *(Variety*, 31/5/78)

Jim Byrnes had already scripted one 'period' western for MTM, *Royce*, without success so on this occasion the setting was contemporary; otherwise, however, this pilot sounds as unlike other MTM products as it was unattractive to CBS schedulers.

Down Home (CBS, 16/8/78) 60 mins.
Producer: Philip Barry. *Writer*: Melvin Van Peebles. *Director*: Fielder Cook.
Cast: Robert Hooks, Madge Sinclair, Beah Richards, Lincoln Kilpatrick, Kevin Hooks, Eric Hooks, Beverly Hope Atkinson, Sonny Jim Gaines, Anne Seymour, Norma Connolly, Tia Rance, Dena Crowder, Edward Binns, William Watson, Paul Koslo, Tim Scott, Woodrow Parfrey, Boyd Bodwell, Mickey Jones, John Gilgreen, George McDaniel, Edward Beagle, Mark Taylor, Andrew Duggan.

Following the success of MTM's first made-for-TV-movie, *Just An Old Sweet Song*, *Down Home* was the first of the company's attempts to spin-off a series from the same story – that of a northern black family moving down south. (See *Just An Old Sweet Song* and *Kinfolks* for further details.) CBS and MTM were apparently keen to come up with a prime-time programme with black protagonists but they were unsuccessful until they decided to place a black protagonist in the uniform of a white genre, the cop show, with *Paris* the following year.

Operating Room (NBC, 4/10/78) 60 mins.
Producer: Mark Tinker. *Writers*: Steven Bochco, Bruce Paltrow. *Director*: Bruce Paltrow.
Cast: Barbara Babcock, Bruce Bauer, Oliver Clark, David Spielberg, James Sutorius,

Janice Kent, Barbara Bosson, Cyb & Tricia Barnstable, Patricia Conklin, Ronnie Troup, Barbara Perry.

> *Operating Room*, an hour long pilot known as 'Doctors & Nurses' while in production, was labeled a comedy-drama by NBC-TV, which used it as a 10 o'clock show when the major league baseball playoff sked unexpectedly opened up Thursday (4th) for regular programming.
>
> The idea was that three single doctors at Los Angeles Memorial Hospital, quite good on the job, spent their off-time indulging themselves in hedonistic relaxation at their Malibu beach house.
>
> There were possibilities for a contemporary *M*A*S*H* premise and flavor, but that possibility was not given much help by a script that did not get its laughs in places where it was reaching for them. *(Variety,* 10/10/78)

Operating Room was one of the pilots produced by MTM as the result of Steven Bochco's arrangement with NBC. It also seems to have served as some sort of predecessor of *St Elsewhere* (for all Bochco's later complaints about the unfounded association between the latter and *Hill Street Blues*); furthermore, *Operating Room* also functioned as an on-air audition for Barbara Babcock and Barbara Bosson, both of whom became *Hill Street* regulars. *Operating Room* concretised a previously insubstantial MTM predilection for medical characters and settings – Mary Richards' fiancé had been an M.D., the husband in *The Natural Look* had been a pediatrician; *Second Start* made medical school its 'situation' and so on. *Variety* noted this pilot's status as a sort of contemporary *M*A*S*H* – a possibility that Paltrow and Bochco were to pursue separately in *St Elsewhere* and *Hill Street Blues*. Mike Post who later wrote the *HSB* theme music also contributed the score here.

Going Home Again (PBS, not tx'd, 1978–9 season)

Robert Sklar, in his book *Prime Time America*, has described the original 'idea' for *Going Home Again*. It seems to have been initially conceived as 'a family saga serial program that would be offered for late-night viewing, from 11.30pm to midnight, Monday through Friday . . . Tinker likens it to the old radio serial *One Man's Family*. It would be built around an older couple with five grown children, and begin in the early 1960s, around the time of President John F. Kennedy's assassination. In fact Tinker says, "I think of them like the Kennedy family".' (Sklar, pp. 85–6). When neither networks nor first-run syndicated stations could be interested in the idea, Tinker took it to PBS and even produced a pilot. According to *TV Guide*, 'Tinker envisions it as a 15-part series – the story of a fictional family played out against real events in the 1960s and 1970s.' (*TV Guide*, 23/9/78, 'What Happened, Pussycat?' by David Shaw, p. 28) *Variety* actually reported that 'MTM Enterprises scheduled a series *Going Home Again* for the Public Broadcasting Service, reportedly the first time a successful commercial producer has agreed to provide an on-going series for Public-TV'. (*Variety* 3/1/79) But it seems unlikely that even the pilot was ever screened.

This pilot produced for PBS is less in the MTM 'quality' style than in the BBC single play format familiar to PBS audiences from the 'classy' British adaptations they would be accustomed to seeing under the omnibus title 'Masterpiece Theater'. It is quite theatrical and appears even more so by being on videotape. The leading actors have theatrical credentials as well.

The plot concerns a movie crew who are making a documentary on the famous writer John David White. We see them outside the White's Victorian house, and the narrative alternates between their story and the saga of the White family, all of whom are about to return home for a family reunion. A possible parallel to the Kennedy family is suggested by the narrative's commencing on 21 November 1963. The White children are introduced in their various locales given in printed titles. Elizabetta White (Libby) is shown at her San Francisco university. She tells her boyfriend she has to go home to Sausalito for her mother's birthday and he says, 'That family of yours. You all think you're so special with all that literary background.' We return to the film-makers who discuss White's work, his fame, and his blacklisting. Then we cut to New York for Evan White, the playwright son. After this, John David White himself discusses the TV film with its producers. He doesn't wish to be 'benignly taken back into the fold'. Meanwhile the TV writer and his associate begin to emerge as characters, discussing their own relationship. She also informs us that the oldest son, now deceased, was aiming for a career in politics (another echo of the Kennedys).

As Libby arrives, we cut to Hollywood where we are introduced to Eben (Doc) White in bed with a woman, discussing her career in the movies. Eben is going to Dallas to cover the Kennedys and his girlfriend will go on ahead to the reunion. She worries that she's not intellectual enough for the Whites, but Eben reassures her that he wants to announce their marriage. After a scene between Libby and Rose in the kitchen, we are introduced to Ethan, who is a monk in Santa Cruz, but a liberal, crusading civil rights activist. Outside the house, the writer and the researcher-lover come up with yet another 'concept' – to make it like a student film. They discuss the other daughter, Margaretta White (Maggie), 'the only one of six determined to be an underachiever.' This is confirmed in the next segment where we see Maggie in Palo Alto mired in a conventional marriage.

In the ensuing reunion, which takes place the day of Kennedy's assasination, the events of the assasination form a backdrop for the family conflicts and the family rituals. The episode ends with a shot of the house and the sound over from the TV of the Kennedy tragedy. This MTM anthology drama was clearly intended to continue. Its extremely literate dialogue and 'Hallmark Hall of Fame' tone and *mise-en-scène* distinguish it from MTM's network TV style.

Mother And Me, M.D. (NBC, 14/6/79) 30 mins.
Producers: Jennie Blacton, Charles Raymond. *Executive producer*: Michael Zinberg. *Director*: Michael Zinberg.
Cast: Rue McClanahan, Leah Ayres, Jack Riley, Ken Gilman, Howard Witt.

Yet another pilot for NBC, once again directed by Michael Zinberg (who was soon to leave MTM and take up office in the comedy development office of NBC where he was to play an important role in the nurturing of *Hill Street Blues*). As the title reveals, this was also another medical comedy, this time concerning the exploits of a young female intern at a hospital where her mother is the head nurse.

Battle Of The Generations: Not Until Today (Home Again) (NBC, 27/6/79) 30 mins.
Executive producers: Michael Zinberg, David Lloyd. *Writer*: David Lloyd. *Director*: Michael Zinberg.
Cast: Darren McGavin, Dick Sargent, Raleigh Bond, Michael Horton, Peter Jurasik, Alexandra Stoddart, David Cohn.

NBC packaged four unsold pilots into one 120-minute slot under the general heading of *Battle Of The Generations*. The title of this episode refers to the previously unknown existence of an apparently illegitimate son of a small town police chief; in this aspect *Not Until Today* looks forward to a series that would focus even more closely on the emotional lives of policemen – *Hill Street Blues*. On this occasion, however, MTM's attempt to incorporate a little social reality into prime-time proved unsuccessful.

> Called *Not Until Today* on screen but referred to as 'Home Again' in the press release, it contained the best writing of the four but not the most laughs. The basic situation of an unknown (and temporarily unwanted) son turning up in the town where Darren McGavin was police chief had considerable poignancy, but was marred by McGavin's overplaying. Michael Horton was quite good as the son, with an assist from Dick Sargent as a priest. (*Variety*, 4/7/79)

Although the theme of illegitimacy is handled rather seriously, this warm comedy is not outside the MTM style. Comic reversals are frequent, as when the police chief tells his son, 'You didn't expect me to confess to him, did you? The man's a priest.' As is typical in a David Lloyd script, there are also media jokes. The boy asks the police chief what he's watching on TV, and he replies, 'I don't know.' 'Why have you got it on?' asks the boy. 'It's my favourite show,' says the chief. The pilot is more 'warm' and less funny than many MTM comedies; these unconventional features may have influenced the network's decision not to buy it.

Bureau (CBS, not tx'd, 1979)

The best available account of *Bureau* comes in Todd Gitlin, *Inside Prime Time* (New York: Pantheon Books, 1983). We quote it here:

> [Gary Goldberg] liked the idea of the romance of journalists in Vietnam, he said, 'and when I started going around, doing the research, [reporters] said that really it was funny over there. As black as it was, there was tremendous humor.'
>
> Goldberg proposed his Saigon news bureau idea to Grant Tinker, and Tinker appreciated the fact that there were, in his words, '*M*A*S*H* suggestions in the thing.' 'I had confidence in Gary,' he went on, 'so we went over to CBS. They had much more reluctance, certainly, than I had, and they wished that Gary would come back with something else. Gary is a very independent guy, and he said, "No, this is the one I want to do." And ultimately they said, "Okay, if you feel that strongly, try it." ' In fact, CBS was sufficiently impressed with Goldberg's work that in 1979 they were ready to offer him and MTM together a series commitment, 'pay or play,' meaning that they would go to pilot and pay MTM for a full thirteen episodes no matter how many or few were aired.
>
> Goldberg wrote what was to have been a half-hour script for a show called *Bureau* – actually about twenty-two minutes – but it came out much too long. At this point Tinker suggested that rather than make 'brutal cuts,' Goldberg open it out to an hour. After all, the style was really too serious for a sitcom. 'I went back to CBS,' Tinker said, 'and I made a very good case for it. I had sold myself and I sold Gary and I sold CBS and I can sell myself sitting here now that it was a good idea.'
>
> Goldberg thereupon wrote an hour-long version of *Bureau*. In the MTM style, workplace relations were central. In something of a reprise of *Lou Grant*, the main characters in this news bureau were the grizzled managing editor, Matthews, and a spunky, go-getting young male reporter, Hartman. Hartman along with other reporters liked to bait the army's buffoon colonel at the daily press conferences universally known as 'the 5.00 Follies.' Hartman said he was in Vietnam because it was the biggest story going, and because he believed in Frank Capra movies – he wanted to tell the people the truth. He got his tips from a friendly, whining army press attaché from Princeton.
>
> The *Bureau* pilot didn't cohere. It lurched between moments of pathos – Matthews lugubrious at a party: 'When all is said and done, war sucks'; a GI dying on the battlefield – and moments of broad comedy. 'Something about the balance of it wasn't right,' Tinker said later. 'CBS was not quite sure what it was. It wasn't a situation comedy and it wasn't a dramatic show. And they had the reservations about Vietnam.' Some roles were indifferently cast; the actor who played Hartman was 'kind of heavy,' Tinker thought. The show tested Below Average, with three major criticisms included in research vice-president Arnold Becker's report: 'First and foremost, viewers simply found *Bureau* a dull, slow-moving program ... too much talk and too little action ... story lines jumbled together.' Second, 'the program sermonized. Most of the talk was on one subject: War is hell. The third major criticism came from those who said they would have preferred to put the discomforting subject of the war in Vietnam behind them.' If *Bureau* were to be salvaged, Becker wrote, 'it is extremely important that each episode include a fully developed central story line ... Credibility should probably be enhanced if the Bureau contingent, most notably Hartman and Matthews, were not so totally

consumed with the moral dilemmas of their time, and . . . the military personnel . . . [did] not emerge as a bunch of single-minded automatons.' Becker told me later he thought *Bureau* 'was so anti-Establishment as to be, I would imagine, offensive to the average American. There were no heroes; the army was the villain. The good guys were the villains and the bad guys were the heroes.'

B. Donald ('Bud') Grant, the head of CBS Entertainment, agreed. Even at the script stage, he thought *Bureau* was not only antiwar but also 'antigovernment, anti-army. It wasn't balanced at all. I had problems with that. We talked with them about it and I think Gary Goldberg felt that we were overreacting, that it would be handled in dialogue and softened in performance. But it turned out that it wasn't.' The film, he said, was 'very well done,' but perhaps he was simply being kind.

'I personally liked *Bureau*,' said another program executive, 'but I don't think I would have put it on the air.' He didn't speak up for it in executive councils. Herman Keld thought the pilot 'preachy' and 'heavy-handed.' 'I cannot think of anybody who liked it' at the scheduling meeting, he said. His personal reaction, moreover, was that *Bureau* 'attacked the integrity of the military' and 'was rather a low blow,' although he insisted, 'I'm not exactly a warlike person. I thought I would rather have the West Pointers, the people who have Honor, Duty, and Country as their motto, than this character who produced the movie, on my side. I was rather upset about the whole thing.' The tenor of the scheduling meeting was that America was simply not going to be entertained by a show set in Vietnam. 'You could read the subtext [of the discussion],' one executive said, 'as really, deeply, about the war.' In short, nothing militated for *Bureau*.

Tinker and Goldberg concluded that the one-hour version was a mistake, but CBS was still sufficiently impressed with Goldberg and MTM that they were willing to try a half-hour version – with the stipulation that it be 'balanced.'

The CBS program executives laid down the law specifically to Gary Goldberg: Build up the army press attaché. As Bud Grant put it, 'What we came up with was a gimmick whereby the press attaché would say to Alan Hartman, "On the record or off the record?" "On the record" means army all the way: "No, we're not napalming that village." But "off the record" with Alan Hartman, there would be that humanity that would show him not as a totally committed army officer but someone who does have some basis of humanity.'

Bureau II was written to suit by two MTM contract writers Goldberg hired, and it was jokey sitcom with the obligatory sound track. The original Hartman begged off to act in NBC's *Kent State* movie, and Tinker and Goldberg went to a much lighter actor. Hartman was now milder, sweeter, and less cynical about the war. The bureau sported a new, ingenue reporter. The press attaché was now so 'humanized' he was wholly implausible, going far beyond the line of duty to help Hartman get his story. The colonel was no longer covering up for army policy in Vietnam; he was now the cliché army brass of every American war comedy. The plot was as frothy as it was simplified: Greedy Vietnamese soldiers were switching toasters for grenades shipped to the front, leaving the infantry – including one GI who saved Hartman from enemy attack – ill equipped in the foxholes. 'It's a situation that could be in any war,' said Richard Dysart, the character actor who played Matthews. 'It had nothing to do with Vietnam.'

No one was happy with this second version. Badly directed and 'not hard funny,' Grant Tinker thought. 'A shitty half-hour pilot,' he called it, then corrected himself to call it 'an okay show but not good enough.' Goldberg didn't like the second script himself. To make matters worse, after all the changes, *Bureau* II still tested Below Average. Arnold Becker's report said: 'Although viewers had no strong objections, neither did they find it particularly enjoyable or entertaining.' They found the show 'slow-moving, without enough action or humor'; the plot, though simple, still confusing and disrupted; the plot resolved too soon, and resolved, to boot, by the army, not the hero. The only character who tested well in both versions was the press attaché. In short, the show had lost its political edge without becoming commercial. *Bureau* was dead.

Carlton Your Doorman (CBS, 21/5/80) 30 mins.
Producers: Lorenzo Music, Barton Dean. *Writers*: Lorenzo Music, Barton Dean, based on a character created by James L. Brooks, Allan Burns, David Davis, Lorenzo Music. *Directors*: Charles Swenson, Fred Wolf.

Animated special featuring the Carlton the Doorman character from the *Rhoda* series. Character voices provided by: Lorenzo Music, Jack Somack, Lucille Meredith, Kay Cole, Lureen Tuttle, Paul Lichtman, Alan Barzman, Bob Arbogast, Charles Woolf, Roy West.

Whether *Carlton Your Doorman* was actually intended only as a one-off special or as a series pilot is uncertain. Certainly, though, it is the only occasion on which an MTM character has been spun off for such a brief moment. It is also the only time that an MTM show has been made entirely in animation – necessitating co-production with Murikami Wolf Swenson cartoon company. (MTM was to reemploy the services of these animators for *The Duck Factory* in the 1984 season.) The Carlton character, who had been only a disembodied doorman's voice in *Rhoda*, had proved so popular that a fan club had been set up by MTM/CBS and in 1976 a record had been released by United Artists with the Carltonesque title, 'Who Is It?' While letters to fans and records could sustain Carlton's facelessness, a TV appearance proved more difficult to handle, since as *TV Guide* has pointed out, Carlton was always a 'somewhat unsavory young man – Music visualises Carlton as in his 20s, blond, and skinny, with sloping shoulders, messy hair and droopy eyelids – Carlton is lazy, Carlton is slovenly, Carlton is a moocher and a lush . . .'

While the context of the *Rhoda* series may have anchored Carlton – and his audience – and even secured him the fans who wrote in for membership cards individually dipped in Ripple Wine – the prospect of a vehicle for him alone may have dissuaded MTM from developing the idea any further. Like *Phyllis*, the Carlton character was a good foil but might prove too abrasive alone. *TV Guide* noted that while 'It is assumed that Carlton will one day be spun off into a show called *Carlton*' it is also recognised that 'If this happens it will supply TV with its most amoral, disreputable and slovenly "hero" . . .' The following season MTM premièred *Hill Street Blues*, whose Belker and LaRue would at least equal Carlton in the unsavoury hero stakes.

Love, Natalie (NBC, 11/7/80) 30 mins.
Executive producer: Judy Kahan. *Producer*: Patricia Rickey. *Writers*: Judy Kahan, Merrill Markoe. *Director*: Peter Bonerz.
Cast: Judy Kahan, Christopher Allport, Corey Feldman, Kimberly Woodward, Kenneth Tigar, Jean DeBaer, Becky Michelle, Darian Mathias.

Another unusually ambitious and 'serious' comedy pilot from MTM dealing with the everyday problems of a young wife and mother. *Variety* noted the 'naturalness' of the performances and the credibility of the situations (making *Love, Natalie* another MTM 'character comedy') and suggested that the pilot induced 'instant empathy from young married femme viewers – and for that reason alone, it may have future usefulness to NBC.' (*Variety* 16/7/80, p. 70) Reviewers also stressed the stylistic invention of the programme which 'included direct asides to the camera'. This combination of social realist 'reflection' and stylistic 'reflexivity' epitomises the MTM house style at its best. Perhaps this is also to the credit of director Peter Bonerz, who had been one of the regular cast members of *The Bob Newhart Show*. Writer Judy Kahan went on to script MTM's children's special *How To Eat Like A Child*.

Brothers (CBS, 30/7/80) 30 mins.
Executive producers: Rick Podell and Michael Preminger. *Producers*: Norman Stiles, Charles Raymond. *Writers*: Rick Podell, Michael Preminger. *Director*: Will Mackenzie.
Cast: Charles Levin, James O'Sullivan, Dori Brenner, Bobby Ramsen, James Hong, Jeanetta Arnette, Chip Fields.

Brothers was the story of two adopted brothers – one, a grocer, married, the other a single lawyer – who end up sharing an apartment. Co-writer Rick Podell, like *Love, Natalie*'s director Peter Bonerz, had first worked at MTM as an actor. In 1984 the American cable channel Showtime launched their first series, also entitled *Brothers* and created by Ed Weinberger and Stan Daniels, but it is uncertain whether there is any connection between the two.

First Time, Second Time (CBS, 25/10/80) 30 mins.
Writers: Bob Comfort, Rick Kellard. *Director*: Asaad Kelada.
Cast: Ronny Cox, Julie Cobb, David Hollander, Sumant, Mary Frann, David Clennon.

Written and produced by the most prolific of the latest of MTM's teams Bob Comfort and Rick Kellard (who were also responsible for *Nichols & Dymes* and *One Night Band*) this pilot concerned a remarried executive whose son by his first marriage won't accept his new mother and whose life is further complicated by an Asian dignitary who comes to stay.

Comedy Of Horrors (CBS, 1/9/81) 30 mins.
Executive producers and writers: John Bonni, Harry Colomby. *Director*: Bill Persky.
Cast: Walter Olkewicz, Deborah Harmon, Richard Roat, Vincent Schiavelli, Jo de Winter, Patrick Macnee (host), Kip Niven, Patricia Conwell, Ivana Moore.

> MTM Enterprises' *Comedy Of Horrors* half-hour pilot attempted to give standard horror material a light touch. The humorous touch was okay in its own way but failed to disguise the triteness of the serious angle of the pilot's plot.
>
> With Patrick Macnee serving as host and audience teaser, the locale was identified as being on a 'scenic but desolate stretch of North Carolina beach' (but never shown). When Kip Niven and new wife Patricia Conwell arrive, they are unaware of the host's tip that only the innocent and pure-of-heart are safe there. With help from a wraithlike ghost, Niven's murderous intent is turned against him in rather pedestrian fashion.
>
> *Horrors* might be a concept worth pursuing, but it failed to exhibit much in the pilot. *(Variety*, 9/9/81)

Another of MTM's generic hybrids – this time combining, as the title indicates, comedy and horror. Having previously succeeded with a three-way hybrid between cop show, soap opera and sitcom in *Hill Street Blues*, and with a horror/cop show crossover in *Vampire*, perhaps MTM's ambitions on this occasion were not so ambitious. Nevertheless, reviews seem to agree that on this occasion MTM failed even to exhibit their customary 'stylistic flair'.

Stephanie (CBS, 8/9/81) 30 mins.
Producers: Alan Uger, Michael Kagan. *Writers*: Alan Uger, Michael Kagan. *Director*: Burt Brinckerhoff.
Cast: Stephanie Faracy, Betty White, Robert Hitt, Jeanetta Arnette, Alvy Moore, Kent Perkins, Steve Landesberg, Kres Mersky, Martin Ferraro, Martin Zagon, Matthew Faison.

> The *Stephanie* pilot concerned the travails of a fledgling host of a Los Angeles TV magazine show (Faracy) as she tried to nail down the job over the objections of the show's creator (White).
>
> Faracy, whose comedy style reminds one of Goldie Hawn, squeezed whatever laughs she could out of her scatterbrained character – being most effective in her interplay with White, again playing the sweet-mannered cold fish that has become her recent typecast.
>
> *Stephanie* didn't make CBS's slate, but was noteworthy for its slick production gloss – an MTM trademark. *(Variety*, 16/9/81)

Stephanie Faracy had co-starred in an unsuccessful pilot for MTM, *Bumpers*, back in 1977. In 1981 MTM produced another pilot vehicle for her, even titling it *Stephanie*. Even the presence on this occasion of Betty White failed to ignite CBS, and though *Variety* noted the MTM trademark of production quality the most obvious 'housestyle' aspect of the pilot was its inclusion of an 'audition' for a job in television.

Nichols & Dymes (NBC, 7/10/81) 60 mins.
Executive producers: Bob Comfort and Rick Kellard. *Writers*: Bob Comfort, Rick Kellard. *Producer*: Lee Sheldon. *Director*: Rod Daniel. *MTM Enterprises and Company Four.*
Cast: Rocky Bauer, Robin Strand, George McDaniel, Kate Murtaugh, Bill Cross, Teddi Siddall, Alan Beckwith, Don Richard Gibb.

> *Nichols & Dymes* (once known while in production as 'Iron Cowboys') was an hour pilot obviously seen as a variation of NBC-TV's *Chips* success. The unlikely production source was MTM Enterprises which has not dabbled in this type of outdoor adventure as a matter of policy, but did a workman-like-enough job on the project.
>
> Rocky Bauer and Robin Strand are the motorcycle pair of country boys who were also Federal agents working undercover (hard to believe) – a twosome prone to getting into trouble.
>
> In short, the MTM skills in execution were once more evident, despite the unfamiliar content for that production house. *(Variety,* 14/10/81)

Grant Tinker admitted to the familiarity of this pilot's premise when he described it as being 'about two guys on motorcycles who are really kind of undercover cops' – adding – 'I think you've heard of that one before.' (Quoted in Howard Rosenberg, 'Grant Tinker's MTM', *Emmy*, Spring 1981)

The Revenge Of The Gray Gang (NBC, 20/10/81) 60 mins.
Producer: Gary Nelson. *Writer*: Michael Norell. *Director*: Gary Nelson.
Cast: Noah Beery, Scatman Crothers, Mike Mazurki, Maxine Stuart, Richard Whiting, Tony La Torre, Pat McNamara, Susan Niven, Nicholas Pryor, Charles Dierkop, Stephen Furst, Adrian Zmed, Peggy Pope, Tom Villard.

In the 1980s MTM seem still to be marked by their emergence in 1970 – the year of the demographic shift in American television advertising and, consequently, programming. Thus the existence of programmes like *Revenge Of The Gray Gang* perhaps, which stress specific sectors of the total audience both in their probable audience and their on-screen protagonists; for on this occasion, the pilot's heroes were a group of elderly retired people of just the kind that CBS disenfranchised in 1969–70 and whose evacuation from prime-time provided the space for new product and new production companies that contributed to the formation of MTM.

Every Stray Dog & Kid (NBC, 21/10/81) 60 mins.
Writer: Joseph Gunn. *Director*: James Burrows.
Cast: Maureen Anderman, Denise Miller, Bruce Weitz, Kris McKeon, Pat Peterson, Jackie Earle Haley, Alan Fudge, Rita Taggart, Veronica Redd, Laurence Haddon, Toni Gilman, Stanley Brock, Todd Lookinland, Steven Spencer.

> A busted hour-long pilot, *Every Stray Dog & Kid* was aimed at the family trade but the pilot, although earnestly dealing with wayward kids from a realistic standpoint, did not deliver enough emotional impact.
>
> The premise was that unmarried Maureen Anderman, an ex-con now working as a writer, had three juvenile offenders placed under her supervision (by means never disclosed – a definite flaw in the concept's believability). Friendly cop Bruce Weitz dumps another youngster on her, which further complicates her time schedule and her plans to marry literary agent Alan Fudge, who has two kids of his own.

The pilot was the handiwork of exec producer Steven Bochco and supervising producer Gregory Hoblit (recent Emmy winners for *Hill Street Blues*), but the impression given was that *Stray* had preceded *Blues* on their production schedule. *(Variety*, 7/10/81)

The presence of Bruce Weitz as a cop in the cast and of Bochco and Hoblit in the credits reveals this as a predecessor of *Hill Street Blues* and as another product of Bochco's arrangement with NBC for the provision of MTM pilots for that network.

One Night Band (CBS, 28/6/83) 60 mins.
Executive producers: Bob Comfort, Richard Kellard. *Writers*: Bob Comfort, Richard Kellard. *Producer and director*: Robert Butler.
Cast: Gregory Cassel, George Deloy, Stephanie Kramer, Brad Maule, Carl Weintraub, Steve Sandor, Linda Hart, Monica Parker, Marji Martin, Patrika Darbo.

MTM has assembled a likeable foursome to make up a C & W band tied up to an unscrupulous manager and broke to boot. Four entertainers, out on a flimsy tour, faced adventures way outside the musical realm – or so it went in this 1981 unsold pilot.

Case at point involved bikers, who were angry at them for having pulled a stunt, and who stole their bus and made them play for their leader's wedding. (*Variety*, 1/6/83)

The presence of Robert Butler as director of this pilot and the inclusion of a musical element in the package reveal the continuities and discontinuities of MTM's house-style in the 1980s. Grant Tinker described this pilot and *Nichols & Dymes* as:

the kinds of things the networks want to buy. They stray off the little narrow path of what I happen to watch and move into other areas because we really need to do that. You get your head flat running against that wall. (Quoted in Howard Rosenberg, 'Grant Tinker's MTM', *Emmy*, Spring 1981)

Ironically, however, none of MTM's stylistic 'strays' have attracted critical attention, awards or audiences in the same quantities as their 'quality' shows like *The Mary Tyler Moore Show, Rhoda, Lou Grant* and *Hill Street Blues*.

Bliss (ABC, 28/6/84) 30 mins.
Writers: Doug Keyes, Chip Keyes. *Director*: Gene Reynolds.
Cast: George Kennedy, Diane Stilwater, Chris Sarandon, Allan Miller, Philip Sterling, George D. Wallace, Anne Haney, Dan Frischman, Barbara Babcock.

A part of the ABC Comedy Special lineup, *Bliss* was reviewed by *Variety* as if that trade paper were writing up an eye-witness account of a state execution. 'There is no bliss in *Bliss*,' said *Variety*. 'Another unsold pilot peopled with nice, gentle and bland characters mixed down with material that has all the impact of a powder puff. The only laughs were on the accompanying track.'

The plot/series premise sees George Kennedy's chocolate factory owner call his daughter back from her executive position in New York to take over the running of his plant. She returns and immediately rubs the factory staff up the wrong way, demanding production growth, an examination of the company books, etc.

Variety wraps up with: '*Bliss* is actually an illustration of why sitcoms are on the decline these days. Small people with small problems. Dullsville. Kennedy loses his fight of trying to make his role an interesting one, while Diane Stilwell as his daughter gives it her best but is also stymied by some dumb material.' *(Variety*, 11/7/84)

Gene Reynolds was invited by ABC to come up with a pilot for them after CBS cancelled *Lou Grant* but, when *Bliss* proved less than successful he turned to NBC and

The Duck Factory. Both these shows, intriguingly, focus on 'factories', as if the allegations about MTM's own expansion and consequent de-personalisation of the production process had actually found its way into the formats – made itself the subject in fact – of their sitcom products. In the case of *Bliss* the setting is a chocolate factory and the title seems to have been a play on the title of the Nabokov novel and Fassbinder film with the same setting, *Despair*. On this occasion, though, MTM's characteristic playfulness failed to find an appreciative audience.

MTM Variety Specials

Mary's Incredible Dream (CBS, 22/1/76) Tape 60 mins.
Producer/creator/writer: Jack Good. *Directors*: Gene McAvoy, Jaime Rogers. *Associate producers*: Richard Briggs, Huw Davies. *Photography*: George S. Dibie. *Music director*: Ray Pohlman. *Music arrangers*: Ira Newborn, Ray Pohlman. *Choreography*: Jaime Rogers. *Art director*: Gene McAvoy. *Costumes*: Peter Menefee.
Featuring: Mary Tyler Moore, Ben Vereen, Doug Kershaw, Arthur Fiedler, Manhattan Transfer.

With Jack Good hot from his *Catch My Soul/Othello* stage rock show MTM Inc. set him to create not only a prime-time Music/Comedy/Variety special but also to stage a non-Mary Richards/*Mary Tyler Moore Show* event for Ms Moore. Richard Hack in his *Hollywood Reporter* review observed, 'Many of course will expect to see Mary Richards of the WJM newsroom singing and dancing. And for that segment of the viewing public *Mary's Impossible Dream (sic.)* will contain an additional element – shock. If MTM wanted to break the mold, indeed she has.' Further insight into this extreme course is related by the *Hollywood Reporter's* applauding review: 'British musicologist Jack Good has fashioned a pastiche of Ken Russell, Federico Fellini and Busby Berkeley techniques, added a few of his own and produced a show which offers Mary singing "I'll Make a Man Out of You" from *Oh, What a Lovely War* (while dressed in green lamé hip boots and little else) and "I'm Still Here" from *Follies* (having aged to about the 60 mark), all done within the same 15 minutes. And so it goes.'

Variety, on the other hand, took a rather negative view of Mary's dream: 'Perhaps it was significant that Grant Tinker's name wasn't on *Mary's Incredible Dream*, though MTM Enterprises turned it out. Tinker and Moore have used their skill and good taste to produce what is arguably the finest American TV series of this decade, and apparently Tinker was able to avoid whatever self-destructive instincts Moore lavished on a special that should have had "nightmare" in its title rather than "dream" . . . the show was nothing but a horror, and TV producers who hear reports the program cost $900,000 react the way film producers do when it's mentioned that *Barry Lyndon* cost $16 million. They hold their heads and moan. The money shows – there were 30 production numbers. Perhaps Moore wanted to break the Mary Richards image and show her variety talents, but she not only starred in a bad wasteful show, she showcased herself in a production so tasteless that it will be awhile before she recovers . . .' (*Variety*, 28/1/76) *TV Guide* confirmed the budget in a report on CBS's apparent dismay with the finished product: '*Mary's Incredible Dream*, the Mary Tyler Moore special . . . became a problem for some CBS executives. It was a lavish, 60-minute program estimated to have cost $900,000, twice the price of the average variety special. "It was very embarrassing when we finally got a look at it," said a network source . . . "It's not exactly your typical variety show format," said another . . .' *TV Guide* also quotes a third unnamed CBS source who explained that 'Mary and her production company are very important to CBS and it becomes difficult to say no or keep the show off the air.' (*TV Guide*, 24/1/76, p. A-1)

Constantinople (ABC, 25/7/77) Tape 30 mins.

Executive producer: Grant Tinker. *Producer*: Jack Good. *Director*: Rita Gillespie. *Writer*: Jack Good. *Music director*: Ray Pohlman. *Conductor*: H. B. Barnum. *Choreography*: Andre Taylor. *Costumes*: Bill Belew.
Featuring: H. B. Barnum Blues and Boogie Band, Lance LeGault, John Valenti, Manhattan Transfer, Doug Kershaw with Slidin' Jake, Kathie Epstein, Mark Atkinson, Tina Turner, Ian Whitcomb.

'Why this show is called *Constantinople* is just one of the mysteries of life,' reported Morna Murphy in *Hollywood Reporter* (25/7/77). 'Called a "fast-paced musical pot-pourri", it is actually a dizzyingly paced miniconcert with rock and country singers whooping it up together for all they are worth. Viewers who tune in to see one of their favorites in action will be disappointed since everybody whizzes by so fast. But as a primer on some very good acts and soloists it certainly gives a taste of musical honey to prime-time.'

How To Survive The 70s And Maybe Even Bump Into Happiness (CBS, 22/2/78) 60 mins.
Producer/director: Bill Persky. *Writers*: Bill Persky, Phil Hahn, April Kelly, Wayne Kline, Tom Sawyer, Sam Bobrick. *Associate producer*: Frank Badami. *Choreography*: Tony Stevens. *Costumes*: Peter Menefee. *Set decorator*: Dom Remacle. *Art director*: Roy Christopher. *Music arranger/conductor*: Jack Elliott. *Editor*: Jerry Davis. *Dance music arranger*: Wally Harper.
Featuring: Mary Tyler Moore, Harvey Korman, John Ritter, Catlin Adams, Candice Azzara, Ed Barth, Allen Case, Gene Conforti, Sam Denoff, Michael Durrell, Arny Freeman, Christopher Guest, Steve Landesberg, Alan Oppenheimer, Henry Polic II, Beverley Sanders, and Dick Van Dyke, Bill Bixby.

This hour-long special provided another insight into the Mary Tyler Moore persona. With *Mary's Incredible Dream* in 1976 she tried, successfully, to hitch off the Mary Richards character with a slam-bam variety spectacular, featuring high-kicks in the style of a cabaret Shirley MacLaine. With *How To Survive The 70s* Ms Moore elevated her position as one of America's finest TV situation comediennes – alongside taking a rather warm and humorous look over her own shoulder. 'This is presented in a variety of vignettes,' observed *Hollywood Reporter* (23/2/78), 'starting with Mary in the middle of a pile of "How To" books, a clever encounter session, a touching dalliance on an elevator with Dick Van Dyke and a particularly telling sequence in a singles bar with Bill Bixby.' *Variety* (1/3/78) also noted 'An insidey segment with jibes at series stars returning to the tube forever and ever in reworkings of their major hits – with a nifty jibe at husband Grant Tinker.'

'Both Moore and Tinker, on a recent New York visit, emphasised that *Survive* was not a pilot, merely a one-shot special ... But despite the contemporary trappings of the sketches and songs and dances, the format still seemed a reworking of the outmoded concept that younger viewers have demonstrably rejected in recent years – and to spring the talented Moore in such a format on a regular basis looks awfully risky, considering what she means in terms of past outstanding achievement in the field of TV comedy.' (*Variety*, 1/3/78, p. 80)

Project Peacock: How To Eat Like A Child (NBC, 22/9/81) Tape. 60 mins.
Executive producer: Edgar Scherick. *Producer/writer*: Judith Kahan. *Director/choreography*: Robert Scheerer. *Music/lyrics*: John Forster.
Featuring: Dick Van Dyke, Darien Dash, Corey Feldman, Andy Freeman, Brandon Goldstein, Paula Hoffman, Rachel Jacobs, Billy Jacoby, Sunshine Lee, John Louie, Arlene McIntyre, Christy Murrill, Georg Alden, Ricky Segall, Rebecca Wolfe, Kimberly Woodward.

The première programme in this prime-time young people's series, on an irregular schedule throughout season. *How To Eat Like A Child* is a comedy-musical based on the book of the same title by Delia Ephron.

Hollywood Reporter stated that *Project Peacock*, a series of twenty prime-time specials for children, originated when Fred Silverman was faced with making a speech to the International Radio and Television Society in New York. NBC's Washington lobbyists suggested that he discuss children's television to counter FCC criticism of the network's shoddy performance in that area. 'How about a high quality children's special each week!' exclaimed Silverman, who instantly called on NBC financial vice-president, Don Carswell, to check the costs. After hanging up the phone he said, 'Let's do it every *other* week.'

Judith Kahan, who had written and starred in the MTM pilot, *Love, Natalie*, was responsible for another one-off here, which *Hollywood Reporter* (22/8/81) described in the following way: 'Sure, it's cutesy. Sure the children featured are adorable and precocious beyond belief. But nevertheless, this *Project Peacock* musical special zeroing in on the not-too-long-forgotten rituals of childhood is delightfully clever entertainment ... Among the "lessons" translated into catchy songs by John Forster are how to stay home from school, practice violin, understand parents, wait, torture your sister, look forward to your birthday, and go to bed like a child!' Only a couple of other observations seem worth adding: first, the presence of Dick Van Dyke whose associations with Mary Tyler Moore and MTM are manifold; and second, the fact that the show was taped at Metromedia Studios – the very company which had syndicated MTM's *Lorenzo & Henrietta Music Show* in 1976.

MTM TV Movies and Mini-Series

Just An Old Sweet Song (CBS, 14/9/76) 78 mins.
Executive producer: Lionel Ephraim. *Producer*: Philip Barry. *Director*: Robert Ellis Miller. *Production supervisor*: Ted Rich. *Production manager*: Abby Singer. *Assistant to producer*: Miranda Barry. *Writer*: Melvin Van Peebles. *Script supervisor*: Terry Terrill. *Story editor*: Jane Parker. *Photography*: Terry K. Meade. *Camera operator*: Ralph R. Gerling. *Key grip*: Stan Reed. *Gaffer*: Alan Goldenhaur. *Music*: Peter Matz. *Title song*: Melvin Van Peebles. *Sung by*: Ira Hawkins. *Editor*: Argyle Nelson. *Art director*: Ray Beal. *Sound*: Warren Welch. *Men's costumes*: Bob Harris Jnr. *Women's costumes*: Aida Swinson. *Make-up*: Ken Chase, Guy Del Russo. *Hairstyling*: Robert Stevenson. *Casting*: Mary Goldberg. *Location casting*: Bonnie D. Reeve. *Technical advisor*: Gil Davis. *Props master*: Gene Cox. *Special effects*: Aubrey P. Pollard. *Titles*: Pacific Title. *Sound mixer*: Keith A. Wester. *Music editor*: Dan Carlin. *Sound effects*: Jack Finley. *Re-recording*: Producers Sound Service.
Cast: Cicely Tyson *(Priscilla Simmons)*, Robert Hooks *(Nate Simmons)*, Beah Richards *(Grandma)*, Lincoln Kilpatrick *(Joe Mayfield)*, Minnie Gentry *(Aunt Velvet)*, Edward Binns *(Mr Claypool)*, Kevin Hooks *(Junior)*, Eric Hooks *(Highpockets)*, Sonny Jim Gaines *(Trunk)*, Mary Alice *(Helen Mayfield)*, Tia Rance *(Darlene)*, Philip Wende *(Sheriff)*, Walt Guthrie *(Winston)*, Lou Walker *(R. Stone)*, Johnny Popwell *(J. T. Dunbar)*, Emily Bell *(Mrs Claypool)*, Ernest Dixon *(Doorman)*.

Melvin Van Peebles' award-winning drama told the story of an urban northern black family and their return to the small southern town of their origin – which fades out with Robert Hooks saying: 'This New South probably ain't what it's cracked up to be but it's better than it used to be. Everything we wanted up there is down here. I still hate the South. The South is up North in them ghettos, but the programme is still the same – ripping off the black man.' 'Its basic theme,' reported *Variety*, 'that life may be better for blacks in the south these days than it is in the north is debatable and probably does not apply everywhere south of the Mason-Dixon Line.' *(Variety*, 22/9/76)

This 'dramatic special,' shown under the 'General Electric Theater' banner, was presented much in the manner of a pilot programme (with its set of 'regular' characters, the introduction of 'neighbours', and its completeness in designing the 'set') as the 'official' pilot, *Kinfolks*. But Van Peebles, in telling a story that 'was specific to the black experience at the same time that it related to the human condition,' deserves the praise that *Variety* awarded:

Melvin Van Peebles has written a small gem of a TV play and a vehicle that should have an afterlife on the stage. It is a sad and negative compliment to say that it was an embarrassment to much of what passes for relevance in the medium. It could have been another rendering of the 'you can't (or can) go home again' theme, but Van Peebles turned it into a parable about the search for new meanings in life. *(Variety,* ibid.)

While *Variety* celebrated *Song*'s 'relevance' and 'parable', the *Hollywood Reporter* described it as 'embarrassing and unbelievable' and accused the script of 'simple-minded dishonesty'. *(Hollywood Reporter* 14/9/76) The fact that it was scheduled as a General Electric Theater special – one of the last examples of 'sponsored' programmes still on the air in the 1970s – is intriguing, particularly in the light of MTM's later attempts to attract corporate sponsors back into prime-time.

Something For Joey (ABC, 6/4/77) 97 mins.
Producer: Jerry McNeely. *Director*: Lou Antonio. *Associate producer*: Roger Young. *Executive in charge of production*: Stuart Erwin. *Writer*: Jerry McNeely. *Photography*: Gayne Reschler. *Music*: David Shire. *Editor*: Gary Griffen.
Cast: Geraldine Page *(Mrs Anne Cappelletti)*, Gerald S. O'Loughlin *(John Cappelletti Sr)*, Marc Singer *(John Cappelletti)*, Jeff Lynas *(Joey Cappelletti)*, Linda Kelsey *(Joyce Cappelletti)*, Brian Farrell *(Marty Cappelletti)*, Paul Picerni *(Coach Joe Paterno)*, Stephen Parr *(Eddie O'Neil)*, David Hooks *(Bishop Sheen)*, June Dayton *(Mrs Frone)*, James Karen *(Dr Wingreen)*, David Garfield *(Dr Klunick)*, Kevin McKenzie *(Mark)*.

'The first TV movie I did there [at MTM],' comments Jerry McNeely, 'was *Something For Joey*, which was directed by Lou Antonio who I'd worked with on *Owen Marshall*. The genesis of *Something For Joey* was really the news coverage of John Cappelletti, best football player of the year who dedicated his trophy to his little brother, Joey, who had leukaemia. And it was an incredibly moving moment. About a month later I had written a pilot for MTM called 'Circus' which was never shot. It was the result of my respect for the enthusiasm of two experts, Fred Silverman and Grant Tinker. Someone had the idea of setting a series in a circus but it was never done; it was about a veterinarian and his family from Indianapolis on the road with a circus. Fred Silverman moved from CBS to ABC and it was never made. It was written as an accepted assignment and that was that.

'My son, Joel, read it and saw it was just an assignment and asked when was I going to do something I really cared about. And I thought about it and decided I would love to do the Cappelletti story. I mentioned it to Stu Erwin, the Executive Vice-President for Creative Affairs at MTM, and through Stu I got in touch with John [Cappelletti]. We met and I explained to him that I would like him to consider the possibility of our doing a film about his trophy speech and his relationship with his brother. I knew nothing about their relationship other than what I had seen on the newscast but I thought no matter what that is there's a drama there. If the brothers were very close that's our story, and if they weren't close but were brought close by that moment that's another story.

'John informed me that Joey was still alive, although ill, and I could see the picture having a very happy ending at that point. He said he wanted to talk it over with his family and then get back to me. That's the last I heard for a while – then the death of my wife occurred and while I was in Wisconsin for the funeral I read that Joey had died. About a month later I got a call from John and he had discussed it with his family and they thought it would be an appropriate thing to do in Joey's memory.

'We then took the idea to all three networks and were turned down flat on the basis that something like it had been done too often before, and that it was too similar to *Brian's Song*. Then there was a change of administration hierarchy at CBS and we re-submitted and this time we got a development deal. I interviewed John and made a couple of trips to Philadelphia to interview his family. By the time I was ready to write the script I had been working on the project for some six to eight months. It took about two weeks of typing and the script was then in almost exactly the final form, word for word and shot for shot. I thought Lou Antonio would be a good choice for directing it and I sent him a copy of the script. He signed aboard and the picture was shot late fall/early winter of that year.

'It got wonderful reviews and it also got an enormous audience – it was the most highly rated of any TV movie of that year. It received a couple of Emmy nominations and everyone at MTM was glad to be associated with it. *Something For Joey* gave MTM a pretty prestigious film as their entree into long form television movie-making [as their first 2-hour TV movie].' (Interview with Tise Vahimagi and Paul Kerr, 1984)

The *Hollywood Reporter*'s review summed up the film perfectly from a technical standpoint: 'Producer Jerry McNeely is writer of the excellent script that shows how courage can transcend tragedy; wonderfully unsentimental direction is by Lou Antonio, photography by Gayne Reschler and music by David Shire add to the subtle impact of the drama.' *(Hollywood Reporter*, 6/4/77)

McNeely's mention of *Brian's Song* above is illuminating in several ways. Douglas Gomery has described *Brian's Song* in a detailed essay about the emergence of made-for-TV-movies *('Brian's Song*: Television, Hollywood, and the Evolution of the Movie Made for Television'), in John E. O'Connor (ed.), *American History/American Television* (New York: Frederick Ungar, 1983). Gomery explains how the 'story concept' formulae function in TV movies, touting social realism and attracting short-lived controversies. In the epitome, *Brian's Song*, the 'story concept' is race relations, the setting is professional sports and the tragic hook is cancer. In *Something For Joey*, the tragic hook is again cancer, the setting once again professional sports (football) and the story concept is strained family relations. Sports have become a recurrent ingredient in MTM drama – from basketball in *The White Shadow* to baseball in *Bay City Blues* and football in *Fighting Back* and *Something For Joey*.

Gomery also compared the evolution of TV movies in the 1970s with that of Warner Bros. feature films in the 1930s: 'topical entertainment reaffirming basic values and beliefs'. (Gomery, p. 217) While Warners tore their stories from the headlines of the tabloids, TV movie-makers – and MTM in particular – seem to specialise in taking their stories from network news. Hence the origins of *The Mary Tyler Moore Show* itself, hence *First, You Cry* (with its real-life news heroine protagonist) and hence, here, McNeely's interest in the Cappelletti story originating in his viewing of a network newscast. (Later, MTM's TV movie *Thornwell* would be a fictionalisation on CBS of one of CBS's own *60 Minutes* stories.) Finally, also like *Brian's Song*, *Something For Joey* incorporated sequences of 'the real Cappelletti's football footage with [actor] Singer's in-uniform appearances'. *(Variety* 13/4/77, p. 48) *Variety* also noted that 'Sponsor IBM had only one commercial break, at the midway point in the drama, and it helped sustain the mood most effectively.' Here once again MTM's ambitions of a new golden age of corporate sponsored quality drama seems to have resurfaced.

Nowhere To Run (NBC, 16/1/78) 98 mins.
Producer: Jim Byrnes. *Director*: Richard Lang. *Writer*: Jim Byrnes, based on the novel by Charles Einstein. *Photography*: Chuck Arnold. *Music*: Jerrold Immel. *Editor*: Gary Griffen. *Cast*: David Jansen *(Harry Adams)*, Stefanie Powers *(Marian Adams)*, Allan Garfield *(Herbie Stoltz)*, Linda Evans *(Harry's new love)*, John Randolph *(Marian's father)*, Neva Patterson *(Marian's mother)*, Ahna Capri *(Ex-Mrs Stoltz)*.

This two-hour drama features David Jansen, in 'an intriguing bit of offbeat casting', as a San Francisco engineer who has devised a system for winning at blackjack as part of an elaborate scheme to escape an overbearing wife.

This appears to be as close to 'mainstream' American TV movie fare as MTM ever produced, at time of writing. The inclusion of made-for-TV movie 'star' names (Jansen, Stephanie Powers, Allan Garfield, Linda Evans) strikes as an obvious would-be ratings achiever – alongside the film's thriller-mystery plot complications.

'Aside from its uninspired title, *Nowhere To Run* emerges as an enjoyable and occasionally quite clever concoction,' wrote *Hollywood Reporter* (16/1/78). 'Richard Lang directed with considerable control of the precarious edges the show balances on between comedy and drama, keeping interest high and the proceedings puzzling until their proper moment of revelation. Producer Jim Byrnes' script (from Charles Einstein's novel) has some beautifully sharp dialogue and very cunning twists. Chuck Arnold's photography can't be condemned, Gary Griffen's editing is wise and Jerrold Immel's music is integral.'

If all this relegates *Nowhere To Run* to the fringes of MTM's output, the presence of Jim Byrnes as writer-producer provides a link with the company; he had previously authored two pilots for them, *Royce* and *The Busters*, two of their most generically mainstream products. Thematically, too, there seems to be some seeds of the *Remington Steele* premise – the construction of a fictional identity – in the plotting of this TV movie.

The Critical List (NBC 11 and 12/9/78) Part I: 98 mins. Part II: 99 mins.
Executive producer: Jerry McNeely. *Production executive for MTM Enterprises*: Lionel Ephraim. *Director*: Lou Antonio. *Associate producer*: Roger Young. *Production manager*: Donald A. Baer. *Assistant to the executive producer*: Kristine Fredriksson. *Post-production supervisor*: Ted Rich. *Production co-ordinator*: Martin Ryan Rosenberg. *1st assistant director*: Peter Bogart. *2nd assistant director*: Carl Dubliclay. *Writer*: Jerry McNeely, from the novels *Skeletons, Critical List* by Marshall Goldberg, MD. *Script supervisor*: Marilyn Giardino. *Photography*: Charles Correll. *Camera operator*: Stephen M. Yaconelli. *Key grip*: Stan Reed. *Gaffer*: Norm Glasser. *Music*: James Di Pasquale. *Editor*: Jerrold L. Ludwig. *Assistant editor*: A. David Marshall. *Art director*: Richard G. Berger. *Sound*: Cloudia. *Construction co-ordinator*: Pat Grande. *Prop foreman*: Richard T. Marino. *Props master*: David Coleman. *Assistant props master*: Carey Harris. *Men's costumes*: Bob Moore. *Women's costumes*: Lynne Albright. *Make-up*: Ben Nye. *Hairstyling*: Jean Austin. *Executive i/c talent*: Meryl O'Loughlin. *Casting director*: Fran Bascom. *Technical advisor*: Chris Huston RN. *Titles*: Pacific Title. *Sound mixer*: Dean S. Vernon. *Music editing*: La Da Music Inc. *Sound effects*: Echo Film Service, Dave Johnston. *Re-recording*: PSS/Jay Hadring.
Cast: Lloyd Bridges *(Dr Dan J. Lassiter)*, Melinda Dillon *(Dr Kris Lassiter)*, Buddy Ebsen *(Charles Sprague)*, Barbara Parkins *(Angela Adams)*, Robert Wagner *(Dr Nick Sloan)*, Ken Howard *(Nels Freiberg)*, Winwood McCarthy *(Ned Josephson)*, James Whitmore Jnr *(Dr Jack Hermanson)*, Robert Hogan *(Jordon Donnelly)*, Scott Marlowe *(Dr Albert Dubron)*, Felton Perry *(Dr Hill)*, Pat Harrington *(Jimmy Regosi)*, Brad David *(Andrew Vivienne)*, Will Hare *(Edmonds)*, Mel Gallagher *(Bednarik)*, Sybil Scotford *(Joanne Larwin)*, Joan Tompkins *(Judge Morton)*, Juli Bridges *(Gale Taylor)*, William Joyce *(Bill Shramm)*, Wright King *(Peter Kenderley)*, Russ Marin *(Ed Moorhead)*, Eugene Peterson *(Sidney Hammons)*, Janice Carroll *(Dubron's nurse)*, Walt Davis *(1st policeman)*, Lionel Decker *(Carl Gorman)*, Robert Kya-Hill *(Judge Graves)*, Janice Karman *(Cathy)*, Colleen Kelly *(Ticket clerk)*, Ray Oliver *(2nd policeman)*, Jane Squier *(HEW executive)*, Ron Trice *(Larry Harrison)*.
Cast for Part II: Lloyd Bridges *(Dr Dan J. Lassiter)*, Melinda Dillon *(Dr Kris Lassiter)*, Ken Howard *((Nels Freiberg)*, Pat Harrington *(Jimmy Regosi)*, Richard Basehart *(Matt Kinsella)*, John Larch *(Sprony)*, Jim Antonio *(Detweiler)*, Joanne Linville *(Nan Forrester)*, Ben Piazza *(Dr Henry de Jong)*, Felton Perry *(Dr Hill)*, James Whitmore Jnr *(Dr Jack Hermanson)*, Louis Gossett Jnr *(Lem Harper)*, Noble Willingham *(Charlie)*, Hildy Brooks *(Rith)*, Regis J. Cordic *(Chairman)*, Steve Gravers *(Senator)*, Jesse Dizon *(Intern Baker)*, Wayne Heffley *(Sheriff)*, George Reynolds *(Andy Simms)*, John Petlock *(Ferris)*, Janice Kerman *(Cathy)*, Hannah Hertelendy *(Hilde)*, Jerry McNeely *(Tom Neubeck)*, George Boyd *(McBride)*, Marilyn Coleman *(Operating room nurse)*, Bryan Clark *(1st man)*, Mike Handley *(2nd man)*, Jody Brisken *(Neonatal nurse)*.

'*The Critical List* was really a strangely structured project,' said the film's executive producer/writer Jerry McNeely. 'It started out as three two-hour films about the same character at different points in his life and the genesis of it was that it was to star the Bridges family – Jeff, Beau and Lloyd. It was to be based on three novels about a doctor, by a doctor I had known for many years. Deanne Barkley at NBC had the idea of doing it for the Bridges family with Jeff as the young doctor, then Beau, then Lloyd as the ageing doctor. I wrote the scripts but once it got finished we found out that Jeff wasn't interested in doing television; and Beau wasn't very interested in being an opening for his father. So I just said what if we do the final four hours. I tried to stitch the two stories together but only the tiniest thread ties them together. We shot on a 40-day schedule, including a week on location in Washington. Lloyd Bridges ended up playing the role in both parts.' (Interview with Tise Vahimagi and Paul Kerr, 1984)

This stitching together of two stories was duly noted by *Variety*'s reviewer:

> Labeled a miniseries by NBC-TV's press releases, the four-hour *The Critical List* played off like two separate two-hour episodes with only the flimsiest of continuity links holding them together. The project has also been identified as a potential future series by the web's top programmer, Paul Klein, presumably as a vehicle for Lloyd Bridges as the physician-director of a Los Angeles hospital. *(Variety,* 20/9/78)

Variety, however, wrapped up the TV-movie/pilot's potential when it considered that 'the script was much talkier than desirable, giving a soap opera veneer to too much of the footage. Bridges was quite strong and versatile in what he had to do, however, and the project's future as a series has to be pegged on his presence.' *Hollywood Reporter* brought the curtain down on *Critical List* with: 'For once, a show's title is perfectly accurate in describing where its overall impact lies.'

It's perhaps worth noting, finally, that *The Critical List* was the first occasion on which MTM were able to accommodate all three of their recurring (and defining) thematics: the worlds of medicine, the media and crime. The *TV Guide* advertisement for the mini-series identified its protagonists as The Medical Director, The Reporter and The Informer . . .

The Critical List was MTM's first and to date only mini-series, though two other mini-series were announced the same year. The first was to be a twelve-hour adaptation of William Goldman's novel *Boys and Girls Together* for NBC, and the second, a project that got no further than pilot stage for PBS, *Going Home Again*.

First, You Cry (CBS, 8/11/78) 120 mins.
Producer: Philip Barry. *Director*: George Schaefer. *Writer*: Carmen Culver, based on the book by Betty Rollin. *Production supervisor*: Ted Rich. *Production executive for MTM Enterprises*: Lionel A. Ephraim. *MTM/Company Four.*
Cast: Mary Tyler Moore *(Betty Rollin)*, Anthony Perkins *(Arthur)*, Richard Crenna *(David)*, Jennifer Warren *(Erica)*.

> One day, well before anything [Carmen Culver] had written had been aired, Norman Kurland casually mentioned that the producer, Philip Barry, might be calling her. Mr Barry, he explained, had read [her script] 'Willa', liked it, and was looking for a writer to adapt a best-selling book into a television feature film starring Mary Tyler Moore. The book, written by NBC correspondent Betty Rollin, was called *'First, You Cry'* and was a touching, personal account of the author's battle with breast cancer. First she read the book and loved it. Then, realising that she'd never seen the legendary Mary Tyler Moore perform, she planted herself in front of the television set to watch several segments of *The Mary Tyler Moore Show.* When the phone call finally came with Mr Barry on the other end, Carmen had already written the screenplay *First, You Cry*, in her head. Philip Barry liked her ideas for *First, You Cry* and hired her to begin a process that all relatively unknown screenwriters must go through. First, he hired her to do only a story line. Then, because he liked that, he agreed to pay her additional money to write a more detailed outline, which is called a 'treatment'. (Quoted in Betsy Covington Smith, *Breakthrough: Women in Television* (New York: Walker and Company, 1981) pp. 62–4)

Culver then went on through first and second drafts to the final, completed script. Then, 'while working on *First, You Cry*, Carmen met and talked with Mary Tyler Moore many times. She met Betty Rollin only once, and then very briefly. "I didn't want to get to know Betty because that would have confused me. I had to think of Mary Tyler Moore as the central character, not the real Betty Rollin." ' The film was transmitted on the CBS network in 1978, some three years after Culver had started work on it, and the film went on to receive a great deal of publicity along with above-average reviews and four Emmy nominations for Outstanding Drama, Best Actress in a Special, Music Score and Editing.

Hollywood Reporter's Earl Davis wasn't sure at first whether the film version could do Rollin's book justice, but then felt that 'Moore is completely convincing and quite impressive in a very substantial stretch for her creative abilities, and her characterisation is crafted every step of the way with a style that marks this lady as a born survivor. Anthony Perkins is nicely understated and ill at ease as Rollin's ex-husband, while Richard Crenna supplies sturdy understanding as a past suitor of Rollin's who wishes to be part of her future. George Schaefer's cohesive direction is of immense aid, never allowing the material to become overly heavy, yet never obscuring the serious ramifications inherent in such a situation. Carmen Culver adapted Rollin's book with honest fidelity and smooth empathy ... it's a sharp assessment of a condition about which this society needs reassurance and discussion, which is precisely what this film accomplishes.' (*Hollywood Reporter*, 8/11/78)

On the other side, *Variety* made it very obvious that *First, You Cry* was not their idea of 'honest fidelity and smooth empathy' by noting: 'Mary Tyler Moore pulls out all the stops in *First, You Cry* – she obviously has a real stake in getting the word out to a mass audience that yes, the loss of a breast to cancer requires traumatic adjustments in a woman's life. The problem is that even though Moore was basing the show on the autobiography of Betty Rollin the two hours came off as artificial and stifling. But although the drama failed to ring true, Moore had some powerful moments, as in the scene where she was told by her doctor that the lump in her breast is probably malignant. She hears the doctor's words, rises from the chair in fear and confusion, collapses, is revived a moment later and then lets out a brief animal howl of pain – which she quickly suppresses and, stunned with humiliation for the lapse in civility, apologises for. The scene was so authentic it mocked the overwrought soap-opera melodramatics that surrounded it.' (*Variety*, 15/11/78)

First, You Cry took its cue, in true MTM tradition, from television news, in this case the true story of a television newsreader's bout with breast cancer. One of several MTM co-productions with Company Four, it is clearly in the TV movie traditions of liberal issue drama alongside MTM's *Something For Joey* (about leukaemia), *The Boy Who Drank Too Much* (teenage alcoholism), *Just An Old Sweet Song* (racism), *Thornwell* (CIA experimentation), and *Fighting Back* (return to football fitness after injury). Their 'serious' themes attracted corporate sponsors in unusual numbers; thus *Just An Old Sweet Song* was transmitted in the 'General Electric Theater' slot, and *First, You Cry* was described by Frank Rich in *Time* magazine as 'essentially a public service drama'.

Vampire (ABC, 7/10/79) 95 mins.

Executive producer: Steven Bochco. *Producer*: Gregory Hoblit. *Director*: E. W. Swackhamer. *Associate producer*: David Anspaugh. *Production manager*: George Goodman. *Post-production supervisor*: Ted Rich. *Production assistants*: Deborah Taylor Harris, Patricia Perillo, Joan Wellman. *Location managers*: Fred Lyle, George Burrafato. *Production executive*: Abby Singer. *Assistant director*: Arne Schmidt. *2nd assistant director*: Ken Collins. *Writers*: Steven Bochco, Michael Kozoll. *Script supervisor*: Wilma Garscadden. *Photography*: Dennis Dalzell. *Camera operator*: Bill Gahret. *Key grip*: Lee Kosskrove. *Dolly grip*: Kris Kosskrove. *Gaffer*: Cal Maehl. *Music*: Fred Karlin. *Ballet sequence*: San Francisco Ballet Company. *Editor*: Ray Daniels. *Supervising editor*: Christopher Nelson. *Assistant editors*: Larry Morrison, Bobby Adye. *Art director*: Jim Hulsey. *Sound*: Greg Harrison. *Construction co-ordinator*: Pat Grande. *Executive i/c talent*: Meryl O'Loughlin. *Casting assistant*: Jackie Briskey. *Transport captain*: Bud Thompson. *Men's costumes*: Bob Moore. *Women's costumes*: Betty Griffin. *Make-up*: Bob Mills. *Hairstyling*: Norma Lee. *Special effects*: Wayne Beauchamp. *Props manager*: Matt Springman. *Titles*: Pacific Title. *Sound mixer*: Jim La Rue. *Re-recording*: Goldwyn Sound. *Music editing*: La Da Music Inc., Bob Badami. *Sound editing*: Mayflower Films Inc., Stevensound.

Cast: Jason Miller *(John Rawlins)*, Richard Lynch *(Anton Voytek)*, E. G. Marshall *(Harry Kilcoyne)*, Kathryn Harrold *(Leslie Rawlins)*, Barrie Youngfellow *(Andrea)*, Michael Tucker

(Christopher), Jonelle Allen *(Brandy)*, Jessica Walter *(Nicole)*, David Hooks *(Casket salesman)*, Wendy Cutler *(Iris)*, Joe Spinell *(Captain Desher)*, Stu Klitsner *(Coroner)*, Scott Paulin *(Priest)*, Byron Webster *(Selby)*, Brendon Dillon *(Father Devlin)*, Herb Braha *(Felon)*, Adam Starr *(Tommy Parker)*, Tony Perez *(Precinct cop)*, Nicholas Gunn *(Dance instructor)*, Ray K. Goman *(Detective)*.

'*Vampire* came about,' said Michael Kozoll, 'when I was lying on a beach in Hawaii with my girlfriend trying to think of some way to write off the trip. And I came up with the notion of a Hawaiian vampire born from the excavation of a new hotel. By the time we went to story meetings with MTM the script was moved to New York and New Orleans and, finally, San Francisco. This is basically another kind of cop show, and if it resembles Richard Matheson's excellent *The Night Stalker* TV movie it was purely coincidental. It was called a "back-door pilot"; whatever that suggests I don't know. The direction I would have taken had this gone to series would have been "I was gone out the door", because I had no desire whatsoever to work on another television series, much less one about a vampire.' (Interview with the authors, 1983)

Hollywood Reporter took it with an average nod: 'There are a couple of riveting sequences and genuinely scary moments in *Vampire*. Effectively modulated sound effects, juxtaposed with shadowy images photographed by Dennis Dalzell, invest the film with a suitably malevolent mood. Fred Karlin's economically tense music and art director Jim Hulsey's darkly opulent and decaying decors also add to the gloom. Supervising editor Chris Nelson's efforts also contributed to the lyrical and erotic aspects of this MTM Enterprises production.' (*Hollywood Reporter*, 8/10/79)

Hollywood Reporter further noted that the protagonists of *Vampire* were ' ... the only happily married couple to be found in a TV movie thus far this season. The wife isn't fat, the husband isn't straying and they don't have an adopted child about to be taken from them. But they have to go and spoil it all by getting involved with a mildewed Hungarian prince (Richard Lynch) who turns out to be a vampire. If it's not one thing, it's another.' This places *Vampire* dramatically outside the 'issues' aspect of TV movies epitomised by *Brian's Song* (racism, terminal disease, etc.) and places it alongside MTM's generic one-offs like *Nowhere To Run*. Like *First, You Cry* and *Nichols & Dymes*, *Vampire* was an MTM co-production with Company Four.

The Boy Who Drank Too Much (CBS, 6/2/80) 97 mins.
Executive producer: Jerry McNeely. *Producer*: Donald A. Baer. *Director*: Jerrold Freedman. *Associate producer*: Shep Greene. *Writer*: Edward DeBlasio, based on the novel by Shep Greene. *Photography*: Allen Daviau. *Music*: Michael Small. *Sung by*: Robert Jason. *Editor*: Anthony Redman. *Production designer*: Ron Hobbs. *Set decorator*: Cloudia. *Sound mixer*: Dean Salmon. *Men's costumes*: Buzz Wiseman. *Women's costumes*: Lynn Bernay. *Make-up*: Brad Wilder. *Hairstyling*: Jean Austin. *Technical advisor*: Ned Dowd.
Cast: Scott Baio *(Buff Saunders)*, Lance Kerwin *(Billy Carpenter)*, Don Murray *(Ken Saunders)*, Ed Lauter *(Gus Carpenter)*, Mariclare Costello *(Louise Carpenter)*, Stephen Davies *(Alan)*, Toni Kalem *(Tina)*, Katherine Pass *(Donna Watson)*, Dan Shor *(Art Collins)*, Michele Tobin *(Julie Seidman)*, Ron Max *(Coach Anderson)*, Marla Frunkin *(Lucy)*, Jerry McNeely *(Spanish teacher)*, Dan Spector *(Murph)*, John Roselius *(Paul Watson)*, Art Evans *(Intern)*, Elizabeth Berger *(Emergency room nurse)*, Nora Boland *(Ruth)*, Shane Kerwin *(Grisdale)*, Naomi Caryl *(Edna)*, Dorothy Dells *(Duty nurse)*, Virginia Bingham *(Kay)*, Mavis Neal Palmer *(Co-al woman)*, Jerry de Wilde *(Co-al man)*, Cheri Heckman *(Melinda)*.

The story deals with Buff Saunders (played by Scott Baio), a skilful high school ice hockey player whose greatest battle is with a bottle not a puck. His father (Don Murray), a former hockey star with a tragic past, is also an alcoholic. Buff's only support comes from his remarkably compassionate friend, Bill Carpenter (Lance Kerwin), who withstands personal sacrifices to help his comrade.

'Ed DeBlasio wrote that script,' commented Jerry McNeely. 'I had a lot to do with the development of it and I was the executive producer. Ed and I worked out a different

The Boy Who Drank Too Much: Scott Baio as Buff Saunders and Lance Kerwin as Billy Carpenter.

structure from the novel on which it was based. It was directed by Jerrold Freedman and shot on location in Madison, Wisconsin, my home town. We took a chance on the cinematographer and employed a young commercials cinematographer [Allen Daviau]. Shortly thereafter Spielberg employed him for the Special Edition of *Close Encounters* and then for *E.T.*' (Interview with Tise Vahimagi and Paul Kerr, 1984)

The team background seems to be a recurring element in MTM drama. On the sports note, this TV movie arrived after *White Shadow*'s basketball team concept and before *Bay City Blues*' baseball team format. This time ice hockey is the backdrop for, as Gail Williams reports, 'a scenario full of fury and emotional confrontations that inevitably lead nowhere.' The *Hollywood Reporter* review continues: 'By the time this tele-feature starring Scott Baio and Lance Kerwin decides it's about friendship we are almost past caring what happens to *The Boy Who Drank Too Much*. With a self-explanatory title like that, you'd think Edward DeBlasio's script, based on the novel by Shep Greene, would be more focused than it is.

The film offers some excellently staged hockey sequences and some fine acting efforts by Baio as the boy battling the bottle, Kerwin as his ice hockey team-mate and Don Murray as Baio's volatile alcoholic father. But the material is just too flat for all the unmotivated nobility that surfaces at the last minute to be convincing.' *(Hollywood Reporter*, 6/2/80)

Fighting Back (NBC, 7/12/80) 96 mins.
Executive producer: Jerry McNeely. *Producer*: Don Baer. *Associate producer*: David Anspaugh. *Teleplay*: Jerry McNeely, based on the book by Rocky Bleier with Terry O'Neil. *Directed* by Robert Lieberman.
Cast: Robert Urich *(Rocky Bleier)*, Bonnie Bedelia, Richard Herd and special guest star Art Carney *(Art Rooney)*.

Fighting Back tells the story of Rocky Bleier, a football player who overcame serious Vietnam War injuries to succeed as a top-rate player for the Pittsburgh Steelers. The film traces his career from tentative professional beginnings, his drafting into the army, through to 1969 when Bleier's right foot was severely injured in an explosion in Vietnam. Medics gave him a 50–50 chance of ever walking again – playing football again seemed out of the question. However, Bleier persisted, rejoining training activities, undergoing another operation, until in 1972 he was back in the regular team. Eight years later Bleier was playing his 12th season with the Steelers.

Jerry McNeely, who acted as executive producer on *Fighting Back*, tells how the project came into being:

> I'd turned down a number of other projects that dealt with injured athletes after *Something For Joey* because I just felt I had been that route. I specifically turned down the Rocky Bleier story right after doing *Joey*. It never got off the ground and they brought it back to MTM some years later, and this time I wasn't turned off by it and we took it to NBC and got a development deal and it was a very smooth project. Almost from the first we had Robert Urich in mind. Bob was a former college football player and what NBC would consider a bankable name, a series star, and so he was more or less a part of the package from as soon as we started. The director of *Fighting Back* was again someone we took something of a chance on – someone from commercials. This young man was called Robert Lieberman and this was his first prime-time film. *Fighting Back* did quite well in the ratings – it was number six for the week. (Interview with Tise Vahimagi and Paul Kerr, 1984)

Thornwell (CBS, 28/1/81) 96 mins.
Executive producer: Harry Moses. *Producer*: Mark Tinker. *Associate producer*: Scott Brazil. *Writer*: Michael de Guzman. *Director*: Harry Moses.
Cast: Glynn Turman *(James Thornwell)*, Vincent Gardenia, Craig Wasson, Howard E. Rollins Jr and Edward Bell.

Thornwell is based on the life and horrendous experiences of a black US army man, called James Thornwell, who was in 1961 accused by army counter-intelligence of stealing classified documents while working as a clerk-typist at a US communications centre in France. Thornwell initially denied stealing the documents but the Army put him through many weeks of hard investigation, culminating with a secretly administered dosage of LSD. Subsequently, Thornwell made several 'confessions' in which he admitted that he stole the documents. However, because of the bizarre way the 'investigation' was conducted Thornwell was allowed to leave the military with the case of the missing documents still unresolved. After his nightmarish experiences under the investigation (and drug-related inducements to confess) Thornwell began suffering from depression and headaches, was unable to keep a steady job and saw two marriages end in divorce. Some sixteen years later, he received a letter from the Government informing him that he had been the subject of drug experiments while in military service. Thornwell got a lawyer on the case – who, through the Freedom of Information Act, learned of the LSD treatment – and in 1981 was granted $625,000 compensation.

Producer Harry Moses heard of the case, followed through with detailed research and produced a startling documentary for *60 Minutes* (which was aired on 25 March 1979). Following the *60 Minutes* episode Moses was besieged by film-makers to do a dramatised version of the Thornwell story. One of the enquiries came from Grant Tinker at MTM, who were interested in producing a TV film, and Moses responded by telling MTM that 'Okay, but now let me tell you the bad news – I come with it. I want to direct it.' Although Moses had no previous experience with directing drama with actors (his professional background being news and documentaries), Tinker and CBS agreed to let Moses direct the project. CBS were putting up the $2.1 million budget and it must have taken a lot of persuading from Tinker to allow Moses the directorial position.

To ensure accuracy, Moses is reported to have based the film on more than 50 hours of interviews with James Thornwell, over 1,000 pages of previously classified Government documents, and a hectic journey across America with scriptwriter Michael de Guzman to talk with various people involved in the real story, including the original army officer who was in charge of giving Thornwell the LSD in France. Although de Guzman tried to keep his script as close to the actual events as possible, memories of those they talked to were, almost two decades later, a little fuzzy. And so, as Moses has pointed out, 'Michael obviously had to invent some dialogue and some scenes may not have happened exactly as they appear in the film.' However, Moses adds, 'all of the dialogue is based on Thornwell's recollections, the documents and what other people told us. There's not one scene in the film for which we didn't talk to one of the participants.' (Above quotes taken from Robert Lindsay's *New York Times* article entitled 'When a News Producer Tries His Hand at a Docu-Drama', 25/1/81)

What should have had the Emmys lining up at the door, given the intensity of this story, sadly didn't. Maybe Tom Buckley's following views suggest why:

> The strengths and weaknesses of the 'docudrama' – the dramatisation of actual events – are demonstrated in *Thornwell*. . . .One can only wish that Mr Moses and the writer, Michael de Guzman, had been bolder in their intentions. Too much of what is on screen is a prosaic recounting of day-to-day army life, fragments of what was still largely a Jim Crow upbringing in South Carolina, and the wordless bafflement and frustration of Mr Thornwell after his discharge. Many questions are left unanswered, and in a docudrama, reasonable suppositions would have been better than nothing. . . . Glynn Turman, who appeared in the screen version of *The River Niger* and in *Cooley High*, does well as the young soldier who tries to conceal his insecurity behind a mask of arrogance. The plump and kindly Vincent Gardenia is not altogether well cast as the head of the team that eventually administers the LSD to Mr Thornwell. This scene, in which he is given the LSD in a liquid mixture, ought to be the climax of the drama. Instead, there is only Mr Turman's almost wordless sobbing. (*New York Times*, 28/1/81)

In Defense Of Kids (CBS, 4/6/83) 100 mins.
Executive producer: Gene Reynolds. *Producer*: Seth Freeman. *Writer*: Michele Gallery. *Director*: Gene Reynolds.
Cast: Blythe Danner, Joyce Van Patten, Beth Ehlers, Sam Waterston, Tony La Taorre, Khalif Bobatoon, Noelle Parker.

The writer of *In Defense of Kids*, Michele Gallery, has described in detail her emergence as one of MTM's and *Lou Grant*'s in-house creative staff, the experience of which clearly coloured her work on her first tele-feature and its concern with social issues:

> I started in television delivering mail on this lot, CBS Studio Center. It was just a temporary job, because at that time which was 1976 there were no women allowed to be mail room 'boys'. I had come onto the lot to speak to somebody about the possibility of looking for work there and I worked there for a few weeks, and then moved to the MTM accounting department and worked there for one season, during which time I went to all

the screenings of *The Mary Tyler Moore Show*. I became a religious audience member of that show. I had done my master's thesis in popular culture on the first four seasons of *The Mary Tyler Moore Show* – kind of a content analysis – those four seasons of scripts, and had come to really admire the comedy writing of the show ... I had thought my career was going to be writing about the way people spend their leisure time and my interest, even now, is how people spend their free time. Because most people in this country spend their free time in front of the television set that became an interest of mine and that's how I came to write my master's thesis on a television show. And that's why I thought it would be valuable to spend some time in this industry. What happened was I was working in Accounts Payable and it didn't matter, I was one of the people making television. From there I went on to be a production secretary on *Rhoda* for a season. And then at that time I got to know Allan Burns and Jim Brooks who were two of the three people who created *Lou Grant*. At the time they were developing that show they realised that since it was going to be more drama than comedy a researcher came in handy to research not only the world of newspapers but the world of stories for the show. And they knew I had a background, they knew I had a master's degree and therefore would not be intimidated by going into the library and they asked me if I would join them, which was tremendous. Gene Reynolds believed very much in research and I spent the first season as a researcher and later in the first year there was an episode of *Lou Grant* that had required a lot of research and was on a very sensitive issue. I think of it as the Hari Krishna show: 'Sect'. Gene Reynolds and Allan Burns asked me if I would rectify the mistakes that were in the script. Which I did and I also rewrote it – I found I was rewriting dialogue. And they liked it. And they gave me a story, an assignment for a subsequent script, and then for the second season they made me a story editor, a term that on *Lou Grant* meant staff writer. I was the staff writer on seasons two and three. I freelanced season four and wrote three *Lou Grants*. And then I wrote four *Lou Grants* for season five and came back on staff [as 'creative consultant']. (Interview with Michele Gallery by Stephen Dark, Los Angeles 1983)

When *Lou Grant* was cancelled in May 1982 (for Gallery's comments on the cancellation see the article by Paul Kerr on *Lou Grant* and *Hill Street Blues* elsewhere in this volume) Gallery collaborated with ex-*Lou Grant* staffers Seth Freeman and Gene Reynolds to write, produce and direct a TV movie in the same 'social issue' mould of the *Lou Grant* series. Thus *In Defense Of Kids* falls in the same category as *The Boy Who Drank Too Much*, *First, You Cry* and *Something For Joey*.

MTM's made-for-TV movies may be seen as falling into two categories. On the one hand there are 'commercial' projects such as *Vampire* and *Nowhere To Go*. On the other there are the movies of social or individual concern such as *The Boy Who Drank Too Much*, *First, You Cry* and *In Defense Of Kids*. The latter concerns children's rights and the question of when the state may intervene in their lives. '*In Defense Of Kids* is a sprightly social issue telefeature,' remarked *Hollywood Reporter*, 'bolstered by Blythe Danner's sparkling performance as its engaging central character.' Danner portrays a contract lawyer for a prestigious law firm who decides to leave her comfortable position in order to establish an independent practice assisting young people with legal problems. *Hollywood Reporter* continues, 'Michele Gallery's teleplay motivates that decision with an amusingly conniving social worker (played by Van Patten) and a fateful encounter with a young streetwalker who has been abused by her father.' (*Hollywood Reporter*, 6/4/83)

Although children feature a lot in MTM's output (*Phyllis*, *The Tony Randall Show*, *Three For The Road*, *The Boy Who Drank Too Much*, *Something For Joey*, etc.), this film, for the most part, appeared to hit on the right note as far as production was concerned: 'When a bunch of talented people take on a subject that is sensitive and complicated, the project is at least promising. Such is the case with *In Defense Of Kids*.' (*New York Times*, 6/4/84)

'Owing to executive producer Gene Reynolds' deft direction, and Gallery's buoyant script, this compassionate scenario is confidently paced and crackles with snappy, credible-sounding dialogue.' (*Hollywood Reporter*, 6 April 1983)

MTM Feature Film

A Little Sex (MTM Enterprises, released through Universal, 1982) 94 mins.
Producers: Robert DeLaurentis and Bruce Paltrow. *Director*: Bruce Paltrow. *Writer*: Robert DeLaurentis. *Camera (Technicolor)*: Ralf D. Bode. *Editor*: Bill Butler. *Sound*: Peter A. Hardi. *Production designer*: Stephen Hendrickson. *Associate producer*: Stephen F. Kesten. *Assistant director*: Victor Hsu. *Music*: Georges Delerue.
Cast: Tim Matheson *(Michael)*, Kate Capshaw *(Tommy)*, Edward Herrmann *(Brother)*, John Glover *(Walter)*, Joan Copeland *(Mrs Harrison)*, Susanna Dalton *(Nancy)*, Wendie Malick *(Philomena)*, Wallace Shawn *(Oliver)*.

This could be considered MTM's idea of Billy Wilder's *Seven Year Itch*, but it never makes the grade. The story concerns a young TV commercials director who tires of sleeping with the permanent gallery of gorgeous women around him and decides to marry his live-in girlfriend. However, not long after he's married he starts to feel the itch again and the marriage starts to slide.

> At this point, DeLaurentis and Paltrow are into a trap they never quite climb out of. Supposedly, most of this film deals with the crisis in their marriage once Capshaw catches Matheson with his pants down with another woman. But what went on during the 10 months they lived together? Surely, Matheson didn't cheat himself to boredom without her finding out? Very late in the picture, a few lines of dialogue try to explain this, but it's too tardy and too little. (*Variety*, 31/3/82)

The location photography is nice (and this is the only area where the film scores over being presented for TV), with the parks, streets, background characters warmly described in much the same way that New York is seen in the Neil Simon comedies, but when this pleasant-looking landscape is populated by the Matheson/Capshaw characters the film takes on the 'slick' appearance of an American TV shampoo commercial. *Variety*'s review banner sums the film up perfectly: '*A Little Sex* – But not a lot of picture.'

A Little Sex was budgeted at 6 million dollars. During its production, both director Bruce Paltrow and MTM president Grant Tinker commented on MTM's move into feature films. As Paltrow put it, 'People will approach this film with a certain prejudice because it's being made by a TV guy for a TV company. But just look at the solid [film] directors who've come out of TV – Sidney Lumet, Norman Jewison; TV hones your craft. This is a conceptual difference, an adjustment of format.' Paltrow's reference to 'golden age' drama directors like Jewison and Lumet is a reminder of MTM's status as something of an industry anachronism in the late seventies and early eighties, attempting to return television to the days of quality product associated with the years of sponsorship, before the rise of telefilms and the invasion of television by Hollywood. Tinker added that '*A Little Sex*, coming to us from a company man, seemed like a good property to get our feet wet. Like most TV people, we've always had a sneaky little interest in movies. But you're always a little scared because you read how dangerous a business it is ....' [and thus] '... We'll never be in the picture business in any volume; our basic business will remain TV.' (quoted in the *Los Angeles Times* 6 May 1981.) *A Little Sex* was finally released theatrically in America in March 1982 but won none of the critical or audience acclaim associated with so many of MTM's TV products. In Britain it never opened theatrically at all, though it was acquired by the Golan-Globus chain, perhaps on the strength of its 'suggestive' title. In 1983, Guild Home Video released it on cassette.